The Beaver Bites Back?

The Beaver Bites Back?

American Popular Culture in Canada

Edited by

DAVID H. FLAHERTY and
FRANK E. MANNING

McGill-Queen's University Press
Montreal & Kingston • London • Buffalo

© McGill-Queen's University Press 1993
ISBN 0-7735-1119-9 (cloth)
ISBN 0-7735-1120-2 (paper)

Legal deposit fourth quarter 1993
Bibliothèque nationale du Québec

∞

Printed in Canada on acid-free paper

Publication of this book has been supported in part by a grant from the Faculty of Social Science of The University of Western Ontario and by the Canada Council through its block grant program.

Canadian Cataloguing in Publication Data

Main entry under title:
    The Beaver bites back?: American popular culture in Canada
    Includes bibliographical references and index.
    ISBN 0-7735-1119-9 (bound). –
    ISBN 0-7735-1120-2 (pbk.)
    1. Canada – Popular culture. 2. United States – Popular culture.
    3. Canada – Civilization – American influences. I. Flaherty, David H
    II. Manning, Frank E. (Frank Edward), 1944–
    FC95.4.B43 1993   306'.0971   C93-090373-0
    F1021.2.B43 1993

This book was typeset by Typo Litho composition inc. in 10/12 Baskerville.

Contents

Preface

The central goal of this volume of collected essays is to examine the impact of American popular culture in Canada and the Canadian response thereto. Three general processes affecting American popular culture are explored: its transmission by means of print and broadcast media and through "live" performances of sport, entertainment, religious evangelism, and other public productions; its influence on Canadian popular culture; and the variety of Canadian responses to it.

While u.s. popular culture is undoubtedly a powerful presence in Canada, as all of us notice in our daily lives, it has evoked surprisingly little scholarly research. The deficiency stems in part from a lack of academic resources. There are no university departments in Canada devoted to popular culture studies. Folklore, the major cognate field, is only slightly better developed, but the country's only two departments – at Laval and Memorial Universities in Quebec and Newfoundland respectively – have concentrated on research in their local areas, which are the parts of Canada least affected by American popular culture. Nor is there a professional society for popular culture studies in Canada.

The lack of study of American popular culture in Canada may also reflect the conventional assumption that Canadians have completely and uncritically adopted it as their own. Such a view precludes examination of what is surely a complex and problematic process of cultural transmission. It also fails to take account of a recipient society's tendency to select and transform the cultural symbolism that it encounters – a phenomenon widely documented in anthropological studies of colonial relations. Elementary examples of this type of selection come easily to mind when one considers Canadian responses to American popular culture. Canadians enthusiastically support baseball, but have an ambivalent loyalty to their own hybrid version of football; consume fast food, but exhibit a preference for their own beer; adopt the sociocultural tastes of the American working class, but sever their ties with u.s. labour unions; and import American entertainment forms, which they re-form – and reformulate – into distinctively Canadian genres.

Of course, these and countless similar examples have themselves become part of Canadian popular culture as well as symbols of its most recurrent image: the sense of an uncertain, ironic, ambivalent, and self-contradictory identity. The salient point here, however, is that our grasp of this phenomenon tends to be anecdotal. There is little ethnographic data or sociocultural theory to illuminate how Canadians actually comprehend American popular culture and selectively incorporate it into their own lives – how, as we tentatively suggest, the beaver bites back.

This volume contributes to Canadian and American scholarship on popular culture; in particular, it should enhance the interest in Canadian popular culture studies noted above. The relevance of such a volume at this time is suggested by the continuing national debate in Canada about various types of free trade, which has evidenced a remarkable demonstration of unity among Canadians for the protection of their "cultural industries." But what are these industries? How do they function as a means of enculturation? What is the relationship between form and content in the communicative process? What factors affect the way meanings are encoded on one side of the border and decoded on the other? What symbols are ultimately important in the shaping of a people's cultural consciousness? Answers to such questions, however provisional and preliminary, should contribute appreciably to Canadian and American Studies and help to sharpen a sense of what "cultural sovereignty" is (or can or should be) within the framework of a relationship as close as that between Canada and the United States.

While concern among Canadians for their relationship to the United States has been historically a national preoccupation, the weight of scholarship has been on the economic dimensions of that relationship and hence on the familiar pattern of domination and dependency. Economic considerations, of course, have a major bearing on the process of cultural transmission. There is no question that the strength of American popular culture lies in part in its enormous economic resources, and that U.S.-controlled multinational businesses are themselves vehicles of cultural communication. Equally, however, culture is not reduceable to economics, and cultural penetration cannot be adequately understood as a mere reflex of economic influence. Given this two-sided caveat, an overall objective of the volume is to examine the complex relationship between American popular culture in Canada and various other aspects of the American presence in Canada, including economic and cultural hegemony. In this sense the volume is also aimed at enriching a body of existing literature on Canada-U.S. relations.

Working towards a general theory of the Canada-U.S. cultural relationship, Frank Manning suggests in the introductory essay that the "Canadian edition" of American popular culture is more than a reflex copy. It can be a creative response, often parodic in tone and subversive in intent, that gives public form to Canadian sentiment and sensibility. From this perspective Canadian popular culture can be understood, at one level, as symbolic protection from, and resistance to, American domination. Ironically, and contrary to conventional wisdom, it may be in popular culture that Canadian sovereignty finds its most meaningful and potent expression.

In this volume authors from a wide variety of disciplines discuss a range of cultural forms and performances – news programs and television evangelism, movies and music, variety entertainment and serious drama, tourist sites and public icons, spectacles and expositions, baseball, football, and Olympic sport. Each example is "made in Canada" and has an ambiguous affinity to American alternatives. As well, each example holds mass appeal for Canadians, who are also on the periphery of the American audience. The contributors develop a rich medley of perspectives on this complex and contradictory relationship, but they strike a common theme: there is, discernibly and distinctively, a Canadian popular culture. This volume is another step towards granting that culture the attention that is its due.

The editors did not force contributors into any particular mould beyond asking them to address some aspect of U.S. popular culture, its impact in Canada, and the Canadian response, if any. Similarly, we regard the varied contents of the volume itself as a striking opportunity for readers to shape, reshape, and reflect on the interactions of American and Canadian popular culture, since the last word has hardly been written on the subject.

This book originated in a conference and lecture series at the University of Western Ontario in London, Ontario, in the 1987–88 academic year, sponsored by the Centre for American Studies and the Centre for Social and Humanistic Studies. Begun in 1984, the Centre for American Studies is an interdisciplinary working unit of Americanist scholars at the University of Western Ontario. The centre sponsors major conferences and lecture series, such as the one that led to this volume. The Centre for Social and Humanistic Studies, begun in 1982, was a forum for interdisciplinary collaboration in areas that broadly overlap the arts and social sciences. The centre's principal program was the publication of the Culture and Performance series, a scholarly investigation of the ethnography and theory of public performance genres.

The editors gratefully acknowledge the significant support and assistance of the contributors to this volume and the participants in the 1988 conference; Frances Kyle, the former administrator of the Centre for American Studies; and Joerg Klauck, our publishing consultant. For essential financing for the overall project, we are equally grateful to the Social Sciences and Humanities Research Council of Canada; the United States Information Service and the u.s. Embassy in Ottawa; the former dean of the Faculty of Social Science, Denis Smith, and his successor, Emőke Szathmary; and the Academic Development Fund of the University of Western Ontario. Dean Szathmary, in addition, provided McGill-Queen's University Press with a grant in aid of publication. Finally, the Woodrow Wilson International Center for Scholars in Washington, D.C., provided a congenial environment in which to complete my editorial tasks.

This is the second co-edited volume that I have published with McGill-Queen's University Press in recent years. I want to acknowledge the supportive professionalism of its executives and staff, especially Philip J. Cercone, the executive director, Joan McGilvray, the co-ordinating editor, and Kathleen J. Johnson, the copy-editor. It has been a great pleasure to work with them and their associates, and I am grateful for their support and guidance on matters large and small.

Frank Manning and I began this project in the fall of 1987 as directors of the respective centres described above. The major conference followed in early May 1988. As my memory and diary remind me, Frank was "the brains behind the operation" with respect to popular culture, a topic that he tried to teach me to appreciate. One of the many pleasures of producing the present volume is the opportunity to bring Frank's brilliant introduction to the attention of readers. In many ways, it is less an introduction than his own considered views (of a New Englander by origin) on how to understand the cultural relationship between Canada and the United States.

We had prepared a complete manuscript for this book by the summer of 1989. At the end of that year Frank's friends were shocked to learn that he was terminally ill. Frank remained determined and attractively optimistic as he struggled with the illness. I dedicate this volume to the memory of a wonderful person and a great friend.

David H. Flaherty

Contributors

G. STUART ADAM was chair of the Centre for Mass Media Studies, University of Western Ontario from 1987 to 1989, and director of the School of Journalism, Carleton University, from 1973 to 1987. He is the dean of the Faculty of Arts and a professor of journalism at Carleton University, and the co-author of *A Sourcebook of Canadian Media Law* (1989).

MICHAEL M. AMES is a professor of anthropology and the director of the Museum of Anthropology, University of British Columbia. He is the author of *Museums, the Public and Anthropology: A Study in the Anthropology of Anthropology* (1986) and *Cannibal Tours and Glass Boxes: The Anthropology of Museums* (1992).

ROBERT KNIGHT BARNEY is a professor of kinesiology and the director of the Centre for Olympic Studies, University of Western Ontario. He is the author of numerous articles, including "Of Rails and Redstockings: Episodes in the Expansion of the National Pastime in the American West," in *Journal of the West* (July 1979).

SETH FELDMAN is an associate professor in the Department of Film/Video, York University. He is the co-editor of the *Canadian Film Reader* (1977) and of *Take Two* (1984), and is a frequent contributor to the *Globe and Mail*.

BRUCE FELDTHUSEN is a professor of law at the University of Western Ontario. He is the author of *Economic Negligence: The Recovery of Pure Economic Loss* (2d ed., 1989).

DAVID H. FLAHERTY is a professor of history and law at the University of Western Ontario and a former director (1984–89) of its Centre for American Studies. He is the author of *Protecting Privacy in Surveillance Societies: The Federal Republic of Germany, Sweden, France, Canada, and the United States* (1989) and the co-editor of *Challenging Times: The Women's Movement in Canada and the United States* (1992).

REID GILBERT teaches English, with an emphasis on Canadian drama, at Capilano College in British Columbia. He has published a number of articles on Canadian drama and poetry, including "'And then we saw you fly over here and land!' Metadramatic Design in the Stage Work of Morris Panych and Ken MacDonald," *Theatre History in Canada* 11 (1990); and "Disattending the Play: Framing and Frame Breaking," *Canadian Theatre Review* 70 (1992).

ANDREW LYONS is an associate professor of anthropology at Wilfrid Laurier University. He is the author of "The Television and the Shrine: Towards a Theoretical Model for the Study of Mass Communications in Nigeria," *Visual Anthropology* 3 (1990). He is the co-author (with Harriet Lyons) of "Magical Medicine on Television: Benin City, Nigeria," *Journal of Ritual Studies* 1 (1987), and the co-editor (with Harriet Lyons) of *Anthropologica*.

HARRIET LYONS is an associate professor of anthropology at Wilfrid Laurier University and the director of women's studies. She is the author of "Television in Contemporary Urban Life: Benin City, Nigeria," *Visual Anthropology* 3 (1990) and the co-editor (with Andrew Lyons) of *Anthropologica*.

JOHN MACALOON is an associate professor of social sciences at the University of Chicago. He wrote *This Great Symbol: Pierre de Coubertin and the Origins of the Modern Olympic Games* (1981), and edited *Rite, Drama, Festival, Spectacle: Rehearsals Toward a Theory of Cultural Performance* (1984), and *The Olympics and Intercultural Exchange in the World System* (1988).

THELMA McCORMACK is a professor of sociology at York University and the acting director of the York Centre for Feminist Research. She is the editor of the JAI Press series on communications research. A former president of the Canadian Sociology and Anthropology Association, she has written extensively on communication and the mass media, political sociology, and women and public policy.

FRANK E. MANNING was a professor of anthropology and the director of the Centre for Social and Humanistic Studies, University of
Western Ontario, until July 1990. He wrote *Black Clubs in Bermuda:
Ethnography of a Playworld* (1973) and *Consciousness and Inquiry: Ethnology and Canadian Realities* (1983); he co-edited *Customs in Conflict:
The Anthropology of a Changing World* (1990) and edited *The Celebration of Society: Perspectives on Contemporary Cultural Performance* (1983).

MARY JANE MILLER is a professor in the Department of Film Studies
and Dramatic and Visual Arts, Brock University. She has written
Turn Up the Contrast: CBC Television Drama since 1952 (1987) and
"Cariboo Country: A Canadian Response to American Television
Westerns," in the *American Review of Canadian Studies* (Fall 1984).

BERNARD OSTRY was the chairman and chief executive officer of the
Ontario Educational Communications Authority (TVontario) until
the fall of 1991. He wrote *The Cultural Connection: An Essay on Culture
and Government Policy in Canada* (1978) and co-wrote *The Age of
Mackenzie King: The Rise of the Leader* (1955). He has served as a deputy minister of both culture and communications for the federal and
Ontario governments.

CHARLINE POIRIER recently received her doctorate in folklore from
the University of Pennsylvania; her dissertation was a conversational
analysis of narrative jokes. She is now at SRI International, where she
is investigating mentoring processes and informal learning and their
implications for the development of distance learning.

PAUL RUTHERFORD is a professor of history at the University of Toronto. He has written *The Making of the Canadian Media* (1978); *Victorian Authority: The Daily Press in Late Nineteenth-Century Canada*
(1982); and *When Television Was Young: Primetime Canada 1952–1967*
(1990).

ROBERT A. STEBBINS is a professor of sociology at the University of
Calgary. His publications on sport and popular culture include *Canadian Football: The View from the Helmet* (1987); *The Laugh-Makers:
Stand-Up Comedy as Art, Business, and Life-Style* (1990); *Career, Culture,
and Social Psychology in a Variety Art: The Magician* (1992); and *Amateurs, Professionals, and Serious Leisure* (1992).

MICHAEL TAFT is an independent folklorist and Adjunct Professor of anthropology at the University of Saskatchewan. His publications include *Blues Lyric Poetry: An Anthology* (1983); *Discovering Saskatchewan Folklore* (1983); *Blues Lyric Poetry: A Concordance* (1984); and *The Bard of Edam: Walter Farewell, Homesteader Poet* (1992).

GEOFFREY WALL is a professor of geography at the University of Waterloo. He is the co-author of *Tourism: Economic, Physical and Social Impacts* (1982) and the editor of *Recreational Land Use* (1982) and *Outdoor Recreation in Canada* (1989).

ANDREW WERNICK is the director of the Trent Institute for the Study of Popular Culture and a professor of cultural studies and sociology at Trent University. He is the author of *Promotional Culture: Advertising, Ideology and Symbolic Expression* (1991).

Abbreviations

ABC American Broadcasting Company
BBG Board of Broadcast Governors (Canada)
BNA British North America Act, 1867
CBC Canadian Broadcasting Corporation
CBS Columbia Broadcasting System (U.S.)
CCF Co-operative Commonwealth Federation (Canada)
CFL Canadian Football League
CHR *Canadian Historical Review*
CNN Cable News Network (U.S.)
COA Canadian Olympic Association
CRTC Canadian Radio-television and Telecommunications Commission
CRU Canadian Rugby Union
CTV CTV Television Network (Canada)
IOC International Olympic Committee
JCS *Journal of Canadian Studies*
MP Member of Parliament
NAFTA North American Free Trade Agreement
NAPBBP National Association of Professional Base Ball Players
NATO North Atlantic Treaty Organization
NBC National Broadcasting Corporation (U.S.)
NDP New Democratic Party (Canada)
NFB National Film Board (Canada)
NFL National Football League (U.S.)
NLPBBC National League of Professional Baseball Clubs

NORAD   North American Air Defence Agreement
PBS   Public Broadcasting Service (U.S.)
PTL   Praise the Lord Ministry (U.S.)
RCMP   Royal Canadian Mounted Police
TVA   TVA Television Network (Canada)
TVO   TVOntario (Ontario Educational Communications Authority)
UNESCO United Nations Educational, Scientific, and Cultural Organization
USOC   United States Olympic Committee

The Beaver Bites Back?

1 Reversible Resistance: Canadian Popular Culture and the American Other

FRANK E. MANNING

A popular Canadian creation myth has it that when the Fathers of Confederation came together, they decided to build a truly great country by borrowing the best of what their ancestors and neighbours had produced. The country they envisioned would combine French culture, British politics, and American technology. But the plan went wrong, and Canada was left instead with French politics, British technology, and American culture.

The continuing debate about free trade between the United States and Canada reveals the extent to which concern about American cultural influence remains a Canadian preoccupation. A 1989 opinion poll indicated that this concern was at its highest level in four decades.[1] The debate became an impassioned national controversy when it shifted from economics to culture, from the rhetoric of "industry" to that of the "cultural industries." Canadians may be insatiable consumers of American culture, but they demonstrated again both a peculiar ambivalence towards it and a strident determination to protect their own identity. That sense of resolution finds expression in the Canadian national anthem's concluding verse, a pledge of vigilant defence uttered in religious language: "We stand on guard for Thee." Appropriately, the opposition sang it as they cast their votes against free trade in Parliament.

This book is a party to Canada's enduring cultural controversy, but we seek to refocus it on issues that others have generally avoided. Our inquiry goes beyond the cultural industries and the question of who owns and controls them to the broader subject of Canada's popular culture and the means through which it is communicated and performed. We deal with sport, music, film, theater, television serials, televangelism, tourist attractions, and a variety of other popular forms. Two issues frame our discussion. The first, readily apparent, is the pervasive presence of American popular culture in Canada. The second is less apparent but more interesting and more suggestive. This is the response of the Canadian audience to that enormous influence, along with the significance of that response in the creation of *Canadian* popular culture. This second issue is the central and integrating theme of *The Beaver Bites Back?*

I challenge the conventional assumption that Canada is a passive receptacle for the phallocentric domination of American culture. The metaphor of a masculine America's penetration of feminine Canada has been frequently evoked by those seeking a vivid imagery for the Canadian experience on a continent shared with an incontinent partner. Margaret Atwood is among those who have been persuaded by it, and she used the theme explicitly in her 1987 testimony before a parliamentary committee on free trade:

Canada as a separate but dominated country has done about as well under the u.s. as women, worldwide, have done under men; about the only position they've ever adopted toward us, country to country, has been the missionary position, and we were not on top. I guess that's why the national wisdom vis-à-vis Them has so often taken the form of lying still, keeping your mouth shut, and pretending you like it.[2]

While Atwood's dramatic use of this extended metaphor may have had deliberate shock value, the statement is consistent with her general position as an interpreter of Canadian literature and society. Canadians, she has argued, are survivors, not winners. Passive endurance is the best that can be achieved.[3]

The position developed in the following pages readily confirms one aspect of Atwood's vision: the aggressive power of American popular culture and its infatuation with a missionary zeal that suits it well for certain types of international propagation. But I challenge the view that Canadians take it lying down. Alternatively, I propose that much of Canadian popular culture is a means both of resisting the cultural encroachment of the southern neighbour and of responding to it as uncertain adversaries. The beaver can, and does, bite back – even though, as Gregory Bateson put it in his celebrated discussion of the complex and sometimes maddening ambiguity of communication, the serious bite and the playful nip may be difficult to distinguish.[4] This very type of ambiguity, and the ambivalence that sustains it, lie at the centre of Canadian popular culture.

CANADIAN POPULAR CULTURE

While the study of popular culture has been most widely identified with the United States, scholars in other countries – developed and developing – are taking an active interest in their national popular cultures.[5] Why, then, has Canadian popular culture escaped sustained study?[6] Part of an answer appears to lie in the distinctive nature of Canadian nationalism and the discourses, political and academic, through which it is expressed.

While American popular culture is generally understood by Americans both as a "given" and as essentially apolitical, Canadian popular culture is, to Canadians, just the opposite: problematic and political. It is problematic because its existence is seen as threatened by American influence, and it is political because it is politically necessary for any government or responsible opposition to appear capable of facing that threat. This, of course, is the reason free trade was ultimately more a cultural than an economic issue in Canada, and, conversely, why it was not an issue at all on the other side of the border. Canadian partisan forces may differ on how to deal with American culture, but that culture, communicated in Canada through all its troubling symbolic stereotypes, holds a place in Canadian political discourse that supersedes, and in fact shapes, partisan differences.

More recently still, domestic cultural controversy has dominated discussion of the ill-fated Meech Lake Accord. The major issue of what has been a volatile national debate was whether the explicit constitutional mandate of one province to "preserve and promote" its culture can impinge upon the rights of citizens or the similar interests of other provinces.[7] In a broader sense, however, this controversy is also contextualized with reference to the perceived American cultural threat. As Bernard Ostry argues in *The Cultural Connection* – a book that reflects a great deal of cultural policy as it developed in the reign of Pierre Trudeau as prime minister – the maintenance of *Canadian* identity depends on the vitality of ethnic and regional cultures. These alone, he proposes, distinguish and protect Canadians from the homogenizing effects of American mass culture.[8]

The politicization of culture in Canada has a variety of implications, which are discussed in this volume. John MacAloon, for example, proposes that Ben Johnson's short-lived triumph at the 1988 Seoul Olympics provided a metaphoric rationale for free trade. He had beaten a disliked, feared, and highly stereotyped American rival, thereby demonstrating Canada's capacity to compete successfully and inspiring a highly placed civil servant to comment that it would be an appropriate time for Prime Minister Brian Mulroney to call a federal election. Alternatively, in 1988 MacAloon described Johnson's scandalous fall from the pedestal as the "Canadian Watergate." It traumatized the country and, like the u.s. Watergate scandal, necessitated a public judicial inquiry for national catharsis.

More familiar if less spectacular examples of the connection between government and culture in Canada are seen in the state's role as cultural policy-maker, regulator, and sponsor. Bruce Feldthusen explores the case in his comprehensive examination of Canadian television regulations during the past four decades, all of them developed and enforced within a vast civil and political bureaucracy of royal commissions, crown corporations, parliamentary committees, and the public service itself. His analysis shows how concern about Canadian content and the viability of Canadian cultural industries has had, over time, bipartisan agreement and support. Specifics are debated, but the problematic quality of Canadian culture, and the resolve to protect it through the agency of the state, are transcendent political causes.

Paradoxically, but perhaps predictably, the unassailable determination to champion Canadian culture has inhibited its study and analysis. What is the culture, anthropologically, that is being defended? The most familiar answer, to echo a theme struck in this volume by Stuart Adam, is the politically tendentious claim that there is not one Canadian culture, but many. Canada is a multicultural society – a social dogma that has virtually become the basis of a Canadian civil religion.[9] Canadian culture is ethnicity in its plural expression, the symbolic total of what the country's ethnic collectivities choose to reveal about themselves through a plethora of media and community events that tourists visit, scholars study, and politicians patronize.

The recognizable factuality of this perspective tends to obscure its limitations. As a national ideology and public value system, the significance of multiculturalism derives from its capacity to represent a clear and simple distinction to the alleged monoculturalism of the United States. The "mosaic" symbolizes a national ideal and a rather self-righteous identity precisely because it contrasts with the cultural sterility and vulgarity that Canadians impute to the American "melting-pot." In the context of Canadian popular culture, therefore, multiculturalism is a symbol of resistance – a resistance that is rendered all the more ironic and potentially ambiguous when Americans, a growing tourist audience at Canadian multicultural events, are there to witness it as paying customers.

The insulation of this process from academic analysis derives in part from the fixation of Canadian social research on one-dimensional models of domination and dependency. The result has been a paralysing blend of radical politics and reactionary scholarship. Domination has attracted far more attention than resistance, particularly the more subtle and ambiguous forms of resistance. Power has been viewed principally as a force that is established and reproduced, not as one that is also subverted, refuted, and avoided. A central concept is hegemony – the culturally sanctioned domination of weaker societies by stronger ones, a relationship that the weak take for granted and unwittingly conspire to perpetuate and validate. Studies of hegemonic systems and processes have themselves become hegemonic, exercising a paradigmatic influence that, as Thelma McCormack points out in her essay, has perpetuated itself despite its dated relevance and limited heuristic value. The reverse concept – counterhegemony – has had fewer adherents and a more peripheral place in academic discourse.

Yet the exercise of domination, cultural and otherwise, is not always what it seems. Examining the impact of colonialism in New Guinea a century ago, anthropologists identified a curious phenomenon. Reacting to the European presence, the indigenous people developed new religious movements known as cargo cults. On the surface the cults appeared to be an escapist attempt to mimic and achieve the "cargo" that the Europeans had introduced – money, goods, technology, modernity. But on a more significant level, the cargo cults were a subversive parody of the European lifestyle as much as an imitation of it. They symbolized a millennial vision in which the indigenous culture would be revitalized and empowered to reverse the colonial relationship. Many have argued that the cargo cults were the genesis of the political movements that led ultimately to national independence.[10]

A cargo cult in Canada? The possibility invites investigation by *Saturday Night Live*. Yet the analogy is useful, primarily because its exoticism helps to highlight a set of dynamics that are structurally comparable to those of the Canada-u.s. relationship. As a symbolic response to domination, the cargo cults were a peculiar and paradoxical blend of imitation and inversion, complementarity and contrast, transfer and transformation. They were also discernibly playful in the dramatic, imaginative, and comic senses of the term; determined resistance was expressed through the theatrics of pretense, and in a tone that combined ridicule of the Europeans with self-mockery.[11] Above all, the cargo cults were a relational phenomenon; the identity and value system that one society ascribed to itself made sense only in conjunction with its cultural construction of the other.

In my judgment, such themes are echoed time and again throughout this volume. Canadians import and eagerly consume American cultural products but reconstitute and recontextualize them in ways representative of what consciously, albeit ambivalently, distinguishes Canada from its powerful neighbour: state capitalism, social democracy, middle-class morality, regional identities, official multiculturalism, the True North, the parliamentary system, institutionalized compromise, international neutrality, and so on. The result is a made-in-Canada popular culture, played primarily to Canadian audiences, but exported to the United States in ways that complete an ironic pattern of reciprocity.

MacAloon develops a conceptual model of this process in his essay on Olympic sport. He proposes that the nationalism of Canadians as well as their development and welfare concerns lead them to want a strong federal state. But the realities of regionalism, provincial autonomy, and institutionalized cultural diversity render that objective unattainable. Canadians do, however, realize their ambition in Olympic sport, which they have built into a highly centralized, state-managed, and officially prestigious cultural system. At the same time, Canadians impute their Olympic imagery on the United States, conceiving their southern neighbour as a reflection of the vision of themselves that they achieve in the field of amateur sport.

A more intriguing aspect of MacAloon's model – for Canadians, at least – is his contention that this cultural exchange is exactly reversed on the other side of the border. Traditional values of local community autonomy and plurality, he argues, lead Americans to want a weak federal state. But that objective is put beyond reach by the requirements of the superpower role, as well as the realities of a complex economy and established, bureaucratically enforced commitments to social justice and equality. Americans do, however, realize their sentiments in their own Olympic sport system, which is decentralized, privatized, and otherwise constituted along lines that make it just the opposite of its Canadian counterpart. Finally, Americans construct their northern neighbour in the image of their own amateur sport culture, conceiving Canada as a country where local initiatives, ethnic traditions, and the spirit of voluntarism continue to play a valued and vigorous role.

Like the cargo cult analogy and the assessment of multiculturalism as an ideology, MacAloon's argument reveals the extent to which Canadian popular culture is a relational phenomenon that assumes its significance vis-à-vis a particular Canadian conception of the United States. The relationship is both symbiotic and dialectic. Symbiotically, Canadian popular culture needs its American partner as an ambiguous and reversible opposite. Dialectically, Canadian popular culture imposes a particular construction on the United States and then defines and redefines itself in terms of ambivalently held differences. That is why, from a Canadian perspective, the two popular cultures are a lode of contrasting stereotypes. Americans are assured believers in their popular culture, bearing it as aggressive publicists and conspicuous consumers, who know that their product is as good for the rest of the world as it is for themselves. Canadians, however, are everything opposite with respect to their popular culture – ambivalent, embarrassed, smugly protective, yet comically selfparodic. As a figure of speech, American popular culture is hyperbole; its Canadian counterpart is oxymoron. Americans are cultural narcissists; Canadians, as Feldthusen labels them in his contribution to this volume, are cultural schizophrenics.

Canadian popular culture is therefore a significant reminder of identity differences that tend to be obscured or minimized in other discourses – those of politics, economics, and defence, for example – between the two countries. Popular culture crosses the border, but it is also perhaps the most prominent marker of what that border, an "open" but highly symbolic boundary, can mean to those for whom its presence is a proximate and pervasive reality.

MEDIA AND MESSAGES

The electronic media, and television in particular, have been at the centre of Canada's cultural debate. Southern Canadians equipped with a simple rooftop antenna, and sometimes less, have been eavesdropping on American broadcasts for half a century. The proliferation of cable and satellite transmission systems during the past two decades has extended the practice and given the practitioners a greater range of choice. Feldthusen reports in his essay that a very high percentage of Canadian households are now equipped with cable, the technological means of receiving from twelve to more than forty channels; the cable menu includes at least four u.s. stations affiliated with the three commercial networks and the Public Broadcasting Service. However, most Canadian subscribers take more than the basic package and thereby have access to about as many u.s. stations as Canadian ones. Those with satellite dishes receive an even larger field of signals, a majority of them beamed from the United

States. American stations now command a third of the English-language audience share in Canada, up from a quarter of that share twenty years ago.

Besides receiving American stations, Canadians import American programs for broadcast on their own stations. The temptation is difficult to resist. u.s. producers typically recoup expenses and reach profit targets on domestic sales alone, and they are able to export programs at a fraction of the production costs. The most popular American imports, the sitcoms and tv dramas, are a particularly good bargain for Canadian stations, as these programs have the highest original production costs. The Canadian stations claim that it would cost them, on average, ten times as much to produce their own programs as it does to subscribe to the American favourites. Ease and economics encourage a course of action that has made the Canadian television environment what Feldthusen calls a "mini-replica of the American system."

Feldthusen is susceptible to seeing a deliberate American design in these circumstances. Specifically, the export of u.s. television encourages the adoption of an American identity in other countries; more generally, it promotes the values of consumerism, which in turn enhance American economic and political interests. Commenting on the international aggression of American popular culture, he constructs a position from sources who identify the American determination "to penetrate the broadcasting systems of all other available states" and to maintain "excitation" and the "manipulation of consumer demand." Margaret Atwood, one suspects, would join in this position.

But does the beaver bite back? Feldthusen, despite his overall views of American domination and Canadian submission, suggests the basis of a limited affirmative response. In a comment on signal substitution, a practice whereby Canadian stations use local advertisements instead of American ones in the programs that they purchase from the United States, he observes that the advertisements often represent Canadian cultural differences, adding a distinctive Canadian style and tone to the overall program package. Adam and Ostry venture considerably further in their essays, arguing that there are substantial albeit subtle cultural differences between Canada and the United States and that these find expression in both national and local Canadian media. For Ostry, the problem is not one of articulating Canadian culture through the media; rather, it is one of making sure that the United States understands that Canadian sovereignty entails independent media.

The issue of broadcast regulations, which has dominated Canada's cultural politics for several decades, is of particular interest here.

Both Feldthusen and Adam point to the failure of the quota system, which now requires that "Canadian content" occupy 60 per cent of the broadcast day on all TV stations. For Feldthusen, the preferred alternative would be a two-tiered policy that gave the Canadian Broadcasting Corporation (CBC) a clear mandate to produce cultural and public service programs and that applied a set of incentives and disincentives to the private stations, with the aim of making it worth their while to develop good Canadian programs. Adam is sceptical of that solution, however, and cites the twin dangers of increased state involvement in broadcasting and the reinforcement of an élite "cultural community" claiming the power to define standards. He favours a generalized approach that respects the freedom of the Canadian broadcasting industry and allows it to become more closely attuned to what is, he insists, a distinctive culture.

In two major areas of popular television, religious evangelism and serial drama, there are suggestions that Adam's vision of a Canadian-oriented broadcasting industry is taking shape. Examined by Andrew Lyons and Harriet Lyons, Canadian evangelistic programs are shown to differ in style as well as substance from the American imports, even though both types enjoy wide credibility among Canadian audiences. Focusing on *The People's Church* and *100 Huntley Street*, Lyons and Lyons argue persuasively that these Canadian broadcasts represent a more Calvinistic concept of religious experience and morality than their revivalistic U.S. counterparts. The Canadian programs communicate both a characteristically restrained ritual style and an emphasis on "works" as the basis of moral assurance. By contrast, the American programs emphasize a flamboyant ritual style as well as an understanding of salvation, which separates the momentary experience of "getting saved" from other ethical considerations – a separation dramatized by the recent conduct of Swaggart, the Bakkers, and other leading American televangelists. These differences are broadly diagnostic of the divergent popular religions of the two countries.

Mary Jane Miller argues a similar point in her comparison of *L.A. Law* and *Street Legal*, two popular serial dramas that deal with the activities of urban lawyers. The former show is produced in the United States by the National Broadcasting Corporation (NBC) and the latter in Canada by CBC. Both programs made their debut in 1986 and are popular with viewers.

Miller contends that the two shows differ in setting, characterization, and world view. The setting of *L.A. Law* is less the city of Los Angeles than a paradigmatic "Yuppieland Everywhere" that universalizes the American experience. By contrast, the Toronto setting of *Street Legal* has no such pretension to generalization; it is simply Toronto. *L.A. Law*'s characters are formulaic stereotypes – competitive, apolitical, and basically unreflexive individuals who see the world in black-and-white terms. By contrast, *Street Legal*'s characters are socially situated types who achieve detachment from their surroundings, question their own circumstances and motives, and recognize the ambiguity and moral halftones of their world. Extending her comparison to the display of credits on the screen, she introduces the now familiar gender analogy. The credits for *L.A. Law* had "an exciting yet claustrophobic feel, tightly framed, full of cement and glass and ending with stamped metal, reflecting a masculine sensibility. *Street Legal* was fluid, with bits of narrative, a rather summery look, and some clearly interpersonal vignettes."

But for Miller, the gender and other distinctive features of *Street Legal* have nothing to do with submission or inferiority. Nor are they a product of ineffective mimicry. She takes issue with a prominent Canadian lawyer for whom *Street Legal* was simply "copycat television." He preferred to have the "tough" and less introspective American lawyers in his corner, and was put off by the Canadian show, which "obtrusively presents both sides of every issue, turning the program into a lawyers' version of The Great Debate."[12] Miller's response is that *Street Legal* functions effectively to convey a sensibility, disposition, and "texture" that are diacritically Canadian as well as, rather more specifically, a characteristically Canadian understanding of the social role of the professional – features that situate the show, as McCormack later suggests, within the Canadian tradition of documentary excellence. The show's value – and even Ruby admits to it – lies in providing the "shock of recognition" that comes from encountering Canadian law on Canadian television. It seems that Canadians appreciate this value, since *Street Legal* now claims a viewer audience of several million, many of whom, one assumes, also have their TV sets tuned regularly to *L.A. Law*.

This line of thought assumes added significance in the light of the importance of media and other means of mass communications in the Canadian context. Communication was, along with transportation, a major theme of Expo '86. More recently, communication has been developed as an underlying subtext of the Canadian Museum of Civilization, which opened its doors in 1989. There is also a rich legacy of media studies in Canada, stimulated by the influence of Marshall McLuhan, Edmund Carpenter, Harold Innis, Northrop Frye, Eric A. Havelock, George Grant, and others. A significant thrust of this work, given its widest popular expression by McLuhan, is the emphasis on form over content: the medium is the message. This position is exactly the opposite of traditional American models of mass communication which, emphasizing content over form, have become excessively concerned with what Robert Merton dismissed as "discrete tidbits of information."[13] The insistence on "Canadian content" for reasons of cultural nationalism is therefore ironic and possibly self-defeating; Feldthusen is on track in dismissing it as a "dream" – an American dream, at that. But the essays of the Lyonses and Miller provide a further refinement. The medium itself, as a combined symbolic and technical form, is not necessarily a homogenizing influence that draws every audience into a global village. Rather, the medium allows for cultural differences, expressed not only through content but also, and perhaps more significantly, through the subtle influences of style, tone, characterization, and direction. Influences of this variety play a crucial role throughout Canadian popular culture, defining its distinctiveness in the light of contrasting conceptions of American alternatives.

THE CULTURE OF SPORT

On 4 June 1988, an exhibition baseball game was played at Beachville, Ontario, between the Beachville Cornstalks and the Leatherstocking Baseball Club of Cooperstown, New York. It was a special occasion, an observance of the 150th anniversary of North America's first recorded baseball game – a match between a local team and one from nearby Zorra township. That historic Canadian event preceded by one year the far better known game played in Cooperstown, where Abner Doubleday is said to have "invented" America's national pastime.

Beachville's anniversary game was played on a rough, overgrown field about two miles from the original site, which is unmarked and now occupied by housing. About a thousand persons attended; adults paid two dollars and minors one dollar for admission. Most brought their own folding chairs, while others sat on the grass, stood, or milled through the relaxed and neighbourly crowd. Local service clubs ran the concessions, selling hot dogs and canned soft drinks. The ambience was like that of a small-town picnic or church fair, and probably not unlike that of the event that was being commemorated.

Played under rules in use in the mid-nineteenth century, the game was no real contest. The Beachville team was overwhelmed by the American visitors, a touring team specializing in exhibition games based on the early rules. But the local fans took the loss in stride. Most seemed gratified that Beachville (population 900) had recently been honoured by a modest road sign identifying it as the "home of baseball." That was also the sentiment of Bruce Prentice, the president of the Canadian Baseball Hall of Fame: "No one here is suggesting that day [in 1838] marked the invention or that it was the first game played. Most everyone has allowed the myth that Abner Doubleday invented the sport to remain. But we are just happy to let people know that we have a history in baseball ... What's really exciting is the game having been acknowledged by the Hall of Fame in Cooperstown, New York."[14]

A Canadian observer cannot help but venture a hypothetical comparison to a similar event, had it been held in the United States. The site, like Cooperstown, would have been enshrined, and the game itself produced as a sacred but highly commercialized event. The national media would have been present, making extravagant claims about the importance of baseball to the United States and the whole world. American flags would have been ubiquitous, and special patriotic ceremonies would have been choreographed to make the occasion a suitable spectacle. In short, the hypothetical American celebration would have been a complete contrast to the relatively unheralded and decidedly non-mythic event that transpired on a quiet Saturday afternoon in a southwestern Ontario town, which, for an overwhelming majority of Canadians, has absolutely no significance.

Yet the radical difference between the public styles of Canadians and Americans is easily obscured by the convergence of their vernacular cultural interests as well as the ambivalence of Canadians towards American popular genres. The double and ironic significance of baseball as "Canada's national pastime" emerges in this broader context. In this volume Robert Barney documents how the game was introduced and nurtured in the early and middle decades of the nineteenth century, chiefly by Americans who migrated westward through southern Ontario and decided to remain in Canada. By the middle of the century there were active amateur baseball clubs in cities and towns from the Niagara Peninsula to the Detroit River. In the 1860s the first professional team emerged in Guelph under the sponsorship of the brewery magnate George Sleeman (the beginning of an affinity between beer and baseball that has persisted). Other professional teams soon followed, and those of Guelph and London were eventually admitted to the International Association, which sought unsuccessfully to challenge the domination of professional baseball by the u.s.-based National League. But the effort nonetheless gave minor league baseball a firm foundation in Canada, and this was extended and strengthened in the following century. In the decade from 1926 to 1935, three minor professional leagues were exclusively Canadian, while Canadian teams belonged to three other minor leagues that included American teams.

The most significant recent development in Canadian baseball has been, of course, the establishment of major league franchises: the Montreal Expos in 1969 and the Toronto Blue Jays in 1977. The latter team has also been the most financially successful franchise in any professional sport. The value of the franchise itself increased by more than 600 per cent during the first decade of the team's existence, and its popularity was the primary reason for the building of the multipurpose SkyDome – a spectacular if controversial facility that has attracted inordinate attention in the American media and seems likely to evoke American imitation. The Blue Jays moved into the SkyDome in 1989 and have subsequently broken all attendance records for major league baseball.

Barney concludes that "baseball stands alone as the sport with the longest and most secure position in Canadian popular culture." It was established earlier than hockey, football, and most other sports played in Canada, and it has maintained and increased its popularity. Even during the 1920s and 1930s, when Canada had major league hockey but only minor league baseball, baseball received as much coverage as hockey in the sports pages of Canadian newspapers. More recently, the success of the Blue Jays has made them Canada's chief national sporting symbol, while writers like the Canadian W.P. Kinsella played a major international role in giving baseball the phenomenal popularity it achieved in the 1980s.

Barney's view is explicitly endorsed later in this volume by Paul Rutherford, who concludes that by the early twentieth century baseball was the most appropriate candidate for the accolade of "Canada's national game." Rutherford makes that observation in the context of a more general discussion of the striking extent to which, at a certain level of their consciousness, Canadians *are* Americans, and "America's mass culture is also Canada's." In turn, this insight echoes a theme struck earlier in Ostry's essay: "America's cultural hegemony over Canada is different from its sway over other countries and cultures. U.S. influence is more pervasive here because we are already in some sense American. The United States does not need to teach us its values; there is always a Canadian ready to do it for them."

Barney documents both the historical basis of Canada's "Americanness" – the early settlement of important areas of the country by Americans – as well as the consequences of that history in generating a long-standing infatuation with baseball. At the same time, Ostry's thesis includes its own antithesis: that the extensive similarities and convergent identities of the two countries motivate Canadians to insist equally on the differences, however subtle and ambiguous. The example of another sport, football, is revealing.

Canadians introduced football to the United States in the 1870s, when students at McGill University began playing a derivative of English rugby that students at Harvard and Yale preferred to their own derivative of English soccer. As the nineteenth century wore on, however, the American evolution of the game diverged from the Canadian, the latter remaining closer to rugby. The result, examined in this volume by Robert Stebbins, was the development of a continuous conflict within Canadian football between "progressive" and "conservative" factions. The progressives, most vocal in the western provinces, have wanted to Americanize the game; the conservatives, strongest in the east, have wanted to preserve its similarities to rugby. The progressives have won most of the battles over the years, making Canadian football increasingly, if belatedly, American in form. Still, the Canadian game retains vestiges and adaptations of rugby that make it unique. As compared to American football, the field is longer and wider; all backs can move in all directions; there is an extra player on each team; and the offensive side has three downs, not four, to advance the ball. If American football encodes the mechanical precision and corporate bureaucratic organization of u.s. urban life in the later twentieth century – a familiar theme in sport sociology – Canadian football has greater speed, excitement, panache, and potential for violence, qualities that give it a striking underlying resemblance to hockey.

Canadian football, then, is just that: Canadian. For all of its accommodation to American influences, it remains a symbol of resistance to complete Americanization. As well, the game is a striking distillation of typically Canadian conflicts (east versus west); compromises (English tradition versus American innovation); and ironies (an export to the United States that was later re-imported and may be exported again). Characteristically – and this is Stebbins's main argument – Canadians are ambivalent about the sport and its ambiguous relationship to the American alternative. This ambivalence jeopardizes the future of the game at the professional level, where the comparison is invidious and commercially threatening. At the amateur level, however, it functions more to heighten the attractive differences of Canadian football, reinforcing its sentimental value in Canadian sport culture. The recent popularity of Canadian university football among paying fans as well as the national media corroborates Stebbins's thesis.

In a sense, the central themes of the baseball and football essays are implied in MacAloon's discussion of Olympic sport culture. Canadians consume American imports but refrain from adopting them completely because they are doubly ambivalent, about themselves and about the American Other. This double ambivalence involves emulation as well as resistance. Hence, in their Olympic culture Canadians project a desired image of themselves onto the United States for two reasons: they are fond of Americans and wish to see them in a Canadian likeness, and they fear Americans and want to have similar resources as a means of withstanding u.s. influence. To accomplish both objectives, they construct a collective identity and sense of national purpose that constitute a double fiction: Canadians cannot achieve it, except in the field of sport; Americans do not recognize it, because they cannot accept it.

As at other levels of his complex argument, MacAloon proposes that Americans engage in a reciprocal reversal of this process in formulating their own identity and the nature of their relationship to Canada. Viewing Canadians as friends, neighbours, and allies within the liberal-democratic capitalistic fold, Americans fail to perceive Canada's Olympic sport culture for what it is: a centralized, state-managed, publicly supported system that is far more similar to models prevalent in the formerly Communist countries of eastern Europe than to the privatized and localized system of the United States. Accordingly, Americans radically misconstrue the Canadian amateur sporting scene, imagining it with reference to a nostalgic view of their own past – a past before the days when "big government" came along to bring the ruin of ethnic pride, community solidarity, and individual motivation. But this misunderstanding of the Other can also be, as in the Canadian instance, a form of disguised envy and resistance. Americans, suggests MacAloon, may be defending themselves against a radical alternative to their own system, precisely because they fear that alternative's potential superiority.

In his classic study of cricket, *Beyond a Boundary*, C.L.R. James expressed his perpetual wonderment for a sport "that could encompass so much of social reality, and still remain a game."[15] The present volume is testimony to other sports having this powerful endowment, the capacity to reflect and reveal society at the same time that they shape and sensitize it, without losing their appearance as a "mere" pastime or, rather more cynically, as a form of mass entertainment that provides bread for the few and circuses for the many. Popular culture scholars would do well to spend less time in the faculty common room and more at the stadium.

STAGE, SCREEN, AND SOUNDTRACK

The significance of sport invites the consideration of other forms of popular entertainment. The term "entertainment," as Victor Turner pointed out, is linguistically suggestive. It means "holding apart," that is, establishing an in-between or "liminal" space, a social environment that is symbolically separate from the workaday world and partially freed from its structures, institutions, values, rules, and conventional understandings.[16] Liminal genres – ritual, theatre, sport, festivity, literature, film, music, and myriad other art forms and performances – enjoy a life of their own, and are able to bring a social system to light and invest it with meaning. Hence the entertainment of society, in both the etymological and colloquial senses, is also the process whereby culture itself is created, comprehended, critiqued, and changed. This general theme is echoed by Andrew Wernick, who concludes his essay with the hope that entertainment forms of the type produced in bars, performance halls, and other "interstitial" venues will realize their inherent "radical possibility" of playing an inspirational role in the creation and renewal of an authentic popular culture.

Reid Gilbert demonstrates textually the importance of entertainment; his search for the iconographic basis of Canadian popular culture leads him through literature, film, theatre, and television. His central argument, posed at the outset as a question and affirmed at the conclusion as a thesis, is that Canadian culture is constituted by a "double iconography: a split between an external [American] set of images appearing in current Canadian popular entertainments and an often inarticulate internal set of images kept private and coded." This relationship makes Canadian culture "a template buried deep in the Canadian psyche over which a daily exchange with American culture is superimposed." He concludes by defining this complex exchange as the "special semiosis" of "a truly Canadian iconography." Canadian cultural forms are inherently ambiguous, communicating dual spheres of meaning: "one the popularly conceived foreign [U.S.] signification with its more and more violent patina, the other an unstated and encoded text perceived at a subtle and usually unspoken level by Canadians themselves."

This line of thought helps to illuminate the plural cultural tastes of Canadians – they consume American cultural products as eagerly as, if not more so than, their own – as well as the paradoxical relationship of complementarity and contrast that binds Canadian cultural forms to American reference points. But what underlies Canada's peculiar cultural predicament? For Gilbert, an answer is rooted in the essentially non-teleological character of Canadian culture. It is a culture without a mythology, without absolute signifiers, without a clear sense of boundaries – in other words, a culture without the fundamental attributes of American culture. Contrariwise, it is specific, pragmatic, localized, episodic, and fluid. The very contrast necessitates continuous comparison: Canadians need to define themselves with reference to an absolute, forceful, and mystified "Other."

Gilbert challenges a field of Canadian cultural critics, Atwood and Gaile McGregor among them, who take the comparison literally and assume that Canada's differences are deficiencies. By seeking absolute values and a defined mythos in Canadian culture, they are effectively imposing an American methodology on the Canadian experience. Worse, failing to find conformity to American cultural standards, they conclude that Canada is a second-rate and subordinate copy. Gilbert's alternative position is that Canadian culture is consciously ironic, parodic, and self-satiric. Canadians laugh at their culture, but they "do not destroy their culture by laughing at it; instead, they affirm it in a complex, inverted manner." Hence, a Canadian "hero" like Billy Bishop, celebrated in John Gray's play *Billy Bishop Goes to War*, has precisely the attributes of an American anti-hero; he is an accidental celebrity, an opportunist without Machiavellian instincts, a modest, rather clumsy innocent abroad, and a thoroughly non-mythic persona, whose shortcomings and failures are as glaring as his triumphs. In Gilbert's view this set of qualities makes Bishop a Canadian icon, a self-satiric figure in whom Canadians see both the prosaic resources of their own character and the comic but futile irony of their attempts to identify with American symbols. Appropriately, Gray's play enjoyed long and successful runs in Canadian cities and small towns from coast to coast, and it continues to be mounted in new productions. On Broadway, the play closed after a few days.

A similar claim on iconic status is made by the autobiographical hero of the Canadian filmmaker Sandy Wilson's *My American Cousin*, a National Film Board production examined in this volume by Seth Feldman. Growing up on a cherry orchard in British Columbia in the 1950s, the adolescent Sandy rebels against the Victorian discipline of her father, a former British military officer, and her equally dominant mother. At the same time she becomes infatuated with her American cousin, who has arrived unannounced from California with his big car, Hollywood-style good looks, rock and roll culture, and surplus of spending money. Begun as an innocent flirtation, the relationship of the two teenagers seems headed for the bedroom until the cousin's parents, who are also caricatures of American popular culture, come to take him home. Chastened and still chaste, Sandy returns to the cherry orchard where she will, one presumes, proceed along her own path to maturity.

Feldman's analysis establishes the film's archetypal significance. Like Canadian football and Canadian televangelism, Sandy is uneasily situated between two worlds: a British past and an Americanized present, the latter appearing to offer the promise of the future. She is also, to cite the gender metaphor that seems to have been destined for this volume, a shy and rather insecure female struck with wanderlust and weakness in her relationship with an aggressive, self-centred male, whose phallic endowment is suggested by his large and powerful red car, an object of exaggerated attention in the film. But Feldman also sees Sandy as a symbol of resistance, a maturing young woman who is far from passive. She flirts with her American cousin but ultimately rejects him, extending her adolescent rebellion against her father's domination to a more mature decision to withstand her cousin's attempted penetration, sexual and symbolic. Finally, as Feldman puts it, the American goes home with his culture, and Sandy proceeds along the course of Canadian self-discovery.

But if the film is an archetype of the Canadian experience, it is one without mythic proportions. As Feldman points out, Wilson's story is about "*a* cherry orchard, not *The Cherry Orchard*." The setting and plot lines are localized and homespun, reflecting their genesis: Wilson put the film together from home movies. Not surprisingly, the story appears at first to have "no particular claim to our attention." Recalling Gilbert's thesis, it is a film devoid of teleological attributes, absolute signifiers, mythic proportions, universal significance, and unambiguous boundaries. Instead, it is a suggestive but unconcluded episode in the life of an adolescent who happens to undergo an experience similar to that of many other Canadians. Sandy is real to Canadians for the same reasons that Billy Bishop is real. She is a figure in whom they can see themselves, a mirror of their uncertain and unconsummated relationship to an intrusive American Other, which has both a powerful capacity to seduce and a recognizable tendency to repel.

These themes are amplified in popular music, examined in this book by Michael Taft. Canadians import specific American musical genres as well as the broader American proclivity for musical syncretism and eclecticism. At times the consequences are comical; blues artists like Lemon Jefferson have a constituency of listeners in Newfoundland, while the Ink Spots are said to stir the souls of Saskatchewan wheat farmers. At the same time, Canadians produce and consume their own music, and even export some of it to the United States – a process replicated in many other areas of popular culture. American, Cajun, and French music have been syncretized in Quebec, for example, while country music from the United States has been mixed with Anglo-Irish folk music to make what entertainers call the "Newfoundland Sound." In addition, Canada has long had what Taft labels its own "home-grown" country music industry. Since the 1930s leading Canadian country performers, many of them Maritimers, have found favour in the United States, reversing the more familiar cultural flow and contributing Canadian content to the eclectic repertory of American popular music.

Canada-U.S. cultural differences find another articulation in Charline Poirier's essay on burlesque entertainment in Quebec and its curious relationship to oral legends about priests. Beginning with burlesque, she proposes that the Quebecois tradition is an inversion of its U.S. counterpart. In American burlesque, women are whores and the story lines involve men buying their sexual favours; in Quebec burlesque, women are wives who have used their family's money to get men to marry them. This difference, she suggests, is consistent with the context of the performance. American burlesque plays primarily to male audiences and features men in the leading on-stage roles; women are scripted as ornaments and objects, although they also exploit men in their role as prostitutes. In contrast, Quebec burlesque features women in the leading on-stage roles and plays primarily to female audiences.

Poirier considers this striking inversion of theme and performance setting in the light of structural differences between Quebecois and American society. Her greater concern, however, is with what she views as gender psychology. This leads her to examine the difference between men's and women's stories about priests in Quebec. Men's stories evoke a sense of historical precision and emphasize abstract principles, authority relations, and the formal social role of the priest. Women's stories are much the opposite: atemporal, personalized, family-oriented, and with an emphasis on the priest as a mediator and communicator rather than as an authority figure. The men's stories, Poirier concludes, are compatible with the underlying character of American burlesque, just as the women's stories resonate with the themes and texts of Quebec burlesque.

Poirier's emphasis on gender differences evokes the recurrent suggestion that Canadian cultural forms are somehow feminine, while their U.S. counterparts are masculine. But Poirier reverses the conventional notation of this argument by emphasizing the cultural independence and political significance of the feminine form. Quebec burlesque depicts "women on top," to borrow a title from Natalie Zemon Davis, the scenario in which gender relations are reversed, with women exercising the dominant position – an image that Davis associates with periods of social upheaval.[17] Couched in this meta-

phor, Quebec burlesque may be seen as a critique of American burlesque, which casts women as sexual commodities and objects of
scatological humour. Equally, it may be seen as a popular form that
precedes the ideological formulation of a feminist alternative to traditional male-oriented power hierarchies, which in Quebec enjoyed
the cultural blessing of both church and state. Politics, as Kenneth
Burke insisted, has its origins in art.[18]

CROSSING THE BORDER

The exposure of Canadians to Americans and their popular culture
takes vivid ethnographic form in the tourist traffic that passes in
both directions across the border. The phenomenon, unlike most familiar examples of international tourism, began long before the de-
mocratization of air travel a quarter-century ago. Rutherford traces
it to the emergence of North America's "car culture" in the 1920s
and the ensuing determination of travel promoters on both sides of
the border to sell their country to the nearest foreign neighbour.

Statistics reflect the enormous impact of cross-border travel on
Canadians. Geoffrey Wall indicates that nearly 90 per cent of foreign visitors to Canada are American, while about 85 per cent of the
foreign trips made by Canadians are to the United States. Going to
the United States, he suggests, is part of the "Canadian experience"
– an insight that applies equally to the reality of playing host to
American visitors in Canada. If, as is so often claimed in the social
science literature, mass tourism is a vehicle of American cultural hegemony, then Canadians are doubly imperilled by the sizable American presence in their country and by their own insatiable interest in
visiting the United States.

Are Canada's tourist sites simply imported Americana, attractions
designed to appeal to the notoriously philistine and monotonous
tastes of the much-maligned American tourist? This is the central
question addressed by Michael Ames in his essay on Expo '86, a "Canadian" spectacle produced as a world's fair but targeted primarily
at Canadian and American tourists. Like the Toronto Blue Jays and
Canada's Wonderland, Expo was initially promoted under the direction of imported American experts. Its first president, an American
who was eventually fired because of his alleged insensitivity to Canadian business and political interests, disclosed a promotional formula drawn straight from the u.s. carnival midway: "You get 'em on
the site, you feed 'em, you make 'em dizzy, and you scare the shit out
of 'em." This outlook was complemented by the adoption of the Los
Angeles Olympic Games as a model, the hiring of American adver-

tising agencies and souvenir-marketing firms (including one that was given the exclusive right to use the Canadian maple leaf on its novelty items), and the granting of major concessions and other business rights to American corporations. The result, as a *Globe and Mail* reporter claimed, was "the largest American fair ever held outside the United States."

At the same time, Ames advises, the fair had a Canadian "style" that underlay its American "appearance," an "infrastructure that was distinctively Canadian, both in character and in organization." He cites three popular conceptions of Canada, each written as a subtext into the script and semantic structure of the fair. The first was the notion of Canada as the Great White North, a terrifying frontier tamed by bush pilots and other adventurers who brought technology and courage to bear on the forces of nature and whose exploits, like those of Billy Bishop, were deliberately depicted in a whimsical, romantic, and comical fashion. The second was the notion of Canada as a "neutral space" offering hospitable welcome to all nations and allowing a diversity of cultures to retain and express their traditions within a supportive environment. The third, rather more implicit but still a pervasive theme, was the notion of Canada as a working partnership of the private and public sectors, an arrangement in which, in effect, governments used public funds and resources to provide low-risk opportunities for private investors to make profit and to gain recognition as successful entrepreneurs.

Ames concludes that Expo '86 was "as American as an apple pie baked in Canada and shared with the world." Its entire production was typical of Canadian popular culture. "American popular themes and institutions were taken over, Canadianized, and sold back to the Americans as something new. This, in fact, is what Canadians do all the time to American popular cultural forms – we borrow from the United States, reconstitute the materials, and then re-export the modifications to American consumers." In this instance, the beaver indeed bites back.

One can go further and consider the question of what American tourists actually "saw" at Expo, and what, more generally, they see in Canada. For example, if MacAloon's analysis of the u.s. perception of the Calgary Olympics is granted, then Americans at Expo would have failed to recognize the themes of state capitalism and international neutrality, but would have endorsed the emphasis on ethnic cultures and communities as a social value reminiscent of their own idealized past. Such a hypothesis is seemingly consistent with Wall's finding that ethnic sites and events, along with cities that are still "safe" because their residents are law-abiding, are among Canada's major attractions to Americans. But the same type of selective perception and comprehension applies to the "Canadian experience" of visiting the United States. Canadians see Disneyland with reference to what they saw at Expo, and they understand American society in terms of their own made-in-Canada popular culture. Like other aspects of Canada's complex and ambiguous relationship to the United States, tourism yields a balance of cultural payments.

At a further level of complexity, one might consider the extent to which Canadians conspire to present the self-images that American tourists expect to see. Again, Calgary provides a handy example. All of its Olympic sites, symbols of extraordinary importance, were geographically situated to represent a meaningful relationship to local places, events, and traditions. The Olympic Saddledome, for example, was built next to the site of the Calgary Stampede, central shrine of the city's imagined roots as Cowtown.[19] The Saddledome is now the "home" of the Calgary Flames, and is served (at Stampede Station) by the city's new LRT, a fully automated, spanking clean rapid transit system built in anticipation of the Olympics. A sign at the station notes the date of next year's Stampede and invites the public – addressed in the southern American vernacular as "Y'all" – to come. Similarly, McMahon Stadium was built on the grounds of the University of Calgary and has since become a campus facility. And the Olympic Plaza, where medals were awarded, was built next to city hall.

There is no doubt that Calgary's interest in the tourist industry plays heavily in the semantics of urban development. Americans were eagerly sought as visitors to the Olympics, and they have since been sought as conventioneers and vacationers. The hosts provide what the guests expect to see: an image (highly sanitized, like those in u.s. theme parks) of the Wild West, examples of civic pride and self-improvement (city hall, the university), and a generalized sense of a community that combines modern efficiency and conspicuous technology with respect for tradition. The more important point, however, is that the process of tourist promotion works to maintain a Canadian sense of difference. Canadians resist American influences, however paradoxically, by representing an image of themselves that Americans favour, precisely because it is an American self-image that Americans feel they have lost but that they still deem valuable. As Dean MacCannell emphasized, tourism is, at bottom, a symbolic system that constructs and ritualizes cultural differences.[20] Irony notwithstanding, Canadian tourist sites function semantically to give the national border a further level of meaning by making it a cultural boundary as well.

ACADEMICS AND POPULAR CULTURE

The 1989 publication of Seymour Martin Lipset's *Continental Divide: The Values and Institutions of the United States and Canada* evoked widespread media attention north of the border.[21] Lipset, an American sociologist who has studied Canada since the late 1940s, was interviewed by the print and broadcast media, including the national networks. The general slant of this extensive coverage – and of the book, particularly as it was promoted by its sponsors, the Canadian-American Committee – was that the free trade agreement does not pose a threat to Canadian identity. Canada, the study concludes, has been and will remain a "distinct" society – the term, ironically, that Quebec appropriated for itself during the national controversies centring on the Meech Lake constitutional accord and its successors. The rhetoric, of course, invites an intriguing analogy: as Quebec is to Canada, Canada is to the continent.

In an important sense, *The Beaver Bites Back?* is aimed both at exploring the type of thesis advanced by Lipset and, more reflexively and theoretically, at considering why its publication became in Canada a media event, a temporary focus of popular culture. The thesis itself is drawn primarily from historical and macro-sociological sources and has a strong Weberian orientation both in its theoretical stance and in its penchant for synthesis, broad comparison, and the integration of disparate fields of data. Lipset builds on the premise that the American Revolution was a historical watershed, dividing the North American continent into two nations: an indelible division, he states at the outset, that "Americans do not know but Canadians cannot forget."[22]

The national differences are alleged to be fundamental and systematic. The United States began as a revolutionary society while the perpetuation of Canada represented counterrevolution. Thus the two societies differed appreciably in what Lipset calls their basic organizing principles. The United States was anti-statist, individualistic, egalitarian, and populist. Canada was statist, collectivist, élitist, and class-based. These contrasting organizational principles bred very different social impulses and historical processes. The United States adopted Whig values of bourgeois liberal democracy and laissez-faire economics, encouraged voluntarism and private social responsibility, embraced an ideological understanding of its national identity and sense of exceptional purpose, and carried the Reformation to its social conclusion by embracing sectarian Protestantism as a popular but strictly "unofficial" religion. Canada, by contrast, accepted Tory values of monarchy and hierarchy, adopted the concept of public political responsibility for economic management and social well-being, embraced a pragmatic, historically conditioned, and compromised sense of national identity rather than an ideological or vocational one, and remained loyal to the Catholic and denominational Protestant churches, allowing them a formal and state-supported relationship to secular society.

Lipset does recognize recent political trends towards convergence on both sides of the border. In the United States, the social legislation that began with Roosevelt's New Deal introduced "Canadian" concepts of state-supported social welfare programs, while the gradual, albeit controversial, introduction of affirmative action programs in the 1970s represented the acceptance of a notion, long entrenched in Canadian thinking, of group rights. Conversely, the Canadian Charter of Rights, adopted in 1982, has certain features of the American Bill of Rights and may eventually give personal rights the a priori status that they have long held in the United States. Still, Lipset emphasizes that these developments are the exception, not the rule. Most changes within each country tend to reflect, if unwittingly, the respective national traditions. The socialism of Canada's New Democratic party, for example, draws from Tory concepts of class hierarchy and public social responsibility, while leftist thought in the United States is typically premised on Whig principles of individual rights, freedoms, and opportunities. Lipset draws a conclusive metaphor: the United States and Canada are trains that began their national journeys at different starting-points and have since been travelling on parallel but separate tracks. There remains a continental divide.

As is readily apparent, many of the general conditions and processes identified by Lipset are both illuminated by and reflected in the contemporary cultural genres and ethnographic practices examined in the present volume. Nonetheless, we differ appreciably in our understanding of the Canadian sensibility. Canadian culture is less the product of its own separate evolution than of its interactive relationship with an American Other. This relationship, as we have seen, is diffuse, ambiguous, and contradictory. It involves imitation and resistance, infatuation and repugnance, collusion and condemnation, submission and subversion, identification and differentiation, and myriad other forms of acceptance and rejection, all of them potentially inversive. In a phrase, the semiosis is a symbiosis; Canadian popular culture "makes sense" only in relation to American alternatives with which it has a counteractive but reversible relationship.

The importance of negation cannot (to use another negative) be overstated. Canadians know, of course, that they are not Americans.

But, to appropriate a term from the dramatist Richard Schechner, they also know that they are "not not" Americans – just as actors realize that they are both "not" and "not not" the character roles that they assume.[23] The basis of this real relationship to a fictive identity is amply evident in this volume. Canada began as a derivative of American history and has since been both a participant in and an audience for the American experience. That experience has been mediated primarily through American popular culture, but its peculiar meaningfulness to Canadians – how they have apprehended and responded to it – is the semantic basis of their own popular culture.

From this perspective one can appreciate why the publication of Lipset's book held a certain brief but shining place in Canadian popular culture. The study was finally important not for what it said but for what it symbolized as an American recognition of Canadian differences. The reality of the American Other was reversed by an American's attempt to reckon with the Canadian Other. In that ironic sense the book had, perhaps unwittingly, a semblance of the Canadian social epistemology. It conceived the continent as a divided duality and it gave the division a continuing lease on life – the very assurance that Canadians pursue through the resistive energies of their popular culture.

The notion of a duality that is both conflictive and complementary also throws light on the persistence of gender imagery as a metaphor of Canadian-American relationships. This metaphor, as noted, runs through the present volume, even though contributors attach widely different values to it. Rutherford evokes the metaphor again in his concluding commentary, tracing its history to Victorian conceptions of a superior Canadian morality. Canada, he observes, was often represented "as a purer and better country (often portrayed as a young if rather stern maiden) than its big neighbour to the south (which was depicted as an older, leaner, slightly seedy male)."

The duality has other metaphorical possibilities. Wernick, for instance, suggests that the Lévi-Straussian raw–cooked model applies, with Canada representing the raw or natural side and the United States being a cooked or cultural imposition – a distinction that many others have seen as parallel to female–male.[24] He further suggests that Canada, a dispersed society of margins and anecdotal pastiche, is quintessentially post-modern, while the United States, centralized and homogeneous, exemplifies a modern society. Interestingly, this distinction has also been compared to the female–male relationship.[25] But the more fundamental point here is that all such metaphors derive from a common figure of thought, what Gilbert calls the "deep template" of Canadian culture. This template premises and predicates Canadian self-understanding with reference to an American alternative and further reckons that very relationship in terms of ambiguous opposition and reversibility.

This perspective points to an indisputable conclusion. Scholars must finally abandon the class élitism and one-dimensional sterility that have trivialized Canadian popular culture as "mere" imported vulgarity, a form of symbolic surrender to hegemonic domination. The complexities of this culture make it intellectually challenging, socially relevant, and, as McCormack pleads impassionately, politically urgent. For the greater significance of Canadian popular culture lies in the predicament that it shares with all of Canadian society: a precarious and problematic relationship to the most powerful image system of the twentieth century. Canadian popular culture has not only refused to default to that powerful Other but has deftly appropriated the relationship as a theatre of self-discovery and creative expression. The failure to apprehend that response in its own right, and through its own rites, is a far greater impediment to Canada's academic integrity than any conceivable American influence.

PART ONE

Communications and Cultural Penetration

This part is especially concerned with the spread of American popular culture through modern techniques of communication. Bernard Ostry, a person with a lifetime of experience as a government official in the national and international politics of culture, first reminds us of the extraordinary tentacles that u.s. popular culture has spread around the world in the second half of the twentieth century, tentacles whose grasp shows little sign of abating. The advent of commercial television in the 1950s hastened this process. Touching on a broad range of topics, Ostry seeks to explain why the spread of u.s. popular culture has been so pervasive. He concludes that the Canadian relationship with powerful American popular culture is special because of the closeness of our respective cultures, our British heritage, and our sharing of the experience of the North American continent. Although Canadians and Americans may have to make an effort to identify our cultural differences, we have created institutions to ensure the survival of Canadian arts and a Canadian voice in the media. Ostry then procedes to explain and defend the existence of the mechanisms for cultural protection that are sometimes attacked within and outside Canada as nationalistic. In his view, "much more needs to be done to help us avoid being swamped by u.s. cultural products to the detriment of our own, whether serious or commercial." Such a nationalist perspective, informed by rich experience, commands careful consideration.

Bruce Feldthusen, a law professor, then takes issue with the nationalist perspective in evaluating the regulatory policies that have proven unsuccessful in addressing the U.S. dominance of the television environment of English-speaking Canada, and concludes that fundamental change will be necessary if Canadian television is to become an effective tool of national cultural policy. In his judgment, Canadians need to awaken from the national broadcasting dream. Feldthusen identifies two basic realities, if not inevitabilities, of the Canadian television environment: first, American television stations broadcast a substantial amount of the programming exhibited and watched in Canada, whether directly or indirectly; second, the great majority of programming in Canada, foreign and domestic, is commercially sponsored. Such U.S. dominance threatens Canadian culture in various ways. The author then discusses what these realities imply for the preservation and development of Canadian national culture, and reviews the regulatory policies undertaken to address them. In evaluating the Canadian Radio-television and Telecommunications Commission (CRTC), Feldthusen concludes that "on the whole, CRTC policy has done little to curb the popularity of U.S. stations in Canada. Moreover, there is little more that the CRTC can do." He points out that commercial television in either country exists for advertising and not cultural reasons, leading Canadian companies to maximize their use of cheaper U.S. programming. Feldthusen argues that "commercial television serves the function of providing unchallenging, and in that sense relaxing, background entertainment," meaning that it is not conducive to the achievement of cultural and public service goals. Feldthusen, like Ostry, is at pains to establish that the U.S. cultural penetration of Canada is indeed part of a worldwide phenomenon. But he also emphasizes that Canadians have established and shaped the dominant commercial TV service that has suited them, with the influence of the United States "primarily latent." Feldthusen pessimistically concludes that "commercial television is the source of our cultural problems, not a vehicle for solving them. The commercial imperative is a powerful and self-sustaining force that cannot be controlled effectively." He ultimately recommends the separation of regulation for commercial and public service television to achieve the appropriate goals of cultural protection.

Stuart Adam, an acute observer of contemporary culture with a background in journalism and political science, takes issue with Feldthusen's conception of Canadian culture, arguing that it should be refined. Adam's argument is that "cultural nationalists will be more effective in the long run if they argue from a deeper understanding and appreciation of the nature and character of Canadian culture." His lament is that "the meaning of culture has shifted away from community and tradition or even scholarly definitions to industrial and media-inspired definitions." He objects in particular to the "commodification" of culture in the interests of a special group within the larger community. Adam suggests that Feldthusen perceives culture more as arts, especially television broadcasting, than as a broader consideration of the Canadian way of life, "a received culture which, if it belongs to anyone, belongs to the people," rather than politicians who argue tendentiously for its protection. A thorough review of the dimensions of culture from a political and historical perspective is unlikely to conclude that the differences between Canada and the United States are marginal. Adam emphasizes the pluralistic aspects of Canadian national culture because of the duality of linguistic communities. The political and historical legacy of Canadians is also British and conservative. Adam explains in detail a variety of ways in which the analysis of Canada's systems of governmental administration, politics, and law reveal substantial differences between the two countries. Among others, Canadians have always accepted a much more powerful role for the state (a point also emphasized by John MacAloon in part 2). Adam concludes that "Canada's national culture is substantially different from American national culture." With respect to Feldthusen's specific suggestions for television broadcasting, Adam warns of creating a system that would further enhance the ability of politicians to interfere with the CBC. The present approach permits independent broadcasters to protect, in effect, the freedom and integrity of the CBC.

Turning to television, Andrew Lyons and Harriet Lyons, anthropologists and self-proclaimed Darwinians and Jewish atheists, examine the differences between Canadian and American evangelical religious TV programming. They argue that the fundamental differences they discover in performative style and the emphasis on different aspects of theology indicate that "in religion as in other aspects of culture, Canadians tend to modify American influences even as they absorb them." The authors compare Canadian and American religious programs televised in southern Ontario. They emphasize, among other points, that televangelism is religion. They highlight distinctive aspects of *The People's Church* and *100 Huntley Street* as Canadian examples of the genre, including its appeal to more middle-class tastes and values than their American equivalents. Lyons and Lyons are particularly insistent that, despite

the élite inclination to denounce televangelism and thus demonstrate our symbolic and educational capital, students of anthropology and popular culture must study such phenomena "as
coherent religious performances, as social facts that must be
explained in terms of other social facts, as events situated in
national and international contexts."

Mary Jane Miller, a specialist in the cultural analysis of TV
drama, concludes part 1 with a comparison of two popular examples
of a subgenre of popular culture – *Street Legal* from Canada and
L.A. Law from the United States. She is at pains to illustrate a process
called "inflection," or the grafting of new ideas, dramatic conventions, and technical advances onto old conventions. Drawing on
the histories of TV drama in both countries, she illustrates how
they have interacted and influenced one another as recent examples
of creative inflection in a familiar adult television genre.

One of Miller's arguments is that most forms of television drama
can be inflected to reflect different cultural values. She compares the first two years of *L.A. Law* and *Street Legal* to demonstrate
"how two different cultures can take a recognizeable genre like
'the professional' and inflect it to match the sensibilities and concerns of audiences in two different countries." In her view *Street
Legal* initially resisted the conventions of television melodrama and
the viewers' desire for narrative closure, developing some of the
ambivalence and ambiguities often characteristic of Canadian
television drama. It is ironic, however, that when *Street Legal* was
revamped in 1988 so that it resembled more closely the American
genre, its ratings went up in Canada. The evolution of *Street
Legal* once again demonstrates the powerful pull of U.S. influences
on Canadian popular cultural products.

2 American Culture in a Changing World

BERNARD OSTRY

That we should be examining the implications of Americanization of culture for the cultural sovereignties of the free world seems apt, especially from a Canadian perspective. To be candid, we should admit that for Canadians the threat of Americanization is quite different from that of all other nations that feel endangered. It is different for us because American culture arrived in our territory with planters and settlers from New England in the early eighteenth century and with refugees from many countries over the succeeding decades. There is undeniably a powerful strand in Canadian culture that is and always has been American.

I shall return to the question of our own cultural predicament. But first I wish to look at the spread of u.s. culture in Europe and other countries. In the late 1920s and 1930s the "Hollywood effect" was extremely powerful, at first less among cultural élites than among the uneducated classes. One example of such cultural influence was the demand for twin beds for married couples. The Hayes Office, Hollywood's invention to ensure its public that even when the industry produced garbage it was "clean," forbade showing two persons in one bed unless they were comedians. Laurel and Hardy could get away with it, but Mister and Missus could not. In the 1930s twin beds began to appear in real-life British and continental bedrooms for the first time.

It was a long time before film was taken seriously as an art form by moviegoers. It was seen as mere entertainment, harmless if one thought enjoyment innocuous, an evil influence if one thought it led to idleness and mischief. Among sophisticates in London and Paris,

American jazz and blues were already serious addictions in the 1930s. And at some British universities, notably Cambridge, American literature was taken seriously for the first time in the same period. Children had been playing the American game of cowboys and Indians for some time. Writers of the calibre of Franz Kafka, Federico Garcia Lorca, and Blaise Cendrars were already celebrating American culture.

None of this American influence threatened anyone except, perhaps, would-be movie-makers everywhere but Hollywood. It was part of the general exchange of culture within the civilization of the west. Americans, for their part, had taken everything from the old world: language, technology, art, science, literature. They read Russian, British, and French novels along with their own; they listened to foreign classical music and admired French painting. They sang their own songs, however, danced to their own tunes, drove their own cars, consumed their own candy, and worshipped their own icons. They identified certain products as all-American: the hamburger, the frankfurter, chewing-gum, Coca-Cola, the saxophone, and the sousaphone. They were developing a new commercial popular culture. Until 1941, when the Japanese attacked them, Americans were largely isolationist: they kept their all-American things to themselves. And until American intervention in North Africa and Europe during the Second World War, few nationals of other countries would have said thank you for any of these all-American products, except maybe the saxophone.

Meanwhile, it was Canadian troops who first introduced American culture to Britain by teaching juveniles to chew gum. Gum-chewing was one of the cultural traits of young camp-followers. With the arrival in Britain and later in continental Europe of large numbers of American soldiers, a large part of the European proletariat became Americanized, taking enthusiastically to Coke, pop music, jitterbugging, Camel cigarettes, Hershey bars, and other exotic folk products they had first learned about from Hollywood films. Along with the soft drinks, they ingested the simple-minded ideology of *Time* and *Reader's Digest*, relentless messages that everything was for the best in the best of all possible capitalist worlds. Because American culture was first taken up by adolescents, proles, and delinquents, European élites tended to despise it. They developed a form of anti-American snobbery, which became known as the anti-Semitism of the intellectuals.

With the arrival of television, American culture – that is, u.s. commercial popular culture – found ever wider acceptance. T-shirts and blue jeans went round the world like a virus, cracking the iron curtain on the way. The American adult's habit of wearing children's shoes became almost universal. European schoolchildren became transformed into teenagers, an alien species who alarmed and distressed their parents. Another surprising development was the appearance of adults with the manners and outlook of teenagers.

In the 1960s the late economist Harry Johnson argued that these cultural novelties should not be regarded as Americanization, but as the preferences of affluent people everywhere. (A decade earlier Johnson, while a fellow of King's College, Cambridge, had amazed his colleagues by wearing striped T-shirts and whittling little figures from sticks with his pocket-knife while discoursing on foreign investment and other economic topics.) But perhaps the new popular culture was both Americanized and the preference of the newly rich young. Americanization owed a good deal to the emergence of a new demographic force, the teenager with purchasing power. Teenagers are themselves a mutant of American pattern, different from adolescents in more traditional cultures.

Viewed in such a light, Americanization could be seen as an aspect of modernization. American ways are taken up, perhaps, because America was in some sense the pioneer of modernization, having cut loose from traditional cultures in the myriad hegiras of emigration. "America" in this sense must surely include Canada.

What is meant by modernization? The essence of the term is an attempt to settle all questions, trivial as well as momentous, by the light of reason. "I have nothing but reason to be my guide," W.B. Yeats wrote, "and so am constantly in doubt about small matters." These small matters might include details of raising children, choices of clothing or food and drink, attitudes to old age, courtship, illness, and death. Even in the most rational enterprise, there is room for irrational choices. Clothing is rational in the sense that it keeps us warm, yet we also use it to announce our sex, even though that would be obvious enough without clothing. Under u.s. hegemony these irrational preferences are most often American in style. Thus dietitians seek to rationalize nutrition, but diets are commonly American fads. Experts invoke platonic entities called vitamins and calories; we believe in them because we have been Coca-Colonized. As for death, reason tells us, even the poets tell us, that it comes equally to us all, yet American funerary customs, essentially rites of denial, have been imitated even in Ireland, where they spoil the fun.

Bruce Russett sums it up:

Altogether, the near global acceptance of so many aspects of American culture – consumption, democracy, language – very quickly laid the basis for what Gramscians would call cultural hegemony ... pervasive American cultural influence was part of the structural transformation of the international system. It meant that in many cases Americans would be able to retain substantial control over essential outcomes without having to exert power over others overtly ... Cultural hegemony ... is among the primary reasons why a decline in dominance over material power has not been reflected in an equivalent loss of control over outcomes.[1]

There is a parallel here with the British empire at its zenith. With a minimum of direction from the centre, imperial officials all over the world took the same line in dealing with their subjects because they were all strongly imbued with the same culture. The so-called public school system had come into being to indoctrinate them from childhood, teaching them to keep a straight bat, to wear a black tie for dinner, and set an example for the natives.

The American empire developed no élite cadre of imperial officials to carry its culture. On the contrary, even in the most obviously colonial of its dependencies, the scattered islands of Micronesia, it sends political appointees as proconsuls, usually men or women without administrative experience, without anthropological training or insight, without a sense of noblesse oblige. Yet it also sent Peace Corps workers, often idealists who identified with the deprived and the underdog, for this too is part of u.s. culture.

It is not in official circles that Americans cultivate a common code of public service. The élites who run the multinational corporations carry it to the heathen. Certain institutions such as MIT or the Harvard Business School are just as influential as the British public schools ever were, with the difference being that no one makes fun of them. These élites are the figures in mohair suits who multiply like hamsters in the corridors of oil companies and other multinationals, diligent, rational, devoted to the firm yet looking out for number one. If Russett is right, they are the carriers of consumption, democracy, language; yet they are also carriers of business culture in a form much more sophisticated than the *Reader's Digest*.

As I hinted earlier, America's cultural hegemony over Canada is different from its sway over other countries and cultures. u.s. influence is more pervasive here because we are already in some sense American. The United States does not need to teach us its values; there is always a Canadian ready to do it for them.

It is because our culture is so close to the American one that we feel we must insist on the differences, small though they may seem. Here we must invite the help of American friends – and our two countries are nothing if not friends – to help create informed public opinion on the meaning of our famous undefended border. There is a notion on the u.s. side that it is simply a line dividing their front lawn from their backyard.

Nothing could more vividly prove the contrary than the difference between the organization of the two democratic systems. Canada is divided between federal and provincial jurisdictions to ensure a high degree of strong pervasive government; the legislative, judicial, and executive functions in the United States are separate to ensure the opposite. Yet we are, by any test, friends. We have been comrades in arms and in the grand endeavours to rebuild a world shattered by war; we have been allies in NORAD and NATO; and Canada does twice as much business with the United States as their next biggest trading partner, Japan. Comrades, allies, and partners, we see the world in almost the same way.

Almost the same, yet not the same. It is the similarity between us, and the difference, and the trouble they can make for us that we would have the Americans understand. In many ways relations between our two countries would be easier if the differences were more dramatic and clear-cut. But we are cut from the same cloth, both offspring of a vanished British empire; both pluralist democracies tempered by constitutions; both speaking the language of liberty and dollars.

It is our resemblances, which we would probably like to think of as superficial but are in fact profound, that make it so hard for Americans to take seriously our claim to be different. And we do claim the right to be different and the right to preserve that difference. We claim the right to develop our unique pluralist culture in our own languages and the right to protect their fragile first growth.

When Americans look at Canadians they see people very like themselves, visibly prosperous, speaking the language of positivism. If they burst forth into prayer, it is normally to invoke the commercial gods of free enterprise or profit. But the differences, however trivial they may seem to Americans, are vitally important to Canadians.

Book publishing is only one example of a cultural industry that is precarious. In 1984 Canadian firms published about 78 per cent of titles by Canadian authors; although foreign subsidiaries published 22 per cent of those titles, they earned 61 per cent of total industry revenues. Although foreign-controlled firms generated about 90 per cent of nearly $1 billion in revenues from the domestic film and video market in 1983, their revenues from the distribution of Canadian films accounted for less than 1 per cent of all such revenues earned in Canada. In English-language television broadcasting, 74 per cent of evening programming in the fall of 1984 was of foreign (primarily American) origin; English-speaking Canadians spent 76 per cent of their viewing time on such foreign fare.[2]

It would not be hard to show that without the institutions we have created to ensure the survival of Canadian arts and a Canadian voice in the media, those arts and that voice would survive only in the way that free literature and art managed to do in the Soviet Union – by *samizdat* publishing and makeshift distribution. The Canada Council and provincial arts councils, the CBC, TVontario and other provincial educational broadcasters, Telefilm Canada, the National Arts Centre Orchestra, the national museums, the national parks, and provincial equivalents have all been agencies by which the Canadian imagination and the Canadian heritage have been assured room to grow. Yet the modest resultant flowering is threatened by the very American agencies that have come near to monopolizing our markets. These companies already have their 70 and 80 and 90 per cent, and unless they can get one hundred percent they cry foul! Restrictive practices! Unfair! Jack Valenti's reactive, if predictable, conduct with respect to our proposed film legislation was a recent example. Canadian cultural sovereignty cannot exist in these conditions.

At the Second Biennial Convergence Conference held in Montreal in February 1987, the head of the CBC, the head of the Australian Film Commission, and a representative from West Germany all charged that the world's airways were being swamped with American programming. Hans-Geert Falkenberg of West Germany said, "The new plague is everyone speaking the same language – an end to cultural sovereignty." Jack Petrik, the executive vice-president of Turner Broadcasting Superstation WTBS (Atlanta), was aggrieved. The time had come, he said, to forget "cultural imperialism." Petrik preferred the term free "cultural exchange"; restrictions on imported programming should end. "The business of producing programming is global," Petrik argued, "distribution is global. Nothing any government can do will change that." Falkenberg countered that free choice was no choice when it was limited to dubbed versions of *Dallas*. A Canadian can only agree.

The vaunted free exchange of culture has little merit when it is all one way. The range of choice on U.S. commercial television is illusory: one may decide to watch Tweedledum or Tweedledee. Nor can there be cultural exchange when access to American markets and airways is cleverly restricted, let alone when Canada has allowed U.S. operators to monopolize access to *its own* markets, airways, and distribution. Attempts on our part to ensure some semblance of fairness are met with angry demands from broadcasters that the u.s. Congress enact punitive measures.

At the end of 1979, as deputy minister of communications for Canada, I had reminded a Toronto audience of the cultural and social anxieties aroused in Canada by foreign control of data banks and foreign domination of media programming. My remarks caught the attention of the Committee on Government Operations of the u.s. Congress, which linked Canada to the Third World in noting that "protection of social, cultural, and political interests are equally important elements of national politics which lead to the creation of barriers to the flow of information."[3] How could one see a barrier in our efforts to make our own voices audible to our own people? We are not restricting information, we are adding to it, and in our own way.

If we choose to set up public bodies to stimulate film production or social welfare programs to protect the old, the sick, and the deprived, that is our business. We are not going to ask the United States to dismantle its defence programs or privatize the Marines, and we must not allow them to demand that TVOntario be abolished, or old age pensions, or medicare.

Flora MacDonald, a former minister of communications, has said, "We want our access to the cultural output of the world around us to be unimpeded. But we want and need a choice which includes our own output, our stories, and our views." This is more than a matter of creative accomplishment; it is also a function of economic viability. "It will remain vital for the Canadian government to continue to aid artists, maintain heritage institutions and operate such a variety of cultural systems of support and regulation (as already exists). A case in point is the new copyright legislation that the government is now in the process of developing. This legislation is designed to further protect and reward creators in light of technological changes that have occurred since the Copyright Act was adopted in 1924."[4] The Canadian government has gratified many writers, incidentally, by paying them increments for lending rights in public libraries. Yet much more needs to be done to help us avoid being swamped by u.s. cultural products to the detriment of our own, whether serious or commercial.

This is not only so that Canadian investors in cultural industries can make money, but to ensure the development of that cultural sovereignty which, as I have argued elsewhere and at other times, we simply do not possess. Hans-Geert Falkenberg imagined a visitor from outer space finding everyone on earth watching identical prefabricated images on a strange glittering box. It is a nightmare which is already with us.

If only for our own survival as a nation, we must ensure the continuance of those measures that prevent the complete dominance of our communications systems and cultural industries. That is why critics pressured the Conservative government to reconsider some of its tax proposals that adversely affect film and other cultural industries. True, there seems to be a principle of differentiation in culture as in biology. Life on our planet takes myriad forms and adapts itself to local conditions, which may vary from field to field, from hilltop to slope. In a recent essay in the *New Yorker*, Alex Shoumatoff reported the extinction of a species of American butterfly whose habitat was no bigger than a football field. The insect was extinguished *by mistake*.

As if it were a reflection of life itself, culture too takes myriad forms, proliferating continuously. Consider just one element in culture, language. At the apogee of the Roman Empire, Latin was spoken over a vast area of Europe. Within three hundred years of the collapse of the Empire, Latin had differentiated into French, Italian, Romansch, Romanian, Spanish, Portuguese, Catalan, Provençal, and langue d'oc. Latin still existed as a written language, but it was dead.

As with language, so with culture as a whole. There is a principle of differentiation which is life. Homogenization, uniformity, monotony, universal hegemony by one culture, especially the culture of business – that is, of American business – are wonderfully ingenious and almost as complex as the most primitive life forms. But they are not living things. Culture, art, and human relations *are* forms of life. We would be crazy not to do whatever needs to be done to ensure that our own tender shoots of art and imagination and individuality are not extinguished by mistake, like the butterfly whose territory was small enough to become a housing estate or a factory.

What is at stake here is our national life. I think of a theme that keeps recurring in Malcolm Lowry's extraordinary novel *Under the Volcano* (1947). It is a sign erected in a public garden. Though it is in Spanish, the narrator reads it in English: "You like this garden which is yours. See that your children do not destroy it." In our own bush garden (as Northrop Frye has called Canadian literature), there are weeds blowing in on the wind, there are bugs, there are caterpillars. It may look just like an American garden, but it is Canadian. We should see that our gardeners do not destroy it.

Yet we are aware that we cannot cultivate our garden or defend it without co-operation. Let the United States recognize that we possess and must defend our heritage by the same right as they possess and defend theirs. Let us work it out together. The leadership of the United States is still needed to stabilize economic and political conditions in our world, as we see in the fields of foreign policy, trade, and finance. We recognize that only by co-operation, negotiation, and the establishment of instruments like the International Monetary Fund, the World Bank, the General Agreement on Trade and Tariffs, and summits can this stability be achieved. The same approach must apply to culture. There can be no further development of cultural sovereignty in our country or any other (as the Europeans are learning) without co-operation. No nation has the right to claim that the cultural world is all free and all theirs. Some of it may be American, but not all. No one, Canadians included, wants to build walls. None of us wants to wage cultural wars. But Canada, like the United States, is committed to the development of cultural sovereignty, to increasing our own access to our own cultural production, and to increasing that production as well. Both countries are vitally interested in genuinely free communications and cultural exchange. Let the leader of the free world learn once more how to give as well as take.

It is my personal belief that the hegemon is not likely to learn the need for concession in bilateral discussions with a weaker partner. The proper forum in which to seek co-operation and collaboration for a country of our stature must be multinational. As a wise Canadian has argued in dealing with a related subject, we need a general agreement on information trade that shall be binding on all parties. Rodney Grey put the argument in the context of computerized information, which is unnecessarily narrow. Information, education, and entertainment are too closely linked in domestic government policies and in the market not to be linked in international trade policy. And cultural development is a matter that concerns, to a greater or lesser degree, all of our allies and partners. Together with them and the leader of the free world we should be able to negotiate better conditions for all of us, to institute something approaching fairness in cultural relations. We need a GAIET, a General Agreement on Information and Entertainment Trade, to walk through freely and proudly.

3 Awakening from the National Broadcasting Dream: Rethinking Television Regulation for National Cultural Goals

BRUCE FELDTHUSEN

INTRODUCTION

Since the earliest days of radio, Canadians have attempted to regulate broadcasting for national cultural purposes.[1] We have tried to ensure that the broadcast media promote Canadian national culture, and we have tried to limit the degree to which American and Canadian broadcasting media transmit American national culture. Despite these efforts, the United States today dominates the television environment of English-speaking Canada, which, especially during prime time, appears to exist as a mini-replica of the American system.[2] In this essay I consider both the threat to Canadian national culture posed by this state of affairs and the regulatory policies that have proved unsuccessful in addressing it, concluding that fundamental change will be necessary if Canadian television is to become an effective tool of national cultural policy.

Television regulation for cultural purposes is premised on the belief that distinctive Canadian culture, especially in comparison with American culture, exists;[3] that it is "worth" preserving;[4] that the Canadian broadcasting environment, with both its Canadian and its American aspects, has a significant national cultural impact; and, finally, that regulation can be successful in achieving national cultural goals. The first two premises are taken as given throughout the analysis that follows. Although I agree with some critics of cultural policy that neither is self-evident, I believe that both are valid premises and legitimate foundations for television regulatory policy.[5]

Their proper proof is simply beyond the scope of this essay.[6] The text concentrates on developing the latter two premises.

The second and third sections are devoted to demonstrating the two basic realities of the Canadian television environment. First, American television stations broadcast a substantial amount of the programming exhibited and watched in Canada. Second, the great majority of programming in Canada, foreign and domestic, is commercially sponsored. I discuss what these realities imply for the preservation and development of Canadian national culture, and I review the regulatory policies undertaken to address these problems. Both u.s. stations and commercial broadcasting are external realities, determined beyond Canada's borders and lying beyond the effective reach of domestic broadcasting policy. Either phenomenon is sufficient to undermine Canada's long-standing cultural and public service broadcasting goals. Taken together, they ensure the domination of American programs and commercial form.

The fourth section reviews Canadian content regulations, the linchpin of cultural regulatory policy since 1960. In common with many other researchers, I conclude that the quotas have been largely ineffective, and I recommend that content quotas be abandoned and that private broadcasters be required to contribute money, not programming, to the national cultural effort.

The final section emphasizes three points and the specific recommendations they entail. First, Canada's effective options are far more limited than we have yet been willing to admit. Second, the cost of direct regulation of private broadcasting will invariably exceed the cultural benefits. Third, only public television can be harnessed to achieve Canada's national cultural goals. Success depends on a concentration of effort. Our obsession with quantity must yield to a commitment to less, but better and different, Canadian programming.

THE FIRST EXTERNAL REALITY: AMERICAN STATIONS

Of the two realities of the Canadian television environment, the influence of American stations is the easiest to explain, both in cause and in effect. Geography is basic. The majority of the population can receive American television stations with, and in some cases without, the aid of an affordable outdoor home antenna. On the supply side, the Americans have always regarded Canada as a natural extension of their broadcasting market.[7] On the other side, Canadian audiences demand the increased station choice and supply of

American programs, which the u.s. stations, now with the assistance of cable carriage, provide.[8] Direct broadcasts to homes from satellites will further enhance this accessibility.

In 1986 u.s. television channels commanded 33 per cent of the English-speaking Canadian audience share, up from 24 per cent in 1968.[9] Between 1967 and 1977 their share in Quebec grew from 3.8 per cent to 8.8 per cent, and stood at 7.5 per cent in 1986.[10] These percentage increases were greater than those experienced by CTV or TVA during the same period and were largely at the expense of the Canadian Broadcasting Corporation (CBC) and its affiliates.[11] There are as many American as Canadian stations available for most cable subscribers, and more for anyone using an MATV or a TVRO system to receive satellite television signals.[12]

This phenomenon is as old as broadcasting itself, which suggests either total regulatory failure or the inherent futility of our cultural regulatory policies.[13] As in the early days of radio, it is explained by the relative ease with which u.s. stations may be received, particularly in densely populated southern Canada, and by the demand for the u.s. programs these channels carry.[14] The increase in the audience share commanded by u.s. stations is explained almost completely by the growth of cable television systems in Canada. Seventy-eight per cent of Canadian households subscribe to cable television systems, which offer at a minimum the three u.s. commercial networks and the Public Broadcasting Service, and often offer optional service with additional commercial and u.s. pay stations.[15]

The Cultural Impact

The influence of u.s. stations poses at least three serious problems for Canadian television policy. First, the American private commercial stations command the overwhelming English-Canadian audience share.[16] As is explained below, this form of television is not conducive to public service broadcasting in any country, let alone a foreign country. Second, these stations carry nothing of particular cultural significance to Canadians. To the limited extent that Canadians would substitute programs of Canadian cultural relevance in the absence of the American stations, their presence represents a loss of opportunity. Third, virtually all the programs broadcast on u.s. commercial stations are American. This not only fails to preserve the marginal differences in the two national cultures; it has the effect of eradicating them.

The claim of significant cultural harm from this degree of foreign broadcasting rests on the double significance of patterns of communication: they are both important cultural patterns in their own right and the means whereby all other cultural patterns come to be transmitted, learned, and shared.[17] Nation-states themselves are perhaps best understood as systems of communication.[18] National cultures develop and persist by virtue of a national communication system, broadly defined: in Harry Boyle's words, "Canada is a country which exists by reason of communication."[19]

Television technology has conquered time and space. It is universally and easily accessible. It has the advantage of resembling direct interpersonal communication far more than other forms of mass communication, giving it an apparent bias to realism and a credibility that is not necessarily warranted. Therein lies the importance of television as a potential object of cultural regulation. One media expert summarizes the role of television as follows:

Television can be seen as a possible teacher of the behaviour appropriate for a variety of positions, conditions and situations; as presenting models of behaviour; as providing information which extends far beyond one's immediate experience; as giving definitions and as supplying knowledge including stereotypes in certain and unclear situations; as offering a wider range of role-taking models than would otherwise be available; as suggesting appropriate values and ideas for particular positions; as portraying many aspects of popular culture which other agencies do not transmit; as playing a part in the socialization process previously carried out by some other agency; as a reward–punishment technique in parental dealings with the child and in several ways in relation to other agencies of socialization, such as the family, school and peer groups.[20]

To the same effect, Peter Herrndorf has argued that "television is awesome as a cultural conditioner. It conditions – in a subtle and often insidious way – our values and assumptions; creates many of our heroes, myths, role models ... and our expectations about life; it accelerates social trends ... and often determines our views about what's good and what's second rate; and most significantly, it conditions our attitudes to our own history, traditions, institutions ... and our sense of self-esteem as a people."[21]

It has been suggested that American programs make a positive contribution to Canadian culture.[22] Given the similarities between the two cultures, it is undoubtedly true that many of the issues addressed on American television, for example, are relevant to Canada.[23] That is, however, part of the problem for a cultural nationalist. These programs strengthen what is common between the two cultures while simultaneously obliterating what is distinctively Canadian. It is the cultural differences, whether perceived as fundamental or marginal, that are at stake in national cultural policy.[24]

Television is as influential through what it does not portray as through what it does. American programs portray nothing distinctively Canadian and everything distinctively American. They are set in the United States. The overwhelming impression is that events of significance occur in Washington, New York, or Los Angeles, not in Ottawa, Halifax, or Winnipeg. Anyone who doubts the significance of setting should consult the chambers of commerce in Hawaii, Dallas, or Miami. All media distort and suppress information. When u.s. television does so, it does so for American purposes. There is such a thing as "American information," upon which Canadians are very dependent.[25] The communication of American behaviour, attitudes, and feelings may be more benign, but it is no less influential.

Moreover, it is likely that American television represents disproportionately the very areas in which there are significant cultural differences between the two countries. This is obviously the case with news broadcasts or public affairs programming with manifest political content. But it is equally true with "value-loaded" television drama, which communicates "very different attitudes and values than exist in Canada (... about conflict resolution; guns; law enforcement; race relations; family life; authority, etc.)."[26] The popular lawyer and police dramas, set in the American legal culture and in a social culture that manifests guns and violence far more than our own, are an obvious example.

It has been suggested that Canadian viewers are capable of recognizing an American viewpoint for what it is and more or less filtering it out in order to retain only that which is of relevance to the Canadian experience.[27] This assertion flies in the face of general research on the impact of television and assumes a willingness and ability on the part of viewers to challenge misinformation. It ignores the subtle nature of socialization and cultural conditioning by assuming that television viewing takes place predominantly in the cognitive, rather than in the subconscious, affective dimension.[28] The argument expects a great deal from young children, who by the age of twelve will have seen 12,000 hours of television, 80 per cent of it American.[29] The filter through which u.s. culture is supposedly passed itself consists of a great deal of American culture.

Finally, the thesis that American programs are destructive of distinctive national culture may be supported from a broader perspective. There is nothing uniquely Canadian about this thesis; every nation in the world subscribes to it to a greater or lesser degree.[30] Perhaps most compelling is the fact that the u.s. government is well aware of the potential of domestic television to alter foreign cultures. It has actively promoted American broadcasting abroad for years under the euphemistic label of "public diplomacy."[31]

The Regulatory Response

It is one thing to demonstrate that the presence of American television signals in Canada is culturally harmful; it is quite another to suggest that anything significant can be done about it. There is virtually nothing that Canadian policy-makers can do to affect either the supply of American stations or the Canadian demand for their programs. Canada cannot afford to match the range of stations and programs offered by u.s. television. It is not practically or politically feasible to attempt to jam the u.s. signals as they enter Canada. In fact, the Canadian Radio-television and Telecommunications Commission (crtc) has pursued the opposite strategy by permitting Canadian cable television companies to carry American stations. The subsequent increase in the audience share enjoyed by u.s. stations has been dramatic.[32] Cable television also contributed to undermining whatever impact Canadian content requirements for domestic stations might have had by ensuring that American competition would be available for all Canadian fare.

In fairness, once the widespread reception of u.s. stations is accepted as inevitable, from a cultural-policy point of view there is much to be said in favour of encouraging cable television as the dominant mode of delivery. It is possible for the federal government to regulate cable companies with respect to what signals they carry and the final form of the signals they transmit to their subscribers. Neither the u.s. stations themselves nor their direct home reception is amenable to effective government control.

The regulators have had to walk a tightrope in limiting access to u.s. stations on cable television. They have attempted to promote and protect domestic television without jeopardizing the attractiveness of cable as the primary vehicle through which Canadians receive access to u.s. stations. This gives the crtc very little room in which to manoeuvre.

The core of cable regulation is tiering, with services offered on separately priced tiers. The basic or primary service tier consists of the twelve channels receivable on a conventional vhf set, plus others, such as the Cable News Network (cnn), that are now being offered as basic services. In effect, the priority rules ensure that all

cable subscribers receive the full range of Canadian television stations, other than pay television, on the basic tier, whether or not they
want it. Since 1972 the CRTC has permitted some cable companies to
offer augmented services on discretionary tiers through the use of a
converter. U.S. commercial stations unavailable on the basic tier are
offered on one. Pay television is available on still another discretionary tier. In pay television fields in which branch-plant Canadian exhibition services have been perceived as financially viable, licences
have been reserved exclusively for domestic channels. Cable companies may carry other American specialty channels which the domestic industry cannot duplicate. Canadian channels must equal or
outnumber foreign channels available on the total service, and the
number of foreign channels on a discretionary tier cannot exceed
five.

The cultural contribution of these regulations should not be overstated. In part, the basic tier regulations are designed to protect local
broadcasters. In many cases, room remains on the basic service for
the three American commercial networks plus the Public Broadcasting Service (PBS). Of course, the CRTC cannot compel Canadian
viewers to watch Canadian stations, but by requiring that a full range
of basic Canadian services be made available, it does improve the
chances that viewers will watch them.

Potentially more promising is the fact that cable carriage permits
the cable companies to alter the signals before delivery to subscribers. In the 1970s the CRTC experimented with a policy implemented
through conditions of licence whereby cable companies would ran-
domly delete commercial messages carried by U.S. stations. This policy was designed to encourage international advertisers to use
Canadian stations and Canadian advertisers to spend their money in
Canada. It was estimated that as much as $60 million annually was
at stake.[33] Program deletion was abandoned in the mid-1970s and
its function assumed by section 19.1 of the Income Tax Act, which
disallows as tax deductions advertising expenses incurred on U.S.
stations whose signals enter Canada. The Applebaum-Hébert report
concluded accurately that both these measures were intended as industrial, not cultural, policy.[34] Even their industrial impact is suspect. Some suggest that the increased revenues generated by these
policies were simply returned to the United States in the form of
higher payments for American programs.[35]

The Applebaum-Hébert Committee was probably also justified in
characterizing the CRTC's signal-substitution rule as industrial policy. This rule permits a station with higher priority to request that its

signal be substituted by the cable operator for that of a station of lower priority, when both stations have simultaneously scheduled identical programming. In effect, Canadian stations may schedule their American programs simultaneously with u.s. stations and then invoke the rule. Thus, cable subscribers receive the Canadian signal, and its advertising, regardless of which channel they watch.

The signal-substitution rule undoubtedly has an economic rationale and effect. It may also be culturally harmful. It provides an added incentive, if one were needed, for Canadian stations to exhibit American programs in prime time simultaneously with the u.s. stations.[36] On a more positive note, it may make some general contribution to Canadian cultural goals if one believes a healthy Canadian private broadcasting industry does so.

In addition, the differences between Canadian and American program packaging may be of greater cultural significance than is generally appreciated. This packaging may consist of more than twelve minutes in each hour. There are no formal Canadian content rules regulating the production of commercial messages, although the CRTC indirectly encourages domestic production.[37] To the extent, admittedly limited, that Canadian advertisements exhibit marginal cultural differences from American, the signal-substitution rule encourages them. At least the local u.s. advertisements, most of them meaningless to Canadians, are replaced with more relevant Canadian commercial material. There are undoubtedly cumulative benefits from exposure to Canadian station identification, news briefs, and public service announcements, although again they are difficult to measure. Promotion of Canadian programs during these periods may increase viewing.

On the whole, CRTC policy has done little to curb the popularity of u.s. stations in Canada. Moreover, there is little more that the CRTC can do. It is pointless to restrict access to American stations on cable if the audience will predictably shift to less efficient, geographically discriminatory, and uncontrollable modes of access.

THE SECOND EXTERNAL REALITY: COMMERCIALLY SPONSORED BROADCASTING

The second reality of the Canadian television environment is the dominant position enjoyed by commercially sponsored broadcasting. This means that the economics of commercial broadcasting incline Canadian broadcasters to favour American over domestic programs. They also incline broadcasters to pursue other strategies which are not conducive to using the medium for national cultural goals.

There are approximately 100 privately owned television stations in Canada, including 26 CTV affiliates, 10 French-language stations in the TVA network, 15 independents, 29 CBC-affiliated stations, and 7 in the Quatre Saisons network.[38] The CTV network alone commands a 30 per cent audience share among English-speaking viewers, or almost one-half of the audience share obtained by all Canadian stations, public and private.[39] TVA commands a 40 per cent audience share in French-language television.[40] Aside from the payments which the CBC affiliates receive for carrying network programming, virtually all the revenues obtained by the private stations come from advertisers who pay for program-interrupting commercial messages.

Publicly owned CBC stations provide the main alternative to private television in Canada. It is true that the very existence of the public CBC network distinguishes the Canadian system significantly from the television broadcasting environment in the United States. However, this view must be tempered by the small audience share enjoyed by the English-language CBC, and by the public network's dependence on the same programs carried by American commercial networks. The CBC owns and operates twenty-nine originating television stations, and the network commands a 20.6 per cent share of the English-language audience and a 41.5 per cent share of the French-language audience.[41] Despite public ownership, the CBC network is also involved in commercial broadcasting and still obtains approximately 22 per cent of its income from net advertising revenue.[42] Thus, within Canada itself there are more private commercially sponsored stations than public, they command a larger audience share than the public stations, and most of the latter themselves carry commercial messages. To this must be added the approximately 30 per cent audience share enjoyed by American commercial stations.[43]

The Cultural Impact

Private television, like any other form of private enterprise, exists to earn profits for its shareholders. Legal restrictions merely establish the parameters within which this strategy may be pursued; they do not alter it. To date, the most profitable form of private television has been commercial television, whereby broadcasting is financed by advertisers who purchase air time over which to exhibit commercial messages. Private commercial television is therefore first, foremost, and always an advertising medium. Its primary goals are not national cultural goals; it is not designed to convey ideas and information; it is not an art form. Nor, contrary to popular belief, is it designed to achieve excellence in entertainment, even so-called popular entertainment. It pursues one basic strategy, seeking to maximize the ratio of viewer time to exhibition cost. The impact of this strategy on Canadian cultural goals is sadly ironic: private Canadian broadcasters will attempt to maximize the number of American programs they exhibit. Private commercial television and American programs complement one another perfectly.

A single television station that broadcasts from 7 A.M. until 11 P.M. daily requires in excess of one hundred hours of programming per week. Such a station could consume the entire works of Shakespeare and Beethoven in less than a week.[44] Few countries, including Canada, have the resources to supply their own domestic needs.[45] They certainly cannot do so at a price competitive with American exports.

The most popular American programs on the export market are the dramas and situation comedies that dominate prime-time scheduling. These programs are designed to maximize the American audience, and hence are popular with the Canadian audience as well. Not coincidentally, they are also the most expensive programs to produce. Typically, one hour of American prime-time drama costs more than $1 million to produce. These costs can often be recovered in domestic sales alone, permitting them to be sold abroad profitably for a fraction of their production cost. Canada can purchase U.S. programs at roughly 3 to 6 per cent of their production cost, and this figure would be lower if competition between Canadian stations did not drive up the price.[46] In 1980 a one-hour episode of *Lou Grant*, which cost $1 million to produce, could be purchased in Canada for $30,000.[47] A conservative estimate of the cost of producing a program of comparable quality in Canada is $500,000.[48] In 1975 an episode of *All in the Family* cost $2,000 in Canada and earned $24,000 in advertising. *The Beachcombers*, a CBC program that attracted the same advertising revenue, cost $65,000 an episode to produce.[49] Exhibiting American drama is highly profitable; showing even popular Canadian drama can be highly expensive. It is obvious why commercial broadcasters in Canada prefer American programs to Canadian; the net revenue differential is staggering. It is equally obvious why the CBC finds American programming an expeditious means of supplementing its parliamentary revenue.

The same "commercial imperative" that attracts American programming also entails certain inherent tendencies that affect the
total commercial television environment: the number of stations;
the length of the broadcast day; the length, scheduling, and tempo
of the programming; and most important, the content of the programs themselves.[50] Although commercial broadcasting is particularly receptive to American programs, these same characteristics will
manifest themselves regardless of the country of program origin.
Susan Crean summarizes the effect as follows:

Mass programming, like mass production, works on the basis of a hypothetical average – the typical taste rather than a cross section of specific tastes.
The commercial imperative disregards diversity and celebrates the middle-
of-the-road, standardizing forms and simplifying content. Programs designed to entertain as many people as possible have to be simple,
conventional, and non-topical, rather than demanding, experimental, or
provocative. The decisive factor is not what will please people the most, but
what will irritate them the least. Mass appeal usually means everyone's second choice.[51]

She understates the case.
This strategy is predicated on more than the premise that television aimed at the lowest common denominator will attract larger audiences; it is also grounded on the fact that it will retain them longer.
Most people watch television, not particular programs.[52] They use it
for companionship, distraction, and background accompaniment to
other activities. A familiar plot performed by familiar characters in
a familiar tempo serves this function perfectly. The viewer can do
housework, read, eat, and even converse without missing anything
of significance. Precisely the opposite is true with an emotionally and
intellectually challenging documentary, for example. The beauty of
the typical commercial television program is that it does not compete
with other household activities. The set remains turned on, which is
exactly what the advertisers want.
Nor is this the entire story. Advertisers would prefer to exhibit the
typical prime-time commercial drama rather than a serious public
service documentary, even if the two shows cost the same and even
if they attracted exactly the same audience share. Past the critical
point of having the viewer turn on the set, high-quality programming is more than a matter of indifference to advertisers; it is a distraction from the advertising messages themselves. Persons engaged
in heated debate or reflective thought are not as receptive to adver-

tising as a "relaxed" passive audience. Social issues of importance tend to be controversial. This is not the type of product association that industry is seeking to generate. No one complains that a particular drama is too simple or too bland; no one expects it to be otherwise.[53]

The television drama or situation comedy has another obvious appeal to advertisers. This type of programming is a form of advertising in itself: it promotes general and specific consumption. Stars live the good life. They travel to exciting places, drive new cars, wear fashionable clothes, and set trends. On other types of commercial programs, such as entertainment reviews or game shows, the advertising content is manifest. A substantial proportion of the so-called morning news programs is devoted to the overt promotion of commercial television itself, Hollywood movies, and consumer products and services. Real life in drama or documentary footage falls far short of consumer heaven.

The analysis of public affairs programming, especially newscasts, is slightly different. First, there is a good deal of it on Canadian television, public and private. In part, this may be explained by the fact that such programming has a relatively low cost of production compared with drama. Nevertheless, much of it is of excellent quality. The CBC comes closest to fulfilling its public mandate in this area. Public affairs programming tends to be more manifestly Canadian than any other domestic production. Canadian audiences demonstrate an overwhelming preference for domestic newscasts over those of the U.S. networks, although the eventual impact of cable-carried CNN remains to be seen.

Despite this encouraging picture of Canadian public affairs broadcasting, the commercial imperative we have been discussing manifests itself here as well. Canadian television news has been characterized as follows:

First, the relative costs of news-gathering in Canada impose a distinct preference for news and information which is American in nature or which is acquired and conveyed by U.S. wire services. Secondly, the economics of producing and marketing news programs disposes the industry towards the dramatic, impassioned, and personalized portrayal of events and away from the impersonal unimpassioned discussion of public problems and social conflicts ...

This emphasis on personal drama is likely to diminish the vitality of long-term disputes over such matters as economic disparities between regions and social classes.

... A short, fast-moving story is less compatible with a dispassionate analysis of issues than with an event replete with emotional turmoil, personal accusations, and counter-accusations.[54]

Commercial television provides unchallenging, and therefore relaxing, background entertainment. Admittedly, there exists a strong consumer demand for such programming, for which public service broadcasting is no substitute. However, there is much to support the thesis that the manner in which and the degree to which this demand is catered has more to do with the needs of the advertisers than with consumer demand viewed as an independent variable.[55]

Obviously, these inherent characteristics of commercial broadcasting are not conducive to the achievement of the public service goals, including cultural objectives, that Canada has proclaimed for its national broadcasting system since its inception. This is true regardless of the country originating the program, and suggests the inherent futility of attempting to harness private television for cultural goals, an objective enshrined in Canadian legislation and regulation for almost thirty-five years, most recently in section 3 of the 1991 revision of the Broadcasting Act. Public service broadcasting celebrates cultural diversity; commercial broadcasting tends towards cultural homogeneity. The former contemplates using television to engage the intellect and the emotions; the latter seeks actively to disengage them. Public service broadcasting contemplates raising individual and social consciousness; commercial broadcasting reduces them to the lowest common denominator.

Commercial broadcasting is another vehicle for American domination of broadcasting, independent of its tendency to favour American programming. Commercial broadcasting as a form was developed and perfected in the United States and exported successfully around the world. Whatever domestic commercial broadcasting can accomplish by portraying and reinforcing distinctive culture, it will do so in a peculiarly American form. There will be a certain sameness in commercial broadcasting, an American sameness, throughout the world. In this sense it is accurate to say, "If you imitate American forms, you get American content."[56]

The Regulatory Response

There are two basic truths against which cultural regulatory policy in this area must be measured. First, as outlined below, it is and has always been inevitable that private commercially sponsored television broadcasting would dominate the public sector in Canada. This is an external reality, and there is no meaningful regulatory failure in this regard. The second truth is that commercially sponsored broadcasting is inherently hostile to national cultural and public service goals, and virtually nothing of cultural significance may be accomplished by its regulation. Thirty years of Canadian content regulation flies in the face of this truth. It is possible, but highly unlikely, that legislators and regulators alike have failed continuously to grasp these truths and to redesign their policy accordingly. A more compelling explanation involves consideration of the other interests at stake, particularly those of the private broadcasters and other persons employed in Canadian broadcasting at every level.

In 1961 Graham Spry, the founder of the Radio League, a remarkable public interest lobby group which supported public radio broadcasting in Canada, described the state of Canadian broadcasting as follows: "It is not a system of national public ownership with local private stations, but a system of local private stations with a lesser public sector serving and subsidizing private stations. The private advertising sector is the dominant sector. The public service sector is the subordinate."[57] His remarks were accurate then, and the influence of public broadcasting has since declined further. Somewhat questionable, however, are Spry's conclusions that this state of affairs constitutes a national failure, a thwarting of the will of the Canadian public and that of successive parliaments from 1932 to 1961.[58]

The Aird Commission, the first royal commission to study broadcast policy, reported in 1929.[59] It concluded that the national cultural interest would be served best by a public radio monopoly. Neither the acts of 1932 and 1936 nor the manner in which they were administered provides much support for Spry's thesis. Neither statute expressly contemplated the public radio monopoly recommended by the Aird Commission, and neither statute adopted the Aird Commission's recommendation on financing. Inadequate financing as much as anything else ensured slow growth in the public sector and the related survival of private commercial radio.[60] None of this should be surprising. Certainly the Canadian population supported a public service option in radio and television, but never a monopoly or anything approaching it. If commercial broadcasting thrives in Canada it does so because of public support, not in spite of it. There is no mystery or shame in this. Commercial broadcasters succeed by offering programs that maximize their audience. By definition, public broadcasting, which pursues a different strategy, will enjoy smaller audience shares in a competitive broadcast market.

The only compelling evidence of a strong federal commitment to public broadcasting dominance lay in the fact that the CBC was given a dual statutory mandate, both as a public broadcaster and as a regulator for all broadcasting. Between 1932 and 1958 the CBC concentrated on expanding the public service on the one hand and restricting the growth of the private service on the other. It appears that Canada was beginning to establish a radio environment in which public radio, albeit commercially sponsored, was assuming national dominance, and in which private broadcasting initiatives were being curtailed.[61]

The Broadcasting Act of 1958 effectively precluded any possibility that public broadcasting would enjoy a pre-eminent position.[62] The statute eliminated the regulatory body's expropriation power and the statutory reference to the public ownership of the airwaves, thereby symbolizing rather than actually effecting a change in the balance of power.[63] The statute also failed to provide for long-term predictable funding for the public broadcasting system. The corporation remains dependent on uncertain annual financing from parliamentary appropriations.[64]

Most important, the 1958 act effected a fundamental change in the regulatory structure of Canadian broadcasting. It stripped the CBC of its regulatory power and replaced it with an independent body, the Board of Broadcast Governors. The BBG was charged with "the operation of a national broadcasting system ... [regulating] the establishment and operation of networks of broadcasting stations, the activities of public and private broadcasting stations in Canada and the relationship between them."[65] The CBC essentially retained its role as a public broadcaster. Private commercial broadcasting has thrived since.

The eventual ascendancy of commercial broadcasting was inevitable from the start. The lack of total commitment to public broadcasting on the part of both the population and the government is as much a reflection of this inevitability as it is a contributing cause. It is wrong to suppose that commercial broadcasting would be greatly restricted today if, for example, the early statutes had followed faithfully the Aird Commission's recommendations, or the CBC had been more generously funded, or the CBC, not the BBG, had been permitted to regulate television in the critical early years. These factors are better regarded as catalytic than causative.

Because most Canadians have always been able to receive broadcast signals from the United States, it has always been impossible for Canada to monopolize its own airwaves. Even a domestic public broadcasting monopoly was, practically speaking, unattainable. By the time the Aird Commission reported, domestic commercial broadcasting was already a well-established, lucrative, and promising industry.[66] Even if it had not been necessary to dismantle an existing industry, the pressures from prospective entrants would have been every bit as great as they were from the incumbents. Given the wealth and power of private broadcasters, and the influential media at their disposal, it is surprising that the CBC, presumably backed by the government, was able to restrict private broadcasting to the extent that it did.[67]

The broadcasters were joined by prospective advertisers. They might have endured non-commercial broadcasting and settled for other advertising outlets if access to broadcast advertising could have been denied to all. Here the presence of U.S. commercial stations played a key role. Manufacturers of products marketed in both countries could use radio advertising on American stations to reach both markets, whereas solely domestic manufacturers could not. They were at a disadvantage even if they used American stations to advertise in Canada, which they did. In both cases, substantial advertising revenues were being diverted from Canada to the United States and away from Canadian broadcasters who were willing and anxious to earn them. This constitutes a major portion of the true cost of public radio policy in Canada, and it was an issue that pitted national industrial and employment policy squarely against national broadcast policy. The cost was simply too great, and in any event pointless, to incur. If the government had somehow withstood the tremendous pressures to expand commercial broadcasting, there would have been more American stations, supported by more Canadian advertising money, directing more commercial messages to Canada, than there are today. The eventual growth of the private broadcasters in Canada reflects the decision that as between foreign and domestic commercial broadcasting, the latter is the lesser necessary evil.

The thesis of commercial inevitability can be established from a worldwide perspective, from which the Canadian experience appears merely as a local variation of a basic pattern of global commercial penetration. Canadian studies focus upon domestic factors – unsympathetic governments, inept regulators, declining Canadian nationalism – as the reasons for the ascendancy of commercial broadcasting in the 1950s and 1960s. World studies focus upon the planned expansion of the American communications system, which began in the 1950s.[68] Canadians view proximity and cultural similarity to the United States as uniquely responsible for our broadcast environment. But commercial broadcasting, and the American programming with which it is intimately associated, exists virtually everywhere. Significantly, commercial broadcasting has penetrated successfully in strong industrialized nations with long-standing state broadcasting monopolies and older national cultures far less similar to the American than our own. Canada's "failure" to maintain an ascendant public system is by no means unique.

Raymond Williams describes a "planned operation" from the United States "in two related stages: the formation, in the United States, of a complex military, political and industrial communications system; and then, in direct relation to this, the operation of this system to penetrate the broadcasting systems of all other available states."[69] In this the American government, no less than the equipment manufacturers, broadcasters, program producers, and advertisers, has been active.[70] Herbert Schiller said, "Nothing less than the viability of the American industrial economy itself is involved in the movement toward international commercialization of broadcasting ... remove the excitation and the manipulation of consumer demand and industrial slowdown threatens."[71]

Whether or not one accepts this conspiracy theory, the patterns of global penetration by commercial broadcasters are too obvious to ignore. Consider Schiller's observations about western Europe: "American and local commercial interests form a temporary alliance which is well financed and relentless in its lobbying efforts. Success in one country immediately jeopardizes a state monopoly in a bordering country."[72] Pirate stations are financed. Satellite broadcasting, itself a part of the planned operation discussed above, is introduced. The British commercial satellite channel, Sky Channel, reaches two million viewers through 106 cable systems in Europe. It broadcasts primarily American programs, exclusively in English."[73] Canada's unique problems begin to appear as merely local differences of degree, not of kind.

Of course, the conscious commercialization of world broadcasting cannot be blamed solely on the United States. It is a strategy employed by multinational corporations whatever their country of origin. And it is a strategy that succeeds in part because of the co-operation of local interests, as has certainly been the case in Canada. The tremendous revenue-producing capabilities of commercial broadcasting are not uniquely appealing to American governments or industry. Canada has willingly provided most of its citizens with better access to u.s. programs than many Americans have. Canadian television has been, almost since its inception, a predominantly commercial venture. Canadians have established the system that suits them; the United States did not have to force it upon them. The influence of the United States is primarily latent. It serves as a reminder to those who think, or have thought, that things could somehow have been different. The similarities between our national cultures, and in particular our national economic systems, account for our embracing in fact, if not in rhetoric, branch-plant American commercial broadcasting. Worldwide experience proves that we could not have prevented our broadcasting system from becoming commercialized even if we had wished and tried to do so.

CANADIAN CONTENT QUOTAS

Since 1960 it has been clear that domestic commercial broadcasting would command the dominant share of the Canadian television market. Therefore, television regulatory bodies have concentrated their efforts on attempts to provide symptomatic relief from two major problems commercial broadcasting inevitably entails – the infusion of American programming and the suppression of domestic programming. Their aim has been to increase the amount and quality of domestic programming shown on Canadian stations in an attempt to achieve the cultural and public service goals contemplated by the Broadcasting Act. The fundamental regulatory strategy has been the imposition of Canadian content quotas on domestic broadcasters. These quotas have constituted the foundation upon which virtually all other non-technical television regulatory policies depend.[74] Quotas have performed dismally as a barrier to American programming and as an incentive for high-quality domestic programming.

The BBG first introduced Canadian content quotas in regulations enacted in 1959. In an explanatory note, the board said:

The Board interprets the reference, in Section 10 of the Act, to a broadcasting service "that is basically Canadian in content and character" to mean that the service is to be so regulated as to ensure its contribution to maintaining Canadian identity and strengthening Canadian unity. It is also expected that Canadian broadcasting will offer to Canadians an opportunity to participate in the broadcasting service.[75]

Nominally, the Canadian content requirements have increased, reaching a maximum of 60 per cent of the broadcast day in 1972 and remaining at that level today.[76] Separate quotas were established for prime-time viewing, defined usually as the period between 6 P.M. and midnight. Since 1972 the CBC has been required to provide Canadian content for 60 per cent of this period, holders of private licenses for 50 per cent. The measurement period, first proposed as one week and first enacted as four weeks, was changed to quarterly in 1964, to annually in 1971, and to semi-annually in 1984.

The quotas are not as demanding as they appear. Their utility in achieving cultural goals depends in part upon Canadian programs being exhibited to a substantial audience. However, the longer the measurement period, the more flexibility commercial broadcasters have in scheduling such programs during predictably low viewing periods and exhibiting the more lucrative American programming during the more popular viewing periods. Similarly, the definition of "prime time" is critical. Before the quotas were introduced, most Canadian stations were already devoting two hours of the period between 6 P.M. and midnight to news broadcasts, so the regulations required little change.[77] A 1980 CBC survey showed that on average the amount of Canadian programming aired by English-language private stations measured 50 per cent on a 6 P.M.-to-midnight basis, but only 25 per cent when measured from 7 P.M. to 11 P.M.[78] True peak viewing time is between 8 P.M. and 10:30 P.M.[79] Thus the effective amount of Canadian programming exhibited to potentially large Canadian audiences is considerably below the nominal figures specified in the quotas.

Quotas raise other problems. Selecting an appropriate level of output independent of market forces is a classic regulatory dilemma, compounded when the output is as variable in kind and quality as Canadian programming. Fifty per cent of prime time devoted to high-quality Canadian drama that attracted a large audience would be a remarkable achievement. The same quantity of culturally neutral game shows featuring Canadian contestants would be embarrassing.

The Broadcasting Act is probably the source of the range of nominal quotas which the regulators have imposed. The act mandates programming "using predominantly Canadian creative and other resources."[80] The 60 per cent–50 per cent quotas currently enforced for private stations in prime time constitute the bare minimum necessary to support the purely technical claim that Canada's television system meets its statutory objective. Outside this context, the nominal quotas appear arbitrary.

Like the Aird Commission's vision of a national radio monopoly, the vision of predominantly Canadian broadcasting appears totally unrealistic in an environment where substantial competition from American stations exists. The regulations dictate the amount of Canadian programming domestic broadcasters must exhibit. Even in theory there is nothing to suggest that they will have much of an impact on the programs Canadian viewers will actually watch. Experience bears this out. Canadian programs, especially drama, attract a small share of the audience relative to American competition.[81] This is largely a function of the economic disincentives to the production of high-quality drama in Canada. Canadian broadcasters cannot afford to compete effectively with the American competition to the extent mandated by the statute. If the goal is popular programming of high quality, the quotas would have to be reduced substantially as part of an overall strategy.

Another fundamental problem with Canadian content regulation is the difficulty in operationally defining Canadian content in a manner responsive to cultural goals. Ideally, it might be preferable to evaluate output directly, judging the programs themselves against a statutory standard supplemented by some objective regulatory guidelines. One insurmountable difficulty is that it is impossible to provide meaningful objective guidelines to guide a screening body. Regulations made under such a framework would always be criticized as subjective or arbitrary. There would be a danger of the regulatory body's imposing a centralized and monolithic, perhaps élitist, conception of Canadian culture upon the viewers. Private broadcasters committed rationally to minimal compliance would insist on objective standards which they knew they could meet before risking production expenses. The artistic community would object to government censorship and the curtailment of artistic freedom. These are all sound objections.

These difficulties have led the regulators to define Canadian content by input rather than by output. They have attempted to promote all cultural patterns manifested within the country, not any particular version of national culture. The emphasis has been on increasing access to the system for all Canadians, as viewers, carriers, exhibitors, producers, performers, and technicians. The key assumption is that communication by Canadians to Canadians will transmit a representative range of national cultural patterns, including but not limited to characteristic or distinctive patterns.

It is questionable whether the open-access goal, even if it could be achieved with moderate success, is sufficiently ambitious to address the cultural problem for which it was ostensibly adopted. As noted earlier, the problem lies at the margin. American programming obliterates the distinctive aspects of Canadian culture while reinforcing what is common between the two cultures. An attempt to address this problem would require incentives to produce distinctive Canadian programming, not a representative range of Canadian content

that would include much of what was common. The hopeless difficulties of attempting to define, let alone operationalize, the concept
of distinctive Canadian culture emerge. Yet without attempting to
do so, we permit the continuous eradication of the marginal differences between the cultures. This is an insoluble dilemma. It is difficult to imagine a screening body's reaching decisions more arbitrary
or less in tune with Canada's express cultural goals than those that
may be reached under the input-evaluation system the regulators
have employed from the beginning. Indeed, the original definition
of Canadian content in the early 1960s was so ridiculous that it called
into question the sincerity of the board that enacted it.[82]

Today's definition of a Canadian program does not contain the
obvious loopholes of the earlier effort. It provides a detailed
weighted-point system that attempts to ensure, as far as regulation
can, that Canadian programs are defined by the degree of meaningful participation by Canadian citizens.[83] For example, a Canadian
production requires at least six "points" based on key functions
being performed by Canadians. A Canadian director is worth two
points, a writer two points, a musical composition one point, and so
on. Ostensibly, this approach is premised on the belief that a substantial correlation exists between Canadian participation and culturally distinctive programming. Quantifiable inputs are relied upon
to generate immeasurable outputs. Ultimately, it becomes a question
of faith, an inherent problem in cultural regulation.

Quotas primarily affect private broadcasters. The CBC routinely
exceeds them, whereas the commercial imperative drives the basic
strategy of the private broadcasters. Whatever they produce will still
be commercial programming with its inherent American character
and hostility to public service programming. The best the quotas can
accomplish is to encourage programs that portray unique aspects of
Canadian culture, albeit in a common commercial form. This is not
an empty goal but a limited one, dictated by conditions for which
neither parliament nor the regulators are to blame.[84]

Moreover, the quotas, at least in their current form, are simply not
powerful enough to overcome the tremendous commercial advantages of American programming. So much is at stake that the commercial broadcasters will always lobby to reduce the impact of the
regulations. So great are the net revenue differentials between Canadian and American programs that the commercial broadcasters
will always prefer to schedule American programs during peak periods. Nothing inclines private broadcasters to produce uniquely
Canadian material. They are rationally inclined to fill Canadian
content quotas with lower-cost programming.[85] They prefer rela-

tively inexpensive news programming to drama production. When the regulators attempt to require drama production, the producers will invest as little as possible. And when they do make substantial production investments, they will rationally attempt to "de-Canadianize" the program in an effort to make it more attractive on the export market.

Studies of the Canadian broadcasting system have had few kind words to say on behalf of the private broadcasters. A comment by the Applebaum-Hébert Committee is typical:

One's expectations of the cultural program content of private television are not very high, and these are usually borne out. Private television uses little Canadian talent and expends few resources to develop new talent. The airwaves and cable are regarded as carriers to be exploited for profit. Few private broadcasters seem to display a sense of responsibility for the development of the arts and other aspects of cultural life in Canada, notwithstanding the content regulations.[86]

Criticism of this sort is accurate but foolish. What else is one to expect? Private broadcasters are not cultural philanthropists; they are in business to earn profits. Canadian content regulations constitute potential obstacles to be overcome. Valid criticism would be better directed towards successive parliaments, regulators, and evaluators who persist in believing, or pretending to believe, otherwise.

The most interesting aspect is the persistence of the apparently futile Canadian content policy for more than thirty years. There are a number of possible explanations, each of which must be considered when assessing the prospects for meaningful change. Faced with overwhelming difficulties in employing our broadcasting system for national ends, an understandable desire persists to attempt what little we can. The claim that our broadcasting system is predominantly Canadian is one of considerable symbolic and political significance. It would take a great deal of political courage to acknowledge the truth and to formulate realistic policy on that basis. Meanwhile, the symbol can be manipulated to serve a number of different interests.

First and foremost, Canadian content quotas are the sustaining force of private broadcasting, not the impediment they are often portrayed to be.[87] The CRTC's ostensible premise is that Canadian culture is best advanced by insuring a lucrative private broadcasting industry, which will then generate Canadian programming of cultural significance. Thus private broadcasters are shielded from foreign and domestic competition, and have until recently been able to earn extra-normal profits.[88] Public debates between the CRTC and the broadcasters symbolize the regulatory commitment to cultural goals. Each new chairman has a new "get tough" policy. In reality, the private broadcasters lobby successfully to ensure that the cost of compliance is much less than the benefits of protectionism.[89] Often they simply fail to comply, with impunity. To this must be added the remarkable observation made in the Caplan-Sauvageau report: "The CRTC protects the industry for its own sake, as an end in itself."[90]

In addition, Canadian content regulation is and has been for more than thirty years the fundamental policy tool of the television regulators. Virtually all of the non-technical television policy regulations are related to and often dependent on this basic goal. It is simply unrealistic to expect a regulatory body to dismantle its entire regulatory structure upon which its credibility, and perhaps even its existence, depends.

It is also possible that Canadian content regulation was never seriously intended to encourage programming of Canadian cultural relevance. Some see it as a "make-work" program, an employment policy in cultural policy disguise.[91] In fairness, securing Canadian participation in the domestic television industry has always been one of the stated goals of content regulation. It may be that employment goals have eclipsed cultural goals over the years. The positive cultural symbols are useful to a government wishing to pass otherwise controversial employment legislation.

In summary, a great deal of commercial television regulation with manifest cultural purposes seems only to benefit the incumbent on-air broadcasters and, to a lesser extent, all persons employed in the television industry. This is exactly what the "capture theory" of regulation[92] or the "economic theory" of regulation would predict.[93] Be that as it may, the travesty lies less in the legislators and regulators having failed to adopt more effective policies than in their perpetuating the belief that any significant cultural goals are likely to be achieved through commercial television regulation, however sincerely and vigorously pursued.[94]

Commercial television is the source of our cultural problems, not a vehicle for solving them. The commercial imperative is a powerful and self-sustaining force that cannot be controlled. The inherent biases of commercial television will manifest themselves within any regulatory framework. The more Canadian commercial television is differentiated by regulation from American, the more self-defeating will be the policy, as more Canadians switch to viewing American stations. The options suggested below may constitute an improvement over the present regulatory scheme, but they do not promise a revolutionary change.

RECOMMENDATIONS

A New Conception of Cultural Policy in Broadcasting

There is a recurrent theme in the history of Canadian broadcasting regulation as old as broadcasting itself. The "National Broadcasting Dream" consists of a vision of the national broadcasting environment in which the external realities somehow disappear. In their place appears a broadcasting environment dominated by high-quality Canadian programming in limitless quantity. Private and public broadcasters co-operate willingly to achieve this goal. Specifics rarely manifest themselves in the dream. For some visionaries it consists of Canadian commercial programming replacing American in domestic popularity. For others it consists of representative Canadian programming reflecting proportionally all regional, linguistic, ethnic, and other subcultures. For others it consists of an alternative to commercial broadcasting, dominated by public service and fine arts programming. For many it consists of all this and more. Not only is this a vision of what will be exhibited but also a vision of what will satisfy the Canadian audience. Indeed, some contemplate a successful export market for the dream. Pity the CBC, and even the private broadcasters, who are expected to make this dream come true.

Notwithstanding its popularity and longevity, the National Broadcasting Dream is just that – a dream. No one can seriously regard the dream as a viable policy goal. If cultural regulation of broadcasting is to be more effective than it has been in the past, the critical first step will be for legislators, regulators, and the public to abandon the National Broadcasting Dream, to acknowledge the external realities of American stations and commercial dominance, and to devise new policies in the light of these realities. In particular, Canadians must abandon their preoccupation with quantity in television production and exhibition and accept that little of cultural significance will ever be achieved by private broadcasters, however they are regulated.

Politicians and broadcast regulators are not incompetent; they can surely recognize the Dream for what it is, and most of them probably have. The existing state of affairs probably represents a series of compromises among a number of different goals and interests, some apparently more effectively represented than national cultural interests. There is no reason to expect impetus for meaningful change to come from the legislators, regulators, broadcasters, or those employed in the industry. The best prospect rests with cultural nationalists, often members of the intellectual and artistic communities, who have proved in the past that they can organize and lobby effectively. Unfortunately, cultural nationalists are often the greatest national dreamers of all. It would be presumptuous to dismiss their vision of Canada; nonetheless, for change to occur they must accept more limited cultural goals in broadcasting, at least in the short run. Otherwise, they will continue to posit a broadcasting dream that serves the very interests they oppose.

The second obstacle to progress in the cultural regulation of television is written into the Broadcasting Act,[95] and was endorsed as recently as 1986 by the last federal Task Force on Broadcasting Policy.[96] This is the notion that the Canadian broadcasting system is a single system composed of public and private elements, and therefore should be regulated by a single authority. Whatever its merits for other (perhaps technical) purposes, this conception is dysfunctional for cultural purposes. It perpetuates the notion that private and public broadcasters are partners in national cultural endeavour, and it legitimizes ineffectual regulations that proceed on this inherently flawed premise. If it is thought worthwhile to fight the commercial imperative of private television for cultural purposes, a regulatory commission can be so charged. To assume that the same problems exist with public broadcasting and that the same agency should therefore regulate both is as harmful to public broadcasting as it is ineffectual for private.

The key lies in recognizing the limits of the private sector and thereby recognizing the needs the public sector must fill. This entails a dual system of private enterprise and public service television. The less they have in common with one another, the better for cultural policy.[97] This proposal would entail dismantling the CRTC and creating two regulatory bodies, perhaps with a common board for non-cultural issues of mutual concern.

The final threshold step requires a clear separation, both in the statutory mandate and the regulations, of industrial policy goals from cultural policy goals. They are seldom the complementary aims assumed in the legislation itself or portrayed in political speeches.[98] This problem has been identified in two recent government studies.[99] If the regulatory schemes of the public and private systems are separated, the public system should be directed towards cultural goals primarily and dominantly, if not exclusively. Industrial policy goals may be left to the private system and scrutinized free from their cultural policy guise.

Specific Private Sector Proposals

As long as we believe that the commercial broadcasters can make a meaningful cultural contribution through program exhibition and production, at least a few minor changes are warranted within the existing regulatory framework. The CRTC could experiment by requiring, through conditions of licence, that particular licensees exhibit a specified number of hours of Canadian programming by category, such as drama.[100] Licensees could be required to devote a specified portion of their revenues to Canadian productions, thus supplying the missing link in the theory that financially sound Canadian television ventures will generate more and better Canadian programming.[101] Prime-time quotas should correspond to true prime-time viewing. American commercial networks, now "free" on the basic tier, could be moved to a separate tier and priced discretely. This would enable the government to tax consumption of American stations directly and to direct those revenues to culturally relevant domestic programming.[102] Many of these options would cost the broadcasters money and contribute to a progressive erosion of the management function of the private broadcasters. None would ensure high-quality Canadian programming, or a substantial audience to watch it.

Alternatively, the private broadcasters could be required to make their cultural contribution in money raised by taxation or licence fee rather than in programming and exhibition.[103] Experience with commercial television over the last thirty years indicates that private broadcasters have far more expertise at making money than at producing and exhibiting culturally relevant programming. The balance in regulatory policy should be shifted accordingly.

If television regulatory policy were being drafted from scratch, it would be tempting to consider abandoning Canadian content quotas altogether. Today this is not a practical or politically feasible alternative. At least as an interim measure, the overall 60 per cent Canadian content quota should be maintained, along with whatever symbolic importance attaches to the weak statutory claim that the system employs "predominantly Canadian creative and other resources."[104] Meanwhile, private broadcasters can contribute to the domestic industry by providing opportunity and training for Canadians. In the long run the quota might be lowered or eliminated entirely with little significant effect.

Prime-time television is the critical issue. This is where regulatory policies and the commercial imperative collide, with the inevitable triumph of the latter. Consider eliminating prime-time quotas: we would lose less than one hour of true prime-time Canadian programming per day, much of it of limited cultural or public service value. This loss would affect a relatively small audience, a proportion of which would watch the CBC instead. Overall industry employment would change little. Most commercial stations would exhibit American programs almost exclusively in prime time, although news scheduling would not change. To an external observer the television environment would appear more American, but viewing patterns would change little. As a matter of industrial policy, such a change makes sense. Private Canadian broadcasters would secure the additional profits that accrue from American rather than Canadian programs. By invoking the simultaneous-substitution rule, they would capture Canadian audiences from American stations. The direct cultural benefit depends on the cultural significance of the difference between Canadian and American program packaging, primarily advertising, but also public service announcements, self-promotion, and station identification, which constitutes approximately twelve minutes per hour and which, unlike the other forty-eight minutes, is amenable to Canadian regulatory control.

A greater cultural benefit might be secured if the government were to tax away the additional profits derived from relaxing the quota and channel those revenues to more promising areas, perhaps as incentives to independent producers, perhaps as additional revenues for the CBC. A tax of this magnitude would be less intrusive on the everyday business affairs of the broadcasters than direct regulation, and would be a matter of financial indifference to them.

A case for a selective excess profits tax stands on its own merits, even if the funds went directly into general revenue, and even if Canadian content quotas remained as they are. Many broadcasters have earned consistently high profits. This is a tribute not only to their expertise but also to a regulatory environment that has shielded them from domestic and foreign competition. These fortuitous profits belong to the Canadian public, although attempts to extract corresponding program services from the broadcasters have proved futile. Direct recapture by taxation is the only valid justification for continuing to restrict entry to otherwise qualified applicants. If the revenues were channelled to other Canadian productive resources, there would exist at least a possibility of cultural benefit. Of course, this taxation regime would not be a matter of indifference to the industry, so the prospects of parliament's venturing this far are slim.

The elimination of prime-time Canadian content quotas coupled with a targeted taxation scheme need not entail abandoning attempts to extract culturally relevant programming from the private broadcasters. The new approach could be coupled with an incentive program that allowed tax credits or guaranteed government advertising commitments to be offered to a licensee who obtained a specified Canadian audience share during a realistic measurement period. Audience share targets would not work under a mandatory quota system, but they could function as credit incentives. The credit could be specific as to program category – drama, for example. Other options are possible.

This approach has number of advantages. Successful commercial production attracts larger audiences than critically acclaimed noncommercial productions. Current mandatory quotas encourage quantity only; the economics of private television discourages expenditures necessary to attract large audiences. Incentives can alter these tendencies. Audience targets are easily measured by independent ratings evaluators. They are easily adapted to the purposes and skills within the industry, and they are far less intrusive than mandatory quotas. One would predict that fewer Canadian programs would be exhibited in prime time, freeing time for lucrative American programs. What was exhibited would be far more attractive to Canadian viewers than present fare and would probably distribute the programming to a broader segment of the Canadian public. At a bare minimum, the credit quota should exceed the total prime time audience that the licensee attracts with its Canadian programming under the present system.

Quality will always remain an elusive goal. No completely satisfactory definition of Canadian programming that corresponds to cultural goals will ever be forthcoming. Subjective output evaluation is not feasible, but objective input evaluation is too often meaningless. For a credit incentive scheme to be worthwhile, several changes would have to be made to the present point system. Points could be awarded for an obvious Canadian setting, physical and social, and for programs that address distinctively Canadian subjects or offer distinctively Canadian perspectives on other topics. Other point values could be reduced accordingly. Admittedly, this would entail controversial subjective judgments and remain subject to some abuse and manipulation. Nevertheless, with industry co-operation this arrangement could work in the context of a selective credit scheme. Without industry co-operation, attempts to secure program contributions from private broadcasters for cultural purposes should be abandoned. The choice is theirs.

Again it must be emphasized that none of these suggestions offers a realistic prospect for revolutionary improvement in attempts to regulate commercial television for cultural purposes. On the one hand, the projected benefits are uncertain and probably small, the best one can expect from commercial television. On the other hand, the projected cost in money and in forgoing programs generated under present quotas is negligible. Why not experiment? More substantial hopes rest, if at all, with the public sector.

Specific Public Broadcasting Recommendations

The redesign of the public system is a topic in its own right, raising many issues beyond the scope of this essay. What follows is based only on the implications for cultural policy that may be derived from the preceding analysis. The general themes are clear. American and domestic commercial broadcasting will continue to dominate the television environment regardless of the policies pursued. It follows that the only policies that promise any hope for harnessing television for cultural purposes are those that encourage the domestic production and exhibition of culturally relevant programming. It follows also that the exhibition capacity of the public service, not the private commercial sector, will be the only effective vehicle with which to pursue such policies.

Canadian television policy has emphasized quantity over quality for too long. Not only have the audience share expectations been unrealistic, but so have the production quotas. A small country such as Canada cannot afford to produce the amount of domestic programming required under current quotas of a quality that will attract large numbers of Canadian viewers or achieve national cultural goals. The exhibition capacity of the public service broadcasting on two channels in two official languages is more than sufficient to accommodate the amount of worthwhile programming that the country can afford to produce. As VCR use increases, the effective exhibition capacity of the public network made possible through time-shifting will greatly increase.[105]

Filling the public network broadcast day with worthwhile Canadian programming constitutes a significant challenge for the future. The exhibition capacity of the private networks is totally unnecessary for this purpose. For the same reason, proposals for additional public television channels – CBC-2 or the proposed TV Canada, for example – are extravagant, unrealistic, and unnecessary. Present CBC capacity is more than adequate to accommodate the type of programming proposed for these stations in a quantity we can afford and of a quality we desire.[106] It remains to be seen whether the public service can and should sustain two public channels in the long run, the basic CBC channel and the relatively new *Newsworld*. The latter's use of "filler" such as fashion reviews lead one to wonder. The proposal for a separate news and public affairs channel is worthy of serious consideration, but only after it is demonstrated that the pool of high-quality Canadian programming exceeds the present exhibition capacity of the public channels.[107]

Admittedly, the quantity of Canadian programming contemplated here, coupled with a projected regular audience share of less than 20 per cent of the Canadian television audience, is a far cry from the National Broadcasting Dream envisioned by the Aird Commission or the Radio League. It does not, however, constitute failure or a cause for national shame. It is simply a fact beyond domestic control. Excellence in programming can still make a meaningful contribution to national culture.[108] If this degree of success is not perceived as worthwhile, Canada ought to consider funnelling its cultural policy resources elsewhere. It is wasteful and demeaning to continue deluding ourselves that more is possible.

Many of the cultural goals posited below may be accomplished through a restructured CBC. Ultimately, the success of cultural policy goals on public television will depend on the network management. It remains to be seen how well it can adjust to a new strategy in which the CBC would not be expected to earn commercial revenues, to generate consistently large audiences, or to compete with private television. To this end, it would be desirable to remove the CBC from the CRTC's regulatory domain to emphasize the entirely different conceptions of public and private television that should prevail. The public service should not be regarded as one arrow in a quiver of television policy. It is an entirely different weapon.

The new public broadcasting regulatory body should have three main attributes:

1 joint regulatory powers with the private broadcasting agency on non-cultural matters of mutual or overlapping concern to the public and private service;
2 a statutory mandate to evaluate critically the CBC's performance, with periodic reports to parliament or cabinet (Although direct regulatory power over the CBC on cultural matters is not contemplated, this would ensure a reasonable degree of CBC accountability. To ensure an effective performance of this function, the general goals described below should be expressed with some specificity in a new Broadcasting Act.);
3 a channel-sharing function with the CBC in which the public agency would be allotted specified access to the CBC exhibition facilities and select independently programs for exhibition on the public channel.

The CBC should be required to abandon commercial advertising in order to counter the inherent biases that form of financing produces. The revenue loss might be offset by increased revenues from parliament, some of which might come from taxes levied on private broadcasters. If not, commercial advertising should be purged, even if it entails reducing the quantity of programming on CBC, perhaps resulting in a shorter broadcast day. Again, qualitative concerns should dominate quantitative.

The CBC should divest itself of affiliate arrangements. The national service should be regional and national in character, not local.[109] Regional broadcasts by cable and satellite are completely feasible. The affiliation agreements are expensive, the affiliates do not carry the full program schedule, and private commercial stations manifest all the tendencies of the unaffiliated private broadcasters.[110] Relaxed Canadian content quotas would ensure the survival, perhaps the flourishing, of many of these affiliate stations.[111] In the case of those dependent on the public service, it is time to abandon a subsidy program whose usefulness has passed. Modern regional broadcasting also requires far fewer originating stations than the CBC now owns and operates. The CBC should sell many of them and be permitted to retain the proceeds and savings for its programming budget.

The overall goal of the public service should be to provide public goods in the form of cultural and public service programming not available on the private networks. This strategy will be pursued in varying ways in different regions. In particular, the French-language network must retain latitude to adopt strategies different from the English-language service in order to achieve the general goals. It would be parochial to require only Canadian programming on the public service, but the majority should be Canadian.

The CBC should not abandon attempts to exhibit popular programming that appeals to large Canadian audiences. Much is to be gained by attracting significant audiences to programming set in Canada and dealing with Canadian subjects. The CBC has proved capable of producing dramas of this nature on occasion. It is simply a matter of recognizing the costs involved in producing popular drama and choosing reasonable quantitative goals based on budgetary constraints.

Much of the public service programming will and should be narrowcasting by each broadcasting hour.[112] Often this programming is particularly suitable for VCR time-shifting. The public broadcasting service should attempt to reach all Canadians, not simultaneously but over the broadcast week. This entails, by definition, programming that will command small audiences. Successful narrowcasting, however, can have a much more intense impact on its audience than lowest-common-denominator broadcasting. Provided that the programming does not cater consistently to the same small audience, this is a desirable goal. Concerts and curling have an equal claim to exhibition time.

Children's programming should be a matter of vital concern. The survival of national culture depends on our ability to communicate with our children. Young children are particularly poorly served by private commercial television. It would be in the general public interest to protect all children, including teenagers, from the biases of commercial television. Both the cbc and the provincial networks have a good record of serving children with uniquely Canadian programming. They should continue to co-operate to ensure that together they provide programming for children of all ages continuously during the critical after-school and weekend morning hours.

The intractable difficulties of defining, let alone producing, distinctive Canadian programming will not disappear automatically in public broadcasting. However, the chances of success would be greatly improved by delegating the task to institutions charged directly and as a matter of priority to attempt to do so, rather than regulating commercial broadcasters who regard the task as an impediment to profit goals. The cbc has already demonstrated some success in this regard, notwithstanding the many other burdens it has been required to assume.

To say that Canada is realistically dependent on the exhibition facilities of the public network does not mean that it is necessarily dependent on the production or exhibition-selection facilities of the cbc. Although the motives behind the Applebaum-Hébert Committee's recommendation that the cbc abandon all but news and public affairs production have been questioned, and the degree to which the cbc's production role should be circumscribed overstated, the basic premise of the recommendation remains sound.[113] Effective cultural policy depends on diversity of participation, and no single institution, however sincere, should be permitted to monopolize cultural expression. The exhibition facilities of the public broadcasting service should be made available for private production. The independent regulatory body charged with the supervision of the service should be allotted hours of exhibition time on the cbc channels and empowered to select programs from the private sector, on the basis of specified criteria, for exhibition.[114] This function should be entirely independent of cbc management control and viewed as channel-sharing rather than regulation of the cbc. It would be interesting to begin by funding this function of the public regulatory body solely from revenues derived from the private broadcasters. The CBC should retain its budget (perhaps increased to offset advertising loss) and be asked to do less, but better, with it.

In one sense the picture of television regulation in Canada is not very heartening. So little of what we have accomplished to date has been effective that it is tempting to consider abandoning cultural policy efforts altogether. Nevertheless, this is a problem in perception which stems largely from our continuous commitment to unrealistic goals. The realistic possibilities are so much more limited that they are, on the surface, deflating. Scaled down as they are, they continue to pose a substantial challenge for the future. If Canada could maintain a public television system that provided something of cultural relevance and public service to all its citizens some of the time, and attracted an overall audience share roughly similar to what it commands today, the public could take great pride in such an achievement. If, as so many believe, a great deal more is possible, further channels could be added later to a sound base. Meanwhile, it is foolish to believe the present state of affairs can or will be cured by more programming alone.

4 Broadcasting and Canadian Culture: A Commentary

G. STUART ADAM

INTRODUCTION

Since the term "Canadian culture" is used promiscuously these days, it is refreshing to see that Bruce Feldthusen (in chapter 3) treats the subject seriously. Feldthusen's major purpose is to justify changes in the methods we use to regulate broadcasting so that we may better preserve and strengthen Canadian culture. But in order to accept the changes, he says, we must understand realistically, and value properly, what we seek to preserve.

In this vein, Feldthusen argues – sensibly, I think – that the "National Broadcasting Dream," which has inspired the systems of broadcast regulation, is, well, a dream. It has been conceived by denying the power and the permanence of the commercial, industrial and, especially, the American influences it is designed to diminish. It inspires the belief that the Broadcasting Act and, more particularly, the CRTC, through its licensing practices and Canadian content regulations, can effectively protect Canada's culture. Feldthusen asserts that the system of broadcast regulation can do nothing of the sort and actually encourages a result opposite to the one intended. So the dream, the product of dedicated patriots, is a source of the very evil he seeks to correct. To give up the dream, Feldthusen says, is to enter a real world in which Americans and commercial interests will continue to be powerful. Because of the power and purposes of these interests, no Canadian patriot should continue to depend on them to promote national culture. In his view, broadcast policy will be more effective when it separates the regulation of commercial television from the promotion of national cultural goals.

Feldthusen's recommendations are provocative and tempting. Like him, I think Canadian culture is worth preserving and strengthening. I believe there are parts of us that cling to an even wider and more seductive dream in which Canada is truly independent. He or anyone else who can overcome the economic ambitions of private broadcasters and the inertia of politicians to change the CRTC's mission and thus encourage a more independent way of life has my support.

However, I think Feldthusen's analysis, particularly the part dedicated to the concept of Canadian culture, should be refined, since it is the starting-point for his argument. He says that by getting that right, we will get the rest right. I agree. But does he get it right? For practical and immediate purposes, the answer may be yes. Policy proposals must be directly and efficiently stated, and there are diminishing returns associated with hair-splitting. Still, I would like to explore some of my reservations and doubts. Very generally speaking, cultural nationalists will be more effective in the long run if they argue from a deeper understanding and appreciation of the nature and character of Canadian culture, and my remarks are intended to promote such an understanding. Despite a dedication to the cause of Canadian cultural and political independence, Feldthusen and others fail to see or describe clearly what they seek to defend. The problem begins with the understanding of the concept of culture itself.

THE CONCEPT OF CULTURE

Raymond Williams says that culture is "one of the two or three most complicated words in the English language."[1] The confusions bred by its complexities pervade every discussion of it. However, Feldthusen indicates that there are two domains in which the word is normally used. The first is the arts – music, literature, painting and the like; the second is the domain of society or, to put it more precisely, a way of life that constitutes a unique society. The first meaning may easily be subsumed into the second.[2] The arts are a storehouse of a society's memory, experience, and aesthetic sensibility, and thereby a source and expression of its way of life. But it is the second and broader concept of culture that Feldthusen is using as he addresses the problem of Canadian culture. He refers his readers to, and adopts for himself, a definition formulated by the anthropologists Alfred Kroeber and Clyde Kluckhohn, who wrote that culture "consists of patterns ... of and for behaviour acquired and transmitted by symbols constituting the distinctive achievement of human groups, including their embodiment in artifacts; the essential core of culture consists of traditional ... ideas and ... their attached values."[3]

Such a definition directs attention to patterns of behaviour and the symbols, myths, values, memories, and ideas that inspire such behaviour. More concretely, it directs attention to Canadian patterns of behaviour and Canadian symbols, myths, values, memories, and ideas.

On the face of it, this definition calls for a straightforward task of assembling and organizing. However, conceptual problems loom. For one thing, the anthropological definition suggests a tradition-based and organic notion of culture rather than a managed and instrumental notion. This should be noticed because on the one hand we are invited to be reverent and attentive to Canadian history and tradition, while on the other we are challenged to be sanguine about a collaboration between the bureaucracy of the modern state and the media in the production of culture. The step into the present requires a recognition, regardless of our final attitudes on the matter, that the meaning of culture has shifted away from community and tradition or even scholarly definitions to industrial and media-inspired definitions.

T.S. Eliot and T.W. Adorno, who have written discourses on culture from radically different points of view, both illustrate how troubling this problem of meaning has become. They provide a single warning that modern uses of the word "culture" are likely to be loaded and tendentious. Eliot says that "culture is the one thing that we cannot deliberately aim at. It is the product of a variety of more or less harmonious activities, each pursued for its own sake."[4]

In an opaque but nevertheless provocative essay, Adorno laments the degree to which modern society – the imperial force of its organization – penetrates and thereby deforms the inner regions of the human spirit. He speaks ironically (our politicians and some of our artists speak earnestly) of cultural industries and argues that by making culture an object the critic "objectifies it once more." In his view, culture's "very meaning is the suspension of objectification. Once culture ... has been debased to 'cultural goods' ... it has already been defamed ... and carries with it the echo of commercial language."[5]

For both writers, but for very different reasons and purposes, culture resides in the almost unconscious, or at least the not self-conscious, foundations of society. Both are conservative. Canadian nationalists are also conservative, whether they are on the right or the left or, like Eliot and Adorno, they are disciples of God or the Enlightenment.

But the discussion of culture in Canada incorporates the spirit which Eliot and Adorno would find alarming. Our politicians and some of our writers tell us endlessly that we have a set of "cultural industries" and, if they are not the property of Canadians as a whole, they are of special interest to a "cultural community."[6] Even Margaret Atwood, a Canadian writer with an international reputation, exhibited an inclination to adopt and use the language of commercialized politics when, in her widely circulated speech to the Parliamentary Committee on Free Trade, she spoke for the "cultural community."[7]

The problem is that when culture is more a commodity than a set of traditional practices – when it is the single product of a special group within the larger community – it belongs first and foremost to its producers. They have an interest in the management and control of the commodity, just as vintners have an interest in the management and control of the production and distribution of wine. But when resources are scarce, how does one conclude that the interests of the producers of culture are superior to the interests of vintners? There is no way to do so unless culture is somehow imagined to be independent of all the interests organized around property and power.

Thus, the more conservative cast of mind and the more conservative language promotes the welfare of artists and writers as individuals rather than as a group with special group-derived rights. This cast of mind and this language promote a notion of entitlement and right derived from the historic community, indigenous values and visions, and the certainty that a people without artists is not truly a people. In short, the concept of culture in modern discourse is coloured by the commercial and political structures within which it is expressed. Although there does not seem to be an easy way to enter the debate on broadcast policy without incorporating some of these new corruptions, we ought to try so that we can see more clearly how, and in the name of what values, we defend Canadian culture.

THE CONCEPT OF CANADIAN CULTURE

Feldthusen says, in one context, that Canadian culture is marginally different from American culture; in another, he says that the difference between it and American culture "may be greater than some suppose." While there may not be a contradiction between these two statements, his stronger belief, and the one on which he depends to make his argument, is contained in the first. In the main narrative he firmly states that what is distinctive about Canadian culture "lies at the margin." This is important, he notes, because American television reinforces what is common between the two cultures. The purpose of defining Canadian culture is to allow us to recognize just exactly where those differences lie and to allow us to stop the "continuous eradication of the marginal differences between the cultures."

The second and more hesitant statement occurs when Feldthusen explains that national cultures may be distinguished from local, ethnic, religious, and regional cultures. His point is simply to remind us that in the social sciences the term "culture" is used to describe the distinctive values, norms, symbols, memories, art, and behaviour of any group. He correctly states that national cultures are conceptually different from other group cultures, that they are especially important among the types of cultures, and that their importance and significance derive from the fact that the political and legal institutions "permeate every other aspect of the national culture."

My position is close to Feldthusen's second statement. It is right to say that political and legal institutions are important elements of any society's unique way of life and, to the degree that they mark a democratic society and engage its adult population seriously, they are important and central rather than marginal. Additionally, I would argue for much the same reason that the political and legal institutions and everything that emerges from them colour the regional and ethnic cultures with which they intersect. This point of view leans heavily on the observation that Canada's system of politics is democratic. To put the matter differently, in a democratic society the political, administrative, and legal systems are in the foreground of life and experience. This point of view also relies on a firm sense of the distinctions between the meanings of culture and the idea that culture defined as a way of life is itself a concept that allows for some sorting and stratification.

To speak briefly of the distinctions between culture as arts and culture as a way of life, it is arguable that Feldthusen sees the differences between Canadian and American cultures more in terms of the former than the latter. Although there is not much in the way of textual justification for this proposition, it strikes me that his perceptions of cultural differences – like those of other advocates of a stronger national broadcast policy – arise out of a consideration of television alone rather than a broader consideration of our way of life. It is as if, for all practical purposes, broadcasting is culture. Obviously this is not the case. That Canadians see much American television is not to be doubted. That the popular cultures of both countries share much – I am thinking here of the Expos and the Blue Jays as well as television – is not to be doubted. However, television and recreation are to popular culture as Van Gogh's paintings and visits to the Museum of Modern Art are to high culture. Both fall mainly in the domain of arts and/or expression and both account for limited dimensions of the broader culture. To form a picture of the culture as a way of life by focusing on the popular culture alone is to omit a great deal from the total picture. The rest of the picture counts for as much, and a thorough audit is unlikely to lead to the conclusion that the differences between the countries are marginal.

The total picture would embrace the distinctive levels of culture. For example, we often say that Canadian culture is part and parcel of western culture. We are likely to admit in the same breath that Canada's culture is North American and that in North America there are Canadian and American national cultures and subcultures, which can be described regionally and linguistically. The extent and importance of the differences between the cultures of Canada and the United States can best be assessed by examining the manner in which the various strata mingle and function in each country. But more important, the stratum of the cultural mosaic that probably matters the most in the analysis of differences is the national culture.

By adopting the term "national culture" I am following Feldthusen's usage. I am not suggesting that there is an official culture that is in the custody of the state or its officials. I am referring to a received culture which, if it belongs to anyone, belongs to the people. Canadians should be wary on this score and listen to such writers as Eliot and Adorno rather than their politicians. Politicians have promoted the view that Canada is merely the sum of its regional or linguistic parts devoid of an organic coherence. This is not to say that politicians have wished regionalism or French-Canadian nationalism into existence; but it has been in the interests of politicians either seeking or defending political power to speak tendentiously of Canadian culture rather than to understand or protect it.

The analysis of Canadian national culture involves first and foremost an examination of the patterns of social and political organization and the memories, values, norms, and behaviour that mark all of Canada, and it involves particularly an examination of the administrative, political, legal, and perhaps educational systems. The analysis would be completed by an examination of the symbols, art, and literature Canadians have inscribed against the backdrop of these systems and, it may be noted, against a backdrop composed of a northern landscape and climate and a once powerful set of religious traditions. Put differently, the starting-point should be history and politics rather than television. The ending-point is television, which remains a problem because of the manner in which it distorts and thereby erodes our way of life.

THE POLITICAL, ADMINISTRATIVE, AND LEGAL SYSTEM

I discuss the political, administrative, and legal system in the singular as a convenience; in fact, they are three systems, not one. However, they are conjoined in a special way as parallel seams in Canadian culture. Having said this, the analyst of Canadian culture must still cross a difficult threshold at the beginning. Two European peoples, first at war and then sharing an uneasy constitutional arrangement, created a foundation for the later development of Canada. A moment of truth – a marriage of event and value – occurred in 1774. The Quebec Act started a process that would eventually guarantee Quebec's religious and educational institutions and its civil law. [8] Later, various statutes, including the British North America (BNA) Act, 1867, and the Constitution Act, 1982, would express precisely what was earlier conceived. The guarantees survived imperial doubts and were incorporated into Canada's constitution.

So a central value, which defines and shapes Canada's political, administrative, and legal system and distinguishes it radically from the corresponding system in the United States, is to be found in its very charter. The so-called national culture of Canada, for better or for worse, is marked by a value that guarantees some of the institutions of two linguistic communities. Canada's national culture is incipiently, even tragically, pluralistic. But the pluralism is often exaggerated; it is only part of the story.

A second value, expressed initially and variously in the behaviour of colonial officials and the actions of United Empire Loyalists and enshrined finally in the preamble to the BNA Act itself, was that Canadian political, administrative, and legal institutions would be British. The preamble of the BNA Act said that the Constitution of Canada would be "similar in principle to that of the United Kingdom." The impulse to independence, the substantial Celtic (Irish and Scottish) elements, which contributed so much to the folk feeling of Canada, the waves of immigration, the lasting acrimony between English and French speakers, even the regional disputes, have not altered the fact that the central political and constitutional values of Canadian culture are British.

The late George Grant argued that much of this legacy is owed to the colonial officials and Loyalists who, he said, brought with them a form of political conservatism that would imprint itself permanently, or almost permanently, on the Canadian imagination. He wrote: "British conservatism is difficult to describe because it is less a clear view of existence than an appeal to an ill-defined past ... Many of the British officials, many Loyalists and later many immigrants felt this conservatism very strongly. It was an inchoate desire to build, in these cold and forbidding regions, a society with a greater sense of order and restraint than the freedom-loving republicanism would allow."[9]

This conservatism accepted where the American republic rejected the notion of hereditary right and royal prerogative. Even Quebec's controversial language legislation of recent years had to receive royal assent in order to become law.[10] More generally, the impulses to create independent and democratic institutions in Canada – impulses that mark the development of all western nations – ran headlong into this conservatism, and the result, inherited from the British, was parliamentary rather than republican democracy, responsible rather than presidential government. The melodrama continues, even at the centre of the language controversy in which, several years ago, Quebec invoked the "notwithstanding clause" of the Charter of Rights and Freedoms to override the guarantees of language rights in the national constitution. By invoking the clause, Quebec's legislature, however imprudently, was using a central doctrine of British constitutional practice, namely, the doctrine of the supremacy of the legislature. In the Canadian version of that doctrine, parliament is supreme in its domain, the legislatures supreme in theirs. Even the American-inspired Charter has failed to lay that doctrine to rest.

The doctrine of the supremacy of the legislature, which carries with it substantial hazards as well as substantial benefits, is expressive of yet another central value that lies at the core of Canadian national culture. Canadians value government and public administration, not as necessary evils to limit the excesses of private interests, but as positive sources of social arrangements and public goods. Until the most recent generation of politicians came to power, Canadians were fundamentally trusting of government. The constitutional expression of this value is found in section 91 of the BNA Act, which empowered parliament to make laws for the peace, order, and good government of the country. But the wider expressions of the value are to be found in the public education and transportation systems, in the public health schemes, and in the system of transfer payments.

Where Americans have allowed private interests to dominate in the creation of the public order, Canadians have allowed their governments – all of them – to take charge.

Progressive Conservative governments established the Canadian Broadcasting Corporation, the Canadian National Railway, and Ontario Hydro. When the Liberal government of Quebec purchased the Beauharnois hydro-producing group in the early 1960s, it was following the same Canadian impulse. So the values of the national culture "permeate" many aspects of Canada's regional subcultures and communities. They are not only expressed at the national level but are pan-Canadian and fundamental – not marginally but substantially different from the values of American culture.

The same could be said of our system of criminal justice, which is uniform because it is federal, and our political parties and civic language. The justice system is traditionally dependent on British practice and precedent; similarly, the political parties show the marks of British Tory, Liberal, and Fabian forebears; and even the notions of liberties and rights have carried different weights and meanings in politics and law. An example of that difference may be found in the way in which Canadians and Americans have conceived of the relationship between the protection of judicial proceedings and freedom of expression. Americans speak endlessly of a conflict between a free press and fair trials. Canadian judges have said, and section 11(d) of the Charter of Rights and Freedoms now states, that an open court is a means of ensuring justice. In other words, the liberty or the right to know is conceived principally as a method of ensuring that the judicial system is subject to democratic review. More generally, Canadians might speak of rights as a means to communitarian ends, whereas Americans are more likely to speak of rights as natural and expressive of individual benefits.

The analysis of Canada's systems of governmental administration, politics, and law reveals substantial differences between Canada and the United States. The earmarks of British progenitors are everywhere, although often denied; the distinguishing values are pervasive and fundamental. They are a basic part of the created environment, just as the climate and the Canadian Shield (not to mention the United States itself) are parts of the natural environment. The distilled experience of Canadian life – the part of culture that is expressed through literature, film, art, and journalism – reveals these elements, which in turn reflect the religious, folk, familial, psychological, and aesthetic values that are common elements in all western countries and cultures. A trick of socalled cultural policy is to encourage opportunities to show these elements and to encourage educators as much as journalists and playwrights to have a value for them. More fundamentally, it is to encourage Canadians to continue to live them.

A contradiction at the heart of contemporary Canadian culture may be noted as a postscript. For reasons that should now be obvious, Canadian national aspirations are often expressed through government. The marriage between French and English Canada was made viable by an important difference in the way some cultural values were received and expressed. French Canadians once saw the church and local community as fundamental to the spiritual and linguistic strands of their culture, as both the expressions and the custodians of the differences between them and English Canadians. The process of secularization and the Quiet Revolution have created opportunities for the further circulation and adoption of what I would describe as pan-Canadian values, in which the activist state is the expression and the custodian of national values and goals. The problem is that it looks increasingly as if there are two nations and two states.

English Canadians have always looked to the state – initially, the federal state – to sponsor their aspirations, and the continuing expression of English-Canadian nationalism is to be found in support for political parties that seek to maintain the prerogatives of sovereignty in the name of national goals. English-Canadian nationalist sentiment, arising out of a cultural attachment to the institutions of state themselves, was expressed in the 1988 federal election through support for the parties that opposed the Canada-u.s. free trade agreement. In the blur of election rhetoric, where costs, benefits, and opportunities and the subject of Canadian culture itself were hailed and carelessly measured and traded, many English Canadians looked to the parties that seemed to promise full sovereignty. French Canada, with an élite of more radical and, one might say, more circumscribed Canadian vision, would see a different community and a different state as the source and expression of their Canadian being.

So Canada's national culture is substantially different from American national culture. It reflects an attachment to values that are sufficiently distinctive to be noticed and sufficiently important to be cherished. Nevertheless, it is true to say that they are threatened in the age of television. Can we do anything about it? Perhaps, but I am cautious about making the cbc the subject of even more political debate. Furthermore, I think we should not depend too heavily on television to answer a problem that is in part the product of television itself.

BROADCASTING AND CANADIAN CULTURE

Feldthusen recommends, among other things, that we should give up the idea expressed in the Broadcasting Act that the broadcasting system in Canada is a single system. We should separate technical and commercial regulation from the regulation of cultural functions. The aim is to give cultural goals the attention and status they deserve. He also says that the commercial system should be taxed to create the funds that would then be devoted to cultural production.

I have two practical objections and an additional theoretical criticism of these proposals. First, there is always a danger that state broadcasting systems will be subordinated to state or political interests. At this stage of our history, when the concept of culture has been so politicized, a new regulator might be even more inclined than the current ones to subordinate culture to the interests of the state or the government that controls it. Such a result is not inevitable, but if this proposal were enacted by the Progressive Conservative government that has been in power since 1984, the same group of politicians who have used and traded on the notion of culture would be asked to implement a new policy that could be administered more for political than for cultural purposes. More directly, it could fracture the already fragile tradition of arm's-length management of the CBC. Curiously, a by-product (not an intention) of the single-system approach is that government and the CRTC, particularly in the area of news and current affairs, are less able to intervene in management if they must deal with the resistance of independent broadcasters as well as CBC's managers. That the government is inclined to intervene and that the CRTC is inclined to pave the way for such intervention may be inferred from a 1987 directive issued by the CRTC to the CBC when it granted a licence to establish *Newsworld*, a cable-distributed news and information channel. The CRTC said that when the licence is due to be renewed it will be interested in knowing what action the CBC has taken to answer public complaints about its performance. Insiders believed that the main complainers were the politicians themselves, or if not the politicians, then powerful lobbies who feel the media are not on their side, though the politicians might be.

The Tory-appointed board of the CBC initially said in response to the directive that CBC management should create a news-standards council – one might call it a political auditor – that would pass judgment on the balance, objectivity, and ethical standards of CBC's news and current affairs programming.[11] This may sound innocuous to public-spirited citizens who believe that CBC's journalistic standards could be improved. However, there is an important difference between arm's-length management and a political auditing system, and that difference goes to the heart of Canadian democracy. So there is, strangely, a benefit to be derived from the single-system concept: journalists and current affairs specialists in television and radio alike, and indeed all creative personnel, are more likely to be judged and regulated by the same presumptions of independence that apply to private broadcasters.

A second practical objection is related to the first. Feldthusen's recommendations call into question the effectiveness of the CRTC and the CBC together. In a manner of speaking, the government and then parliament decide annually whether the cost of nation-building or nation-maintaining institutions is justified. The practical effect of a campaign that promotes the notion that they are ineffective may be to convince the government and parliament to reduce their support. When money is tight, they may decide to give up and save.

Once again, such a result is not inevitable. However, because the independence of the CBC is fundamental to our national well-being, its legitimacy should not be called into question. We have been through this before. As the government of Brian Mulroney, early in its first term, prepared the way for cuts to the CBC's budget, a political attack was launched on the quality of the corporation's programming. The cuts were made and the hardships within the CBC were substantial. But the debate on programming quality now seems to have ended, and it is again a matter of business as usual. Still, the cost to the public treasury for the CRTC and the CBC is in the range of $1 billion, and the government and parliament together could easily justify cuts in the name of stringency and a belief in the CBC's ineffectiveness.

Finally, there is the matter of broadcasting, and especially television, itself. The broadcasting media may be seen as sources of culture and a set of opportunities to express it. In some senses they are; in a more fundamental sense, they are not.

Broadcasting provides images of life and ideas. With degrees of quality and competence, the public and private media provide narrative accounts of the here and now and abbreviated versions of ideas and issues. The process of production, however good and high-minded, is almost always more industrial than craftlike. It is more the work of committees than individuals, and it works best when it is articulated to other institutions, such as schools, theatres, and legislatures, in which the impulses and values of culture find clearer expression. To turn the matter around, if the institutions in which the impulses of culture should be first and most clearly expressed are themselves debased, television cannot provide much of a remedy. A society that looks too longingly at the broadcast media for cultural nourishment may be in trouble. It follows, as I have said above, that politicians and policy-makers who expect too much from the broadcast media are probably not interested in culture at all.

I have argued that there is an independent culture in Canada. It is important that the broadcast media be incorporated into it and that they provide opportunities for our best journalists, filmmakers, and artists to inform, entertain, and divert us on our own ground. As Feldthusen points out, the competition of u.s. broadcast systems for audiences in Canada puts American diversions and information in the foreground and deflects attention from our own territory. This is regrettable, even if it is inevitable. However, if it is Canadian culture that one seeks to defend in the age of television, one should not depend too heavily on a broadcasting response to a broadcasting problem.

At this time in our history, cultural nationalists should focus much of their attention on education systems and curriculum. They are potentially much more important than broadcasting to the transmission of the social and political heritage. Canadian television is like all national television systems; it is more likely to promote loyalty to the state than an attachment to values. Yet it is values and meaning, not power alone, that provide the foundations for culture.

5 A Sweet Hope of Glory in My Soul: Television Evangelism in the United States and Canada

ANDREW LYONS AND
HARRIET LYONS

Television evangelism is an aspect of American mass culture that is both more frightening and more comforting than some of its other manifestations. It is frightening because of its (perceived) links with distrusted trends in American politics. It is comforting because few middle-class Canadian intellectuals are in danger of actually having to admit to a liking for the stuff. In this latter sense, it differs from *Miami Vice* and Coca-Cola, and we need neither Dallas Smythe nor Mel Hurtig to protect us from it.[1] We can monitor its penetration into the Canadian market, compare it with its home-grown imitations, and worry about its effects, secure in the knowledge that it is others who may be led astray by it. We can ask the Canadian Radio-television and Telecommunications Commission (CRTC) to restrict it, with no concern that Canada will be duller if it disappears. We suggest below that we must be acutely aware of class-based attitudes towards television evangelism, on the part of both its devotees and its opponents, if we are to understand the phenomenon in its entirety, whether in Canada or in the United States.

We approach this essay as anthropologists, as Darwinians, and, more personally, as Jewish atheists, who are often made fundamentally uncomfortable by fundamentalist Christianity. We often have trouble being relativists ourselves when dealing with the evangelical movement; and yet, paradoxically, part of this essay is a plea for relativism. When fundamentalist millennialism exists among "others," relativism comes much easier. The anthropologist may even be converted, and that conversion regarded as legitimate "participation" (for example, Jules-Rosette).[2]

Our aim here, however, is neither to condemn nor to convert. Instead, we will investigate the roots of the discomfort experienced both by anthropologists and by other members of the North American hegemonic class, correctly identified by fundamentalists as secular humanists, when confronted by evangelical Christianity, particularly in its televised version.

Ethnographically, we are broadly concerned with a comparison of American and Canadian evangelistic broadcasts. Despite the popularity of American programs in Canada, their made-in-Canada counterparts display significant differences in performative style and emphasize different aspects of theology. An examination of these differences reveals that Canadian religious culture reflects distinct national and regional social histories. In religion as in other aspects of culture, Canadians tend to modify American influences even as they absorb them. What the evangelists call conversion can be placed in a different context in Canada.

That context encompasses theological traditions such as the notion of redemption and the doctrine of predestination. We suggest that Calvinist notions of sin and predestination have retained much of their efficacy in Canadian Protestantism, including some of its fundamentalist branches. They have been much diluted in many forms of populist fundamentalism in the southern United States. The anthropologist James Peacock draws a similar contrast between the southern and northern regions of the United States.[3] The latter area is both culturally and geographically closer to Canada.

RELIGIOUS BROADCASTING IN SOUTHERN ONTARIO

There is a considerable level of penetration of television evangelism, both American and Canadian, on Canadian airwaves. On a sample Sunday in March 1988, the *Globe and Mail*'s TV guide listed a total of 36.5 hours of Christian religious programming, distributed over 10 hours of broadcasting time. One and one-half hours of this period were devoted to a live transmission of a regular Sunday service, filmed on location at a different church each week; another one and a half hours were filled with three televised Roman Catholic masses. The remainder of the Christian broadcasting schedule might fairly be described as evangelistic. Virtually all stations available to regular cable subscribers in the Toronto area offered some program(s) of this type, with the exception of CITY-TV and the Toronto affiliate of the CBC.

The American evangelist Jimmy Swaggart (presumably in reruns) had by far the largest share of Sunday airtime; his hour-long program was aired nine times in five different time slots on nine stations, four American and five Canadian. Other well-known American televangelists received less exposure: Oral Roberts's half-hour program was shown once simultaneously by two American stations. Jerry Falwell was aired twice, for an hour, by a Canadian and an American station. Robert Schuller, less a household word among the unconverted than those three, was shown four times, three times on American stations, once on a Canadian one.

Canadian programs with significant airtime included *100 Huntley Street*, with a one-hour slot early Sunday morning on CBC's Wingham affiliate, and *The People's Church*, aired by four stations, including CTV and some CBC affiliates, in two consecutive one-hour slots. Dr. John Wesley White's Christian commentary on current events, another Canadian production, received five half-hour showings at three times on five stations. *Circle Square*, *100 Huntley Street*'s children's program, was also shown simultaneously on three stations. Other offerings in the Sunday diet of television evangelism include *Day of Discovery*, *Hymn Sing*, *The Worldwide Church of God*, *Hour of Power*, and a variety of minor programs.

On weekday mornings, Jimmy Swaggart, *100 Huntley Street*, and *Circle Square* each received several airings. Saturday mornings were similar to weekdays, with some additional time for Jerry Falwell. Christian broadcasting disappeared from the airwaves by evening on Sunday and early afternoon on weekdays, though the international version of *100 Huntley Street* was shown late at night on a Buffalo station. Televangelism is not a prime-time phenomenon in Ontario, as it is in some parts of the United States.[4]

TELEVANGELISM AND NATIONAL DIFFERENCES

North American religious broadcasts follow a number of formats. Some of these are modifications of traditional liturgies, while others are derived from secular programming. The principal formats include the live or videotaped services, shortened or modified to fit the sixty-minute time slot, the ministerial address, the documentary, and, in the case of the troubled PTL Club, an adaptation of the familiar talk-show and variety presentation.[5] The most common form is the sixty-minute service. Swaggart and Schuller use this format, as does The People's Church in Toronto.

A typical broadcast includes the following phases:

1 Introduction: a theme hymn with a view of the place of worship.
2 First hymn: the service may or may not be in progress. We might note that in comparison with the typical Protestant Canadian or North American church service, the central or liminal portion of the service is highly emphasized at the expense of the beginning and end.[6] The structure of ritual has been shown to display much consistency from culture to culture. Typically, rituals include an opening phase, marking out the special status of the occasion, and a closing stage, when participants return to normal life. The central or "liminal" period is the period in which the real business of the ritual is usually accomplished. Arnold Van Gennep and Victor Turner have characterized the liminal period as one of heightened emotion, alteration, or reversal of normal social relationships, and a time when individuals are prone to the direct experience of the sacred.[7] It should be noted that nearly all the hymns in these programs are very well known.[8] The television audience is to be put at ease, not challenged by the unfamiliar. The choir is dressed in bright-coloured robes.
3 The choirmaster or assistant pastor introduces the minister, who says a few words, and introduces
4 the second hymn.
5 There will be one or two more hymns. One of them may be led by a guest singer. At the end of one of them,
6 an advertisement will be placed on the screen, possibly coupled with a tape-recorded appeal by the minister asking viewers to write for booklets, tracts, etc., to an address shown on the screen.
7 A 15- to 20-minute sermon.
8 More hymns.
9 An appeal for donations coupled with a reminder about literature available by mail.
10 Final hymn.

If American evangelical services are compared with those at Toronto's The People's Church, several differences become apparent. Swaggart, for instance, is expensively attired, although his costly suits might not be described as in good taste with their bright colours and loud checks. In contrast, the Reverend Paul Smith of The People's Church is attired in a natty but clearly inexpensive dark blue suit. Swaggart moves across a stage and gesticulates with raised hands to emphasize his points. Smith does not move across any stage and, in the main, uses his voice for emphasis. (Occasionally in all such services a single chord on the organ will be used to emphasize a rhetorical point which carries a high emotional load.) Swaggart's church is vast, although not as gaudily impressive as Schuller's Crystal Cathedral. Smith's is an ordinary modern church; in the 1988 Easter service a crude backdrop representing the Green Hill of Calvary appeared behind the minister and part of the choir.

A more notable difference is in the behaviour of the congregations. On one winter morning, both congregations sang the same hymn. Swaggart's congregation sang with gusto, "This is my s-t-o-r-y; This is my s-o-n-g." Faces registered emotion, bodies swayed. Smith's congregation sang with some fervour, but faces registered little emotion and bodies were still. There are also theological differences, which are at least as important as the differences of style. Television religion *is* religion, a fact its critics often lose sight of. We feel that Gregor Goethals makes this mistake when she claims that television has de-emphasized "The Word" in evangelical broadcasting.[9] Television evangelists preach "The Word," and they do so in tropes with perduring histories.

AMERICAN HISTORY AND CALVINIST THEOLOGY

Michael Kenny, in his masterly study *The Passion of Ansel Bourne*, notes a number of theological developments that occurred in the United States in the late eighteenth and early nineteenth centuries. These developments transformed the various forms of Calvinism that the early settlers had brought from Europe into a singularly American form of evangelical Christianity.[10] The transformation thus wrought, Kenny argues, created a theology particularly congenial to the American national ethos as it was developing then and has continued to develop. Some of the developments Kenny identifies are pertinent to the subject under discussion insofar as they may shed some light on the scandals that have plagued television evangelism in the United States and on certain differences in style between Canadian television evangelism and the u.s. version.

Swaggart, in one sermon broadcast before his fall from grace, took as his text Psalm 98, which, he said, described the emotions of Pentecost, or the receipt of revelation. Speaking of verse 5, "Sing unto the Lord with the Harp," Swaggart suggested that the King James translators had introduced a meaning that was both overly restrained and incorrect. He suggested that "Sing the Lord" would be a better translation both linguistically and doctrinally. Knowledge of salvation came directly and emotionally, and the saved should not merely worship God: their testimony was vital in proclaiming God's presence in the world.

We find here an expression of some of the key notions of evangelical Christianity, particularly as that tradition has been understood in the United States. We also find some hints about the nature of the distrust that members of the mainline churches bear towards evangelicals, a distrust brought to light in charges that evangelists are too emotional, hypocritical, and intolerant, that they oversimplify texts, and that they are ludicrously extravagant in the claims they make for Jesus (for example, the power to heal and to intervene directly in people's lives.) Let us briefly enter this theological controversy, not to take religious sides but to gain a broader understanding of the differences between American and Canadian evangelism.

The developments that Kenny notes concern the central doctrines of salvation and predestination. The latter, which holds that a majority of souls are condemned to eternal damnation, was both too pessimistic and too determinist a notion to suit a world view centred upon individual initiative, undertaken in a spirit of hope – what William James called "the religion of healthy-mindedness."[11] By contrast, anxiety about salvation was a legacy of Calvinism too deeply rooted in the American character to be ignored. The result of this conflict was a variety of evangelical Christianity in which hellfire was still a real possibility, its avoidance still dependent upon divine will; but the form in which that will manifested itself changed in certain significant ways. Election was not an ineffable secret to which God at best gave clues, but was announced by an overwhelming signal: the born-again experience, in which the sinner was drawn to confess his sins and his inherently sinful nature and to accept Christ as his saviour. This experience came to be more significant as a guarantee of salvation than a blameless life peppered with good works; indeed, the deeper the pit of iniquity that a confessing sinner could acknowledge in his own soul, the more convincing his testimony might be to himself and other believers.[12] Kenny, who is concerned with the psychiatric malady of split personality, seizes upon these facts to argue that the u.s. version of evangelical Protestantism predisposed many of its followers to accept the notion of a kind of double self. The dichotomy between the sinner and the saved soul interests us because it may provide a historical context for some of the recent revelations about the "secret life" of TV evangelists and the surprising willingness of their followers to accept and forgive their sins.

American evangelical preaching and witnessing stress the inadequacy of mere works to achieve salvation (though abstention from sin after conversion might be a sign that the conversion was genuine). A certainty that one has heard the word of God is far more significant. Susan Harding has provided an excellent discussion of the contemporary born-again experience from an anthropological perspective; she stresses many of the same points advanced by Kenny.[13]

THE PEOPLE'S CHURCH

The preaching of the divine word to congregations in North America, Spain, Britain, Russia, South Africa, and the Third World was the life work of the late Oswald Smith, the founder of The People's Church in Toronto.[14] Smith, the son of a telegraph operator for the Canadian Pacific Railroad, became an assistant pastor at Dale Presbyterian Church in Toronto in 1915, and resigned as acting pastor in 1916.[15] His fundamentalist Calvinist convictions, love of gospel songs, disdain for orthodox hymn books, and commitment to evangelism quickly made him a maverick who wandered from congregation to congregation, from sect to sect, from Canada to the United States and back again. From time to time he had no congregation. In the late 1920s he began a brief association with the Worldwide Christian Couriers, an organization headed by the Chicago preacher, Paul Rader. In 1928 he founded the Cosmopolitan Tabernacle, later The People's Church, in Toronto. Its position was simply put:

We stand for the Salvation of souls, the Edification of believers and Worldwide Evangelism; and we emphasize especially the four great essentials; viz,
– Salvation
– The Deeper Life
– Foreign Missions, and
– Our Lord's Return
There will be no church membership. We are separate from all churches and denominations, reaching out for the thousands of people who never enter a church door.[16]

Reading this statement, one is reminded of some of Razelle Frankl's remarks in a recent and remarkable book: "There were additional changes that signaled an emergency institution. Urban revivalism was detached from congregational and denominational activities and practices, and the role of the professional revivalist evolved as a specialized calling or career. A professional revivalist had one major function, namely to gather converts to Christ. Other pastoral tasks were secondary or outgrowths of this mission. His organization developed from his calling rather than his being ready to serve a pre-existing congregation."[17] Frankl's central hypothesis is that modern televangelism is distinct from its predecessor, urban revivalism, because it has fused the old traditions with newer techniques of mass media salesmanship. We feel that she, like many other critics, may be concentrating too much on form (or packaging) and too little on content.

Radio broadcasts from Smith's church began in 1930 and were carried by the Toronto stations CKNC and CKCL. By 1936 the broadcasts were heard on forty-six stations from coast to coast. Smith quickly learned one necessity of broadcasting: "His meetings were started precisely on time, not one minute before the hour, or one minute after, and they always concluded on time – with radio, this was a necessity."[18]

Television broadcasts began in 1973. By this time Smith's son, Paul, had assumed the role of pastor. Paul Smith was educated at Bob Jones University in Tulsa, Oklahoma, and Union College in British Columbia, went through a period of doubt, reconverted, and became a Baptist minister before rejoining his father's church. In 1979 "The People's Church" offered its services to a congregation of 2,600 on its premises and 180,000 Canadian viewers. The Canadian edition of *Reader's Digest*, an authoritative source in popular culture, identified it as Canada's largest church. Its founder, whom Billy Graham described as "the most remarkable man I have ever met," died in 1981.[19]

Is *The People's Church* a peculiarly Canadian phenomenon? The concepts advanced by Paul Smith and Oswald Smith merge, as perhaps Anglo-Canadian culture does, American and British traditions into an interesting syncretism. Presbyterianism (in Oswald's case) and Baptism (briefly in Paul's) are, of course, generic North American as well as British religions. The Northern Irish and Scots Presbyterian tradition is particularly strong in Ontario and has doubtless had a strong effect on the formation of culture and character in the province. On the one hand, some part of that tradition was arguably diluted with the foundation of the United Church. On the other hand, Oswald Smith and his son have had very strong ties with American evangelicals, and both have preached in the United States. Nonetheless, as the following analysis of one of Paul Smith's sermons will show, the Calvinist tinge in the message from Sheppard Avenue is more than most contemporary American viewers would find palatable, although Jonathan Edwards, the eighteenth-century

New England minister, might have found its conclusion, if not its allusions, unexceptional.

The reverend Paul Smith's Easter Sermon, "The Camouflage of Sin," exemplifies a number of features that characterize the preaching of *The People's Church*. Recalling a fashion show he was induced to attend with his wife when he was a young preacher, Smith said that he had come to the conclusion that it was a "camouflage show." Every dress was trying to hide something. Demonstrating the artificiality of his shoulder pads, Smith declared "Sin is like a fashion show." He was not, he said, an "Evangelical, Hellfire, and Bible preacher – just a Bible preacher ... If you go to a church that doesn't preach you're born in sin, they're not teaching you the Bible." Man, he went on, is born in sin and likes to sin. People make excuses for sin: "I can't help it; I came from a bad environment." To refute this, Smith talked about two former members of The People's Church, a brother and a sister, products of the same environment, one of whom became a missionary, the other Canada's leading bank robber.

You can be saved in thirty seconds, Smith announced, by inviting Christ into your heart, but "people postpone that to have a fling first." Smith's father, the founder of The People's Church, once talked of a man who planned to ask for salvation as he died. This is taking advantage of God. Madalyn Murray O'Hair, the well-known champion of atheism, had a son who preached in The People's Church. He wrote of his mother's going out in a storm, while pregnant, to challenge God to strike her dead. Smith compared her to a grasshopper who did not believe in trains because he had jumped on a track without being hit. "God's got her number; God's got my number, and God's got your number," admonished Smith in falling tones. "The beauty of the Gospel is that there is forgiveness for sin ... When God knocks on the door, one must admit one is empty and let him in."

This sermon contains elements of both traditional Calvinist theology and an evangelical emphasis on the conversion experience. On the one hand, salvation through individual rebirth in Christ is deemed to be essential. On the other hand, the importance of "works" is not minimized, as it is with some evangelicals. Much more time is given over in the sermon to man's sinful acts and his love for sin than to conversion itself, and when conversion is mentioned Smith suggests that it is the pleasure of sin that causes people to postpone conversion, implying that conversion is invalid if it is not followed by virtuous behaviour. Moreover, Smith's overall message is one of discipline and self-abnegation, not one of emotional expansiveness, even under the influence of the Holy Spirit. This message is consistent with his sober suit, his restrained manner, and the relative simplicity of the church itself. He assumes that most of his listeners will reject the call to repentance and salvation, and dismisses as unbiblical preaching that does not stress the pervasiveness of sin and the likelihood of damnation. As if to underline the message, the keynote hymn that began the Easter Sunday broadcast service was entitled "Wasted Years."

This is a different emphasis from the generally upbeat, worldly preaching of the Swaggarts and the Bakkers; Jim Bakker once declared, "We have a better product than soap or automobiles, we have eternal life."[20] There is little in *The People's Church* broadcasts that would fit George Gerbner's characterization of television evangelism as "the commoditization of Christianity," despite appeals to viewers to send in for tie pins and booklets.[21]

The activities of The People's Church are compatible with a stress on works as well as on faith; money collected from members and viewers goes towards the church's activities in famine relief and development projects, as well as towards its work in spreading the gospel. Guest preachers are people who have accepted hardship assignments with no glamour, preaching among prisoners or in the former Iron Curtain countries. The People's Church appears to have close links with the Salvation Army, an organization at least as concerned with alleviating the suffering of the unfortunate as with the salvation of their souls.

100 HUNTLEY STREET

Other Canadian religious programs have an orientation similar to that of *The People's Church*, although the broadcasting format may differ. A case in point is *100 Huntley Street*, a religious talk and variety show, produced by Crossroads Christian Communications, a company that receives some mainline church support despite its strong Pentecostal ties. A typical broadcast contains a number of musical spots featuring hymns by resident or guest performers, a five-minute sermon, a film section on a problem of concern to Christians, and a conversation between the host, David Mainse, and a guest or guests concerning that problem. A regular feature is the portrayal of the life of a born-again Christian or lay evangelist. Sometimes this involves simply an interview between Mainse and his guest (for instance, a newsreader on local TV) in which the conversion experience is described. On other occasions the talk-show segment will be preceded or followed by a film clip (such as a Christian railroadman singing country songs against a background of engines, rail, grass, and blue sky.) Social issues discussed vary from Third World poverty to drugs, homosexuality, and cults. Generally speaking, the content of the program, and particularly its emphasis on conversion, suggests a conservative rather than a liberal Christian position. Unlike its American counterparts, however, it is not primarily a vehicle for the charisma of a particular preacher. Furthermore, controversial issues (such as capital punishment or partisan politics) seem to be avoided. In general, despite an obvious and strong American influence, *100 Huntley Street* conforms to Reginald Bibby's description of the difference between Canadian televangelism and the American product: "The style of religion is much more low-key; there are few efforts at empire-building."[22]

Crossroads' children's program, *Circle Square*, features playlets and discussions centred on moral problems, and involves regular adult and child characters. During one session viewed by Harriet Lyons and our children, the dramatization and discussion concerned the need to have courage to differ when friends encourage one to join them in petty theft. A significant indicator of the program's style is the fact that neither of our children identified the program as "Christian" or "religious," just "boring" and "goody-goody." One might note that the children have more experience with Christianity than their history with us might suggest, having been adopted from a Pentecostal foster home.

A Canadian religious program with a somewhat unusual format is presented by John Wesley White, whose name probably indicates either his or his parents' doctrinal orientation. White's program, apart from musical interludes involving a soloist and a white grand piano, focuses almost entirely on his talking head as he ponders the Christian significance of current affairs. Referring to a woman who had been quoted in the press as saying she was not afraid to die because she would be joining Elvis Presley, White stressed the superiority of Christ to Elvis as a saviour, since Christ could not lie, steal, and "immoralize."

Like other Canadian televangelists, therefore, White tempers his desire for the acceptance of Christ as a saviour with some emphasis on morally correct behaviour and attitudes. He has referred to the people who wished to reject the Tamil refugees as "rednecks," and he has extolled the good works of people like Mother Teresa. Although he is given to the use of sports and automotive metaphors in his effort to sound contemporary, his underlying message is much the same as what one hears in the broadcasting of *The People's Church* or *100 Huntley Street*. White is, in fact, a frequent guest on the latter program.

REFLECTIONS

We have attempted to demonstrate some pertinent contrasts between the American and Canadian varieties of religious broadcasting. Yet we also recognize that these contrasts are clouded by regional differences in both countries. Swaggart, Roberts, Pat Robertson, and Bakker are all products of the American south and, although their following is national, it is clearly strongest in the so-called Bible Belt. In central Canada, where established churches are strong, fundamentalism is relatively weak, although there are "Bible Belt" pockets such as our own twin cities of Kitchener-Waterloo. In Alberta some fifty years ago, the Social Credit party rose to power as a result of radio evangelism. Indeed, the Canadian west presents, and presented even more strongly in the past, a pattern somewhat different from other regions, one that is more American in style.

Nonetheless, there remain important national differences. In his recent book *Fragmented Gods*, Reginald Bibby points to striking differences between u.s. and Canadian religious statistics.[23] In the United States Protestants outnumber Catholics by more than 2 to 1 (57 per cent to 28 per cent). Furthermore, more than 20 per cent of Americans are "conservative" Christians – that is, fundamentalists. This figure is important because televangelists appeal primarily to lapsed or even active members of conservative denominations. The growth of the religious right in the United States has therefore derived from existing strength rather than mass conversion. In Canada, by contrast, 47 per cent of the population are Catholic and 41 per cent are Protestant. Catholics constitute not only the majority group in Quebec, but the largest denomination in Ontario.[24] In the west, of course, and most of the maritime provinces, the majority is Protestant. Bibby emphasizes that only 7 per cent of Canadians belong to conservative Protestant groups, and that the number has remained constant for over seventy years.

With respect to religious programming, Canada has zigzagged uneasily between the Reithian and American models of broadcasting.[25] The British Broadcasting Corporation, under its first director, Lord Reith, many of whose policies were continued by his successor Sir Hugh Carleton Greene, sought assiduously to elevate popular taste. Its standards of propriety were so stringent that it was nicknamed "Auntie." While u.s. television has had a certain bland-ness imposed upon it by advertisers who fear to offend potential customers, its channels have in large measure been open to the highest bidder. Evangelists who pay for time have been comparatively free to set their own programming agendas.

The CBC, as a public entity, has been subject to certain constraints deemed appropriate to its role. It must be seen to favour no particular church, no particular creed, no particular region, and neither of the two main language groups. It has also been required to give air time to expressions of Canadian culture. Recently it has been subjected to governmental pressure in order that it may be rendered profitable. The CBC offers evenhanded coverage of various mainline denominations and will accept paid religious broadcasting, although the latter is more evident on local affiliate stations than on the main English stations broadcasting from Toronto. One should note that several southern Ontario affiliate stations have recently become independent of the CBC. Commercial networks such as CTV and Global follow the American model in broadcasting, and the effect on the content and quantity of religious broadcasting is predictable. The advent of Vision TV will be discussed below.

In Canada, public and commercial networks and producers of all kinds are subject to obvious budgetary restrictions, which do not affect the broadcasting industry in the United States. Much Canadian programming is superb, but is produced on budgets that are ludicrously low by the standards of the three major U.S. networks and their affiliates. American fundamentalist broadcasters pay for their air time both in the United States and in Canada. Economically, at least, the presence of Swaggart on Canadian stations may be regarded as "Coca-Colonization." Canadian religious broadcasters cannot compete with their U.S. rivals, and this fact has an effect on the style of production. For example, in a *100 Huntley Street* telethon that we monitored, the campaign's goals, objectives, and achievements were detailed on a blackboard rather than in credits flashed on the screen.

Another issue transcends national boundaries and must be taken into account in reflecting on any academic analysis of evangelical religion. This is the matter of what Pierre Bourdieu calls class "habitus," and it has much to do with attitudes to religious broadcasting in both Canada and the United States. Television evangelism appeals not only to a rural audience, but to an urban audience with rural roots and a nostalgia for a real or imagined past of imagined moral superiority. It feeds on, breeds on, anomie and, of course, its aim is the restoration of moral order. As Frankl observes, it is rooted in a tradition of urban evangelism.[26] Its audience is unsophisticated and just as suspicious of sophistication as sophisticates are suspicious of evangelism. While evangelism boasts wealthy and prosperous converts, such as the Bunker Hunt family and many prominent entertainers and politicians, its primary appeal is to the working class and to that most despised of groups, the marginal petite bourgeoisie.

This is particularly true of the American programs. One cannot help but suspect that the reaction of Canadian as well as American academics and professionals to television evangelism is a manifestation of the class "habitus" of the North American haute bourgeoisie. In Bourdieu's terminology, "habitus" denotes the emotional, cognitive, stylistic, and even bodily dispositions of a class or cultural group.[27] Taste cultures are products of the habitus. In adolescence or at university many of us learned that we should prefer Schoenberg or at the very least Bach to Tchaikovsky, even though we possessed not an inkling of musical theory. We work hard to learn what we ought to like, and by cultivation we learn to like it "instinctively."

Taste cultures do not begin and end at the Peace Bridge or somewhere between Detroit and Windsor, although in Canada taste culture includes certain class-bound attitudes to things labelled "American." We did not produce Swaggart in Canada, but we know well where to place his performances in our hierarchy of ideological and rhetorical taste. Just as Bourdieu's intellectuals knew "instinctively" that Kandinsky was "better" than Utrillo, we know that a pope exercised good taste by using funds accumulated from tribute or surplus value to pay Michelangelo to paint the Sistine Chapel, but Jim and Tammy Bakker were aesthetic and moral reprobates when they used their funds to construct a religious theme-park.

It should be understood that the remarks above constitute neither a defence of Catholicism nor an attack on Pentecostal "extravagance." We grind axes for neither. Rather, we wish merely to note that the current debate concerning television evangelism is part of the debate over mass culture. Emotional sermons, possession by the Holy Ghost, "singing the Lord," healing, and discussions of spiritual rebirth and Armageddon are in "poor taste." Of course, one should know what is appropriate in a particular context. A friend of ours, a German refugee, was dismissed from his post as a rabbi in suburban Westchester county in New York state in the early 1940s after he delivered his first sermon on Hegel's phenomenology of spirit. Jonathan Edwards, for that matter, was dismissed from his Northampton, Massachusetts, church (which now bears his name) because of his refusal to accept a compromise that would have allowed those

who were not converted, but earnestly awaited conversion, to participate in the Lord's Supper. Scholars who ridicule contemporary
evangelists revere Edwards as a master of rhetoric, though they certainly do not share his ideas.

We are in Bourdieu's debt because he pointed out the obvious,
that the critique of mass culture, irrespective of the political preten-
sions of its authors (Marxists such as the Frankfurt School or Dallas
Smythe, democratic socialists such as Richard Hoggart, or conservatives such as S.I. Hayakawa or Ernest van den Haag), is ultimately itself the product of habitus rather than "independent" reason.
Bourdieu's aim was not merely to relativize taste but to extend the
ideological and supposedly superstructural referents of "class" so as
to portray better its hidden injuries. If we join in a superficial de-
nunciation of television evangelism, we may demonstrate our symbolic and educational capital, but we will gain little as students of
anthropology or popular culture. It is necessary to study evangelical
services on television as coherent religious performances, as social
facts that must be explained in terms of other social facts, as events
situated in national and international contexts.

The emphasis on symbolic capital, in Bourdieu's terms, perhaps
slights the degree to which the distribution of genuine political
power in both Canada and the United States is directly linked to
some of the issues we have raised. The haute bourgeoisie does not
merely wear its claim to value "reason" above "emotion" as a badge
of good taste; rather, through the theoretical foundations of liberal
democracy, it asserts its entitlement to political power upon this
basis. Many people with left-wing convictions genuinely fear that
some of those who would use televangelism for political purposes
are manipulating the rhetoric of the lower and lower-middle classes
in their attempt to build a populist base for a challenge against civil
liberties and such related social changes as the move to greater racial
and sexual equality.[28] In Canada these threats tend to be specifically
associated with a spreading American influence, and, as we have
seen, home-grown television evangelism does appear, for whatever
reasons, to conform more closely to middle-class tastes and values.
In both countries, however, the sense of disempowerment fostered
by taste culture may lead to reaction from those whose preferences
command little status.[29]

The scholar who wishes to understand the translation of American television evangelism into a Canadian idiom must be alert to
many nuances and may be rewarded for such alertness by a better
understanding of the broader relationship between the two cultures.

EPILOGUE

Since this brief study was completed, television evangelism has ceased to be front-page news. Jimmy Swaggart's programs are now broadcast on very few stations (they appear on two small independent stations in our viewing area). Jim Bakker of the *PTL Club* is still in prison in the United States. Pat Robertson's bid for the U.S. presidency in 1988 fizzled out fairly rapidly. In 1992, however, President George Bush called upon Robertson to aid in his attempt to win support for his re-election on the theme of "family values." Although this appeal failed to win the election, the opposition that has greeted President Bill Clinton's attempt to remove the ban on gays in the U.S. military is evidence that some of the anxieties of the religious right are shared by a wider segment of the electorate.

The major development in religious broadcasting in Canada during recent years is the appearance of the cable station Vision TV. Except on the weekends, Vision TV devotes most of its prime-time viewing hours to more or less secular programming. However, John Wesley White, Falwell, *The 700 Club, 100 Huntley Street, The People's Church*, and the Benny Hinn Ministries are all given program time. So too are programs on non-Christian religions and ecumenical discussion. There is a space for Canadian liberal as well as fundamentalist Protestantism – for example, *Harpur's Heaven and Hell*. There are serious documentaries, such as the series *North and South*, and reruns of British situation comedies, such as *Bread* and *Last of the Summer Wine*. Except for some of the weekend broadcasts, for which sponsors presumably pay, Vision TV has attempted, with considerable success, to attract educated viewers, and has aimed at balance among the various religious communities that make up its audience. In general, Vision TV conforms more closely to the model we have described for Canadian religious broadcasting than to the patterns of U.S. television evangelism.[30]

6 Inflecting the Formula: The First Seasons of *Street Legal* and *L.A. Law*

MARY JANE MILLER

Generic theory goes back to Aristotle's definition of tragedy. As is well known, his influential description of tragedy fits *Oedipus Rex* very well but does not adequately describe *Antigone* or *Oedipus at Colonnus*, most of the surviving plays of Aeschylus and much of Euripides – that is, much of what we know of as Greek "tragedy." Yet the term is not meaningless as a way of analysing Greek drama, or Shakespeare, or some contemporary plays. Theatre is a public art. When its context changes, the concepts that define a genre alter over the centuries. With Racine true Aristotelian tragedy appeared only nineteen centuries later, where none in the French language had existed before. Thus the critical theory shapes the forms as the form has reshaped the theory. This process is often called "inflection," or the grafting of new ideas, dramatic conventions, and technical advances on to old conventions. Pushed far enough, the dramatic form may no longer be a Western in Science Fiction dress like *Star Wars*, but a new hybrid form, or perhaps a new genus altogether.

In this essay I take advantage of the simultaneous launch of two series, one American, *L.A. Law*, one Canadian, *Street Legal*, both of which focused on the private lives and professional successes and failures of lawyers, to locate differences in the two cultures that affect both the processes of production and the aesthetic of the programs. In so doing I have not observed the rather rigid distinctions between "generic conventions" and "formula" drawn by John Fiske in his useful book *Television Culture*, because I am not exploring as a sociologist might "the industrial and economic translation of conventions ... essential to an efficient production of popular cultural commodities."[1] As someone who has analysed a considerable portion of the Canadian television drama that has survived since 1952, I have always insisted on the aesthetic dimension of the medium. Television drama is called "product" by everyone in the business who is too young to remember when "mandate work" at the CBC included drama as well as news and current affairs. Call television drama an "art form" now and those who make it, as well as those who make decisions that shape it, shudder. Nevertheless, as I demonstrated in several chapters of *Turn Up the Contrast*, superb one-act plays of great emotional and sometimes technical complexity have been found within the series format since the CBC first started to make series in the late 1960s.[2] Such moments are more likely to happen when the conventions of the particular series genre are stretched or inflected because the episode contains unpredictable elements.

Long before any organized discussion of the genres of television drama existed, newspapers described half-hour plays that were common to American, British and Canadian television in the 1950s as "mysteries" or "cop shows" or "comedies" or "westerns." Series in all such genres have waxed and waned in popularity ever since.

For most of our recent history, large numbers of Canadians have watched American television either directly from American stations or as imports on CBC and CTV. Our familiarity with the latest in the evolution of American genres is a given for writers, directors, and producers of Canadian television. Yet not until the third season of *Street Legal* did the CBC use the same series production systems as the Americans did. Rather, the CBC followed the British model because it had neither the money nor the conviction that the hour-long series dramas should aim for twenty or twenty-two episodes a season. John Kennedy, the head of TV drama for much of this period, firmly believed that even if the money were available, the creative juices would dry up and the quality would be superceded by tired formulaic writing, shooting, and acting – even for international hits like *Seeing Things*.[3] This attitude created the possibility that teams of producers, writers, directors, and designers could put the mark of their own sensibility on a series without complete exhaustion and subsequent dilution setting in. The first two seasons of *Street Legal* corresponded to the production conditions that prevailed at the CBC for hour-long series from 1966 to 1988. Subsequently, the American model has prevailed: sixteen to twenty-two episodes are created by a stable of writers, two or three producers, and many directors, and given continuity by an executive producer and a creative head. As with most American television, the result is often a rather institutionalized (or is the word formulaic?) style and treatment of subject-matter.

In the eighteen years since Horace Newcomb wrote his influential book *TV: The Most Popular Art*, which described the earlier development of American television genres, tastes and trends have changed the picture substantially.[4] The western disappeared, reappearing only sporadically. The fairly rigid cop show format pioneered by *Dragnet* opened up in the 1980s to include multiple plotlines, many characters, and the structure of a serial – with overtones of the metaphysical horror fantasy in the cult hit of 1990, *Twin Peaks*. The cop show's only rival in durability, the sitcom, has broadened its base to include wryly complex little fables like those in *Cheers* and *Roseanne* or the more challenging quirkiness of plots and characters of the hour-long 1990s dramedy, *Northern Exposure*. Nevertheless, the formula of the more traditional problem/complication/resolution format of popular shows like *Evening Shade, Cosby, Major Dad*, or *Doogie Howser* prevails in the 1990s as it did on *Fibber McGee and Mollie* in radio in the 1940s.

Newcomb used the descriptive category "Doctors and Lawyers: Counselors and Confessors" for the equally durable series drama focused on the traditional professions. His account of the early American development of that genre may be summarized as follows: programs such as *The Defenders* (1961–65), *Owen Marshall: Counselor at Law* (1971–74), and *Storefront Lawyers* (1970–71) focused on social problems that often raised questions such as "whose rights should be protected" or "who is responsible."[5] Newcomb argues that even though the emphasis remained firmly on the stars of the show (still a sine qua non of most series television), such dramas reflected the concerns of all sections of society, all ages, and and all types of individuals – and in Canada, I would add, from a mildly liberal, completely middle-class perspective. It is worth pointing out that in few episodes of *The Defenders* and *Owen Marshall* did the producers even venture to reject narrative closure. The quality of these series depended largely on the persistence of writers like Reginald Rose and producers like Herbert Brodkin and David Victor, all of whom already had track records in high-quality anthology television. Thus the lawyers did not always win their cases, and bad guys were not always punished (and, in a few instances, were not defined as melodramatic villains). These series did provide some examples of inflection of their conventions.

Still, the basic conventions of the genre prevailed. The writers (who in the American system are often co-producers) had to blend the personal and professional lives of the protagonists; the young male heart-throbs had to have older mentors; conversely, the wise though fallible older stars needed attractive young protégés. By the 1980s women were also included as acceptable protégées although they were very rarely mentors. In the background there was always a professional family of secretaries, clerks or nurses, associates, and sometimes friends. The genre, particularly as it flourished in the 1960s and 1970s, stressed the proper mixture of compassion, skill, and emotional concern as essential components of the apprenticeship. Throughout its history this genre of "professionals," or "doctors and lawyers," has presented most social ills as largely personal in origin and thus usually capable of correction if the behaviour of the characters changed appropriately. In American series drama of this kind, the political and social dimensions are largely ignored. Even when the "whodunnits" like *Perry Mason* and *Matlock* are excluded as belonging to a different genre called "mysteries," lawyers' cases in the genre under discussion are derived from the highly emotional areas of criminal and family law. Corporate and real estate law do not have the story value required by series television. Yet within these boundaries, there is still a strong informational component in some of these dramas.

DRAMA IN CANADIAN TELEVISION HISTORY

The following brief review of Canadian television history is intended to demonstrate that there is a context, a practice of inflecting or making hybrids of American genres, largely forgotten by those who make television, those who make the decisions about television, and the viewers.[6]

In Canada the CBC came late to filmed series television, thanks both to an unofficial understanding with the National Film Board (NFB) that the latter would do film drama and to the fact that anthologies both as populist as *GM Presents* and as élitist as *Festival* and *Q for Quest* continued to flourish after their American counterparts had vanished. Not until 1966 did Ron Weyman, a CBC producer, invent *Wojeck* (1966–68) and *Quentin Durgens MP* (1967–69). The two programs, which overlapped in their time slots in the 1968–69 season, featured respectively a young idealistic coroner and a young idealistic member of parliament. They were followed by an older cynical newspaper reporter in *MacQueen: The Actioneer* (1969–70) and a young idealistic doctor (with an older mentor) in *Corwin* (1970–71).

At about the same time, the United States provided a good example of trying to have it all ways. *The Bold Ones* (1969–73) was an umbrella title for four different series rotating in the same slot in various combinations: *The Doctors*, *The Lawyers*, *The Law Enforcers*, and *The Senator*. The doctors and lawyers survived the longest. However, *Wojeck* bore very little resemblance to the American one-hour "professional" format focused on a doctor or a lawyer or occasionally a teacher. The producer Ron Weyman (an ex-NFB employee who had started *The Serial*) saw drama in terms of contemporary stories told in a cinema verité style.[7] Most of his work, particularly *Wojeck*, broke the conventions set by the American genres. For example, some episodes of *Wojeck* did not place the star in the foreground at all. Sometimes the guilty were not punished. Often the problem was not solved, because those guilty of indifference to old people or bigotry towards homosexuals or racism towards an Indian were the viewers. It was superb, disturbing television – ironic, visually and verbally literate, and filmed on location (since the CBC had no sound studios for film). *Wojeck* regularly questioned the values of the polity whose tax dollars supported the CBC. By midseason the audiences were huge and increasingly enthusiatic about a series that was Canadian, contemporary, and visibly different. *Wojeck* was the product of a small team of directors with considerable experience in CBC anthologies, including Paul Almond, George McGowan, and Ron Kelly, with the producer Ron Weyman, the writer Phillip Hersch (and two other writers in the second season), and the actor John Vernon. It also profited from a core group of actors (such as Jack Creley and Kate Reid) who had learned their craft in CBC television adaptations of demanding classics as well as routine playlets.

Only Americans who lived in the border states saw something so consistently atypical of their own genre as *Wojeck*. However, like many Canadian productions it was shown in Britain. British viewers had their own roster of "professional" shows and American imports to compare with this odd swan-duckling, and the reviews make interesting cross-cultural reading. The direct cinema style and Vernon's rugged looks, abrupt demeanour, and colloquial language confused the British critics, who had not seen a face or an acting style or a program like *Wojeck* before: "The close-ups of ugly faces coupled with the message that the world is made up of acned predators or gooey do-gooders with strong jaws and steely eyes had me cringing in my shoes. But before then I had succumbed to the gloomy impact"; "It has taken me two weeks to get used to [it]. The number of actors and small parts is much larger than usual and the facial types somewhat bewildering"; "Told with the truth of a newsreel, it was dazzling and deeply depressing. One must admire it. But the programme puzzles me – it's neither entertainment nor social drama"; and, of course, in the rotund tones of *The Times*, "The episodes I have seen have set off from fairly reasonable premises and then gone rather [further] than we hoped, a little way beyond credence, but always with the best of social intentions."[8]

By the time *Wojeck*'s stepchild *Quincy* – an American show about a crusading coroner – appeared, those differences had disappeared.[9] Since it now looked much like many other formula police-procedural cop shows, the drama could slip smoothly into the flow of American prime time without a ripple. However, we find in *Halliwell's Television Companion* a comment, tucked at the end of a wry little entry headed "doctors," that demonstrates that Canadians could imitate American genres with alacrity – although, in the 1970s at least, with little success. Philip Purser commented on this subgenre of the "professionals":

The classic formula in medical-men series comprised one young doctor who had to learn that Experience and Wisdom still count, [an] irascible old mentor who had occasionally to acknowledge that New Ideas can work, and a little medical propaganda ("If only she had come to see us six months earlier ..."). *Dr Finlay's Casebook*, derived from A.J. Cronin's stories, may have set the formula, but Dr Kildare pursued it most determinedly, with every episode balancing one happy outcome against a less happy one and the theme music picked up on church bells if anyone actually died. Handsome and boyish in his white bum-freezer suit, Richard Chamberlain's Kildare won every mother's heart, and it was said that his chief rival, Dr Casey, was deliberately created – all scowls and hairy forearms – to woo the American matron from dream son to dream lover ... Dr Simon Locke applied the formula to a Canadian setting. Consult these practitioners individually.

Dr. Simon Locke appeared in 1972 in a derivative independently produced series called *Police Surgeon*, which tried to be both cop show and doctor show. Its short run reflected its lack of popularity.

Unlike CTV, where *Police Surgeon* first appeared, the CBC was relatively free of the pressures to get ratings and sponsors. Is it a coincidence that in those first few years of series television in Canada the product was both distinctive and very popular? It is true that the next generation of shows that Toronto produced, *MacQueen: The Actioneer* and *Corwin*, were more derivative and less popular, in part because Ron Weyman's energy was at a low ebb, as was the general morale in the drama department. However, in Vancouver Philip Keately produced two seasons of a series called *The Manipulators* (1971–73), about parole officers who were professional social workers. The series, although uneven, continued the indigenous inflection on purely formulaic characters and plots. After *The Manipulators* the "professionals" genre disappeared, although the first season of its successor, *Sidestreet*, portrayed the police team as social workers as well as crime-solvers.[10] From 1973 until the late 1980s the CBC had only one hour-long time slot available for filmed series drama, and that was filled with cop shows, some derivative, some less so.

There was one exception. In 1982 *Judge*, a half-hour taped series intended primarily to develop new directors and writers, appeared. As with *Wojeck*, the problems posed by the writers did not always have solutions, nor were the rights and wrongs of the cases necessarily clear. The series was badly constrained because it was a training slot, taped in a small studio on a limited budget. Moreover, it was eventually assigned a time slot (7 P.M. on Saturday nights) completely unsuitable for adult material. *Judge* tackled issues such as the right of Jehovah's Witnesses to affect the health of their children. (Religion is seldom referred to on comparable American television series.) Other scripts looked at the failure of the child welfare agencies and the rights of a father regarding a foetus (years before the Chantal Daigle case). The series clearly resembled an anthology, since only the judge, one colleague (a female judge), and (very rarely) the judge's wife appeared on a continuing basis. The show had nothing in common with the daytime syndicated American series also called *Judge*, which shows real judges and real complainants looking at trivial cases of civil law in gossipy detail. Good scripts and Tony Van Bridge's talent made *Judge* work. Nevertheless, the CBC did not give the series the support it needed for reasons that had nothing to do with ratings or quality and much to do with the economic and political pressures on the corporation in the 1980s, as well as the disappearance of one hour of late prime time into the fold of news and current affairs when *The National* and *The Journal* went to air in 1982. The "professionals" did not reappear in an hour-long series until *Street Legal* in 1986.

STREET LEGAL AND L.A. LAW

The first two seasons of *Street Legal* provide the most recent example of creative inflection in a familiar adult television genre. Both *Street Legal* and the American series to which it was so often and so inappropriately compared, *L.A. Law*, were launched in the 1986–87 season. In many ways the comparison was predictable. Canadian television critics' colonial reflex made them relate *Sidestreet* to *Kojak*, a very different kind of cop show; *Empire Inc.*, a show about business ethics and familial relations over six decades of Canada's radically changing social and economic history, to the serial-soap *Dynasty*; and the hybrid comedy-cop show *Seeing Things* to every sitcom on the dial, just because it was dotted with wisecracks and the odd pratfall.

In the present instance the comparison was also not particularly appropriate.[11] *L.A. Law* is about a large, well-established Los Angeles law firm housed in corporate splendour in a glass tower. The series was modelled on two successful open-ended serials of the early 1980s – a cop show, *Hill Street Blues*, and a doctor show, *St. Elsewhere*. Both borrowed from serials to provide multiple plot lines. Both provided closure in one or two plot lines in every episode, and both had a dozen featured characters and a determination to show the grittier, more cynical sides of police or hospital work. *Street Legal* began as a series focused on three partners in a small law firm housed in an old building on Queen Street West in Toronto.[12] In the beginning, all of the main plot elements were rounded off in a single episode.

Many Canadian television critics seemed to pair these two shows simply because they were both about lawyers. Following a familiar pattern, some predictably concluded that because *Street Legal* did not resemble *L.A. Law* it was not as good, and therefore Canadians could not make that kind of program.

I do not propose to argue either that the early years of *Street Legal* were better than *L.A. Law* or that we should not make serials based on the American *Hill Street Blues* prototype, because most forms of television drama can be inflected to reflect our different cultural values. However, common sense suggests that we should not try to imitate without inflection overly familiar genres or especially huge successes like *Magnum, P.I.* After all, there are few Vietnam veterans and no palm trees in Canada, and only one Tom Selleck in the world. Why would Canadian viewers look at imitations of American hits when, thanks to cable, earth dishes, or simple proximity, 90 per cent of them can look at the real thing by changing the channel? In the hundred-channel universe that is just over the horizon thanks to direct broadcast satellites, viewers will be able to look at almost fifty years of television series, serials, and specials in what will soon be re-run heaven.[13]

A comparison of the first two years of *L.A. Law* and *Street Legal* demonstrates how two different cultures can take a recognizeable genre like "the professional" and inflect it to match the sensibilities and concerns of audiences in two different countries. Maryke McEwen, the former executive producer of *Street Legal*, told a reporter that the strength of her series would be characters, not (as in

American television counterparts) a focus on dramatic situations.[14] The content of the first two seasons of *Street Legal* and *L.A. Law* arose chiefly out of the subject – the law – and the genre – the "professional." Both series stressed the work family. Children other than clients were rarely seen, parents and siblings not at all.[15] Both series featured a wide range of litigation. Nonetheless, the correct nomenclature for a Jamaican pattie or the guilt or innocence of a dog whose owner produces the dog's droppings in court as evidence would not make it into the subordinate plot lines of the more upscale *L.A. Law*. (In fact, this subplot would not have made it past the executives who, until the early 1990s, were the rigid guardians of CBS network standards.) *L.A. Law* was more likely to focus on domestic disputes in its minor subplots, such as a mother-in-law making harrassing phone calls to her ex-daughter-in-law. Canadian writers and producers have significantly more freedom than their American counterparts, including those in public broadcasting. (For example, the final shots of the one-hour special abortion episode of the CBC's *Degrassi High* were deleted before it was broadcast on PBS in 1991; nonetheless, the image of a pro-life demonstrator thrusting a plastic fetus at Erica and Heather reappeared as a visual motif in later episodes.) Canadians have far less excuse for producing formula-ridden mediocrity.

Los Angeles is familiar to the television audience. In its early years *L.A. Law* did not do much with the setting except to show us more varied domestic interiors than usual, reflecting the emphasis on the divorce cases, the personal love affairs of the lawyers, and the real estate deals. The series is set in "yuppie anywhere with nice weather," presumably so that the maximum number of viewers can identify with it. *Street Legal* also has to contend with a familiar setting – Toronto, which is not only the setting for all but one of the cop shows and professionals shows ever made in Canada, but also masqueraded successfuly as Anywhere U.S.A. in CTV's *Night Heat* and *Adderly*, as well as in dozens of American movies. The designers and directors tried to freshen the series by making it Toronto-specific: they used Charles Pachter prints on the walls, recognizable restaurants, details of Queen Street West, Toronto Island, and Cabbagetown, with particular emphasis on the ethnic and class mix in the streetscapes and public places.[16]

The opening credit sequences of both series demonstated some of the differences in tone. *L.A. Law* opened with a blank screen and a soundtrack of blues played on a saxophone. The viewer heard the sound of a car trunk lid slamming and saw a closeup of a vanity licence plate with "L.A. LAW" on it – the logo used between acts. The music shifted to updated Dr. Kildare/Ben Casey music reminiscent of the professionals shows of the 1960s, fully orchestrated with chimes and major chords in an upbeat mode. The visuals began with jumpcuts: first a long shot of anonymous high-rises in a skyline, then a shot of one building; cut to a scan of glass and concrete windows, pan up, and cut to boardroom. This was followed by a sequence of interior shots of characters on the move in impersonal settings. The third sequence was a slower-moving montage of the series stars in closeup and a final, more poetic, shot of the skyscrapers lit up at dusk.

Street Legal's opening credits, for the first two years had a more relaxed feel than *L.A. Law*'s. The sequence reflected the less formulaic approach characteristic of those early years. The music was light and syncopated, with a driving but low-key rhythm under a male voice from which a viewer could pick phrases like "sidewalk symphony" and the refrain "you gotta move." The visuals began with rapid sequences of a subway train coming out of a tunnel toward the viewer, traffic flowing towards and away from the city skyline, concrete curves, and a street in a city park. The camera shifted to a whiteface clown in a piece of street theatre, four Hindu men going past a colourful mural, a bag lady using a drinking fountain to wash. The third sequence was made up of vignettes of the three original characters – Carrie walking swiftly through a sidewalk crowd, then framed against a bookstore window; Chuck window-shopping, then framed against the signs of secondhand shops; and Leon in full black robes and white tabs whizzing by on his bicycle. They converge on their walkup office, kid around about who goes in first (a light-hearted reference to the changing relationships of working men and women), and exit. Cut to the show's logo – the city at sunset in long shot with the words "*Street Legal*" scrawled across the screen.

The credits for *L.A. Law* had an exciting yet claustrophobic feel, tightly framed, full of cement and glass and ending with stamped metal, reflecting a masculine sensibility. *Street Legal* was fluid, with bits of narrative, a rather summery look, and some clearly interpersonal vignettes. I suggest that this is because Maryke McEwen had a different view of the genre, reflecting a different cultural context. In 1988 new opening credits were devised for the revamped series; "revamped" is an apt term, given the introduction of Olivia's stereotyped witch/whore character in contrast to Carrie's wife/mother. The increasing objectification of all of the principal women characters and the emphasis on sexual relationships, power grabs, and serial storylines brought the show closer and closer to the *L.A. Law* look and feel (a decade earlier, *Sidestreet* also evolved into the more

American formula cop show). It must be admitted, however, that the changes sent the ratings up as the differences, the inflections on the genre, diminished. In a series that belongs to a genre dominated in North American broadcasting by a long history and large quantity of "American product," it appears that adding more elements from the American generic codes does boost ratings.

In the first two seasons the parts of the narrative that focus primarily on the law in both series varied widely, ranging through all types of criminal and civil law cases. However, the differences between the two series (and perhaps between the two broadcasting traditions) may be seen in their treatment of the same subject. For example, both series looked at the integration of the mentally handicapped into ordinary society. In one episode of *L.A. Law*, Benny, the mentally handicapped office boy (played by a non-handicapped actor), confesses to the murder of a prostitute because he had blundered into a tryst with her and then realized it "was a bad thing." In a somewhat contrived misunderstanding, which reveals the fears of those who know of his great strength and childlike emotions, Benny confesses to "doing a bad thing" when accused of her murder. The lawyers, particularly Arnie, the selfish swinger, who is his closest friend, require several twists of the plot to arrive at the truth and exonerate him. Benny is a recurring character, and there have been many opportunities to explore his adjustments to the working world, and the others' adjustments to him, since that early episode.

A *Street Legal* episode called "Romeo and Carol" cast two mentally handicapped actors. Jimmy and Carol are in love. Carol's mother tries to get a court order to prevent Jimmy from seeing her daughter. Various plot developments show that they cannot really cope on their own; for example, when they run away they become lost, and Carol takes some food from a convenience store, and they end up (briefly) in jail. Yet the drama also makes the case that they have the right to be in love, because, as Carol says, "I can learn, if I'm taught right." At the hearing the mother's lawyer presses Carol to explain what a mortgage is. The lawyer's questions demonstrate the difficulties that they will face as a couple. Yet Carol's direct, simple reply to his badgering – "Stop doing this to me. All I ever wanted was to be with Jimmy" – puts the other side of the case succinctly. There are no easy answers to such questions of competing rights and responsibilities. Regrettably, the episode concludes with a concession to those who need reassurance. The social worker assures Leon and the viewer that "they'll be fine," which undercuts to some degree an hour of careful, complex, and entertaining exploration of the issues; the ending reiterates the prevailing convention of narrative closure.

Both episodes show how stereotyped responses to individuals can lead to injustice. Both show how other characters are educated to the needs of such people. *L.A. Law*, however, presents the issue as part of an entertaining melodrama, one storyline among several in the episode. *Street Legal* concentrates on the single issue, and addresses it on a much more realistic level. A murder of a prostitute in the mean streets of Los Angeles is not the focus of *Street Legal*. Knowing how to function in a strange environment at night is much closer to the basic question whether someone with Down's syndrome can lead a life of his or her own. Because the executive producer of *Street Legal* used mentally handicapped actors, something the constraints of American series television at that time made unlikely, *Street Legal*'s point about their abilities and worth was subtly reinforced. Canadian anthology and series television has dealt with contentious issues such as homosexuality (*Wojeck* 1967), child abuse (*Twelve and a Half Cents*, 1970), and racism in the schools (*The Education of Phyllistine*, 1964) years and sometimes decades before the executives who policed American network standards would consider introducing these topics to prime-time audiences, particularly if the issue was not easily resolved by the time of the last commercial break.

Not only was there closure in most of the plot lines of *Street Legal*, but the fact that there were only three protagonists meant that the original narrative structure was far less choppy. Having two or three plot lines, which is standard narrative strategy for an hour-long program, means that there can usually be light relief. However, in the sensitively handled episode in which Carrie is sexually assaulted by the enraged husband of a battered client, the only distraction was Leon's problems with a street-smart and rebellious black adolescent. The writers floundered with that story line and it was dropped.

Closure of the plot elements does not mean however that *Street Legal* comes in neat packages while *L.A. Law* has more of the untidiness of real life. Both shows continued to be open-ended in many of the narratives involving the personal lives of the characters. Even in "the case of the week" the "conclusions" could be ambivalent, more often though not exclusively in *Street Legal*. In the assault episode just mentioned, at the turning-point of the action, Jean, the battered wife whose low self-esteem prevents her from leaving her husband, begs Carrie not to testify against him: "Thanks for realizing it wasn't him ... he's a good man. Don't hound him. It's best for both of us." The mixture of fear, delusion, and complicity imprisoning the other woman makes Carrie decide that she must testify after all. She does so in a harrowing but underplayed scene that focuses both on Carrie, the lawyer who is finding out what it is like to be a witness forced to relive an assault, and on the damage sexual assault can inflict even on a self-confident and highly trained professional. She hears the guilty verdict with great relief. Cut to the stunned face of the husband; cut to Jean looking at Carrie, frozen in reproach; cut to Carrie steeled against that look. The man will be out of prison in seven months.

In the 1987–88 season opener, *Street Legal* looked at the then new and often sensationalized issue of surrogate motherhood. Carrie appears on an open-line radio talk show (with an Ontario "in-joke" featuring a walk-on by Tuffy, CBL radio's former resident cat). The story then focuses on her client, a nineteen-year-old girl who now wants to keep her baby because it will offer her unconditional love. She had been persuaded into the arrangement by a drug-abusing boyfriend who decamped, and she now lives with Chris, a sound engineer with a rock-and-roll band. In the first hint that this will be a complex treatment of the issues, "Chris" turns out to be a woman. Other scenes establish that the New Wave ambience of Toronto's Queen Street West may not be ideal for a baby. But just as the cards seem stacked against the young mother's obtaining custody (she is arrested for scalping tickets and resisting arrest), we see her giving birth in a very graphic, unromanticized scene which, without sentimentality, begins to restore the balance. The designer nursery prepared for the child and the elaborately coiffed matron's longing for a baby do not now seem quite such a counterweight, at least as far as the viewer's sympathies are concerned. Yet the teenaged mother and her lesbian partner, convinced that they have no hope of victory in a court, are prevented from vanishing only by Carrie's assurance that they will destroy the fighting chance they do have by running away.

In court we watch Chris, the breadwinner, put aside the chip on her shoulder to try and win the baby for herself and the mother. Carrie forces the wealthy matron to admit in anguished humiliation that she cannot face the pain of childbirth. Now we know the reason for the surrogate contract, and it is not, according to society's conventional androcentric wisdom, particularly acceptable. By now the audience cannot predict how the judge will rule. No one is absolutely right here. Without verbal explanation (a completely realistic touch which compels the viewers to sort out their own reasoning), the judge rules for the wealthy husband and wife. We see reaction shots. Carrie announces that she will appeal. Cut to Carrie going up the stairs to their funky but comfortable apartment to supervise the transfer of the baby – only to find the rooms stripped to the walls. The young mother, her partner, and the baby have disappeared.

Cut to the parents-to-be coming into the empty room. Close-ups of their pain and Carrie's rueful glance. The closing credits roll.[17]

Narrative closure with "feel-good" endings is a temptation for the CBC as well as for American networks. McEwen, the executive producer of *Street Legal*, told me that she and Nada Harcourt (now head of development for creative series television at the CBC) had considered another, more formulaic ending. To cover that option McEwen had the director shoot another scene in which Carrie, once more on the radio talk show, receives a call from the mother and her lover telling her that they and the baby are just fine. Fortunately for the strength of the drama, McEwen decided against the pat conclusion.

When McEwen went on to other projects, she was replaced by Brenda Greenberg, a producer with American experience. As with *Material World*, the only sitcom to survive at least four seasons in the late 1980s and 1990s, American credentials for key personnel seem to be highly valued by CBC decision-makers. At about the same time, the drama department was refocussed and reorganized in the wake of a new round of budget cuts and increased dependence on advertising dollars. Although it was true that the schedule carried much more Canadian drama programming than it had in the late 1970s and early 1980s, ratings were also more important than ever before. Is it coincidental that *Street Legal* now emphasizes the personal lives of its characters rather than the problems of the law and its interactions with people? In 1992 Leon's marital problems with Alanna received more focus than his defence of native land claims.

I asked McEwen about this more obvious concern with the personal lives of the stars, which she had articulated as she prepared for the 1988 season. I was told that because the series had increased to twenty episodes per season from eleven, the show required more story possibilities if it was to stay fresh. In the following two seasons the show was much more heavily advertised; posters on billboards and in bus shelters asked provocative questions about the characters' love lives. The show was given a more visually sophisticated style, and plots were given a higher ratio of "jolts per minute." Whether through imitation (conscious or unconscious), in response to audience expectation, or, perhaps more likely, the producers' conviction that a "look" sells a program, *Street Legal* came to look not unlike *L.A. Law*. Whatever the reasons, if one uses the criterion of ratings, which did indeed go up, the strategy worked.

From the beginning, *L.A. Law* excelled in the presentation of the personal lives of its characters: ambitious, prickly Grace and smooth but sincere Michael; Douglas and his screaming wife; Arnie the cruiser, who specialized in divorces; senior partner Leland, his ex-mistress, and his very competent secretary Iris; and the attractive young singles, Victor and Abbie. In the 1991–92 season a powerful and vicious woman was introduced, then dropped down an elevator shaft at the end of the season.

Yet one of the reasons that *L.A. Law* has survived so long (it has re-peatedly been nominated for an Emmy as best dramatic series) is that the producers and writers will depart from the formula on oc-casion. For example, early in the series the tall, gorgeous lawyer Ann married the short, fat, and unexpectedly rich lawyer Stewart. The conflicts, insecurities, joys, and work life of this couple were rich in humour and careful observation of credible characters. The culture clash of criminal defence lawyer Carrie Barr and crown counsel Jean-Marc Boisvert could also have reflected such complexities, but Jean-Marc disappeared (with thirty seconds' worth of explanation) after the summer hiatus in 1988–89.

By contrast, *Street Legal*'s other single, Leon, was not young, hand-some, or distinguished, and his only real romances (one with an un-reformed but attractive hippie) were neither well worked out emotionally nor credible as plot complications. Although he had a gift for friendship, which is a running motif in the show, the writers had trouble with Leon and romance, perhaps because his character as conceived resists formula solutions. His marriage to Alanna, a conservative corporate lawyer who became a judge, should have sparked some real ideological conflicts. Instead the issues that arose were chiefly domestic, neither topical nor interesting, with some spurious suspense thrown in. In 1992–93 the show went into its sev-enth season, now without Carrie Barr. It is not difficult to predict that Olivia's machinations will continue to be in the foreground, that her romance with Chuck will heat up again, and that new characters will be added to provide further love triangles with a dash of murder or other titillation. But will the series focus again on widowed crown attorney Dillon Beck? Will Leon be allowed to address more se-rious reality-based political issues? Or will the focus continue to be on Chuck's sleazy clients, power grabs by Olivia, tension over whether they will live together or marry, and Chuck's access to their daughter?

The opinions of two Canadian lawyers who reviewed both shows in April 1988, before the transformation of *Street Legal*, are of inter-est. Clayton Ruby, a well-known criminal lawyer, said that he would want the Americans, not the Canadians, in his corner.[18] He said that *L.A. Law* was "gripping ... There is rarely a false note in the writ-ing ... [The characters] know what they are doing, they are ethical, they are tough and they are compassionate." Ruby called *Street Legal* "copycat television" (apparently unaware that it was conceived and in pilot a year before *L.A. Law*). He lamented that even though "the issues are dramatic and the characterizations tightly delivered ... it is so abysmally scripted that it presents a good case for sending its own writers up the river." Since good characterization is dependent on good writing, the statement is illogical. Moreover, Ruby does not like the fact that "the series obtrusively presents both sides of every issue, turning the program into a lawyer's version of the The Great Debate." The series did not present two sides of torture in South America or illegal corporate takeovers, but, as we have seen, it did resist the conventions of melodrama and the viewers' desire for narrative closure.

By contrast, Jeffrey Miller regards the generic u.s. television lawyer as "a health club super hero, larger than life. *L.A. Law* could be *Wonderwoman*, as kitted out by Nieman Marcus or a Brooks Brothers *Superman*, on those rare occasions when '80s men are not stereotyped on the show as bastards or wimps ... Canadian TV on legal themes – *Street Legal, The Judge* [sic], *Seeing Things* leave a taste in your mouth ... maybe a little bitter, maybe a little sour one of chronic insecurity. Just as in everything else, Canada finds itself in the grey area, playing a lonely game of 'Who am I' in the glare of the whiter than whites of the u.s.a. and the shadow of the blacker greys of the u.k. and its shows like *Rumpole of the Bailey*."[19] After much praise of *Rumpole*, Miller returns to *Street Legal* with the comment that the counsellors on this series "are no worse but conscientiously no better than we are, on the assumption that the audience expects its lawyers to put their pants on one foot at a time, too, eh?"

In 1990, Paula Kulig interviewed several lawyers, including the legal advisers to *Street Legal*.[20] Some deplored the extent to which the characters were emotionally involved with their clients. Tom Carey, a criminal lawyer, said "It's refreshing to see a show when the defence lawyers are for the most part sympathetic," although he also accurately described the 1990 ad campaign as "sexist." Another lawyer preferred *L.A. Law* because it is "amusing, believable," and because lawyers at MacKenzie and Brackman are concerned with their billings. (In the 1990–93 seasons, one of *Street Legal's* running plot lines has concerned the firm's financial problems.) One lawyer praised the grittiness of *Street Legal*, enjoyed the more balanced trials in *L.A. Law*, but found the *Street Legal* lawyers to be far more ethical than those in *L.A. Law*.

These reviews may tell us more about the various ways lawyers think about their work than about the programs themselves. During the run of the series, lawyers could be found to argue either case. Nevertheless, both reviewers experienced a shock of recognition when they encountered Canadian law on Canadian television, and that seems to me to be the point of the CBC's doing this kind of TV drama.

Finally, in the early years of both series there was that difficult-to-define element that is sometimes called texture. Any Canadian viewer can tell which country a show is set in within the first ten minutes. The American lawyers on *L.A. Law* are intensely competitive, with more tension and edge in their dialogue; yet despite the presence of Victor, the obligatory angry young man, they are less likely to question the rules governing success in their world. After all, they belong to a successful corporate firm with many partners. Most of them are cynics with hearts of gold, of course, even the selfish womanizer, but all of them are intensely ambitious and almost completely apolitical. Back on Queen Street West, Chuck Tchobanian's ambition to become a corporate lawyer was treated as both understandable in a second-generation Canadian and attainable for a lawyer of his ability. Nevertheless, his aspirations were often portrayed as foolish (he gets naively involved in the boxing world, wants a vulgarly exotic car, etc.) or, worse to a Canadian audience, a little crass. Carrie's successful drive to be the perfect criminal lawyer was linked to her failed marriage and to being a woman in a man's world, but she was kept from being the too-perfect token woman by plots that emphasized her naiveté about the long reach of political torturers in Latin America or the corrupt use of corrupt informers. Leon was their mentor and their conscience, the champion of the cases that most clearly involved ethical questions. Very little was made of his Jewish roots until his wedding, and then the subject was dropped.

After several years *Street Legal* still does not feature highly dramatic legal battles with stirring emotional climaxes in every episode, and *L.A. Law* is still too often inclined to pile on the emotional climaxes without much preparation. There were three murders in the first two seasons of *Street Legal*, and there have been few since. Though action and violence are not emphasized as such, there is more of both in *L.A. Law*. I suggest that Canadian viewers would find so melodramatic a structure unbelievable in a series set in Canada, though perfectly acceptable in American television or in the Americanada of *Night Heat* and *Adderly*.

INFLECTIONS AND OTHER EVOLUTIONS

As I have suggested, *Street Legal* changed over the years, as has *L.A. Law*.[21] Deborah Hastings called *L.A. Law* "one of NBC's proudest dramatic achievements," although she pointed out that the momentum, the black humour, and the executive producer, along with most of the stars, had gone by the end of 1991–92.[22] New stories from the original writers were commissioned for the second half of the 1991–92 season, including an episode with "an unwanted and videotaped office kiss, the shooting of a serial rapist and murder, the offer of sex in the office restroom and references to douching." Hastings calls this episode a response to a statement by Warren Littlefield, the president of NBC entertainment, that *L.A. Law* was missing "those personal stories that are just as important as the [legal] cases. We're not delivering the punch I want in the personal stories."

From the changes made to *Street Legal* in 1988–89, I infer that the director of CBC's English television entertainment (and now a vice-president), Ivan Fecan, who was a protégé of NBC's Brandon Tartikoff in the 1980s and a much more "hands-on" director than his predecessor, issued the same kind of critique (and implied directive) to *Street Legal*'s producers. A CBC press release issued on September 19, 1989, quoted the new executive producer, Brenda Greenberg: "This season then will be more in-depth character development along with harder-hitting, real-life story lines. Romantic love triangles, betrayals and tensions within the firm will make this season of *Street Legal* sizzle." Two years later, on November 9, 1991, *Starweek* writer Bill Taylor was protesting that "rather too much attention [was] paid to the legal eagles' nesting habits in bed rather than on the bench," but he did put the show "head and shoulders above *L.A. Law*." And so it goes in the popular press. Sometimes critics love the glamorous amorality and greed that often gets its Canadian comeuppance in *Street Legal*. Others prefer their amorality apolitical and choose *L.A. Law*. Some like socially conscious, nationalist, and topical issues, others the brisker, more extreme, yet still morally complex characters of *L.A. Law*.

The fact that *Streat Legal*'s ratings improved when interpersonal problems took precedence over professional issues and legal and ethical questions suggests that the American formula for success upon which *Street Legal* came to depend does satisfy more viewers. They like the sizzle. In fact, according to Sid Adilman of the *Toronto Star*, 1.368 million people watched Carrie's wedding, for reasons perhaps best expressed by one of Canada's favourite icons, Peter Gzowski. His article in a women's magazine is headed "Steamy 'Street Legal.'"[23] He points out that originally the program "spent more time in court. It was a valiant effort to Canadianize an American format" (an effort that included a cameo performance from Gzowski when Leon visited *Morningside*). In his mind, as the seasons rolled on, "everything got steamier and more fun." Since Olivia arrived, the series "has taken our minds off things. And that, after all is what television does best" – an accurate and unapologetic description of one of the uses of television and the most probable "dominant" reading of most series in the professional genre.[24]

In the fall of 1987, when the CBC was deciding to take the plunge and do a full twenty episodes of *Street Legal* for 1988–89, McEwen and two assistant producers visited the production units of *Cagney and Lacey* and *L.A. Law* in Los Angeles to find out how they got twenty-six episodes on air on schedule. They found that some of the Hollywood practices were adaptable to the different circumstances of working for a crown corporation in another country, and others were not. So too with this most recent Canadian version of the professional genre. Some conventions are adaptable, others must be inflected or ignored and new ones invented. The electronic border is not closed, but neither has it disappeared. *L.A. Law* and *Street Legal* demonstrate that.

I have discussed one or two "deviant" readings of *Street Legal* among the critics and viewers who have expressed an opinion – "deviant" because based on cultural assumptions other than those of the makers of the program and their audience as constructed by their expectations of the genre, or based on incorrect information. My own reading is "resistant" to the "dominant" one. I prefer the more sober first two seasons of *Street Legal* because I read them in the context of *Wojeck*, *The Manipulators*, and *Judge*, all of which placed in the foreground the legal and moral tangles of our courts and the public lives we lead. After the death of docudrama in the anthology *For the Record* when it was cancelled in 1985, serious discussion of topical issues could only appear in series television, and those opportunities have diminished in the last three seasons of *Street Legal*. Before it became less ratings-conscious, the series did set "taking our minds off things" as a primary goal. But it did not tell us what to think or feel, did not depend on a high jolts-per-minute ratio, and took time over its dramatic crises, which were carefully explored and often ambivalent or ambiguous in outcome. It was a distinctive inflection on a genre within an established tradition of successful variations. In the hundred-channel universe on our immediate horizon, there should be room for both the spicy *L.A. Law* and the tarter flavour and after-bite of the early years of *Street Legal*.

PART TWO

American Sports
and Canadian Society

Part two opens with a fascinating comparative essay by John MacAloon, an American anthropologist with a strong interest in the comparative study of Olympic sport. His broad concern is "the recovery and analysis of patterned difference" in the conduct of contemporary popular cultural studies, in contrast to familiar claims of "homogenization" as mass culture's distinctive feature. In particular, he contests the almost automatic assumptions made about the similarity of the Olympic movement in Canada and the United States. MacAloon views the topic of popular culture as highly politicized in Canada because of nationalism and demonstrable or feared u.s. domination, which at the least leads to certain misconceptions about the United States and may obscure profound cultural differences. MacAloon's central argument concerns the existence of "profound" differences between Canada and the United States in the sport–politics relation centring on the role of the state. He describes Canada's Olympic sport system as "state-centred and state-driven," with the federal government as the "leading institutional actor." The government is massively and directly involved in Olympic sport, a fact that does not and cannot penetrate American popular culture and consciousness. In the United States the federal government has no formal, central role in sport. Americans (and indeed many Canadians) find it unimaginable that they could be so different from Canadians when it comes to the organization and promotion of Olympic sport.

Robert Barney, a historian of sport, next explores the historical roots and the subsequent evolution of the "American" game of baseball into a Canadian national pastime. He explores the importation of the game through American immigration, the embrace of codified playing rules from the United States, the organization of baseball clubs and the development of intercommunity and tournament play based on American models, the rise of professionalism in emulation of American patterns, the minor league phenomenon, and the implantation of a major league identity in Canada during the last twenty years. Barney's essay describes a fascinating process of a cross-border commingling that began in the nineteenth century. First, immigrant Americans brought the game of baseball with them. Then Canadian teams imported u.s. baseball rules; thereafter they started to play American teams, winning foreign attention with their skill. Professional players were then imported from south of the border, after which Canadian teams joined u.s. leagues and continued to participate in them. Canadians also avidly followed American teams and made native heroes of some of their famous players. Comparing the popularity of baseball and hockey, Barney argues that "baseball became institutionalized and ritualized in the lives of Canadians more rapidly and indelibly than any other sport," thus preparing the way for the successful advent of the Montreal Expos and the Toronto Blue Jays. The author believes that residents of Canada have always had a love affair with baseball and that it has a central place in popular culture.

In the final essay in this part, the sociologist Robert Stebbins presents Canadian football as standing at the centre of the popular cultural ties that bind in the society; yet he explains that English Canadians have always had ambivalent feelings about this sport, especially in comparison with the u.s. variant. The availability of American NFL games on television and in local press coverage leads "some Canadian fans to conclude that the game played in Canada is inferior or at least less glamorous." To show how the proposition about ambivalence is tenable, Stebbins considers five value conflicts – about rules, ideals, rights, quality, and familiarity – that have undermined wholehearted acceptance of Canadian professional football from the beginning. He describes a fluid movement of teams and rules across the border in the second half of the nineteenth century (much as in baseball). Both American and Canadian football emerged from British rugby, but the latter retained more rugby-like features, in part out of resistance to "complete Americanization." In the early to mid-twentieth century, conflict among Canadian rugby-football teams was over such issues as professionalism versus amateurism and its relationship to excellence. Some of the "professionals" were in fact Americans, a situation that continues to the present day.

7 Popular Cultures of Olympic Sport in Canada and the United States

JOHN J. MACALOON

The old debates about the scholarly dignity of popular culture studies have been overwhelmed by the explosion of such work in the social and human sciences over the past fifteen years.[1] Indeed, it is sometimes difficult to recall what all the fuss was about amid the currently rich harvest of case studies, the transformation of whole disciplines (such as history), emergent boundary-defying intellectual programs (such as critical cultural studies),[2] and a diffuse postmodernism indexed by a studied transvaluation of high- and low-cultural values. Culturally oriented sociologists and anthropologists, long bemused by the category "popular culture" itself, have turned to the study of "public culture" and its flows across conventional national and international boundaries.[3] Investigators in several fields are moving on to broader theoretical and methodological matters. Three such matters are of special concern in this essay.

The first has to do with ways of thinking across domains of experience that are separated in cultural common sense and in the scholarly division of labour that tends to reproduce it. The aim is to divine the systematics of social life in novel fashion. In Pierre Bourdieu's work, and particularly in his monumental *Distinction*, we have one powerful exemplar of these new directions.[4] Bourdieu distinguishes such fields as politics, art, sport, dress, movies, and consumer goods solely in an attempt to recognize relational patterns of taste among them, revealing intersections and disjunctions of social, cultural, and economic capitals in a non-reductive way. Many anthropologists, however, continue to insist on the constitutive primacy of culture,[5] and interpreters of more pluralistic and ideologically egalitarian North American societies may have a harder time determining the systematics of difference than scholars of more hierarchical France.

This is the second main challenge today, the development of concepts and methods that permit cross-genre, cross-institutional, and cross-national analysis without falling back into a priori and monolithic reductionisms of the sociological or political-economic sorts that vaporize important diversities of cultural formations and popular experience. The third challenge is to develop truly comparative studies of similar popular cultural forms within diverse societies and social segments and, where interaction is direct, of models of intercultural exchange among them. In sum, it is the recovery and analysis of patterned difference that must be stressed in contemporary popular cultural studies, in contrast to familiar claims, right-wing or left-wing, of homogenization as mass culture's distinctive feature.

THE "CULTURE CONTROVERSY" IN CANADA

In Canada, popular culture has been for some time a public problem in Joseph Gusfield's sense. In the contexts of Canadian nationalism and of demonstrable or feared U.S. domination, the politicization of the category has had the signal effect of helping to legitimate it in scholarly, parliamentary, and street-corner discourses. As both cause and consequence, the "culture industry," "culture ministries," and "cultural policy" exist as bounded and named objects in the Canadian social world to a much greater extent than they do in the American. At the same time, certain misconceptions linger and are even reinforced by the politicization of the category, equally among those who regard the colonization of Canada by U.S. popular culture as a fait accompli and those for whom Canadian popular culture represents an important site of resistance to American cultural hegemony.

The first is an assumption of a certain transparency in the cultural products themselves. Discourses centring so thoroughly on ownership, appropriation, diffusion, and colonization may produce their own form of mystification in which cultural goods are reduced to mere instrumentalities. Economic and political values are substituted for cultural values. The meaning of things, which renders them marketable in the first place, is either taken for granted or treated as a mere "externality."

The second problem lies with the related assumption of an identity of meaning and value of cultural objects in the two different societies. The same logic that makes capitalism capitalism and the liberal state the liberal state, Canadian or American, reduces the problem to one of homogenized power and profit, domination and resistance, and thereby tends to make the objects of exchange intrinsically or fundamentally homogeneous too. Cars are cars, books are books, films are films, sport is sport. Profound cultural differences – supposedly the object of protective concern – may thereby be obscured, with objects of trade becoming subjects of ignorance. Comparative differences of meaning inscribed in, and potentially revealed by, putatively common items of cultural attention and value are rendered invisible. Misrecognition of the Other becomes a consequence of defence against the Other.

Progressive Canadian intellectuals regularly and rightly complain of American ignorance of Canada. Less frequently, in my experience, do they imagine that this might be an active process of American resistance against representations of envied or feared Canadian institutions, values, or practices. Neither do such Canadian voices seem to worry very much about their own possible misconstruals of "The u.s." We Americans tend to be taken as simple givens, transparent obviousnesses, by such discourses. Or else Americans and the American state are simply identified in a certain style of Canadian prose, without much compunction about the imperialism involved in such a rhetorical move. By such means is sameness often vigorously reproduced by its most proudly avowed enemies.

Third, ways in which the cultural productions of Canadians and Americans are equally constrained by and responsive to actors, agencies, and events beyond their borders tend to be overlooked in discourses that overstate the purely bilateral character of the relationship or reduce its complex multilateral engagements to abstractions like "the Free World" or "the international capitalist order." The synthetic result of these mistaken assumptions can be to eliminate the possibility of generating, through comparative popular cultural studies, more general interpretive paradigms with the potential for illuminating broad political and economic processes themselves.

"NORTH AMERICAN" OLYMPIC SPORT AS A PARADIGM OF CONSTRUCTIONS OF THE OTHER

In both Canada and the United States, Olympic sport is an economically, socially, and culturally prestigious object of mass attention. Olympic sport as an item of popular culture appears to be shared in the double sense of common participation in the international organizations and competitions of the Olympics and of common cultural constructions and interpretations of that participation. Popularly conceived relations between "sport" and "politics" exemplify these commonalities, and in few other domains in both countries is academic discourse so little distinguishable from the popular. Nevertheless, as I intend to show, there are differences between Canada and the United States in the sport–politics relation centring on the role of the state, differences so profound as to destroy any taken-for-granted notion of "North American" Olympic sport. These differences, however, are generally unknown, unrecognized, or actively concealed between and among the general populations of the two countries. Canadians and Americans regularly fail to perceive and explore their Olympic difference, and they misread their neighbours in terms of a projected similarity that does not exist.

To be sure, there are some infiltrations of prior American practice into Canada – aspects of the mass marketing of the Olympic Games, for example. But at the same time, Canadian developments infiltrate American practice: the rationalization and bureaucratization of coaching and administration, the "carding" of athletes, and congressional investigative hearings in imitation of the Dubin inquiry into drug abuse, to mention a few recent examples. Unidirectional colonization is *not* the hallmark of the relationship in this domain of popular culture. Moreover, historical flows of particular practices generate and are generated by a totalizing structure of intercultural relations that, when taken from the point of view of organization, administration, and the explicitly political dimension of the political economy of sport, is profoundly inversive. This symmetrical inversion, however, is largely secret and silent, hidden from popular consciousness on both sides of the border. Far from simple errors or ignorances, these misrecognitions of the North American Other are in fact illusions in Freud's specific sense of the term, wish-fulfilments projected onto the neighbour of what each society wants but otherwise does not want or cannot have for itself.

In a simplified nutshell, Americans want a weak federal state (and gain one in Olympic sport) in favour of local community autonomy and plurality. But the requirements of a complex and large-scale economy and of commitments to social justice and equality mean that a weak federal state is precisely what Americans cannot abide. Canadians want a strong federal state (and gain one in Olympic sport) in favour of national prestige, social welfare, and economic development. But the requirements of bilingualism, multiculturalism, and provincial and local autonomies mean that a strong federal state is what Canadians cannot abide. Each society turns to and constructs the neighbour in terms of its own obscure object of desire. This essay is devoted to demonstrating the presence and power of this paradigm, both heuristic and structuring, in the context of Olympic sport. In concluding, I will show how it contributes to organizing, mediating, and understanding properly politico-economic relations between the United States and Canada.

BEN JOHNSON AS A FIGURE OF CANADIAN POLITICAL SPEECH

In Seoul's Chamsil Stadium in 1988, alight with the glow of Ben Johnson's victory, a high sports official in the Progressive Conservative government (call him "Mr. R.D.") rushed up to a Canadian Olympic Association (COA) official and exulted that "now Mulroney can call the [federal] election." This statement is in some way or other comprehensible, that is to say interpretable, on both sides of the border. Indeed, at the poles of its potential meanings, the interpretants that Canadians and Americans would bring to bear upon it are largely identical. However, from a popular cultural point of view, most of what lies at the centre of this utterance and its discursive setting for a Canadian would make little sense to an American.

Emotional outbursts in the flush of stirring events are hardly unknown among Americans. In the case of sport, transcendent performances – and, a fortiori, world record-smashings under global gaze and impossible pressure in archetypically individual speed events – are physically and morally experienced as testimonies to individual "character," "will," "seizing the day," and "triumphing over circumstances." Such ritual performances of the "ideology of excellence"[6] are culturally constituted, officially and popularly privileged, and emotionally esteemed interpretants in both Canada and the United States. Citizens of both societies take it as equally "natural" that the victory of one's co-national and performatively "representative" athlete is especially inspiring. In a public logic centred on "identification" with the athlete in such mediations and circumstances, it is not incomprehensible or even surprising that an enthusiastic celebrant should spontaneously and expressively seize on some connection, however farfetched or irrational, between his own occupational or social interests and those of the victor. Judging by American mass media coverage and public conversation, it seems to me unlikely that many Americans appreciated the added meaning for Canadians of Johnson's victory as a victory *over the United States* in the person of ("brash," "arrogant," "too easily dominating") Carl Lewis. But as a victor *of us all*, Ben Johnson as sign nonetheless carried sufficient surplus of meaning to render such effusive utterances as that of Mr. R.D. "understandable" – that is to say, human and in its excesses "forgivable." However, if this much be shared by both Canadian and American interpreters of his assertion – "now Mulroney can call the election" – the specific content of its predications between sport and politics introduces strangeness for Americans in what is contextually familiar to Canadians.

This is not to say that R.D.'s statement might not call out surprise, scepticism, even hostility among Canadians, as indeed it did for its original addressee. But I suggest that it does so primarily as hyperbole, whereas for Americans auditors it is not hyperbole in the sense of an exaggeration of recognizable or taken-for-granted relations between sport and politics. I will concern myself with the situational factors that make for this difference after pointing out the other compositional figures of speech embedded in this discourse, which likewise make possible the comparing and contrasting of cultural perception.

In the statement, athletic victory is expressed not only as a metaphor for politics (footraces are like politics), but as a metonymy (contiguity in time: *now* the election) and synecdoche (Johnson's victory is a part standing for the whole of the Conservative electoral campaign, including U.S. relations in the context of the debate over free trade between the two countries). Indeed, the hyperbole of both occasion and utterance threatens explicitly to move the assertion out of figurative speech entirely and into a conceptual identity (Johnson's victory *is* federal politics). Now metaphoric predications of politics as sport are perfectly common in the United States, and related metonymic and synecdochic ones, though less frequent, also appear (for example, the Los Angeles Olympics in 1984 as the "Reaganite Olympics"). However, as we shall see, it is in these figurative modes that institutional and contextual factors generate barriers against mutual recognition and understanding between Canadians and Americans.

With respect to simple assertions of transitive identity (sport is politics, and politics sport), commonality between the two national popular cultures generally returns. In both cultures we commonly speak of politics "enabling" or "contaminating" and "interfering with" international sport, or of sport "reflecting" political structures or "reproducing" and "reinforcing" political socialization or, perhaps less frequently, of sport as a moral and metasocial "critique" of existing political arrangements. But regardless of the verbs chosen to link the two domains – and the metaphors underlying them: disease, pollution, the mirror, the servomachine, the sermon – the separation of the domains of sport and politics remains at its deepest and most constitutive cultural level quite intact.[7] (After all, were they not constitutionally separate things, there would be no need or possibility of such figurative locutions.) Indeed, there is almost an obsession with reinforcing these boundaries in the customary speech of North Americans. Beneath the rhetorical surface it can be discovered equally among neo-Marxists decrying the "sports-media-industrial complex" and its reproduction of the alienating and exploitative ideologies of late capitalism (proportionately more audible in Canada than in the United States, incidentally) and among conservatives lauding sport's representation of excellence, democratic equality before the rules, social mobility, and individual motivation to achievement. Here the two poles meet of u.s. – Canadian interpretive commonality made visible in respect to the utterance about Johnson.

Politics, after all, is the realm of necessity, of those really real realities of power and economic condition; sport, however profitable or engaging, remains in the end, like art, voluntary activity categorized socially as an aspect of civil society, not of the state, and culturally as belonging to the realm of play and entertainment, of, as we moderns say, "the merely symbolic." To suggest anything else – that is, to conduct a discourse in which distinctions between things labelled "sport" and things called "politics" are the problem to be solved rather than the premises of inquiry – is to be thought a mad person, a comedian, a romantic poet, a totalitarian, or perhaps an anthropologist. I am suggesting that Americans compelled to take R.D.'s statement as a literal and substantive assertion would have no recourse but to conceive him instantly under such labels (probably one of the first two), whereas Canadians in the same circumstances could pass through a wider range of plausible meaning-structures before being forced to the same interpretive position. Critical differences are, in other words, contained within and concealed by similarities in the apparently common cultural object of Olympic sport. What are these differences and to what are they attributable?

Starting from within the utterance, the first thing to note is that in the United States elections are not "called"; they occur on a fixed schedule. This calendar happens fatefully to coincide with Olympic years, but unlike both the games and federal elections in the Canadian parliamentary system, it is inconceivable that American presidential elections would ever be negotiated, postponed, or cancelled. In their timing, they are not subject to strategizing. Elections are the one fixed star in American political and civic life, and all other transient, episodic, or happenstance events are oriented in American public space and time around elections, never vice versa. The Canadian situation is obviously quite different. National elections are called and potentially rescheduled in terms of other events and developments. Indeed, at the time of the Seoul Olympics, the strategic tussle among the political parties over when to call elections in the light of public opinion on free trade was a dominant public issue. Thus in Canadian political space and time there is no a priori ground of disconnection between the possible timing of national elections and other epic events judged to have an effect on the national mood. As the former are subject to political judgment and negotiation, so the latter are subject to interpretive judgment about their concrete political effects. That Mr. R.D.'s assertion might be judged hyperbolic by many Canadians merely reveals that the predications contained in it are, generally speaking, conceivable, plausible, and possible.

Special contextual features of Johnson's victory bring it further into contiguity with relevant political things, creating conditions for the shift from metaphor to metonymy. I have already mentioned the salience for Canadians of the fact (unappreciated by most u.s. audiences) that it was "the Americans" whom Johnson conquered. The simultaneous argument between the government and the opposition parties over free trade was being fought out largely in a vocabulary of nationalism, often overwhelming any empirical concern with a practical calculus of economic advantage for either signatory to the treaty. New Democratic and Liberal voices accused Prime Minister Brian Mulroney and his Tories of selling Canada out, of placing it in a position of never again being able to "win" over the United States. The government, for its part, argued that free trade was the best means of protecting nationalist aspirations by creating conditions for Canada to better compete with the United States and in the world market. The nationalism of the opposition was labelled as reactionary, weakening, and demeaning to a contemporary Canada aspiring not to isolationist peculiarity but to visibility on the world stage. Ben Johnson, the Canadian, was, on the day of his victory, the most visible and celebrated person on the planet. (As, tragically, he was to be again a few days later.) He had actually achieved what both parties claimed to be seeking for Canada entire.

Johnson stood as part to whole, a synecdoche for nationalist politics in the idiom of nationalist sport. The coa official to whom the Conservative political official expressed his exultation in Chamsil Stadium is in fact a well-known ndp adviser, a former legislative candidate, and a potential sports minister in any future ndp government. I cannot say whether Mr. R.D.'s choice of interlocutor was motivated in part by partisan hostility and personal rivalry, or whether it reflected instead a spontaneous presumption of a shared delight in the national importance of the victory just achieved for all Canadians. Because both parties to the conversation were involved in electoral politics, that delight was understandably expressed in a political idiom. Perhaps the gesture contained both meanings, it being the feature of emotive master symbols to join otherwise disparate and contradictory significances.[8] In any case, the gesture reflected and reproduced a nationalist "return to the whole" achieved by the ready translation of Ben Johnson's victory from civic metaphor to national political metonymy and synecdoche.[9] As the political situation in Canada added meaning to Johnson's victory, so athletic triumph added meaning to the political situation.

Additional domestic situational factors were literally embodied in Johnson's victory and tied sport discourse further to political discourse. Scores of millions of Canadian taxpayers' dollars had been poured through Sport Canada into Olympic sport by a series of Liberal and Conservative governments. But the funding leading up to 1988, and particularly the "Best Ever" program to develop and virtually promise Olympic medals to the Canadian public, had been appropriated and spent under the Mulroney regime. Though this program had been generally supported by all three parties, the onus of "failure" would flow especially to the party in power just as elections approached. Moreover, a potentially damaging ambiguity in the Conservative party's policy had developed and was receiving fairly wide publicity in this Olympic year. On the one hand, the Mulroney government proclaimed a continuity with prior policies supporting federal involvement with sport. But on the other hand, the government was believed, like Margaret Thatcher's government in Britain, to favour increasing "privatization" of sports development and funding efforts in line with its general laissez faire ideology. Olympic success could be claimed by the opposition as owing to the innovations of previous Liberal governments and maintained in 1988 in spite of Tory tinkering, while failure could be ascribed directly to the present government's efforts at devolution.

Though otherwise a considerable triumph, the Calgary games had reproduced the trauma of Montreal in 1976 in that no Canadian had won a gold medal. Now in Seoul, day after day passed without a Canadian's winning a medal of any kind. As I, along with other observers on the scene, can attest, the agitation of Canadian government sports officials grew visible and extreme. In marked contrast to Los Angeles, where under the Liberal government of John Turner and the sports minister Jean LaPierre (and, of course, with the socialist countries absent) an unexpectedly rich and nationally celebrated harvest of Olympic medals had been won, in Seoul all those millions of dollars and accompanying government rhetoric shockingly threatened to go without payoff.

In normal circumstances in a state-centred and state-driven sport system, the government presents itself for praise and blame as the leading institutional actor. Where such a system happens to be present in a liberal democracy like Canada, additional contextual features are brought to bear. Blaming the government is already a general public habit, and relatively strong inhibitions exist against too overtly attacking the athletes themselves, who "after all" and by assurance of the ideologists of excellence are just individual "kids doing their best" in most difficult circumstances. In the United States, where the government is unavailable for Olympic blame, and the athletes are similarly protected in discourse (and in any case never fail to win many if not quite enough medals), public rancour over losing (notably to the former Soviet Union and East Germany) traditionally flows toward the United States Olympic Committee (USOC), the sports federations, and the coaches. In Canada, by contrast, the COA, the sports governing bodies, and the coaches were enjoying in 1988 a relatively favourable reputation given the remarkable successes of the early 1980s.

Therefore officials of the sports ministry and Sport Canada, and the Mulroney government to whom they stood as part to whole, had every reason to be distressed. Johnson's overwhelming victory understandably came as a massive relief to them, compensating in its epic quality for the modest number of medals Canadians would go on to win in Seoul. Mr. R.D's assertion, delivered with smiles of palpable relief, had the particular meaning that he might now be assured of keeping his own job, given, of course, a Mulroney victory in the election that was "now safe to call." Indeed, within two days the prime minister himself, in statements to the press and on the floor of Parliament, was explicitly interpreting Johnson's victory as evidence that Canada could compete internationally under a regime of free trade, private initiative, and government co-ordination. (Johnson's well-publicized wealth from "private" corporate sponsors in combination with Sport Canada's efforts were alluded to here as a model.) A few days later, on October 1, 1988, the Canadian federal election was called.

Canadians would rightly judge absurd any suggestion that the timing of the election was singularly or even largely attributable to Johnson's victory. Such an utterance would belong precisely to that conceptual identification of sport and politics that can no more easily be entertained in the Canadian popular imagination than in the

American. However, recognizing meaningful plausibilities in a government official's assertion that Johnson's victory made it safer to call an election is another matter indeed, one that Canadians could entertain in ways that their southern neighbours could not. It is to American conditions that I will now turn, after a brief summary comment.

As Donald Macintosh has written in a volume which revealingly has no published American equivalent as yet, "improved performance by 'made in Canada' athletes in international competitions provides Canadians with sport heroes who are not part of the North American 'professional' sport package. It is our view that this has played a role in countering the threat to Canadian identity of the pervasive mass culture of the United States."[10] Macintosh, like Bruce Kidd and other Canadian sport researchers, understands this fact as both cause and consequence of the massive and direct Canadian government involvement in Olympic sport. That involvement is certainly known (reportable and interpretable) in some degree to a majority of Canadians and unknown, as I will go on to point out, to an equally large proportion of Americans. This inversive symmetry provides the master key to the differing comprehensibility to Americans and Canadians of both the exemplary episode of Johnson and the broader strutures embodied in it.

AMERICAN DIFFERENCE AND PROJECTIONS OF A CANADIAN OTHER

In the United States there is not, nor has there ever been, such a thing as a government ministry or minister, much less an assistant deputy minister, of sport and fitness. Indeed, there is no u.s. governmental office of any kind, executive, legislative, or federal bureaucratic, having sport as its raison d'être and official responsibility. There are no regular federal budgets for international or national sport and the few, irregular, and relatively tiny appropriations for sport are always publicly presented as indirect (tax incentives and checkoffs, security assistance, property transfers, one-time start-up grants), not direct allocations of public funds. The two political parties have never included sports policy in their electoral platforms, have no official sports advisers or appointees, and communicate irregularly and privately with Olympic officials. The rare assertive occasions of Democratic and Republican differences over sport go largely unnoticed in the media or in public discourse and in any case are attributed not to principled party stands but to the transient peculiarities and interests of individual politicians and situations.[11] It is almost unknown among Americans that the United States Olympic Committee is a congressionally chartered organization, and it is perceived by no one as a governmental or even, to use the sociological expression, a quasi-non-governmental-organization (QUANGO), as Sport Canada or the British Sports Council is so perceived among Canadians or the British.

On occasion there have been U.S. congressional hearings on sport matters; there was in recent memory a President's Commission on Amateur Sports; presidents and vice-presidents declare open Olympic and Pan-American Games held on American territory; and, of course, the Carter boycott of Moscow in 1980 and to a lesser extent the Reagan State Department's reactions to the Soviet boycott of Los Angeles were matters of public discussion. But all of these episodes are popularly understood as historical transients, and mass media discourse inevitably follows this interpretive program. In declaring Peter Ueberroth its 1984 Man of the Year, *Time* noted the echoes of Reaganism in his achievement. Ronald Reagan, who had just been overwhelmingly re-elected, finished second, and not a word was mentioned in the magazine about any presidential connection with the Olympics (although, for example, the Reagan re-election campaign raised over $15 million in Los Angeles during the games). As perceived in American popular, public, and official cultures, the official policy of the United States with regard to Olympic sport is that there is no policy. That is to say, so the popular logic runs, since there is no governmental involvement, no explicit, ongoing, and valorized state interest, and since Washington is the index of "the political," therefore there is no public political policy (except of state non-involvement).

To be sure, mainstream American politics and successive administrations have been anti-communist and therefore episodically concerned with medal-counts in relation to the socialist countries. But in American popular culture this interest is preferentially attributed to wider civil society, and any government interest is conceived merely as a derivative sharing of popular concerns. In Olympic sport matters, "the American People" and civic and commercial organizations lead; the government only, if at all, follows. Keeping the state out of sport and keeping sport as a defended, even indexical, matter of civil society or "the private sector," are the proud and controlling emblems of American popular conceptions of Olympic sport. Controlling, because it is absolutely remarkable how little of the very real U.S. state and party interests and operations in sport have entered even the American mass media, much less popular consciousness. Proud, because Americans know only too well that the state runs sport in the socialist countries, whereas America is, because it must be, different from them. For a quarter of a century every solicitation from the usoc, nearly every relevant article in the popular press, and much academic work has repeated the claim that our athletes and Olympic organizations "get not a penny from the government" and are free of its influence and control. Most Americans believe this. In the United States the patriotic and nationalist values of Olympic sport have required, to a comparatively large measure in fact and entirely in popular culture, that the national government be absent.

The contrast with Canada (not to mention other liberal democracies) could not be more striking or more significant in grasping the origins and reproduction of mutual misperceptions. Americans rightly understand Canada as a capitalist liberal democracy like the United States, and, as numerous Canadian writers have pointed out, do not normally concern themselves with other political, cultural, social, and historical differences between the two nations. As a consequence, the central and intensive state involvement in Olympic sport in Canada does not and cannot penetrate American popular culture and consciousness. It has been inconceivable that our fraternal allies, neighbours, and (from a nuclear-defence point of view) dependents, the Canadians, could be so unlike ourselves and so like the former Soviets and East Germans in this significant area of political culture. That Canadians might be like the British, the French, or the former West Germans in this regard does not penetrate American popular consciousness either, since the sports systems of those distant countries are a still more irrelevant object of attention, even during the Olympics. In ironic consequence, American popular discourse about American exceptionalism actually masks how exceptional the United States truly is in this regard.

A vignette not only shows how long Canada has been hidden behind a screen of American Cold War perceptions of the former Soviet Union and how in u.s. sport the culture of intellectuals is little different from public culture, but also shows how pervasive American localism and the focus on professional sports add additional factors of indifference and misperception. Several years ago I was lecturing at a conference at Indiana University summoned to compare Soviet and Eastern European with American popular culture. To make a point about the apparently transnational popularity of international sport, I remarked that anyone in Bloomington could reproduce for me the imagery of sport's "Big Red Machine." Heads nodded throughout the audience and, for a moment, I believed my point was made. I was, of course, referring to the popular American model of Soviet sport as a highly rationalized and state-run system that converts promising children through merciless training, medical intervention, and the promise of material comfort into medal-winning machines to be used for national solidarity and propaganda purposes; a system in which coaches are paid by the medal, athletes forsake legal rights accorded as a matter of fact to other workers as the price of obtaining credentials for competition, and selection to teams is made on the basis not of maximal participation but of likelihood of winning. But as I drew this portrait, the heads stopped nodding and members of the audience seemed momentarily confused. Only later was I informed that in the local culture of Bloomington "the Big Red Machine" is what everyone calls the Indiana University basketball team.

Like all jokes, this one (at my expense) showed that all meaning is contextual, and culture is in large measure the constitution of a revealing hierarchy of contexts. It is perhaps archetypically American, as Alexis de Tocqueville long ago pointed out, that local community contexts can strangely displace international ones that one might expect to be more encompassing. At an international conference of intellectuals explicitly concerned with national cultures, even with the epic Cold War opposition between east and west, the local referent of "Big Red Machine" could for some Americans spontaneously supplant the international referent, doubtless in part because the topic of sport remains odd and even intrusive in scholarly debates, whereas it is constitutive for the self-conception of Hoosiers, including university intellectuals who could not otherwise care less about sport. In fact, I was not mistaken in my assertion that any American on the campus could reproduce the American imagery of the Soviet sport system. But as "big" in popular consciousness as that Red Machine might be for three weeks in every four years, for the rest of the time it was nothing compared to the real Bigness of the local Red Machine.

I do not wish to downplay the role of the famously general American insularity, ignorance, and reverse hegemonic self-absorption in accounting for such facts. But the point to be stressed is that we are here in the presence of one powerful American cultural code, in which the "neighbourly and proud" local community stands as a model of and for the state and not vice versa, as Tocqueville's French successors from Pierre de Coubertin to Hervé Varenne and Michel Crozier have repeatedly pointed out about the United States[12] The proof lies in the fact that in conditions of neighbourly sameness the logic of local sociability and friendliness can encompass even state-level differences and oppositions. Later in the same speech I noted that in many of its aspects the American popular cultural construction of the Soviet "Big Red Machine" in sport fit better the big red maple-leaf liberal democracy to our north. Here the remark was met not with cognitive dissonance but with difficulty in recognizing any referent at all. Surely I could not mean that Canada was a state-centred, state-driven, and almost fully rationalized Olympic sport system? In popular American culture, it was and is simply unimaginable that we could be so different from Canadians in a performative and ideological context of at least periodically great importance to us.

A second vignette from a more public, mass-attentive context reproduces the finding, while pointing to what Americans do prefer to make of their "neighbours" to the north. In the one hundred hours of ABC network coverage of the Calgary Olympics and the millions of printed words that swirled about it, and in the context of a vigorous debate about the sources of American "athletic failure," American media managed completely to avoid discovering how shockingly differently Olympic sport is organized in Canada. Moreover, there is not the slightest sign that American popular cultural formations broader than what is constituted by the media managed to recognize this either. If Canada's "Best Ever" campaign had resulted, as it was supposed to do, in fifteen medals instead of five, perhaps there would have been more American curiosity about the Canadian sports system. But even if this had been the case, one would confidently predict that the attention would have been focused on athletic technology, fund-raising, coaching development, medical facilities and such, not on administrative hierarchies and not at all on governmental involvement.

ABC broke its silence on Canadian state involvement in sport on only one important occasion. In a trenchant irony, the agent of this transient attention, which occurred during coverage of the closing ceremonies (that is, when the games were over), was Peter Jennings, a Canadian citizen. Beginning in Los Angeles, ABC had acknowledged the foreign affairs implications of the Olympics by stationing Jennings, its main news anchor, next to its main sports anchor during the opening and closing ceremonies broadcasts. (ABC's motives for this practice also have to do with ratings wars in news programming.) The effect has not been salubrious. As in Los Angeles, Jennings was again poorly prepared, rather "American" in this parachute journalism, uttering such idiocies as that the ancient games began in the shadow of Mount Olympus, and devoting many of his comments on the succession of teams in the parade to telling American audiences which countries were friendly to the United

States. (The Canadian anchor as the American network's resident and most highly marked Cold Warrior and hegemonist.) But in the Calgary context, the oddity of his behaviour was even more marked. Despite direct invitations by his enthusiastic colleague to do so, Jennings studiously refused to identify himself fully as a Canadian, acknowledging only that he had been "born in Canada." Whether any personal ambivalence was present in addition to career concerns I cannot say, but signs of his uneasiness showed frequently. Jennings completely bollixed Brian Mulroney's name ("Mul-door-oney") in introducing the prime minister during a one-on-one, prime-time interview in which Jennings avoided not merely partisan political questions but any serious inquiries as to what the prime minister thought of the particular significance of this event to Canada. During the closing ceremonies, Jennings came as close as ABC was to get to hinting at the extent of Canadian state involvement in amateur sport. The camera focused briefly on Otto Jelinek being pushed in a sleigh around the ice during the celebratory pageant; he was identified as "minister of sport" in an on-screen graphic, over which Jennings added the vague remark to his colleague and audience, "That shows you how seriously they take sport up here, Jim." The whisper passed, and the culturally constituted and media-reproduced silence returned instantly.

I hasten to add that on the other side of the paradigm, ABC's commentators did mark purported Canadian difference for Americans in another way. It was repeatedly emphasized how, in contrast to the "Hollywood-style" opening ceremonies in Los Angeles with their "paid professional performers," the Calgary ceremonies were put on by and starred "ordinary citizens," members of the local community "who have given their time and commitment to making this celebration a success." This refrain was uttered over and again in various keys and was not limited to the organizational and technical success of the "people of Calgary's" commitment to a wonderful Olympics or even to the broader cultural perception easily anticipated, perhaps even shared, by eastern Canadians that Calgary is a terrific party town, that "out there" men are men and women are women, that the city is a brawling democratic and egalitarian place where no one puts on airs or stands on ceremony. (Mayor Ralph Klein came direct from central casting not as a politician but as the embodiment of his community.) Still deeper themes organized this discourse: a perception of community solidarity, sociability, resourcefulness, hope, commitment to family and children, and – in the key idiom Varenne sees as the United States' preferred solution to its own social structural contradictions – love. ABC's only exploration of any recent Canadian political or economic history was a quick treatment of Alberta's cycle of boom and bust. No national issues like the free trade deal or the upcoming election were ever touched on. But this served as negative background to making community life all the more remarkably an object of admiration, shored up, of course, by the western frontier backdrop that retains its symbolic hold over national U.S. folk culture.

Of course, ABC did not explicitly make the point that Calgary, and by extension Alberta and Canada, are superior to the United States in that they continue to possess what we fear we have lost, community spirit in the face of statist tendencies and threatened economic and political decline. And a well-meaning though patronizing commentary about how puzzling and inappropriate the "Canadian national inferiority complex" is in the face of these happy conditions somewhat undercut the general interpretive motif. However, it remained naked in its prominence. Beyond the sport and the medal count, it is what the American reading of the Calgary games, at least in the mass media construction of them, came to be. Putting these two observations together, the general message in the Olympic context was once again, "In Canada, they have no state worth mentioning; they have rich civic and community life filled with solidarity, a life worth admiring and even envying." Whatever the empirical merits of this constructed portrait of Canadian society and culture, it is impossible not to see in it a projection of one particularly desired American view of America, a reading whose implications extend well beyond the immediate context of Olympic popular culture.

CANADIAN COUNTERPROJECTIONS

An ethnography of speaking within the Canadian Olympic sports community conducted over thirteen years indicates a frequent misperception and overestimation of the U.S. governmental presence in American Olympic sport inversely parallel to the American underappreciation of such a presence in Canadian sport. Such Canadian expectations extend from the top to the bottom of the system. Once I had occasion to communicate potentially important information to the most internationally visible of Canadian Olympic officials. His response was to wonder what the U.S. State Department's judgment on the matter was and whether a contact there could be arranged, despite the fact that there is no officer or office in the U.S. State Department particularly informed about or continuously concerned with Olympic affairs, a situation which the Canadian sports officer's experience had previously and painfully confirmed for him dozens of times. His own habitual contact with Canadian government foreign affairs officials on such matters led him once again to expect a similar relationship in the United States, where it does not exist. This same effect is also to be noted among Canadian academic critics of Olympic sport, the most informed of whom either hold official positions within Canadian sports bodies or are in regular communication with them. (This is inconceivable in the American Olympic system where, since William Milligan Sloane died in the 1920s, no truly accomplished intellectual, much less any critical one, has ever been welcomed into the USOC inner circle.) Several of these Canadians are socialist in their politics and Gramscian in their theoretical commitments, leading to the expectation that they would pay careful attention to the empirical differences in the state–civil society relation. Yet in their writings and conversation they also frequently assume a state-involved and public centralization of American Olympic sport that does not exist.[13]

In Canada, although there has been a regular circulation of persons among the COA, Sport Canada, and the federal and provincial ministries of sport, they remain distinct institutions, regularly engaged in negotiations, conflicts, consultations, and co-operative agreements, sometimes highly politicized and publicized. As a consequence, Canadian sports officials and sports critics frequently assume that similar relations exist in America between the USOC and various political authorities. But in the United States there are no national or state governmental offices of sport and no "Sport America," and in my experience USOC officials are frequently surprised or disoriented to receive requests from their Canadian counterparts for statements of official U.S. government sports policies. Demurrals or vague "civic" responses, however, do not prevent such requests from being repeated. An additional situational factor helps account for this Canadian behaviour. In recent years, high USOC officials have had military backgrounds (executive directors Colonel Don Miller, General George Miller, and former Colonel Harvey Schiller) or cabinet-level backgrounds (former USOC president William Simon was Nixon's secretary of the treasury), making it easy for outsiders to mistake their judgments and counsels on Olympic political matters for formal state policies. Present Olympic leaders are also only too eager to cultivate contacts with the White House, senators, and congressmen and to drop names in the hearing of outsiders. Personal networks of information and influence among political élites are an important part of the American system, but it is a mistake to take them as evidence of institutional and formal state involvement in sport.

Past causes célèbres like the Olympic boycotts likewise create flows of misinterpretation into channels of Canadian domestic experience and projected expectation of the American Other. U.S. Secretary of State Cyrus Vance's hectoring of the International Olympic Committee (IOC) at Lake Placid, President Carter's 1980 boycott campaign and Vice-President Mondale's arm-twisting of the USOC, White House operative Michael Deaver's actions with regard to the Soviet boycott of Los Angeles, and President Reagan's activities at those games – episodes that sometimes received more media coverage and comment in Canada than in the United States – all have contributed to foreign misperceptions of a continuous U.S. government involvement in Olympic affairs. On matters of state funding, some Canadians were quite aware, Los Angeles Olympic Organizing Committee rhetoric notwithstanding, that some $90–120 million of public funds in the form of government services went into the Los Angeles games. Indeed, the unexceptional character of this from the point of view of Canada, where federal and provincial governments put hundreds of millions of dollars in direct grants into the Calgary games, helps blind Canadians to the fact that most in the American sport community, and certainly the general American public, believe that the Los Angeles games were "entirely privately funded," that once again, from the U.S. point of view, the federal government properly kept out of sport.

While in all liberal democratic societies the state is the master symbol and measure of centralization itself, harmonic concentrations of other forms of status may contribute to associational misperceptions of government activity. For example, according to Pierre Bourdieu's model, athletic capital, economic capital, and political capital may coincide to quite different degrees in diverse societies. In Canada, present and former officials such as IOC members Richard Pound and Jim Worrall, COA president Roger Jackson and vice-president Ken Read, COA education committee chairman Bruce Kidd, Sport Canada chief Abby Hoffman and sports minister Otto Jelinek are former Olympic competitors: an athletic élite turned into an organizational élite and developing thereby, as noted earlier, governmental affiliations or associations. Moreover, at least in the period from 1984 to 1989, not a few Canadians-in-the-street could recognize the names of such Olympic officials.

The situation in the United States continues to be very different. Top leaders of Olympic organizations who have been Olympic competitors are the exception rather than the rule. Organizational capital has consorted less with competitive athletic capital than with (at least among the "volunteer" leadership of the USOC) economic or social capital of a distinctly local (civic) sort. Most important, it is extremely difficult to find any American citizen not directly involved with international sport who can name *any* present American Olympic official or, when offered names like Anita DeFrantz, Harvey Schiller, or Leroy Walker, recognize them as such. With regard to their national political and financial capital, William Simon and lately George Steinbrenner offer exceptions to the general pattern and enjoy some public name recognition, but none at all as Olympic officials. Few ordinary Americans can spontaneously report their association with Olympic affairs. Even Robert Helmick's acquisition of a public name through scandal quickly faded. The general rule still holds of a comparative absence of concentration of multiple kinds of capital in the administrative centres of the American Olympic movement, and of a popular cultural perception that undervalues even the level of government and financial élite involvement that does exist. For us, Olympic sport preferentially should be and therefore is perceived to be an affair of local communities and public-spirited citizenries. Yet the general image of an American colossus in Canadian popular culture appears to lead Canadian populations to a different and less accurate conclusion. They see big television, big money, and big medal counts and therefore assume big government and big élite involvement to be the typical pattern in the United States, as it is in Canada.

While such misperceptions are demonstrably common in the Canadian sport community, I cannot comment on broader popular speech and conceptions in Canada with the same degree of confidence. Extensions to Canadian popular culture as a whole of this paradigmatic finding of an overestimation of American centralization in sport must remain propositional until Canadianists take up the challenge of confirming or refuting it. However, the hypothesis is not without additional support in the form of Canadian journalistic discourse, which mediated between public opinion and the subculture of official sport, during the Ben Johnson "trial." Selections of Canadian press reports from the Dubin inquiry record and the composition of it into popular melodrama make the point clearly, while simultaneously revealing a key Canadian ambivalence about its own system, at least when it generates such an overwhelming tragedy as the Ben Johnson affair.[14]

Within months of Johnson's disgrace, the peremptory announcement of the commission of inquiry, the Conservative electoral victory, and the signing of the free trade agreement, our Mr. R.D. found himself in the dock as one of the opening witnesses before Mr. Justice Dubin. He and other government officials were called upon "to set the stage" by laying out the structure, organization, and funding of Canadian Olympic sport. As our model would predict, this phase of the hearings received no coverage in the U.S. press. Indeed, American press coverage during the later phases of "dramatic revelations" at the hearings never extended even as far as terse "backgrounders" on the Canadian government's involvement in Olympic sport. As far as American popular and public cultures are concerned, there still is no such involvement. Moreover, other than the fact that the principals happened to be Canadian citizens and the hearings were unfolding in Canada, little was considered distinctively Canadian in any aspect of the American press coverage.

To be sure, steroid abuse in the Olympics is hardly unique to Canada; as intended, the Dubin inquiry revelations had international significance. However, specifically Canadian institutional, historical, and political factors contextualizing and constituting the event and the inquiry were subsumed in American media under a logic that generally reduced them to individual (Johnson, Charlie Francis, Dr. Jamie Astaphan), occupational-ethical (coaches, athletes, doctors), technico-legal (test protocols, lawyers' briefs), and purely local community (Mazda Track Club, York University, Toronto) meanings. "National implications" for Canadians meant, in this American construction, no more than civic sadness, pique, or outrage felt by masses of individual Canadians, but not serious governmental entailments. When Abby Hoffman was forced out of her Sport Canada position in October 1991, in part as a result of the Dubin aftermath, the event was not mentioned in the U.S. press.

If "Canada" was not especially present in American coverage of the Dubin hearings, "America" was remarkably present in the Canadian coverage. Understandably, a reaction by some Canadians to the situation was an attempt to code it as a "foreign body" intrusive in Canadian society in order to rationalize or soften the blow of otherwise having to accept it as a native phenomenon. One form of this was the regular marking of any foreign affiliations of Canadian citizens implicated in the scandal. Ben Johnson's processual passage from "Canadian," to "Jamaican-Canadian," to "Jamaican" – perhaps reversed in his final emotional statement that he would only run in the future for "my country, Canada" – was only the most obvious example. Many other Canadians were carefully identified in press stories as "Polish-born," "Jamaican native," or "St. Kitts-based." The second form involved repeated attempts to implicate or shift certain responsibilities to foreign nationals: Spanish and Swedish IOC officials, Italian track authorities, East German drug suppliers, and Soviet state agencies. But the foreign body beyond all others, in both the testimony and the Canadian press constructions of it, was the United States.

Johnson's coach Charlie Francis played on Canadian anti-American sentiments in his own defence. He had learned all about drugs from Americans, every notable American track champion from Seoul (not directly named, for legal reasons) was on steroids but had not been caught, the USOC actively helped its athletes beat the watchdogs through non-punitive testing rehearsals, Ben Johnson's urine sample had been sabotaged by a mysterious American seen conversing with Carl Lewis after the race: on and on it went. Other witnesses rarely seemed to miss an opportunity to point out that Americans were doing it too, and – since they had not been caught at Seoul – doing it better. The underlying defence was, of course, that for Canadians "to be competitive" with the "big players in the world" – the same reasoning that structured general politics at the time – they, like the Americans, would have to accept the "free market" in athletic technology.

Until it could no longer be maintained even in fantasy, Canadian newspapers repeated the American saboteur theory, speculated at length whether American witnesses from avowed "steroid gurus" to Carl Lewis himself would testify (Lewis had volunteered to do so), and printed every available response from the American individuals and institutions Francis and his athletes had accused. Some of the accusations and innuendos, like those made against Lewis, were reprehensible and purely self-serving; others were known by American insiders to be true, and activist Americans were grateful for the goad they gave U.S. sport authorities to reform themselves. Indeed, the USOC medical director Dr. Robert Voy seized the occasion to resign publicly in protest over the slowness of drug reform in the United States.

Voy's resignation may have been more fully covered in the Canadian press than in the American, and Senator Joseph Biden's congressional subcommittee hearings on drugs in U.S. sport certainly were. This is crucial evidence for the general paradigm of intercultural relations I am seeking to demonstrate. In the United States, as in Canada, a vast public and popular discourse on steroids and sport ensued. But its most marked federal engagement – the Biden committee hearings called in imitation of the Dubin inquiry – received less publicity in the United States than a variety of local episodes and legislative and judicial initiatives. The vast majority of Americans have never heard of the Biden hearings or of the anti-steroid treaty, modelled on the international nuclear freeze treaty, that was subsequently concluded between the USOC and the then-Soviet government Sport Committee. Interestingly, this crucial step towards levelling the international playing field went largely unnoticed in Canada too, perhaps because it contradicted the constructed image of organized high-level American drug-pushing and made Canadian government efforts to pass an anti-steroid resolution at the United Nations seem platitudinous and ineffectual.

Otherwise, Canadian constructions of u.s. sport in the context of the Dubin inquiry have rhetorically portrayed a centralized, concentrated American system of élites assumed to have governmental aspects or to operate like the government, even if no such evidence can be produced. The decentralized pluralism, the diffuse civic consciousness, even the organizational anarchy of the American system, not to speak of its proud popular hostility to any government engagement, never comes through. Big Brother is Big Brother, the American state is the American state: all concentrated power in this domain, as in the political economy and culture industry, always threatens Canadian independence. Moreover, the United States simply could not be so different from Canada in the organization and functioning of Olympic sport.

For Canada, the real drama of the Dubin inquiry lies precisely in Canadian reactions to the Canadian state presence in sport. State-level organization of nationalist, political-party, and cultural interest in sport success created special conditions for steroid abuse in the first place. Any Canadian who still doubts that the Sport Canada and sport ministry professionals were not aware of it and chose to turn a blind eye to it in favour of medal-counts is benighted indeed. But individual athletes, coaches, and federation officials have been the ones disgraced or punished.

In his final report Mr. Justice Dubin did not shrink from assigning government entities a share of the blame. But neither did he pursue individuals in the ministries and Sport Canada or issue calls for dismantling the system.[15] The ambiguity of the report's attitude towards state-centred sport echoes the current ambivalence of Canadian public opinion on the matter. It is hard to judge the future, but my own guess is that the disturbance of national consensus was only temporary.

CONCLUSION: POLITICAL CULTURE AS POPULAR CULTURE

Olympic sport is equally important in the popular cultures of Canada and the United States, and the realms of Olympic sport and electoral politics are popularly conceived as categorically disjunctive in both liberal democracies. If such cultural similarities told the whole story, familiar scholarly and popular models of cultural analysis reducing the interactive situation between the countries to a simple calculus of power relations, colonization, hegemony, and counterhegemony might be adequate. I have tried to show, however, that the differences in the social organization of Olympic sport and its relations with national politics in the two countries, as well as in intercultural perceptions and misperceptions between them, are so profound as to require more complex and sophisticated treatment. The result of this analysis is an interpretive paradigm, which in each society orders and constitutes cultural understandings of the neighbour in terms of domestic self-perceptions. In turn, this mirrored image, in its accuracies and distortions, influences the struggles of institutional and individual actors to command the definition of the domestic situation and to manipulate it to advantage.

The discovery of such paradigms of and for intercultural understanding and action offers alternatives to survey data, public opinion polls, and deductive critical theories in excavating the dynamics of popular consciousness in large-scale social contexts. If, however, the power of such paradigms is limited to isolated realms of cultural and organizational life – Olympic sport, in this case – their value is quite specialized and restricted. Static "value-theorists" and those who are cynical about the constitutive power of cultural formations in politico-economic life will find it easy to continue to ignore them as purely local and marginal phenomena. The challenge for cultural analysts is, first of all, to insist on the deep congruences between the concepts of "popular culture" and "democratic political culture," and, second, to demonstrate that root paradigms derived from the study of the former illuminate structures, issues, and events consensually taken to belong to the latter field.

This challenge cannot be fully taken up here. I would like to conclude, however, by claiming that analysis of the public debate over the free trade agreement – the most significant bilateral issue between Canada and the United States in contemporary times and an object of special territorial claims by political economists – would show it to be configured by exactly the same paradigm of understanding that organizes binational Olympic discourse. At the time the agreement was signed, u.s. press coverage (there was little American popular discourse independent of the media) highlighted the potential impact of the treaty on local Canadian communities (Ontario auto workers, the Quebec hydro-electric industry, maritime fishermen, British Columbia wood products companies) but paid comparatively little attention to the institutional dramas and entailments on the Canadian federal level. These were largely reduced to a simple and personalized pro-and-con political joust between Mulroney's Conservatives and the opposition parties, circumscribed by the elections.

Perhaps some Americans were led to wonder why some Canadians could be so fearful of free trade, of a deeper alliance with the United States against our common rivals, and suspicious of American intentions. But the issue certainly did not generate any concerted exposure to, or exploration of, Canadian historical, social, political, and institutional differences from the United States. This constructed and familiarizing portrayal of Canada was shaped as well by the framing of discussion of the domestic origins and impacts of the treaty in the United States, which largely boiled down to its possible economic impacts on American local communities. Washington-centred political and commercial élites were to Americans obviously responsible for the initiative; the treaty was a state-level production. But, as ever, the state's perceptions and interests tended to be (wishfully) treated as secondary to what might or might not be good for "the American people."

In Canada, although once again I am forced to be more cautious in my impressions, neither the potential impact on American local industries and communities nor the dominance of this point of view over American public conceptions of what was at stake was highlighted in Canadian perceptions and discourse about the other party to the agreement. Instead, the emphasis was on "Washington" as the central actor, understood as the Reagan–Bush executive branch and the Congress, or else on a cabal of influential big businesses (which in some popular Canadian views amounted to the same thing in the state-centred American colossus). At the same time, Canadian ambivalence about a strong Canadian federal state was never more in evidence. On the one hand, that state embodies the social welfare system that the free trade deal is thought by its opponents to threaten. On the other hand, that state had perhaps arrived at such a point of concentrated power that the current government could, so it was said, sell Canada lock, stock, and barrel to its neighbour. In raging against such perceptions, Tory leaders argued that they had shown that the state was strong enough to deal on equal terms with its powerful neighbour while, at the same time, humbly serving the future interests of the rich variety of local and provincial communities that compose the so-called Canadian mosaic. The proponents of the treaty too reflected this ambivalence in their discourses.

Of course this is a simplified portrait, and much of it needs to be confirmed and elaborated by careful and extensive study of the discourses so summarily depicted. But my point is at least plausibly to suggest that, in certain contexts and circumstances, popular interpretive paradigms recognized in one domain of sociocultural life are actively organizing public understandings of other domains, and therefore can contribute in new ways to analysing the problems we take to be distinctively political. This assertion is a methodological one for the future of popular cultural studies, but it is also a claim about the nature of political culture in the North American liberal democracies.

8 Whose National Pastime?
Baseball in Canadian
Popular Culture

ROBERT KNIGHT BARNEY

Late in the American depression, in 1939 to be exact, my father's daily woodcutting chores (like millions, he was jobless), complemented by my impatient stacking of the split pieces, inevitably were accompanied in summer months by an imposing New England cultural ritual – afternoon radio broadcasts of Red Sox games from Fenway Park in Boston. Jimmy Foxx was my first baseball hero. I never saw him play, but the descripton of his feats by Jim Britt, the play-by-play announcer, were magnified several times over by my imagination. By the summer of 1941 the nation's economic woes had abated. America girded for war. My father got a real job. He celebrated his first pay-cheque, I remember, by taking me to Fenway Park to see a Red Sox game.

In ensuing years Fenway became my cathedral, Ted Williams and Dom DiMaggio my bishops. Beyond my immediate family, I came to worship baseball most. From the start I had visions of someday becoming a major-leaguer. I lived baseball, breathed it, immersed myself in its every facet. And there were millions of American boys just like me: we were all preoccupied with baseball.

What does this have to do with baseball in Canadian culture? In effect, everything, because the glorious diamond spectacle has developed a cultural identity in this country similar to its embellishment in the fabric of American society. In recent times the phenomena of the Montreal Expos and the Toronto Blue Jays have raised popular interest in baseball to a feverish pitch; indeed, the fortunes and misfortunes of the two clubs as members of the major-league fraternity have roused the interest of Canadians from coast to coast in a way that few other events have. Although baseball can count legions of older fans, it is a game that has particular appeal to children and young adults. Much of the success of the major-league experience in Canada can be traced to the enthusiasm that young Canadians exhibit at now being able to grow up carrying on a diamond love affair with a home team. Nonetheless, there is reason to believe that most Canadians enraptured by the mystique of baseball know little about, much less have an appreciation for, the game's roots and subsequent evolution in Canada. This essay attempts to explain those roots and comment on the extraordinary popularity that baseball enjoys in contemporary Canadian times.

BASEBALL'S CANADIAN ROOTS

At least six distinct areas must be explored, however briefly, in developing the theme of this essay and to explain why baseball has evolved to the point where it has become a legitimate Canadian national pastime. These considerations are (1) the importation of the game through American immigration; (2) the adoption of codified playing rules from the United States; (3) the organization of baseball clubs and the development of intercommunity and tournament play based on American models; (4) the rise of professionalism, emulating American patterns; (5) the minor-league phenomenon; and (6) the implantation of a major-league identity.

Baseball has been embedded in America's cultural genes since the children of English settlers in colonial America paused in their daily routines to muster ball and bat and play at various versions of what we know today as baseball.[1] To be sure, the rules were different from those we know now, even different from locale to locale, but there were mainstream commonalities that kept the game in a perspective of "sameness." Balls were tossed and struck by bats, runners ran to bases or goals, players were put out, tallies were scored.

In isolating baseball's genesis in Canada, one's natural urge is to postulate that if the game's roots were entrenched in American colonial children's play, then certainly the concept of baseball must have arrived north of the forty-ninth parallel in the cultural baggage of United Empire Loyalist youngsters, whose parents, loyal to the crown, left the United States and immigrated to Canada during or after the American Revolution. However, such a hypothesis lacks substantive evidence.

The first wave of Loyalists settled in established areas of Canada, including the farmlands and communities in what became New

Brunswick, Nova Scotia, and Prince Edward Island. Baseball's earliest presence in Canada arose elsewhere – in southwestern Ontario, from the Niagara peninsula westward to the Detroit river. This was an area of both later and limited Loyalist settlement. It was, however, a region of intense American immigration following the war of 1812.[2] When Americans looked westward for a feasible route to what would one day become Michigan, Illinois, Wisconsin, and Minnesota, the shortcut corridor across southwestern Ontario between the Niagara and Detroit rivers did not escape their notice. A virtual highway developed over which a steady stream of Americans moved westward in search of better economic substance and new lives. It proved impossible for British administrators to keep them out. Landholders in southwestern Ontario, with little prospect for development under normal conditions of settlement, saw a ripe opportunity for healthy profits from the sale of farm and settlement land to Americans. Thus the area came to resemble a giant filter, which thousands of Americans permeated as they travelled west.[3] Thousands of others elected instead to remain in the area and build their homes and new lives in Canada.[4] The resulting American majority, endowed as it was with Yankee customs, ideas, and political thinking, in time helped to stimulate the rebellion of 1837.

A notable early American cultural contribution to the area was baseball, which was played by children and young adults alike. The reminiscences of Adam E. Ford, who lived in the area as early as the 1830s, provide insight into the intrusion of American cultural customs and, as well, establish the earliest documented reference to Canada's baseball heritage, a legacy that today has grown to immense proportions.

Adam E. Ford was born in Oxford County, Ontario, in 1831. During his youth he saw baseball games played by older youths and adults; later he played the game himself. When Ford was fifty-five years old and residing in Denver, Colorado, his reminiscence of baseball events in Oxford during the 1830s, 1840s, and 1850s was published in the popular American weekly, *Sporting Life*. Ford provided legitimate and graphic descriptions of local baseball rules as they had evolved in the locale by the 1830s. His account described the equipment used, the names of players, and the players' prowess.[5] Equally important, Ford's reminiscences offer insights into baseball's circumstances well before the time of his youth, and into modifications to the game that occurred during his adult years. Combining Ford's recollections with known events of immigration and social development in southwestern Ontario establishes a starting-point for understanding baseball's roots in Canada.

The advent of telegraphic communications and, by the mid-1850s, the development of railway networks expanded the world of isolated inland Ontario communities. It was only natural that local baseball teams sought the challenge of competition with teams from other communities. Mutually agreeable, trans-regional, written rules became essential. The so-called New York rules, originally drawn up by Alexander Cartwright in 1845, modified in the late 1850s and throughout the 1860s by the National Association of Baseball Players (an American organization), provided the necessary standard for Canadian intercommunity play.[6] In 1859 the Hamilton Young American and the Toronto Young Canadian baseball clubs competed in Canada's first intercommunity baseball game using the New York rules. By 1861 the town of Woodstock had embraced the same rules as the standard for competitive play.[7]

American baseball's playing rules, originally set in place by amateur authorities, in time gave way to rules formulated by professional elements: first, the National Association of Professional Base Ball Players (NAPBBP) in 1871 and, in 1876, the National League of Professional Base Ball Clubs (NLPBBC). In each instance the playing rules of the professional organizations became the standard for Canadian clubs.[8] The New York Knickerbocker Club was the first baseball organization in America. In 1845 it established a constitution and formulated a set of rules. Throughout the 1850s baseball clubs proliferated in the northeastern United States, particularly in and around New York City and New England.[9]

The first baseball club organized in Canada was the Hamilton Maple Leaf Club. In 1854, drawing on the model of American baseball organization pioneered by the Knickerbockers, the Maple Leafs struck a constitution, formed an executive, set annual dues, and arranged for a place to play.[10] In 1856 a baseball club was organized in London, Ontario. J.K. Brown, a French millinery-shop owner, became president of the first executive. Practices for the club's twenty-two members were held twice weekly on the military reserve grounds. Woodstock's Young Canadian and Ingersoll's Rough and Ready baseball clubs were organized in 1860.[11] Clubs were subsequently organized in other southwestern Ontario towns, among them Dundas, Guelph, Stratford, and St. Mary's, and intercommunity competition blossomed.

The organization of baseball tournaments was an inevitable extension of intercommunity play. Spurred by community pride, competitive tournaments involving several teams became popular in the late 1860s. Cash prizes, together with handsome symbolic trophies, prompted tournament appearances by teams throughout Ontario.

The city of Woodstock was a leader in organization and participation, an influence duly noted by a popular American sporting publication. The Woodstonians, reported the *Clipper*, "hold a high position in the advancement of matters pertaining to the American National Game."[12] Baseball tournaments often occurred at fairs and exhibitions. Ultimately, however, the zeal to play on competitive terms in regional tournaments led to the advent of professional baseball in Canada.

CANADIAN PROFESSIONAL BASEBALL

Intercommunity rivalries and the quest for tournament prizes and championships spurred efforts to acquire and retain the players needed to guarantee success. Thus Canadians quickly emulated the American model of professionalism. The practice of ballplayers performing for "cash or kind" dates to the early 1860s, at which time many of the more successful American clubs employed professionals.[13] In 1869 Cincinnati's Red Stockings fielded the first all-professional baseball team.[14] By 1871 professional ballplayers had established the first professional league, the National Association of Professional Base Ball Players. Player control of professional baseball lasted five years, after which power and authority passed to club owners. The National League of Professional Base Ball Clubs was formed in 1876; it is known today simply as the National League. The Montreal Expos became a member of that august body in 1969, exactly ninety-three years after its origin.

There is no doubt as to which town, team, and individual was responsible for ushering in the era of bona fide professional baseball in Canada. The town was Guelph; the team was the Guelph Maple Leafs; and the individual was George Sleeman, a wealthy brewing entrepreneur and a zealous civic leader. Guelph teams played intercommunity baseball as early as 1863. The Maple Leafs were organized in 1864 and, by 1871, had developed to the point where they deserved their reputation as Canada's best baseball team.[15] Their desire to test themselves with more demanding challenges led them to seek matches with American teams. In 1871 the Maple Leafs invited the Forest City Club of Cleveland, a member of the Professional Players League, to play a match game in Guelph. Before a reported crowd of five thousand, Guelph lost the contest by a run, a loss rationalized by a claim of conspiracy about an umpire's decision in the final inning. The following year the Baltimore Club of the same league visited Guelph. This time Guelph triumphed by a run.

Its success roused American awareness of Canadian baseball expertise: "Beware of those upstarts from the North," commented an
American baseball columnist.[16]

Sleeman, who had gained a measure of local baseball fame
through his efforts in organizing and developing his Silver Creek
Brewery nine for local competition, eventually was invited to head
the Maple Leafs. He was quick to ensure that Guelph's premier team
retained the good players who were sought by teams in other Ontario communities (and by some American clubs). Sleeman also
displayed initiative and perseverance in acquiring outstanding
personnel at positions not already capably filled.[17] In this way the
Guelph Maple Leafs were able to triumph consistently over all Canadian competitors. As well, the Maple Leafs held their own in games
with professional teams from the United States, including contests
against the best clubs of the era – Philadelphia, New York, and
Boston.[18]

When other Ontario baseball clubs sought to achieve a competitive
balance, professionalism spread across the province. The most determined of Guelph's challengers was the London Tecumseh Baseball Club. A heated rivalry developed between the two cities and
their ball clubs. London, with greater financial resources, acquired
the necessary players to bring Guelph's domination to an end.[19] A
new baseball scene evolved, one in which professionalism in both
large and small contexts became a fact of life.

Canada has experienced more than a century of minor league
professional baseball history. Exactly ninety years before the Expos
became Canada's first team to make it to "the Bigs," Guelph's Maple
Leafs and London's Tecumsehs were admitted to the International
Association, a grouping that baseball historians acknowledge as "the
first minor league."[20] In reality, it was not a minor league at all.
Rather, it was the first of several unsuccessful attempts to challenge
the National League's dominance of urban markets and the best
playing personnel.[21] After several failed attempts, a bona fide com-
petitor, the American League, was established in 1901.

London's powerful Tecumsehs won the inaugural International
Association championship in 1877.[22] Since then, minor-league baseball in Canada has been an established fact. By 1912 Canadian-based
teams were playing in four minor leagues. In the decade 1926 to
1935, Canadian teams were represented in five minor leagues. Two
of those leagues, the Class B Eastern Canadian League and the Class
D Colliery League, were composed entirely of Canadian teams
staffed with players who, for the most part, were just beginning ca-

reers in professional baseball. The remaining three leagues featured both Canadian- and American-based teams. They were the Class B Western International and Michigan-Ontario Leagues and the Class AA International League, an organization featuring many of the élite players of minor league baseball who were on the brink of graduating to the major leagues.[23]

THE POPULARITY OF BASEBALL

Spurred partly by minor-league activity and partly by general interest in big-league competition south of the border, the Canadian preference for baseball was pronounced. A content analysis of the sports pages of five major urban Canadian newspapers published between 1926 and 1935 ranked baseball virtually even with ice-hockey as the most reported and highlighted sport. The sample reflects a coast-to-coast perspective (Halifax, Montreal, Toronto, Winnipeg, and Vancouver). Only in Montreal, a city infatuated with hockey, was baseball decidedly second in newspaper attention. In Toronto and Vancouver baseball reigned supreme over hockey. In Halifax and Winnipeg the two sports were about evenly reported.[24]

Canadians played, watched, and became passionate fans of organized baseball long before professional hockey came to occupy a similar status. Though I use the terms loosely here, baseball became institutionalized and ritualized in the lives of Canadians more rapidly and indelibly than any other sport. Baseball's adherents came from all socioeconomic classes, ethnic groups, and geographical regions. Canadians became avid followers of major-league teams and annual pennant races in the United States long before the National Hockey League and the Stanley Cup were conceived. Ned Hanlan and others notwithstanding, Canadian sporting heroes were American big-league baseball stars – the likes of Cap Anson, Napoleon Lajoie, Honus Wagner, Walter Johnson, Christy Mathewson, Ty Cobb, Babe Ruth, and a host of others.[25]

Thus by the second half of the twentieth century a rich baseball culture of significant longevity lay like a freshly plowed field ready for seeding by entrepreneurial efforts aimed at Canadian major league membership. This point cannot be stressed enough. The first success, of course, came in the form of the Expos. Montreal had joined the International League in 1912 when that league's classification was double-A. The Royals, as they came to be called, became celebrated in baseball history as the ball club from which Jackie Robinson vaulted to the Brooklyn Dodgers of the National League, the

first black to play modern major-league baseball.[26] In 1969 the
Expos joined the National League. For a decade they played in
old Jarry Park, gathering a supportive following of French- and
English-Canadian fans alike. Today's Expos are at home in the
unique confines of Montreal's Olympic Stadium.

SELLING THE BLUE JAYS

The entry of the Toronto Blue Jays into the American League in
1977 produced the full flowering of the Canadian baseball heritage
planted over 150 years ago. Drawing support from the largest population centre in Canada, enjoying extensive exposure in Canadian
and American print and electronic media, employing a marketing
strategy similar to that which had spelled success for Ray Kroc's
McDonald's hamburgers, capitalizing on a natural geographical
rivalry with the Detroit Tigers, and playing in baseball's more glamorous division, the Blue Jays became "Canada's team." In their inaugural season they lost 107 games, and finished 45 games behind
the eventual World Series champion New York Yankees. Yet they
attracted 1,701,039 fans to their home games and recorded a profit
of $1.5 million.[27] Fifteen years later the Jays had a world series
championship in hand, and had broken all-time major league attendance records by attracting over 4 million fans in each of the 1991
and 1992 seasons.

The orchestrator of Blue Jay mania was Peter Bavasi, the son of
the respected and successful Buzzy Bavasi.[28] Peter had accepted an
appointment as director of the San Diego Padres' minor league operations. When Ray Kroc bought the Padres in 1974, he named
Buzzy Bavasi club president and Peter Bavasi vice-president and
general manager. From Kroc, the impresario of McDonald's, young
Bavasi learned about "selling the sight, sound, taste, touch and
smells of a product." To Kroc, that meant marketing Big Macs. To
Peter Bavasi, it signified the essence of marketing Blue Jay baseball.
Kroc's parting message to Bavasi as he left California for Toronto
was to "sell the sizzle if you don't have the steak ready."[29]

Bavasi's strategy from the beginning was to seek public involvement in Blue Jay development. A "name the team" contest was the
first order of business. The name "Blue Jays" won; "Toronto Island
Ferries" did not.[30] The next priority was the creation of a team logo.
Bavasi sought a symbol as easily recognizable as Kroc's golden
arches. The cocky Blue Jay, superimposed on a baseball with a red
maple leaf stuck in its "ear," became a national symbol of recogni-

tion. Saturation marketing of the logo led to its appearance on everything from toys and clothing to baby bibs and frozen pizza packages. Youngsters, in particular, wore the emblem with pride.

The Jays finished dead last in each of their first three seasons, but in the process set a standard for being a well-managed, financially sound enterprise (despite the sad state of the Canadian dollar against its American counterpart).[31] The franchise increased in value from $7 million (its approximate purchase price) to an estimated $40 to 45 million (u.s.) in 1986.[32] Twenty-eight radio stations carried Blue Jay baseball in 1977, twice that number a decade later.[33] All of this took place while the team played in a venue described by many as the worst in major league baseball. This state of affairs was rectified in 1989 when the Blue Jays moved into the luxurious SkyDome, a stadium that would not have been built if major-league baseball had not been present in Toronto.

PASSION AND PASTIME

Are Canadians attracted to baseball because of the nature of the game itself, or is fascination generated by its status as a modern sports spectacle? Certainly, mass media attention to baseball and increases in discretionary income and leisure time have all had a dramatic impact on the ritualization of certain components of the sport. One such component is reflected in the growing number of "sports" bars, in which worship of particular major league teams occurs. In dimly lit, often loud and raucous confines, legions of steadfast male and female fans gather to drink beer, munch peanuts and popcorn, and root for their favourites. The game is projected live from the stadium on huge television screens. In effect, thousands of baseball fans across Canada experience the atmosphere, the drama, and the camaraderie that go hand in hand with watching the home team perform in the stadium. There are a few qualities missing, of course, but the absence of sunshine, green spaces, and even hot dogs appears to be only a minor irritation. Another ritual practice is the annual spring migration of Canadians (particularly residents of Ontario) southward to Florida to witness spring training. But the recent success of baseball in Canada, and indeed its status as a major spectacle, is not solely due to television and marketing and increased leisure time and disposable income. The ritualization of baseball in American culture took place long before the advent of television, radio, and, for that matter, the newspaper sports page. The Canadian experience has scarcely been different.

In a rich baseball atmosphere that has witnessed the rise of the sport from early nineteenth-century immigrant play to modern major-league competition, Canadians have demonstrated a consistent desire for baseball – playing it, watching it, reading about it, glorying in its triumphs, bemoaning its tragedies. The fascination with baseball has always been present in Canada. Jacques Barzun, a critic of American social and cultural values, once remarked, "If you want to know the heart and mind of America, learn baseball."[34] His observation applies equally to Canada. And although Americans may have planted the seeds for baseball's heritage in Canada, Canadians themselves have been the sport's fertilizers, harvesters, and consumers. The thoughts of the celebrated Canadian novelist W.P. Kinsella express at least one reflection on the place of baseball in a cultual context. Though Kinsella's words were written with respect to the United States, they could just as well apply to Canada:

I don't have to tell you that the one constant through all the years has been baseball. America has been erased like a blackboard, only to be rebuilt and erased again. But baseball has marked time, while America has rolled by like a procession of steamrollers. It is a living part of history, like calico dresses, stone crockery, and threshing crews eating at outdoor tables. It continually reminds us of what once was, like an Indian head penny in a handful of coins.[35]

Although an extrapolation of Kinsella's message to Canada is a pleasant ending to this essay, I am reluctant to conclude without stating my firmly held belief (one supported by evidence) that baseball is as much a Canadian national pastime as hockey or any other sport. Contemporary Canadians may find that hard to fathom, believing as they do that interest in baseball derives from the fact that two Canadian teams are now members of the major leagues. But, as I have tried to demonstrate, baseball has dominated during all eras of modern Canadian sporting history. Other sports rose to challenge baseball's pre-eminence during particular periods – cricket and curling before 1875, rowing and lacrosse in the latter part of the nineteenth century, hockey and football in the twentieth century – but baseball has consistently remained the primary public focus.

Baseball stands alone as the sport with the longest and most secure position in Canadian popular culture, and its future appears secure. In all probability, Vancouver will someday join Toronto and Montreal in the major leagues. More and more Canadian youths will ply their talents in the diamond sport, expanding the already considerable numbers now populating youth leagues. An added boost to Canadian baseball interest is the extraordinary popularity of slow-pitch softball (baseball played with a larger ball on a smaller playing field), an activity that draws players and fans of all age groups and both sexes. Playing ball and becoming immersed in its culture is the activity of millions of Canadians, young and old, male and female, rich and poor, French and English, easterner and westerner alike. No other "Canadian" sport has demonstrated such wide appeal.[36]

9 Ambivalence at the Fifty-five-Yard Line: Transformation and Resistance in Canadian Football

ROBERT A. STEBBINS

English Canadians have always been ambivalent towards their second national sport, that master-symbol of Canadian popular culture, Canadian football. People who are uncertain hold contradictory attitudes or emotions towards the object of ambivalence, such that actions that would be taken with reference to it are often inhibited by the more or less equally strong contradictory orientations. In this essay I will argue that, given their ambivalence about their game at the professional level, Canadians are restrained today by their own feelings from at least one important football-related act: buying tickets to games. This ambivalence, however, has been present since the last quarter of the nineteenth century, when football began to develop as a distinct game by separating itself from rugby and soccer. Thus, other factors are necessary to explain why more than a century of ambivalence is only today making itself felt at the gate.

One might wonder how an assertion of national ambivalence is tenable, given the mania accompanying Grey Cup week, the period of the national football championship, an occasion held by many Canadians to be one of the major unifying national events of the year. Moreover, English Canadians do take a routine interest in their professional football as it is served up in the press and as it drifts in and out of talk at work and at home. The progress of the local team is a popular topic of conversation, and discussion of its performance unfolds in the lore of great games and great names of the past. These are cultural ties that bind.

Yet all this talk now takes place alongside the highly appealing coverage by the mass media of National Football League (NFL) games in the United States. On television such coverage has become technically impressive, constituted as it is of instant replays, zoom shots, and split-screen comparisons and co-ordinated by colour commentary from American football heroes at prime time; Canadians are easily able to compare the two versions of the game. The sophisticated coverage and a seemingly greater precision in the execution of plays in American football lead some Canadian fans to conclude that the game played in Canada is inferior or at least less glamorous. Canadian newspaper coverage of NFL football, although hardly the technical display found on television, does consume a noticeable amount of space. When combined, television and newspaper coverage of American football are such that the Canadian Football League (CFL) tries to avoid competing for television viewers who might just forsake Canadian games for more attractive ones telecast from south of the border. To what extent the expansion by the CFL into the United States will affect these tendencies remains to be seen.

To show how my proposition of ambivalence is tenable, I shall consider five value conflicts that have undermined wholehearted acceptance of Canadian professional football from the beginning. These are the conflicts of rules, ideals, rights, quality, and local familiarity. The first two, although not entirely dead issues, are of only minor importance today. In the past, however, they set the stage for contemporary ambivalence, an orientation that is substantially influenced by certain reporting practices in the mass media.

EARLY VALUE CONFLICTS

Ambivalence did not just develop concurrently with the game of football; it is endemic to it. Past and present contradictory events and practices in football have fostered and continue to foster this orientation. Moreover, the Canadian game is unique among modern western sports in that it was derived from two established and influential sports, namely, American football and British rugby. From the beginning, then, Canadian football has always had reason to question its identity as something distinctly Canadian. At the outset it was a set of haphazard modifications of an upper middle-class British sport that was adopted and modified at the same time, with more publicity and fan appeal, in the United States. All this was happening against the backdrop, in the late nineteenth century as now, of efforts by English Canadians to shape a distinct national identity for themselves separate from Britain and the United States.

The Conflict of Rules

The first of the five value conflicts was the conflict of rules: British rugby versus American football. Members of an English garrison stationed in Montreal during the 1860s played rugby against civilian teams composed principally of McGill University students.[1] The game caught on quickly at McGill and in English-speaking Quebec. By the early 1870s Quebec boasted the best rugby teams in Canada, if not in North America.

It must have been Quebec's reputation for rugby that led Harvard to challenge McGill to a two-game series in May 1874. By this time McGill students were playing with an egg-shaped ball. Their game consisted of running, kicking, passing, and tackling. There was a concept of offsides and the use of free kicks and drop kicks. Harvard preferred the "Boston game," a variant of association football played with a round ball with which the players could run. The Boston game was unpopular with other American schools, which forced Harvard to search elsewhere for competition. It won the first game using its rules and its ball. The second, played according to McGill's rules, wound up in a 0–0 tie.

This series is frequently cited as a turning-point in the history of American football. The Harvard team greatly preferred McGill's rugby to their own modification of soccer. Another match was played in Montreal in September of the same year. Harvard won this first game of intercollegiate football in Canada by a score of 3 to 0. It set out at once to persuade the students at other northeastern colleges and universities in the United States that rugby was superior to soccer, the Boston game included.

A game between Harvard and Yale in 1875 was sufficient to convert the latter to rugby. During the following year the Intercollegiate Football Association was formed in the United States. The game it organized was rugby; the game it excluded was soccer, which by 1877 had disappeared from American campuses, not to return until shortly after the turn of the century.

Although Harvard introduced rugby to American collegiate circles, the early transition from rugby to present-day American football occurred at Yale. During the 1880s and 1890s Walter Camp, first a player and then a coach for the Yale team, either introduced or formalized the use of the scrimmage line, the quarterback, eleven men on a team, the calling of signals, and the practice of giving up the ball unless it advanced five yards or more (later to become ten yards) by the fourth down. Except for the number of players and downs, all these changes soon drifted up to Canada.

Thus, in the waning years of the nineteenth century, Americans rapidly transformed rugby into American football. In Canada, owing to the strong British influence, the transformation of rugby to Canadian football was slower. The Rugby Union was established in Britain in 1871, an act that brought needed standardization to the rules of the game. The organization became a model for rugby unions in Quebec and Ontario. Now a set of official rules and regulations existed, backed by a bureaucracy to enforce them.

The history of changes in Canadian football is primarily about the outcome of the struggles between what Frank Cosentino calls the "traditionalists" and the "liberals."[2] The traditionalists wanted rugby to remain as it was in Britain; the liberals wanted the game to evolve more or less as it was developing in the United States. Obviously, the liberals, who were strongest in western Canada, where ties to Britain were relatively less important than in the Canadian east, won most of these struggles, although they sometimes had to wait several years for success. But the liberals did not win them all.

The present Canadian game is distinguished in part by certain rugby features and by a legacy of resistance to complete Americanization. Hence Canadian football is not simply football as played in Canada; rather, it is a uniquely Canadian version of the game that evolved through protracted compromise. Of course that process itself is characteristically Canadian, as is the ambivalence that it evokes.

It is not always known how quickly changes in the rugby game in the United States came to Canada. The University of Michigan used the snap-back with the hand or foot from a single line of seven forwards against the University of Toronto in 1879.[3] Canadian teams were using quarterbacks in fourteen-player teams by the turn of the century. These innovations spread from Yale University to other American schools and subsequently to schools in Canada. A new scoring system put into use in Canada in the 1880s consisted in part of a four-point touchdown, a two-point conversion, a one-point safety touch, and a one-point rouge. The rouge is awarded to the kicking team when it misses a field goal, or when the receiving team fails to run the ball out of its end zone following a punt.

The first three decades of the twentieth century saw numerous changes to the game and its equipment. By 1909 the first year of Grey Cup competition, teams were allowed substitutions for injured players during the first half of the game, and by 1915 during the entire game. By 1921 the number of men per side had dropped to twelve. Centres had ended the practice of heeling the ball and were directly "snapping it back" between their legs. Thus the other two men of the front three forwards were no longer needed. And, despite its roughness, football in Canada was not played with built-in shoulder pads until the early 1920s. At this time headgear was still varied: some players wore a helmet, some wore a cap, and some wore no protection at all.

Frank Shaughnessy, the American-born-and-trained coach of the powerful McGill teams of 1912 and 1919, is usually credited with bringing the huddle to Canada. It was not used by any other team until 1925, and then only amid great controversy. Those opposed to the innovation held that it slowed the game too much. Those favouring it felt this disadvantage was outweighed by the secrecy it provided for calling signals. Before the huddle was adopted, signals were called at the line of scrimmage within earshot of the opposing team.

The Conflict of Ideals

Paralleling and to some extent connected with the conflict of rules was the conflict of ideals: amateur sport versus professional sport. This clash was already apparent in the late nineteenth century. The Canadian rugby unions organized competition among the adult senior, intermediate, and junior teams sponsored by various athletic clubs in Quebec and Ontario. Disagreements between them over certain rules and regulations continued until they became affiliated in the late nineteenth century with the Canadian Rugby Union (CRU). The CRU soon became the most powerful football body in Canada, and remained so for the next sixty-five years.

During the 1880s and 1890s games were played, sometimes sporadically, sometimes regularly, between various colleges and universities in Ontario and Quebec. A league, the Intercollegiate, which was finally formed in the late nineteenth century, also promptly became affiliated with the CRU. The Intercollegiate teams competed for the oldest annually awarded football trophy in Canada: the Yates Cup. The winner of the cup advanced to the CRU playoffs for the dominion championship against the senior winner of the rugby union playoffs.

Intercollegiate teams won the majority of dominion championships through 1924. Even the "Big Four" – the four strongest senior teams from Montreal, Toronto, Hamilton, and Ottawa and the forerunners of today's professional teams in those cities – were unable to dominate the major university teams. The Big Four were themselves a cut above the other senior teams in the rugby unions; hence the other unions were weakened beyond recovery when the Big Four pulled out in 1907 to form their own rugby union.

However, the university teams sometimes refused to compete in the CRU playoffs. Between 1900 and 1904 they boycotted the dominion championship on the grounds that the rugby unions were using professionals. Further rule changes and further standardization were demanded of the CRU before the universities would return to the dominion championship in 1905. But professionalism continued to be a problem. A model already existed in the form of the English Rugby League, which commenced operation shortly before the turn of the century.

By the early 1930s the growing professionalization of Canadian football was a trend to be reckoned with. Professionalism of individual players, though not of teams as a whole, had become common. Historically, the commonsense notion of professionalism stimulated discussion, some of it acrimonious, on whether it was good or bad for football. One of the criteria used to differentiate amateurs from professionals since the late 1920s has been excellence. It was generally believed that professionals were the better players.

Another criterion was player remuneration. Occasional charges that football players were being paid were heard before the turn of the century. By the early 1930s, however, it was widely believed that the senior teams were paying from two to five players on a per-game basis. Most of these men were Americans. Since no contracts were signed, the fiction of amateurism could persist at the executive level of the rugby unions. Still, it was clear enough to the eastern universities, when they played the senior teams, that some of the men on those teams were professionals. The university teams withdrew from Grey Cup competition in 1934. And there were other signs about that time suggesting that professionalism was a growing force in Canadian football: promoters tried to establish a professional league in 1932; a professional team called the Crosse and Blackwell Chiefs actually competed for several seasons against professional teams in the United States. The Winnipegs, a senior team, had nine American players on its roster in 1935.

By the late 1940s the ideal of amateurism, to which the CRU demanded allegiance by all member teams, was being ignored. The wealthiest teams – the Big Four and the western senior teams – neither embraced professionalism nor renounced amateurism. Behind the scenes, they had the money to acquire more fine players than the teams in the other eastern senior leagues. Those leagues, by now composed mostly of teams from the smaller cities in Ontario and Quebec, suffered much the same fate from the late 1930s onward that the university teams had endured ten to fifteen years earlier: a noticeable gap in excellence between them and the big city teams, accompanied by declining fan interest.

The CRU made three decisions in 1946 that unwittingly fostered the further growth of professionalism. First, it abolished the rule that an imported player had to live in Canada for a minimum of one year to qualify as a player for a member team. The new rule stated that he need only be a resident by 21 August of the year he played for his team. Second, it authorized five imports from the United States for each team. Third, all linemen were allowed to block up to ten yards beyond the line of scrimmage. Because earlier CRU rules had prohibited downfield blocking, Canadian linemen had little experience with it. This inadvertently encouraged the further importation of American players, since they were familiar with this technique.

With contracts still a rarity, Canadian teams began to hire American players with increasing frequency in the early 1950s. The collapse of the All-American football conference threw many good players out of work. The CRU's response was to raise to seven the number of imports allowed. About the same time, Canadian teams began a bidding war with the NFL in a drive to acquire some of its more talented players. And while NFL officials were protesting the "raids" by Canadian teams, certain NFL coaches and managers were trying to lure players from these same teams to play in the United States. The demand for players had raised their value and hence their salaries. As a result, the financial gap between the rich and poor teams in Canadian senior football grew still wider, and what Bruce Kidd refers to as the "Canadian dependence on and subordination to U.S. commercial football" began to develop.[4] Later this movement of players became much more one-sided, with Canadian teams scrambling to acquire as many of the best Americans as CFL regulations and team budgets would allow, but with no equivalent demand for Canadians from the United States.

The Canadian Football Council was established to exempt the senior teams, which were by now openly professional, from the restrictions imposed on amateurs. Yet the council was part of the CRU, an amateur organization. This lingering anomaly was eliminated in 1958 with the formation of the independent CFL.

MODERN VALUE CONFLICTS

Against this background, three present-day value conflicts continue to foster ambivalence towards Canadian professional football. As I will point out later, sports reporting in the mass media helps foster the conflict and ambivalence of today. One is the conflict of rights: the employment of Canadians versus the employment of Americans.

In a study of Canadian amateur and professional football players, I found that one important career contingency is the position a man has played in junior or university football.[5] Although there are occasional exceptions, the general rule is that Canadians hoping to play professionally are much less likely than Americans to be invited to a training-camp as quarterbacks and somewhat less likely than Americans to be invited as defensive backs or wide receivers. Likewise, with certain exceptions, Americans are much less likely to be invited to a training-camp in the position of kicker and the positions in the offensive line.[6] The regulation stating that a team must have no more than thirteen imported players on its active roster (plus three quarterbacks, all of whom may be imports) suggests that this contingency might be different if there were no such restriction.

Another contingency bearing on employment is physical limitations. Some players, although equal to their competitors in ability and experience, are lighter or smaller. Depending on the positions they seek, these men receive few invitations to try out for the professional clubs or, if they do somehow get to a professional camp, are quickly cut. Several interviewees pointed out that many Americans in the CFL were unable to pursue a career in the NFL, not because of a lack of ability but because of weight or height limitations.[7] Canadians who are eliminated from the professional ranks for these reasons, of course, have no alternative professional league.

The strategy of flexibility is also of interest. By remaining flexible and useful – that is, by being willing and able to play several positions – certain categories of players influence their own employability. This strategy, which is open mostly to Canadian linemen, helps teams achieve the optimum mix of talented Canadian and imported players. This strategy benefits Canadian linemen and American backfield players.

The Conflict of Quality

One of the principal reasons for wanting to hire American players, or "import players" as they are more neutrally called in football circles, is embodied in the fourth value conflict, the conflict of quality: Canadian mediocrity of play versus American excellence of play. My study of Canadian amateurs and professionals showed that the competitive nature of training fosters certain malevolent practices.[8] Many rookies are vying for the same position. When differences in ability and experience are slight to non-existent, other criteria must be brought to bear if individual players are to distinguish themselves or be distinguished from their competitors.

To this end, colleges and universities are ranked according to their reputations in football. When players come from a school with a poor reputation, this is taken as a sign that they are poorly qualified to play professional football. Such players may deny the truth of this reasoning; still, imputations of this sort do little to bolster their self-confidence in a highly competitive situation where self-confidence may be the determining factor in performing well enough to make the team. The ranking system generally accords Canadian schools a lower reputation for football than American schools. Supporting this evaluation are the facts that, on the average, Americans start playing football on organized teams earlier than Canadians, and that they have better football programs in high school and, to a lesser extent, in university.

In other words, imported players, as well as coaches and managers, generally believe that experience at a school in the United States validates their claim that they are better than Canadians, especially if the school has a strong football reputation. The following comments by a Canadian offensive linemen with five years' professional experience and four years at an American college indicate that at least some Canadians also accept this ranking system:

If you're a Canadian, you're looked down on. They'll look down on you if you're a Canadian and played Canadian college football or a Canadian who played in the States. Like I told you before, there's a ranking. [The coaches will] take you sight unseen if you played in the States ... I'm just as bad myself. I say Canadian college football sucks and all that, yet this attitude may cost us a great football player once in awhile. But I'm a victim of that myself. I look down on Canadians until they prove themselves otherwise. But I've seen some great Canadian football players.

In general, imported players wind up in the so-called skilled positions, which are presumed to require the most speed, agility, and dexterity. These are quarterback, running back, cornerback, and wide receiver.[9]

The Conflict of Local Familiarity

Related to the two preceding clashes is the issue of local familiarity. "Local" refers here to the local community or national Canadian talent or both. Local talent is better known by Canadian football fans than imported talent (at least initially) because it receives greater press coverage and, on the community level, has greater visibility. The imported players (with a handful of exceptions such as Rocket

Ismail and Doug Flutie) are not the well-publicized stars of American college and professional football; those men normally wind up in the NFL. Compared with their Canadian colleagues, players coming from the United States are less well known to Canadian football fans.

In time, imported talent can become local by being present for a couple of years or more. Thus it is possible for this value conflict to disappear once a team establishes its roster. Unfortunately for the reduction of ambivalence, established rosters are uncommon in the CFL. When a team is having a lacklustre season, the tendency for many coaches and personnel managers is to trade and cut players in an effort to find a winning combination. Although it is doubtful they can reach their goal by these means, there are other undesirable consequences as well.[10] One is the destruction of fan allegiance, which may well be tested by a team in the throes of two or more losing seasons. But the problem is exacerbated when attempts to start winning include bringing in large numbers of new players about whom the fans know little. At this point many fans begin looking for other outlets for their attention and money.[11]

The mass media are implicated in all of this. Modern reportage on matches and events relating to them tends to centre on two phenomena: great plays and great names. Play-by-play commentary as well as pre- and post-game reviews of sporting events discuss and recall outstanding athletic actions, especially those of the stars. In Canadian football, stars are most likely to be import players, since they are rendered most visible of all team members by their passing, catching, running, and defending in the backfield. Thus fans who follow their team in the newspapers and on radio and television hear much more about American than about Canadian players. Such ambivalence can only worsen the conflicts of rights, quality, and familiarity that the fans are experiencing today.

CONCLUSION

The central proposition of this essay is that English Canadians are ambivalent towards Canadian professional football, an orientation that has been around since the beginning of the game and that is indeed endemic to it. This ambivalence is embodied in five specific value conflicts, which have emerged through certain contradictory events and practices over the history of the game, three of which have been sharpened by the reporting practices of sports journalists. And, as mentioned in the introduction, ambivalence may also be furthered by the coverage (particularly the televised coverage) of NFL football and the invidious comparisons this practice makes possible with the Canadian game. One important inhibiting result is low attendance at the games.

There are without doubt other explanations for poor ticket sales. Even if ambivalence were somehow suddenly eliminated, other factors such as attractive alternative forms of leisure, high ticket prices, and scheduling problems appear to have a bearing on fan attendance. It might even be found, through further study, that fan allegiance is as strong as ever but is now being expressed in ways other than going to games. Talk about team performance, watching televised games (when they are not blacked out), and identification with one's team may still be high.

It would be interesting to know what role, if any, amateur university football in Canada plays in this situation. Except for the clash of rules, which is comparatively weak today, university football is free of the conflicts and the consequences of mass media reporting considered here. Are fans today more attracted for this reason to amateur university football? Has amateur football buoyed Canadian interest in the game and given the professional version a longer lease on life than it might otherwise have had? University teams are largely created from local players who often enjoy a four-year tenure there and whom local fans come to know. But fans who want more of the advanced level of football than a university team can provide (about five home games) must turn to a professional team in the hope, as futile as it may be, that a measure of roster stability will eventually take root.

Whatever the answers to these questions, the reduction of ambivalence does not lie in trying to change the psychology of the fans. If my argument is correct, they are responding to inherent conflicts and contradictions that only changes in Canadian football will resolve. The next move lies with the CFL, not with the people who buy tickets. Unfortunately, the league has done little or nothing to combat the ambivalence of fans stemming from the two modern value conflicts. Rather, its officials are on the verge of increasing it by expanding into the United States (a team in Sacramento will play in the 1993 season), a change that will surely reduce the number of Canadian players after the present contract with the Canadian Football League Players' Association expires.

From a more detached perspective, however, Canadian football can be seen as a master-symbol of Canadian popular culture. It is an historical compromise between British and American influences, one that is today uncertain of its loyalties to the former but stubbornly wary of becoming too much like the latter. It is ironically fitting that a "second sport" enjoys this stereotypical symbolism, and it is characteristically Canadian to be whimsically ambivalent about the whole matter. Canadian football, one suspects, will survive – whether we like it or not and despite the mass media.

PART THREE

Stage, Screen,
and Soundtrack

In the first contribution to Part Three, Reid Gilbert, a literary
scholar, examines various images of Canada in popular entertainment under the rubric of "Mounties, Muggings, and Moose."
He reviews them as components of Canadian national identity –
in effect, the popular sense of self that popular entertainments
project. Gilbert's treatment is suffused with the complex interactions
of American and Canadian popular culture; he even suggests
that the Canadian sense of self is split between "an external set of
images" in popular entertainments (which he describes in detail
from films and TV programs) and "an often inarticulate internal set
of images" that is kept more private and coded. Gilbert also use-
fully reviews, from a critical perspective, various literary efforts to
investigate the nature of Canadian culture and identity, and
warns in particular of the danger of measuring such matters by
foreign norms. That risk is especially great in relation to the U.S.
culture of glamourized violence; for a Canadian "to voice his culture
in anything but similarly horrific pictures is to admit to a culture
that is impotent." Canadians run a significant danger of concluding
that their popular culture is a failure if they adhere too closely
to American models of cultural success and, indeed, to U.S. images
of Canada. At the same time the process of "borrowing" from
the dominant culture to the south is ongoing and powerful. In pur-
suing his quest for Canadian cultural identity in films, plays, TV
programs, and depictions of the RCMP, Gilbert advances a variety
of thoughtful notions, including the "contention that Canadian

culture is, at base, self-satiric." Canadians' search for a more sophisticated cultural image of themselves continues, and their "cultural signifiers appear to be less anchored than those of many other nations."

Michael Taft, a folklorist, next explores the emergence of Canadian popular music in a North American environment in which influences and borrowing, the amalgamation of forms, and eclecticism, syncretism (fusion or combination), and preference predominate. Taft illustrates and explains the eclectic character of the sources of blues and popular music for African-American and white singers. He is able to document the incursion of black music, blues, bluegrass, and country and western into parts of Canada where they are hardly native. Taft's basic argument is that even Canadian popular music has had highly varied roots, resulting automatically and inevitably in syncretism. Despite the fact that Canadian popular music is heavily influenced, perhaps even dominated, by American traditions, "as a region of North America and as a culture in its own right, Canada has produced its own syncretistic musical traditions. These forms of music distinguish Canada from the rest of the continent, since its regions have produced blends of music not found in the United States." Taft shows that preference, like syncretism, serves as a marker of regionalism in popular music.

In the third essay in this part, Seth Feldman, a film critic, reviews how much the Canadian film industry, if it can even be called that, continues to be dominated by Hollywood, even to the extent of making the "American product." He examines the history of what he calls "Canadian cinema's cultural surrender" and considers how that process might begin to be reversed. Feldman reads Sandy Wilson's 1985 film *My American Cousin* as a metaphor for the "Canadian ambiguity towards the American presence as a whole and the manner in which that ambiguity expresses itself in cinema." It is the story of the disillusionment of a young girl in British Columbia in the 1950s when she is visited by her Californian male cousin. At other levels Feldman regards the film as illustrating the substitution of American for British Canada and the youthful experience of most non-Americans in realizing that they live in the wrong country: "The teenage rebellion – the first assertion of an adult self – is a pledge of allegiance to American style." Feldman then presents the history and practice of Canadian film as a moving away from "the adolescent infatuation with American expression." From the industry's beginning, Americans have financially dominated the film scene in Canada by ownership of theatre chains and distribution rights and by insistence on free trade in (u.s.) movies. Only the Quebec film industry and the products of the National Film Board have offered alternatives to American rule, although the latter failed to build any bridges to the former. Otherwise, in Feldman's view, the private film industry in Canada has largely made "American" films and TV programs. Feldman's essay ends with reflections on how this situation can be altered.

In the final essay in Part Three, Charline Poirier, a folklorist, investigates gender relations and narrative voices in Quebecois performance traditions. She begins by noting differences in the performance of burlesque in the United States and Quebec (for example, one audience is male, the other female). She explains the differences in story lines between Quebec and u.s. burlesque by an intertextual analysis of voices: male and female narrative voices strongly agree over characters' stereotypes, but they disagree as to the dynamic tensions between the motifs – that is, how they differ in their thematic interest. Poirier's examination of story lines offers an interpretation about inverted sex roles that is consistent with contrasting patterns of social and sexual politics. In Quebec, women have had a particularly powerful social position, just as men have been traditionally dominant in American society. For further support of this analysis, Poirier introduces her study of the defining circumstances surrounding characters and themes in the legends told by Quebecois men and women about Roman Catholic priests. She says, for example, that "in men's narratives, the priest stands in opposition to men and their desires; he is God's soldier and his work is to maintain the equilibrium of religion and society." For this, he is given some supernatural power over aspects of the life of his parishioners; the priest is the "extraordinarily powerful ruler." For female narrators, "the communicative powers of the priest are at the centre of their concern, and the duty of the priest is to serve as a bridge between the living and the dead, between the natural life, the religious life, and the eternal life, between the human and her God." Poirier concludes with respect both to burlesque and storytelling that there are "crucial differences between u.s. and Quebecois entertainment traditions."

10 Mounties, Muggings, and Moose: Canadian Icons in a Landscape of American Violence

REID GILBERT

Any attempt to define the effect of pop entertainment on a Canadian sense of national identity immediately comes up against four major questions. What is the sense of national identity that popular entertainments reflect? To what extent can any sense of self be unitary in a multinational country whose minorities are asserting their individual vision? How do the images of self that fill Canadian popular entertainments differ from those that present America to Canadians in the entertainments that flood across our long, peaceful, but highly porous border? What has been the effect on a contemporary Canadian sense of self of seeing the strong, urban, and often violent images that fill American film and television?

The present discussion largely ignores the crucial second question, recognizing that enormous changes have occurred in Canada in the past five years – changes that question the very possibility of a central national identity – but recognizing also that the prodigious effect of foreign popular culture in Canada not only renders an internal sense of self elusive but urges the struggle to find one even in the face of the growing suggestion that the odyssey is unauthentic to the Canadian experience.

Within the academy, social and literary critics are beginning to question the persistent Canadian effort to define the nation; in the majority popular culture, however, images from outside continue to provoke the feeling that something describable must exist and that it must be measured against foreign, particularly American, norms.

The popular sense of self, which this essay discusses, grows from the tradition that has marked Canadian education and both popular and scholarly introspection since Confederation. Work is now underway that begins to deconstruct this model, urging a very new look at what Canadians should actually seek in viewing themselves; nonetheless, the dualistic and often negative self-image and the subtle fluidity of signs that have marked Canadian iconography and methodology are still potent forces in the popular imagination.

At first glance it seems that Canadians view their own culture against a set of attitudes which they see as desirable by virtue of their apparent acceptance in the dominant American culture. There is, however, also evidence of a more intricate, double iconography: a split between an external set of images appearing in current Canadian popular entertainments and an often inarticulate internal set of images kept, private and coded. Is Canadian culture in fact a template buried deep in the Canadian psyche over which a daily exchange with American culture is superimposed?[1]

To view national identity as something that can be categorized, that has absolute signifiers, is to suppose a teleology which, as Lionel Rubinoff has suggested, is not authentic to the Canadian experience. In an essay written as early as 1969 for a collection of opinions on the subject of Canadian national identity, Rubinoff granted that "there are some Canadian intellectuals who take the search for Canadian destiny more seriously, and who indulge in an eschatological brand of the philosophy of history," but he suggested that "Such intellectuals ... betray once again the enormous influence of European and American culture on the Canadian consciousness," an influence which, in Rubinoff's opinion, Canadians "ought to be far more critical of than we apparently are."[2] He posits that while a thinking Canadian may not easily take for granted his or her involvement in the human condition, worrying about the progress of history, "the efficacy of advanced industrial society and the pathological implications of what Marcuse has aptly called 'the technological a priori,'" the same thinking Canadian is likely to take quite for granted the fact of being Canadian – feeling no tension and no suspicion, and prescribing no boundaries on what frames this experience.[3] In this the Canadian has traditionally differed, I suggest, from the American. I say traditionally differed, because, as Rubinoff foresaw, a new academic growth industry arose in Canada in the 1970s: the investigation and selling of Canadian culture in terms exactly contradictory to those outlined above, and therefore perhaps more appropriate to European or American cultural analysis.

A CANADIAN MYTHOS

A number of studies have searched for a defined Canadian mythos: Margaret Atwood's *Survival* led the way in 1972, followed by books like John Moss's *Patterns of Isolation* (1974), Robin Mathews's *Canadian Literature: Surrender or Revolution* (1978), Gaile McGregor's 1986 study *The Wacousta Syndrome*, and Mathews's *Canadian Identity: Major Forces Shaping the Life of a People* (1988).

In a highly negative review of *The Wacousta Syndrome* in *Canadian Forum* magazine, Frank Davey charged that studies such as these "seem to be motivated by the u.s. myths of origin and transcendent national identity ... The most professedly nationalistic of our recent cultural books appear American in their fundamental assumptions: that a culture must have a unitary, monolithic identity, and that this identity is to be found in that culture's earliest moments, the experiences of its settlers or its time of revolution."[4] If, as Davey argues, an analysis like *The Wacousta Syndrome* takes as its evaluative norm the culture and the analytical methodologies of another nation, it must necessarily fail to define legitimately what constitutes Canadian culture. As long as Canadians measure their culture against foreign norms, they will continue to believe their own ethos "lack[s]" something, find it "to have 'missed out,' to be 'captive,' to show 'inability' and 'failure,' to be 'flawed,' 'incapable,' 'inadequate'" – all terms Davey quotes McGregor as using in her study and all attitudes found in Atwood's pioneer work.[5]

Atwood's *Survival* was eagerly applauded as the beginning of a definition of recurrent themes in Canadian literature; but even her most enthusiastic first critics accused Atwood of selecting examples to fit a thesis and of being reductive; in the light of Davey's objections to the new study some fifteen years later, Atwood can be seen to have twisted her examples into a thesis that may be inappropriate to the country it explores. Further, the study inculcated a Eurocentric vision, which was at the time the only accepted version of literary history and the chief reply to fears of American colonization. If popular entertainments have changed in the 1990s, it is in their presentation of alternative images to the mainstream Caucasian, patriarchal, Anglo-European icons; if they have failed to change, it is in their continued aping, at least superficially, of American urban life.

Atwood's theme of survival, of existence in exile from cultural roots in Europe, has been the common view of Canadian culture since Northrop Frye's early writing on the subject. In modern terms, the theme continues past political colonialism into the alienation from human security and power that is often seen in contemporary Canadian literature. It has also been present in Quebecois literature and in the repetitive images of isolation, harsh weather, and deprivation (physical or spiritual) that have formed recurrent motifs in Canadian novels, plays, and films. But these themes have also dominated much western literature, and Frye himself noted that Canadian poets had begun, by the 1960s, "to write in a world which is post-Canadian, as it is post-American, post-British, and post-everything except the world itself."[6] A critical distinction may exist between Canadian poetry and fiction (which, as D.G. Jones pointed out as early as 1970 in *Butterfly on Rock*, use images characteristic of "western culture generally") and Canadian popular drama and television, especially in the 1980s when the theatre began to congratulate itself on achieving an unashamedly "commercial" maturity.[7] But in all genres it is now clear that the easy assumption of the exiled Canadian may seem entirely true only to those who see Canada from the outside.

Canadians themselves may not feel that they are isolated from a historical past until they make their graduation trip to Europe or to their grandparents' Asian homelands and discover an architecture that feels at once foreign and familiar. Canadians themselves may not feel isolated from the corridors of power until the TV news tells them that the United States has secret plans to administer the Canadian government in the event of nuclear attack, or until they see the country excluded from real participation in a major international decision, as in Alan Stratton's play *Rexy!*, where the audience is shown Mackenzie King as a prime minister who can be a crushingly powerful politician at home but is a puppet in the hands of Winston Churchill and Franklin Delano Roosevelt.[8] When they are confronted with the established *teleos* of these other cultures and the power it brings, Canadians notice the absence of a similar central design at home; but in their daily lives in Canada do they sense the absence, or do they continue a "phenomenological viewing" of their country, which does not require such a pattern?[9] Is it only because they are told that such a pattern should exist that Canadians have begun to search for ways to codify themselves?

For reasons of bilingualism and multiculturalism, Canadian studies are very often regional studies, and religion, education, class, and gender also create cultural élites that must be examined individually. Naturally this is true also in the United States, as in most countries, but Americans seem always to have measured subgroups against a national definition. Canadians, by contrast, have always viewed local cultural signifiers – understanding them intuitively perhaps, and in terms of a set of local connotations, but not automatically seeking for a central definition. That Canadian scholars have tried to do so may be, as has already been suggested, more a reflection of an education system that teaches foreign values and foreign sociological methodologies than any authentic prompting of the Canadian sense of place or being. Even the critics I have cited as applying inappropriate methods to their studies recognize that doing so damages their findings: Atwood herself admits that if "the viewer is given a mirror that reflects not him but someone else, and told at the same time that the reflection he sees is himself, he will get a very distorted idea of what he is really like."[10] Robin Mathews, speaking from a more political viewpoint, goes further: "In surrendering the possibility of Canadian community and in taking on the language (which means the terms of reality) of u.s. life, the writers find themselves accepting u.s. terms of behaviour." The result is a Canadian who sees himself "as negro," a simile that reminds one of Pierre Vallières' view of the doubly colonized Quebecois as the *White Niggers of America.*[11]

It is the more chilling that Canadians should take on "the terms of reality of u.s. life" as that reality becomes progressively more violent and the images in which that reality portrays itself become images of violence made glamorous, images in which the power grows from the violence and becomes synonymous with it. The Canadian is now faced not only with a measure against which his culture seems to be lacking in power, but a sense that to voice his culture in anything but similarly horrific pictures is to admit to a culture that is impotent. It is here that Canadian popular iconography has been most resistant to deconstruction and reconstruction, even in the eventful period since 1990, when other manifestations of the national identity have been shaken.

In *Why We Act Like Canadians* Pierre Berton attempted to discuss his own sense of identity in a series of snapshots of Canadian life outlined in letters to his penpal "Sam." He is able to define himself only against what differs from the experience of his American alter ego, exhibiting the familiar negative sense of being Canadian, which Jim Christy deplores as "beating the same horse" of hackneyed nationalistic definition.[12] Berton, however, recognizes that a definition based on anecdotes may come closer to a real portrait than the categorizations assembled by the critics whom Davey and Christy repudiate and whom I have used as examples.

If Canadian culture exists, then, more as a collection of impressions than as a common definition, how can the nation express those impressions in its art or popular entertainments? And, more important, if Canadians have been told by their educators and scholars that they should be able to define themselves in terms of one stated thesis or another,[13] and if they see in the movies and television that beam across the border the measure of a foreign culture that seems able to do so, often with cruel power, what is the effect on the Canadian sense of cultural success or failure? What, indeed, will develop in such a climate as icons of the Canadian national identity?

If, as has often been suggested, the Canadian sense of self is essentially the sense of a lack of defined self – an identity as anti-identity – then no easy iconography can be formed. If, as Christy suggests, "a definition is irrelevant, [and] the intuitive feeling of being Canadian is what matters," then we need an iconography "felt" rather than heraldic. The formulation of a set of images of that which is not may be understandable from an intellectual point of view, but it is complicated to picture, especially in popular entertainments. The poet may be able to express it in a language that captures the mute power of the country, employing some post-modern "vocabularies ... [which] embrace ... the earth" itself, but Malcolm Ross's figurative language does not easily translate into symbolic language, into the signs upon which entertainment and myth-making rely.[14] And it does not easily satisfy the need for the familiar and homely.

So Canadians, in trying to express themselves, have separated a documentary sense of their history, the making of which they value as a Canadian talent, from any mythic sense of themselves. The documents may be largely fictional, as the popularity of the short story of personal reminiscence and the lyric poem attest, but they are still local and episodic; they do not claim to speak for all Canadians. In order to express a single, collective personality, then, Canadians turn either to borrowed images or to satirical images of themselves, representations of that which they view as true phenomena of their culture but which they have been taught to devalue. When measured against foreign criteria, the individual images Canadians feel as part of their disparate and undefined sense of themselves seem not sufficiently cohesive or simply second-rate copies. Living with a sense of failure for not having created what they have been told they need – and what studies like *The Wacousta Syndrome* suggest is lacking – and convinced that their gentleness is weakness, they invert their icons into satirical self-portraits or the personae of losers. Within these visions, however, resides a second set of icons, much more subtle in nature, which speaks to the Canadian of his true self.

The most successful of Canadian popular entertainments, plays like John Gray's *Billy Bishop Goes to War* (1981), which enjoyed astonishing commercial success in small towns as well as cities, and *SCTV*, which enjoyed enormous popularity and propelled a number of Canadian comics to international fame, bear out the contention that Canadian culture is, at base, self-satiric.[15] A film such as Jean-Claude Lauzon's *Un Zoo, la Nuit*, which enjoyed significant popular success and swept the 1988 Genie awards, demonstrates the curious desire for an American violence in which to picture an urbanized Canada. The history of Canadian commercial theatre and much of the history of the strong amateur tradition supports the notion of borrowing.

In *Frontier Theatre* Chad Evans describes the typical entertainments of the Pacific coast and the Yukon during the nineteenth century, especially during the gold rush. British Columbia in that period serves as an excellent example of the colonial borrower, since it still felt its close association with England (of which it was still two direct colonies), felt connections to eastern Canada (from where the railroad would soon stretch, bringing Confederation), and to the United States, whose citizens poured into the Klondike in search of gold. Each influence formed part of a borrowed culture that still exists to some extent: from visiting English naval parties came a tradition of "effete British dilettantism"; from eastern Canada came a tradition of travelling shows, bringing European culture to the hinterland; and from America came a glossy progression of vaudeville shows.

Evans suggests that the American influence was more significant than the others, denying the "idea British Columbia came about as part of a central, national design"; he argues instead that the "predominant face" of cultural influence was "commercial American."[16] Initially the immigrant society sought to replicate the English and eastern models; if it had no "strong prerogative of place" with which to form authentic images, it was certainly prepared to falsify a "mock-culture ... [a set of] pretentious false-fronts"; but these were, Evans suggests, "destined to be blown away by the shifting dreams of gold-seekers." These frontiersmen demanded the "variety entertainment [which] controlled a large share of the mining audience," the professionalism, and in fact the vulgarity of the American shows. The Boar's Head saloon in San Francisco in 1850 "featured a sexual exhibition given by a 'pretty-waiter-girl' and a wild boar," and the boys in the Klondike wanted the same.[17]

The preference for American borrowings can be documented in central Canada as well. In the light of the earlier contention that the Canadian sense of self has been conditioned by criteria appropriate to the United States, the pattern of borrowing and a subsequent need to borrow becomes cyclical and insidious. No wonder that today, despite the fact that remnants of all three influences remain part of the popular sensibility of Pacific Canadians and despite a new respect for an earlier, indigenous ceremonial iconography, few trendy British Columbians would readily admit to the old English or Native cultural markers which seem less "up-end" than the copies of American TV shows with which the CBC now tries to woo them. For the large number of new Canadians now arriving in the region from the Orient, of course, the residual British images are either inappropriate or viewed through other colonial filters; the other remnants evoke no memories, and the American images seem fresh and full of the promise of the North American dream.

U.S. TELEVISION

That American TV is the chief influence on popular Canadian culture goes without saying. It is less clear whether that influence is the result of choice or necessity. A major government task force on television presented some surprising statistics in 1986 which, *Maclean's* suggested, explode a myth: the notion that Canadians do not watch their own TV. Brian D. Johnson and others claimed that "viewers watch Canadian programming in almost direct proportion to its availability." Their figures are highly revealing. "During an average week of English-language TV, 28 per cent of the programming available is Canadian – and 29 per cent of what the audience watches is Canadian. Figures for drama match precisely: two per cent of TV drama is Canadian, and Canadians spend two per cent of their viewing time watching [it]."[18] That these correlations surprised the investigators shows how much the popular imagination in Canada expects to find a preference for American shows and the degree to which it has been conditioned to consider it unlikely that Canadians will elect to view themselves. The figures also remind one of the paucity of Canadian dramatic programming; if 2 per cent of available drama is locally produced, 98 per cent is not. Finally, the *Maclean's* article fails to consider the extent to which new Canadian programming copies the American models that make up the remaining 71 to 98 per cent of viewing time.

Significant changes to the CBC's schedule and program mix in 1992, which stressed news reportage and moved the major newscast to an earlier time slot, underline the perception of the national broadcasting network's role. It seems that Canadians trust their own news, trust themselves as honest and reasonable reporters; it seems also that Canadians are generally prepared to leave the bulk of their entertainment to Americans, who, they believe, do it better. (A si-

multaneous decision to broadcast Canadian movies in the time slot
following the news, however, speaks of promising changes in this
attitude.)

In *Turn Up the Contrast*, a study of drama produced or shown on
the Canadian Broadcasting Corporation, Mary Jane Miller discusses
the series *Cariboo Country* (1960–67), a series she calls "absolutely distinctive [and] ... a conscious alternative to the pervasive form of the
American television Western."[19] Citing not only the show's content
and sense of myth but its realistic documentary style, Miller shows
how the program differed from the American *Bonanza* against
which it competed in a Saturday-night time slot. She contends that
the program "summarizes some of the perceptions which distinguish
Canada from the United States," working with a "very different history of western settlement ... [and] divergent literary traditions." She
also reports, however, that the series was not always broadcast across
the entire CBC network, that although the CBC "initially showed only
two American westerns in the 1960 schedule ... [it] picked up several
... more during the seven year run of *Cariboo Country*," and that while
the American westerns ran approximately twenty-six episodes per
season, *Cariboo Country* averaged seven or eight.[20] With a forward-
looking attitude to women and to Native Canadians, without "stars,"
and without the heroic model of the mythologized American cowboy, the show offered less violent, less ritual action. Depicting a
rather stoic population dealing with real issues of survival, the show
did not adhere to what Richard Carpenter has called the "large, simple, general patterns" of the U.S. western, patterns which are highly
marketable and which, to repeat, Canadians have been conditioned
to expect.[21] While the program attracted a large following, it has not
entered the national image bank as Ben Cartwright and the boys
from *Bonanza* have. It is clear that "unlike the American networks,
the CBC ... did not consider its audience to be homogeneous" and,
therefore did not engage in active national myth-making.[22] But it is
also clear that Canadians seeking such myths will accept the rituals
of their neighbours as entertainment, will overlay the homogeneity
of American life on their own silent sense of regional self, and will
look to U.S. imports for the collective experience their own more
pragmatic culture does not provide.

It is interesting to conjecture whether Canadian viewers distinguish between the representation of an amorphous "North American" experience, which seems to satisfy them, and American
depictions of Canada itself. In an episode of the American mystery
series *Murder, She Wrote*, broadcast in October 1987, the action
moved to Quebec City, or at least to an American writer's idea of
Quebec City. As the Canadian dramatist John Lazarus pointed out

in a letter to the editor of the *Vancouver Sun*, "not a word of French, nor a single Quebec, Parisian, or even fake-French accent [was heard in the program]. Except for an excess of Canadian flags, making us look as flag-happy as our good neighbors, the location might have been Cleveland during a royal visit." Patrick McGoohan, "with relish and chutney, [played] a pompous and incompetent [British] lawyer described by a fellow Quebecker [with a Brooklyn accent] as 'the best in Canada.'"[23] Of even more interest to a student of iconography, the show also depicted dozens of Mounties wearing their red serge on ordinary patrol and court duty, an identifiably British tone in decor and home life, and barristers in wigs.

It is nothing new for Hollywood to present Canada in false images; Pierre Berton's *Hollywood's Canada* made that clear, as have later studies: but it is significant in an age of television, where the false and foreign signification of Canadian icons is beamed into Canadian living-rooms coupled with the generalized images of North American life, which, it is argued, Canadians accept.[24] How confusing for the Canadian mind to separate these two sets of responses; yet it appears that Canadians can do just that. Reaction to the *Murder, She Wrote* episode was negative, not only from letter-writers like Lazarus, who saw an ominous "omen for the future of Canadian culture under free trade," but from ordinary viewers who scoffed at the program the next day. Canadians know the Mounties are not always ceremonial heroes, even if not all of us are sure whether or not Canadian lawyers wear wigs in court. Canadians perceive the false depiction of icons they hold dear, but somehow assimilate them into an equally false depiction of North American life which they then accept. The increasing slickness of CBC dramas has not prevented Canadians from seeing their falsity; it has, however, assisted in the assimilation.

Indeed, portrayals of the RCMP are a prime example of this compartmentalization. Mounties remain both a central icon of Canadian pride and a source of common Canadian humour. Tourists may buy picture postcards of handsome Mounties dressed in red, but Canadians also send them to each other as camp or ironic jokes. Individual Canadians know of problems and abuses within the force: a recruitment drive in the 1980s attempted to broaden the ethnic and gender mix in the force to redress historic inequality.[25] The series of royal commissions on the RCMP (from the 1960s to the 1980s) were, in Edward Greenspan's words, "an eye-opener. They showed there was nothing unusually fair or decent about the force, that it was not an elite."[26] Still, citizens of Canada respond to the power of the image even while rejecting it as phony. The controversy over the decision to allow Sikh recruits to wear turbans as part of the dress uniform indicates that Canadians are reluctant to alter the icon but realistic enough to admit the need for change in a nation of changing demography.

By arresting Charles McVey, who had been selling billions of dollars' worth of western technology to the Soviet bloc, Corporal Daniel Fudge became a brief hero of the RCMP. A *Los Angeles Times* article (reprinted in the *New York Times*) attempted to demystify the RCMP, quoting Greenspan's remark that "the Mounties are a ... great Hollywood myth," and pointed out that it "took fifteen years to get Parliament to approve a separate intelligence service which handles ... some ... functions that are handled in the United States by the Central Intelligence Agency and the FBI."[27] The article quoted Corporal Fudge: "I hardly ever wear red serge. Once when I was in Ottawa and saw a Mountie on a horse and in red serge, I grabbed a couple of snapshots myself." After his counterespionage triumph – an act that at the time seemed somehow American in its victory for western technology over communism – Fudge appeared at the White House in his red coat. The reportage was pure myth-making, but Americans took the photos. It is also worth noting that Fudge failed to deliver the criminal to a judge within the prescribed time limits, and the spy was released; another Mountie, who was not dressed in red serge and has not been presented at the White House, later rearrested McVey near Vancouver.

One is reminded of the sad final scene of Sharon Pollock's play *Walsh*, in which the Mountie major who fails as a human being finally comes to realize that the politicians want to see him in the *role* of the Mountie; he stages a false Indian attack on a train carrying officials.[28] Canadians are drawn to the documentary nature of such a story: they see the falsity of national public relations and they reject it in foreign examples, but in the idiosyncratic admixture of the Canadian psyche they also see in it part of themselves. No wonder Canadians turn to their own news programs: these have the feeling of dispassionate reportage that seems central to the Canadian mind. And Canadians watching the news feel no need to extend the facts into myth, no need to compete with the stronger sense of national storytelling of other nations.

CANADIAN CHILDREN'S PROGRAMS

The national news programs are presented not during the dinner hour, when local news is seen, but in mid- to late evening, when young children are in bed and adult Canadians can sum up the day with a sober look at the world. In the morning, however, their children watch u.s. cartoons, with their complex links between mythic character and marketing.

There are a number of excellent Canadian children's programs. However, they intermingle with u.s. imports, breeding the schizophrenia or, as has been suggested, the fluidity of perception of young Canadians. *Sesame Street*, for example, which is often considered an inappropriate model for non-urban, middle-class American children, is even less appropriate for the majority of Canadian children. Yet its popularity in Canada refutes this fact; *Sesame Street*, recognizing its Canadian audience, introduced three Canadian muppets, including an otter and a beaver, animals that are undeniably Canadian icons. The cbc children's series *Under the Umbrella Tree* demonstrates that the pattern of laying an American borrowing over a Canadian sense of the world continues: the show "deals with reality, is non-violent and non-sexist," and features a hero who is a "tough little" creature who "looks remarkably like *Sesame Street*'s frog-host Kermit." In one episode, when a storm plunges his apartment into darkness, the hero, Iggy, "is scared just like the not-so-tough."[29] This honest and vulnerable figure has successfully competed in the Saturday morning ratings wars with popular American animals who often exhibit violent behaviour and who generally embody images of power (except where they parody it). In 1992 the program was still broadcast weekly.

Iggy's survival suggests again the deep structured affinity of Canadians for honesty, even in an anthropomorphic vision of animals. The English tradition of *Wind in the Willows* and the American tradition of Walt Disney are both alien to an indigenous Canadian view of animal characters. Unknown to many Canadians is the extensive collection of late nineteenth-century Canadian animal stories by writers such as Ernest Thompson Seton (1860–1946), tales of real animals who struggle to survive in a hostile northern environment.[30] Indeed, even Margaret Atwood, who, it has been suggested, was one of the first critics to impose American methodologies on Canadian literature, herself wrote in a poem entitled "The Animals in That Country:"

In this country the animals have the faces of animals.
Their eyes flash once in the headlights and are gone.
Their deaths are not elegant.
They have the faces of no-one.[31]

Such animals, however, seem like failures when viewed against the urbane Toad of Toad Hall, the endearing Mickey Mouse, the crafty and always successful Bugs Bunny, or the impossibly violent Road-runner.

There was an attempt in the heady years of Canada's centenary to introduce a commercially successful Canadian animal icon, the Ook-pik. Based on the Arctic owl, the fluffy creature had a brief moment of fame and remains in the affections of middle-aged Canadians. But the Ookpik never enjoyed the mad popularity of the later Cab-bage Patch doll sold to Canadian children by American television marketing, which had consumers literally in tears, beating each other away from the limited stock available in Canada's department stores. More telling is the way Canadians have forgotten Ookpik since 1967 or how they pass him to their children as another unin-teresting Canadian animal. In his highly acclaimed book of chil-dren's poems, *Alligator Pie*, Dennis Lee wrote that "an Ookpik is nothing but hair. / If you shave him, he isn't there. / ... He has noth-ing at all on his mind."[32]

An *SCTV* spoof of Canadian broadcasting had great fun with its version of a series of Canadian-government-produced shorts about animals. A video crew at the side of a highway films while a dry voice-over reads, "The woodchuck is a nocturnal animal ..." The shows caricatured the dull educational spots and their equally dull series title, *Hinterland Who's Who*. Throughout the *SCTV* program, the action repeatedly cut back to this film crew and, finally, to a pass-ing car (part of another skit) as it ran over the woodchuck. The image of the director leaning over the mangled corpse of the animal while trying to resuscitate it is one of the funniest moments in the series. But the poor woodchuck, who was indeed one "flash" in the headlights and then was "gone," became an object of rather cruel humour. Because it has "the face of no-one" it is rejected, and short films about it which provide useful information, but do not turn the animal into a mock human with star quality, are considered boring. The loon of *Hinterland Who's Who* is not Woody Woodpecker.

It is here that our trust in our own documentary reportage and our suspicion of our own stories must again be noted. Contempo-rary conservationist writings, such as the novels of Farley Mowat, which depict Canadian animals in realistic terms, do exist and are read, but images from those tales have not become commonplace in popular entertainments, on TV, or, generally, in commercial theatre. Again the response to such works is to separate them from the main-stream of Americanized entertainment, to locate them as "serious" and naturalistic – therefore documentary, and therefore simultane-ously "ours," boring, and unstated. The animals in these true sto-ries often meet violent deaths, but that is not violence which can be glamorized.

AMERICAN VIOLENCE

The desire to make violence glamorous is a profound reality of twentieth-century life, and nowhere is it more obvious than in American popular entertainment. As Canadians seek a more sophisticated cultural image, they appear ready to incorporate this treatment of violence into the complex of their self-perceptions. Lauzon's film *Un Zoo, la Nuit*, touted as a breakthrough in Canadian cinema, juxtaposed pure American violence with highly sentimental and self-satirizing icons of Canadian life. The sordid world of the Montreal drug trade is shown in images reminiscent of the *film noir* tradition. There is heavy rock music; the visual landscape is filled with high-tech amplifiers, stereo equipment, and answering-machines; the milieu is filled with drugs, motorcycles, leather, corrupt vice cops (not dressed in red serge), muggings, prison bars, and pick-up bars; the value system is commercial, predatory, misogynistic, and negatively homosexual in an extension of male combat and violence. By contrast, the older world of the protagonist's father is pure Canada: it is innocent; it centres on escape to the wilderness of one's childhood; the milieu is filled with crumpled old fishing-hats, mist rising off northern lakes, '57 Buicks, failed drunks; the relationships are heterosexual (and often unsatisfying), and the central truth is, at the end, love of family and peace. In this film the protagonist, by entering the exciting and lucrative drug subculture, also accepts its norms, just as he accepts its dress codes, its symbiotic relationship with corrupt policemen, and the advances of homosexual prostitutes. The narrative is resolved only when the protagonist enlists the help of the most physically attractive and the most amoral character in the film, his American cellmate, who can seduce the weak and despicable undercover cop and who can plan and carry out a brutal murder. After the cop is killed in a sleazy sex hotel without a French name but with filmic connections to every evil Chinatown in u.s. cinema, this murderer assures the Canadian protagonist, "Remember, you always have an American friend."

In a simultaneous plot in *Un Zoo, la Nuit*, when the boy comes together with his dying father, the desire to kill is also present, but it is a complex fantasy, full of pioneer memories and mild competition with more recent immigrants – a desire to kill the biggest moose in history. Contemporary Canadians find themselves laughing at the old man and yet, like his son, they are unable finally to reject him. The image of the gangster son in leather jacket and chains, reclining in the back of a canoe while his old father tries to call a moose to its death by imitating the call of the female animal, is at once ridiculous and strangely moving. The flatness of the scene on screen, the mist, and the clichés all function to reduce the fishing sequence to a joke and present it in sharp contrast to the adrenaline rush of the inner-city action. The Canadian audience looks for proof that the protagonist can survive in the North American criminal subculture and finds it in his suitcase full of cash, which the father refuses. And yet the same audience realizes that the relationships in that world are empty, that people connect only by message machine, and that, in it, sex is another commodity. In the end, the old man's value system seems to win out, although the protagonist's attitude is enigmatic.

What is significant is the role played by conscious acting-out and social myth in the lives of the Canadians. In a funny but touching scene, the emotionally sick young Canadian and the physically sick old Canadian come together by watching a film of moose-hunting which the boy brings to his father's hospital bedside. Running on an old 8-millimetre projector, so unlike the high-tech equipment in the urban loft of the drug dealer, this echo of *Hinterland Who's Who* provides a vehicle for the men to understand what binds them. In a moving series of images of Quebec life (such as the washing of his father's dead body) and a tender series of images of true male love in which the son lies naked, cuddling his nude, dead father, real touching occurs. It is expressly because the audience can laugh at the falsity of the nostalgic moose-hunting and because Canadians visit their zoos to view more exotic animals that it understands what it is to be Canadian.

BILLY BISHOP GOES TO WAR

It is the highly satirical nature of the Canadian sense of self that is finally the most interesting and the most complicated aspect of the Canadian national character. The *SCTV* woodchuck skit works exactly because Canadians want to laugh at what seems to them drab or second-rate in themselves. In laughing, however, they accept the existence of the prosaic wildlife lesson in their view of things. Canadians do not destroy their culture by laughing at it; instead, they affirm it in a complex, inverted manner.

John Gray's play *Billy Bishop Goes to War*, mentioned earlier, presents a Canadian hero who not only displays a set of borrowings, but is himself heroic by default. By fulfilling the role of popular idol, Bishop becomes a subtle satire of the very Canadian need for heroes who resemble the heroes of others, and an important example of what might be a true Canadian hero. He is an icon, it might be argued, only for the mainstream male Canadian of British ancestry, but he echoes a psychology that is common among Canadians of many backgrounds and communities. It is in the subtlety of his portrait, not in his surface characterization, that he points to a Canadian attitude.

At the outset the play seems simple enough: a single actor-narrator and a piano-player who sometimes acts as foil tell the story of Billy Bishop, a young Canadian fighter pilot, who becomes a hero in a daring raid on enemy territory. Celebrated in London, he returns home as a war hero and becomes a major figure in the Canadian military establishment. At the end of the play he delivers a recruitment speech that glorifies the battlefield as a place for young men to do heroic deeds. It is obvious that this is a play of characterization; all other considerations are secondary to the portrait of Bishop, which is highly dramatic and which first led to the play's popularity in Canada, encouraging Mike Nichols to take it to Broadway. For Canadian audiences, however, the portrait is powerful beyond its theatricality: many Canadians find in the characterization of Bishop a potent icon for their own sense of themselves.

Billy Bishop has been performed from coast to coast in Canada; it has enjoyed long runs in the major cities, and is still mounted in the 1990s. On Broadway it closed in a few days and moved to a smaller theatre. Reactions to the New York experience vary: the author found it devastating, while some commentators suggested that the move was a shrewd commercial decision. Nonetheless, it is clear that despite warm praise by the critics, American theatre-goers viewed the play merely as a war story and could not experience the empathy with the hero that Canadians feel without articulation. The popularity of the play is not explained by any previous affection for Bishop among the majority of Gray's countrymen; indeed, as Barbara Gamarekian wrote, Bishop was "virtually unknown to young Canadians" when the play (and a subsequent series of films and TV programs about him) first appeared. Eddy Rickenbacker, by contrast, is "part of [the] mythology [of all young Canadians] as a result of American films." There is also, as Mel Gussow noted in the *New York Times*, "a measure of Richthofen and Snoopy in the portrait" – both heroes of foreign countries, one of them another anthropomorphized animal who is much more droll than the poor squashed woodchuck.[33] This portrait borrows not only the power of these external First World War flying aces and the fantasy of adventure they still seem to evoke (despite a number of films determined to explode the myth); it also contains within itself the key to Bishop's appeal to Canadians and the reason for his lack of appeal to Broadway theatre-goers. Bishop is an accidental hero. He is also an opportunist who is at the same time totally non-Machiavellian.

If the play draws Bishop as the "transatlantic innocent in corrupt Europe," it also creates confusion or irony in his growing awareness that he is indeed a hero.[34] For if, as the actor who collaborated in the writing said to a newspaper reviewer, the Bishop of the play "didn't *know* he was a hero ... he was just trying to stay alive," the text itself suggests that he became aware of it by the end of the war and certainly by the time of his recruitment pep-talk in 1941. And if, as Gray suggests, "he was a sort of small town juvenile delinquent who, though just scraping to survive and hang on, became the toast of London," he also came to know, in the same way that the small-town gang leader does, that "I really was Number One now."[35] Despite Gray's desire to interpret his character as having been unknowingly swept into fame, the play makes it clear that Bishop was not unaware of how fame could be gained and, when he did find it thrust upon him, enjoyed the adulation with obvious glee but without any personal sense of change or purpose. In this sense he is a hero without guile. He differs from the protagonist of *Un Zoo, la Nuit* who understands the new role into which crime has initiated him. Reviewing the Edinburgh production of *Billy Bishop* in *The Scotsman*, Allan Massie called Bishop the "hero as anti-hero." But this term implies, again, an absolute hero against whom he can be measured as negative, or as anti-signifier. If Canadians insist on borrowing such absolute measures, then Bishop may be a modern "anti-" figure. But as himself, Bishop is more.

The Bishop character is complete within himself as a gently satirical, ironic Canadian, proud of his status but unsure how he reached it. He is also kept aware of his position by characters who represent the military establishment: they remind him that while he is, as he himself says, "a dignitary," he is "a colonial dignitary. There is a difference." Bishop's worldly London patroness notes in a song, "You're a typical Canadian, / You're modesty itself" and Bishop sings, "Nobody starts no wars on Canada / Where folks tend to wish each other well." This well-wishing and ever-present sense that others have "a lot more class than me" is mixed in Bishop with a delight in the hunt, a need for the kill – an important shading of the stereotype of the peace-loving (and peace-keeping) Canadian. This enigmatic mixture makes Bishop an ideal war pilot, but a clumsy guest at embassy balls. It also explains his love of flight, his feeling that "once ... in the air, I felt a lot better. In fact, I felt like a king!" And in showing that the loser, once alone and free in an environment he can control, can scream "at the top of my lungs, I win, I WIN, I WIN!" it appeals to the Canadian audience who, in European courts or American executive offices, feels less than secure.

By ending the play with the recruitment speech of 1941, in which the older Bishop returns to enlist new victims for war, Gray underlines his characterization of the hero as well as his secondary theme of the futility of war: "Makes you wonder what it was all for? But then, [both as ordinary men and as Canadians] we're not in control of any of these things, are we?" In the final irony of this closing speech, the ideals of battle have taken over; Colonel Bishop now sounds like a conventional hero, but the diction is cliché-ridden and the substance false. He has become like Major Walsh; he is as false as the bogus barrister of *Murder, She Wrote*. It is the reprise of the theme song that causes this puppet-hero to become personal for a moment and to question "what it was for." His final line reinforces his attitudes, but it also intensifies the irony of these attitudes in his unintentional pun: "All in all, I would have to say, it was a hell of a time!"

Now Bishop is a figure much easier to paint. But he is no longer a bona fide hero to Canadians, even though he has learned to appear as heroic and is now as polished as the members of the foreign military élite who earlier belittled him. It is in that personal aside that the plain-speaking Canadian boy (probably unaware of the force of his own pun) recaptures his personal worth by setting aside the very power of the image which he (and his audience) would have assumed made him more significant, more a figure from the non-satirized borrowings to which Canadians have trained themselves to turn.

The negative view of the old Bishop is pointedly satirical: it shows the falsity of a Canadian who willingly dresses up in the symbols of others. The satire implicit in the portrayal of the young Bishop is gentle and affectionate. While recognizing his failure to be a British general or to be as fine as those at the embassy balls, Gray shows Bishop's "phenomenological viewing" of the world around him.[36] If there is a hero in the play it is the young Bishop, and if he is a hero he is both existential and unformed; he is both seduced into the role of hero and naive in the enjoyment he feels in portraying that which he knows, at base, he is not.

CONCLUSION

Canadian cultural signifiers appear to be less anchored than those of many other nations. They float in and out of a documentary denotation and a complex connotation in which they may be sign-vehicles of more than one signifier at the same time: one the popularly conceived foreign signification with its more and more violent patina, the other an unstated and encoded text perceived at a subtle and usually unspoken level by Canadians themselves. And, by refusing for 125 years to be anchored in a particular official signification, they may always have pointed to the post-modern notion that no single identity exists or may be allowed to claim priority. This may be the special semiosis which links the images and patterns that form a truly Canadian iconography.

To measure such versatile signs is, of course, extremely difficult, except against some fixed set of values which may explain the critical and popular desire to use markers from other countries, from cultures motivated by established teleologies or cultures whose values have been assimilated as part of the colonizing process. But the popular entertainments of Canada do not allow their viewers to sidestep the fluidity of their own identity, do not allow Canadians to make into heroes characters who are both heroes and failures, historical figures and borrowed myths, figures of affection and self-repudiation, figures that may themselves be agents of cultural hegemony but are also victims of foreign domination. Alone in the air, fishing in a leaky old boat, or by the side of the road, Canadians know they have the "face[s] of no-one," and yet they recognize the face as one of many they call their own.

11 Syncretizing Sound: The Emergence of Canadian Popular Music

MICHAEL TAFT

Making categories is a long-standing academic tradition; breaking them is an equally old popular tradition. In attempts to understand the nature of popular culture, categories seem essential, if only to reduce this vast area of creativity to manageable chunks: cinema, literature, theatre, food, architecture, and song, among others. Yet gingerbread houses shaped like wedding-cakes sold in bakeries, children's books that play music, and films that mix live action with animation show the mutability of any strict classification of popular culture.

At least for the purposes of analysis one might be able to separate one popular culture genre from another, but the categorizing of subgenres remains a difficult problem. One purpose of this essay is to examine some subcategories of North American popular music in order to determine how well academic distinctions stand up in public practice and preference. This study also explores the eclectic and syncretistic roots of both u.s. and Canadian popular music and the fluid interactions between them.

The history of popular music in North America is one of influences and borrowing, of the amalgamation of forms, of eclecticism, syncretism, and preference. All modern forms of popular music – rock, country, and Broadway musicals, among others – grew out of combinations of older forms – blues, gospel, hillbilly, cowboy, jazz, vaudeville, operetta – which in turn were amalgams of still older traditions – minstrel, ballad, hymn, and grand opera. Added to the cross-influence of subgenres is the history of the interaction of different ethnic music – African, Latin American, British, French, Jewish, among others – which accounts for the phenomenon of North American popular music.

THE ECLECTICISM OF BLUES SINGERS

Before we approach syncretism it is necessary to understand eclecticism, since the amalgamation of musical forms cannot occur without a variety of music available to the public. As an example, consider African-American pre-war blues – both a traditional and a commercial form of song that has had a far-reaching effect on North American popular music. Tracing the roots of the blues from African traditions through slave songs and work songs has been a tried-and-true approach to the genre: virtually all students of the blues have launched their studies from this historical base. Yet the emergence of the blues as a song form in its own right (c. 1890) did not isolate the blues from other song genres, nor did it prevent further syncretism or eclecticism.

From its inception the blues was only one among several song forms performed by so-called blues singers. The kinds of songs from which the blues evolved remained in the repertoire of blues singers, since neither they nor their audience were purists.[1] The eclectic nature of blues singers' repertoires was not merely a function of their personal aesthetics. As professionals, the singers had to learn to cater to the different types of audiences they faced. The blues singer Rosa Lee Hill explained it this way: "We played the blues for them that wanted to hear it, and them that like church songs, we'd play them. Just like we'd go to their house, they wanted blues, we'd play it. And if we go to white people's houses, they wanted waltzes, foxtrots ... we'd play that for them. And when we'd go to older people's houses, they wanted church songs, well, all of us would get together and sing and play that."[2] Carl Martin, another blues singer, gave a similar explanation of his repertoire:

When you play music for your living you play what people want; that's the way I always tried to figure for myself. Anything they want – if it was weddings, dances, breakdowns, churches, anything they sent for me to come and play. That's why I learned to play so well, 'cause I practiced all kinds of music. Then when I came to Chicago, I go to the Polish neighborhood, go to the Irish neighborhood, I go to the German neighborhood, go in the Italian neighborhood; I had to learn to play all their musics.[3]

Similarly, Johnnie Temple and the McCoy brothers played polkas and Italian music for the Capone gang in Chicago.[4]

These statements bring out a further fact about blues singers: although in some contexts they catered to all-black audiences, in other contexts they played for white audiences and with white musicians. Several scholars have noted this black–white interchange.[5] Given this fact, it is understandable that blues singers were influenced by white song traditions and that they readily added white songs to their repertoires. For example, Jimmie Rodgers, the white hillbilly singer, had a large following in black communities, and blues singers not only bought his records and knew his songs but on occasion even accompanied him in live performances.[6]

Music, then, was one of the few areas in which blacks and whites could comfortably interact. This is not to say that music promoted harmony between the races; rather, the two cultures were able to understand and appreciate each other's song traditions, and their tastes tended to overlap to a great extent. The performer, whether black or white, had to understand this fact and had to shape his or her repertoire accordingly. Robert Johnson is often thought of as the archetypal blues singer, but Johnny Shines's description of his repertoire should come as no surprise: "Robert didn't just perform his own songs. He did anything that he heard over the radio, ANYTHING that he heard. When I say 'anything,' I mean ANYTHING – popular songs, ballads, blues, anything."[7]

The non-blues repertoire of blues singers included many different types of songs. First and foremost among those were probably religious songs. Record companies were generally receptive to this portion of the blues singers' repertoire, and most of the major race-record blues artists recorded some religious songs: Willie McTell, Charley Patton, Robert Hicks, Lemon Jefferson, Memphis Minnie, and Bessie Smith, to name a few unlikely "gospel singers."

It must be remembered that, as Rosa Lee Hill said, gospel songs were sung because of the popular demand for them, and not necessarily out of any religious conviction. Son House made this point: "And me and Charley [Patton] and Willie [Brown], nary a one of us wasn't sanctified, but we's making out like it, you know to make the record ... So on the record people didn't know no better. They figured we's three sanctified guys. We wasn't nothing but ol' whiskey drinkers and blues players."[8]

Popular white songs also formed a large part of the blues singer's non-blues repertoire. When the musicians played before a white audience, it was necessary to know these songs:

Dewey Corley, who worked with both the Memphis Jug Band and the Beale Street Jug Band, recalls with amusement the "stag" parties at the Peabody

[Hotel]. They were patronized chiefly by businessmen, who left their wives at home. Everybody became very drunk and very generous; the tips over-ran the musicians' wages. The music most in demand at these parties was sentimental stuff and current popular hits, with occasional fast dance-numbers; and the jug bands could provide this sort of fare as efficiently as they could play the blues.[9]

Sam Chatmon had similar memories: "Now when we [Mississippi Sheiks] moved to the Delta in Hollandale here, in '28, we got to playin' up at Leroy Percy Park for the white folks all week. 'Eyes of Blue,' that's what we played for the white folks. 'Dinah,' that's an-other for the white folks. But we played blues for coloured."[10]

Supply and demand affected the eclectic repertoires of blues sing-ers, especially since they played for both black and white audiences as well as for different ethnic groups. But their repertoires were also shaped by their own aesthetics, which might take them far afield, not only from the blues but from other traditional forms of black music. Leonard Caston described part of his aesthetic: "Things like 'Dark Eyes' and Chopin 'Till the End of Time'; I mean I don't play it ex-actly as written but I have my own version on it. And 'Moonlight So-nata' and you know, those classical things that I do on piano."[11]

THE ECLECTICISM OF POPULAR SINGERS AND THE GENERAL PUBLIC

The eclecticism of blues singers is matched by that of other popular performers, whether bluegrass musicians, country singers, or rock performers. Elvis Presley's repertoire, for example, ranged from covers of African-American rhythm and blues songs to mainstream rock and roll to songs, such as "Love Me Tender" and "It's Now or Never," inspired by European classical traditions.

Perhaps one reason that the eclecticism of popular singers has been largely overlooked is that record companies tended to impose their own aesthetic, or their own sense of what the public wanted to hear, on the performer's aesthetic: "One seldom obtains documenta-tion of the full repertory of commercial folk artists, but it appears that most of them recorded commercially only a portion of their repertory. The same artists, when approached by field collectors, of-ten gave a different portion of their repertory."[12] Neil V. Rosenberg later pointed out that only when performers become celebrities can they impose their aesthetic on the record companies.[13] Radio sta-tions' practice of broadcasting only certain kinds of music has also had a stifling effect upon research into popular eclecticism.[14]

The eclecticism of North American popular performers reflects the general public's attitudes towards music. Perhaps only enthusiasts and academics are purists. Depending upon the context, almost any form of music may become popular with the public, which means that notions of élite music or class-based music are difficult to defend when discussing North American preferences. This is not to say that all forms of music are equally popular with all segments of the public; Arnold Schoenberg's twelve-tone compositions or Thelonious Monk's progressive jazz may well lie outside the range of preference for most people. Yet even avant-garde music may find public acceptance as movie or television theme music, or in combination with more readily accepted musical forms. Bluegrass music gained wider public acceptance through the television show *The Beverly Hillbillies* and the films *Bonnie and Clyde* and *Deliverance*; classical Indian music entered public awareness when it was used by the Beatles.[15]

That eclecticism is a by-product of neither commercial nor cosmopolitan environments is evident. As stated above, commercial record companies, as well as radio, television, and the other mass media, spend considerable energy trying to identify markets; their business is to categorize populations and types of music and then fit the proper music to the proper group of people. But the public taste as often as not defies their best efforts. After all, only a small percentage of recorded popular songs become hits.

While some might associate a catholic taste for popular music with an urban populace, the fact is that rural and even highly isolated North Americans exhibit an eclecticism in this regard. To go back to the example of black music, the blues and related forms are found in homes in communities far removed from the southern United States and the black communities of America's cities. For example, in 1975 I found a collection of blues and rhythm-and-blues records in a junk store in Halifax; the 250 or so 78 RPM recordings had obviously belonged to a single person. Perhaps the owner was a member of the black community in Halifax, which might partially explain how such a collection found its way so far from its "roots." In fact, race-record hits by the likes of Ma Rainey and Lemon Jefferson were sold by mail order as far north as Nova Scotia.[16] Perhaps this explains how a Lemon Jefferson recording turned up in St. John's, Newfoundland, where there is no black community; yet the fact that such a record surfaced at all seems an indication of a greater eclecticism in Newfoundland than one might imagine.[17]

Along the same lines, I witnessed an even clearer example of white rural eclecticism in Canada when visiting the small hamlet of

Lancer, Saskatchewan, in 1984. A community concert given as part
of the annual Chokecherry Festival featured a country and western
band from the region and a comedian whose persona might be
termed "native" to rural Saskatchewan. This concert, however, also
included the black American group, the Ink Spots. I noticed no
drop in the level of appreciation when this group came on stage; on
the contrary, the rural farmers and ranchers showed their knowledge of the Ink Spots repertoire by clapping after the first few bars
of the songs and even singing along on occasion.

The incursion of African-American popular music into Canada is
not surprising when one considers the great impact that black music
has had on all of North America. Black artists from Bert Williams to
Ethel Waters to Michael Jackson have gained a Canadian following,
but this would not have been possible without the willingness of the
Canadian public to expand their musical horizons.

Bluegrass, another phenomenon of the southern United States,
has also found its way into Canada. Just as this white American regional music has had less impact in the United States than the blues,
bluegrass has had a proportionately smaller impact in Canada – but
it has a following nevertheless.[18] Country and western, a related
form of music, has become one of the most popular American imports in Canada. Once again this popularity is not limited to urban
Canada or to those parts of the country bordering on the United
States; if anything, country and western music has gained its strongest foothold in rural Atlantic culture and in the prairie provinces.[19]
The acceptance of country and western music by Canadians has perhaps been more profound than their acceptance of blues or bluegrass, in that a home-grown country music industry has flourished
in Canada for many years. From at least the 1930s Canadian country
artists have reversed the "invasion" from the United States: the two
most prominent examples of this reverse flow are Hank Snow, born
in Nova Scotia, and Wilf Carter, a Nova Scotian who became an Alberta cowboy before starting his songwriting career.

The eclecticism of North Americans, Canadians included, goes
beyond blues, bluegrass, and country music. Such popular forms
may seem to be naturals in this regard, since all three stem from
home-grown North American traditions. Yet as we see from
Caston's statement quoted above, so-called classical European traditions should not be ignored in the overall study of North American
popular music.

Although it may seem to be a contradiction to call classical music
"popular," popularity lies more in the context, function, and meaning of a musical form than in its structure or history. European classical music may have originated as an aristocratic, élite tradition, but

in the New World it quickly became accessible to the masses. Many small towns in the United States and Canada boasted opera-houses, or at least church and community halls where travelling performers, including classical virtuosi, played before the public.[20]

One rural and small-town tradition that was especially instrumental in popularizing both exotic and classical music was the chautauqua, a travelling tent show that brought cultural events to the countryside. The chautauqua was well represented in Canada and undoubtedly gave scope to the eclectic tastes of Canadians:

The musical groups that travelled the Canadian circuits over the years were also many and varied. Among them were Negro quartettes; various Hawaiian groups; the Russian Cathedral Choir; the Plantation Singers; "The Kilties" and other Scottish groups; the Swiss Alpine Yodellers; a Schubert quartette from Toronto offering only the works of Franz Schubert; many different opera singers and concert soloists; the Elias Tamburitza Serenaders from Croatia in Jugoslavia; Italian tenor Umberto Serrentino and his Venetian Strollers; and the Toronto Operatic Artists with a program divided into three sections, "In the Drawing Room," "In the Chapel," and "In the Studio," with operatic music and song appropriate to each.[21]

Whether or not as a result of these organized performances, classical pieces turned up regularly in the Young Co-operators song columns in the *Western Producer* newspaper of Saskatchewan. These columns served as a clearinghouse for popular song among adolescents in the prairie provinces. Although most of the over 75,000 songs mentioned in the column between 1927 and 1975 are non-classical, the works of Beethoven, Chopin, Tchaikovsky, and Dvořák, among others, appeared with considerable regularity.[22] Indeed, many of the correspondents attributed their interest in classical music to local concerts and travelling musicians.

The popularity of classical European music has survived the demise of the chautauqua, as evidenced by Leonard Bernstein, the Boston Pops Orchestra, Liberace, and Victor Borge, all of whom have marketed their "élite" music to the masses. The same people who enjoy these modern "chautauquans" enjoy country, rock, and other less "classical" forms of music.

ECLECTICISM IN CANADIAN POPULAR MUSIC TRADITIONS

Examples of eclecticism in Canadian popular music traditions abound, at least at the general level of the community or region. Surveys of the eclectic nature of individuals, families, and communities are less common. Although scholars have conducted surveys of popular aesthetics in music, most of them concentrate on only one subgenre of popular music.[23] Surveys of the listening habits or record collections of Canadian individuals, however, tend to support my thesis of eclecticism. For example, E.A. Howes recalled the music preferences of his childhood home in rural nineteenth-century Ontario.[24] Traditional songs from the British Isles as well as North American logging ballads figured in Howes's description – "Kathleen Mavourneen," "Lord Thomas and Fair Eleanor," "The Banks of the Little Eau Pleine," "The Jam on Gerry's Rock." Songs from the American Civil War, such as "Marching Through Georgia" and "Bonnie Blue Flag," were popular, as were minstrel songs and sheet-music tunes such as "Ellie Rhee," "My Old Savannah Home," "Juanita," and "Silver Threads Among the Gold." While these may all seem to fall under the category of "old-timey" songs, such a designation represents a modern view rather than one contemporary with Howes's Ontario childhood. In fact, these songs cover a variety of nineteenth-century subgenres of popular music and show one Ontarian's eclecticism not only in types of song, but also in national and ethnic origins.

Lester Sellick's survey of his personal record, sheet music, and songbook collection offers a twentieth-century perspective on Canadian eclecticism. This Prince Edward Islander's recordings included private records made by members of his family as well as Don Messer, the Mamas and the Papas, Rosemary Clooney, Nana Mouskouri, Kenny Rogers, Guy Lombardo, Elvis Presley, the sound track to "My Fair Lady," Lawrence Welk, Wilf Carter, Harry Belafonte, the Wurzels, a bird-dance album, a polka album, Benny Goodman, Liberace, American square dances, Caribbean dance music, the Irish Rovers, and Herb Alpert, to list only a portion of his total collection. Among his sheet music was "Edelweiss," "Bali Ha'i," "How Great Thou Art," and "Who's Gonna Take You to the Prom?"; his songbooks included *Irish Songs, Irving Berlin's Best, Praise and Worship Hymns*, and *Popular Waltzes*.[25]

Among people whose musical tastes are dominated by eclecticism, syncretism becomes inevitable. In rather short order North Americans have blended the various musical traditions that surrounded them into new – or perhaps more accurately "New World" – forms. All African-American music is syncretistic, being a blend of African and European traditions, and the various subgenres of black music continue this syncretism by blending and reblending earlier forms. For example, rhythm and blues is a blend of blues and gospel, just as rock and roll is a blend of rhythm and blues and country and western (among other ingredients). That African-Americans sing Euro-American songs while whites sing African-American songs is syncretistic in itself.

CANADA'S SYNCRETISTIC MUSICAL TRADITIONS

It is partly though studying the phenomenon of syncretism that one might differentiate one musical region in North America from another. Although, as is made obvious by many of the examples given above, Canadian popular music is heavily influenced, perhaps even dominated, by American traditions, as a region of North America and as a culture in its own right Canada has produced its own syncretistic musical traditions. These forms of music distinguish Canada from the rest of the continent, since its regions have produced blends of music not found in the United States.

Perhaps the most dramatic example of Canadian "otherness" is the popular music of Quebec. The overlay of the French language on North American forms – for example, rock, country, and gospel – is syncretistic in itself, while the influence of music from France adds to the blend. Benoît L'Herbier has written that "Quebec songs had external sources which nourished the process for more than 300 years."[26] Quebec and Acadian popular music are in many ways more closely allied with Louisiana Cajun music than with the popular music of Ontario or the maritimes, yet Quebec music is not zydeco (the indigenous music of Louisiana Cajuns); its syncretism does not include the black and Latin influences that have shaped Cajun traditions.[27]

In English-speaking Canada as well there is strong regional syncretism, and it is hardly a recent phenomenon. For example, Ronald Caplan's study of a turn-of-the-century Cape Breton obituary verse writer discovered a mixture of Gaelic laments, New England Puritan traditions, ballads from the logging-camps, and literary poetic forms, all of which explain the particular style of the songwriter, Andrew Dunphy.[28] Despite the seeming isolation of northern Cape Breton in 1900, there was nothing "pure" or homogeneous about the music found there.

As a modern example, Newfoundland popular music is anything but pure. I have described elsewhere the blend of styles and materials in which Irish and country and western music are combined with traditional Newfoundland music that accounts for the Newfoundland "sound."[29] Newfoundlanders have especially taken to country music, blending it with traditional musical styles to create a fusion as distinctive to that island as western swing is to the southwestern United States.[30] Newfoundland popular performers, like the blues singers discussed above, recognize the eclectic and syncretistic nature of their audience's taste by being prepared to offer a large variety of musical forms when performing. At a club or dance the artist may have to perform everything from traditional Anglo-Irish music to current rock and country hits to calypso and reggae in order to please all members of his or her audience.[31] To be successful, the Newfoundland composer or recording artist must discover the most appealing mixture of musical traditions for island audiences.[32]

Similarly, Canadian ethnic and immigrant artists must confront a situation in which their audiences are moving away from old European musical forms and towards New World traditions. This phenomenon demands, once again, a syncretistic approach, as Robert Klymasz points out with respect to popular Ukrainian-Canadian music; "sounds you never heard before" is an apt description not only of the music Klymasz has in mind, but of much ethnic and regional popular music in Canada.[33] The Canadian group the Romaniacs, while making fun of various eastern European ethnic traditions, nevertheless demonstrates only the most recent trend in a syncretistic movement that might be called "ethnic fusion."

Taken as a whole, Canadian and American popular music form a single New World phenomenon in which European barriers to syncretism in music have crumbled. Perhaps because of the democratic tradition of these two countries, where movement between socioeconomic class is always a possibility and where strict caste systems are virtually non-existent, different kinds of music no longer have rigid associations with one group or another.[34] Classical music is no longer the preserve of the aristocracy or the wealthy; black or white music is no longer racially distinct; ethnic music is no longer in the sole possession of its originators. Syncretisms, in Herbert Halpert's words, "generated their own dynamics."[35]

Yet, as demonstrated above, North Americans are not uniform in the way they mix their music. Syncretism allows for musically distinct regions of the continent, including many areas that are purely Canadian in their regional nature. Taken together, these Canadian regional syncretisms define the national "popular music," although one could as easily divide the continent into musical regions which have nothing to do with geopolitical boundaries: New England-Maritime-Newfoundland syncretisms, Prairie-Plains syncretisms, Arctic syncretisms, or Pacific Northwest syncretisms, to name four possibilities.

Further complicating the musical map of North America are regional preferences for different kinds of music. Although syncretism is a mark of such music, the public is certainly aware of the various forms of music available to it. Yet when forming their aesthetics, not all people in Canada and the United States choose all forms of music in the same proportions. For example, most regions, and even many small communities, have a collective repertoire of purely local songs composed in a specific area, which have special meaning to members of that community, which may actually define that community, or which act as anthems for its members.[36] Sheldon Posen's recent study of the function of *The Chapeau Boys*, a locally composed logger's song, as the anthem of Chapeau, Quebec, shows how a community's repertoire of song can include items that would be foreign to most other parts of North America.[37]

REGIONAL PREFERENCES IN MUSIC

The larger question of preference concerns the particular proportions of one or more types of song, singer, style, or performance that mark one region off from the next. Do all communities in North America choose the same proportion of country, rock, jazz, classical, and other forms of music in arriving at their own eclectic repertoires? Clearly not.

Evidence from the song columns of the *Western Producer* demonstrates the effect of preference on repertoire, as the following example should make clear.[38] The popularity of Bob Dylan between the years 1965 and 1975 was continent-wide at the very least. One writer's contention that Dylan "probably has the title of most influential pop songwriter of the 20th century locked up" may be an exaggeration, but he certainly is one of those American celebrities known even by those who have no interest in folk revival or rock music.[39]

No doubt adolescents in the prairie provinces were as aware of Dylan's music (and personality) as any other North American group. Yet despite airplay on radio stations and mass media publicity, Dylan's songs were relatively rarely requested or discussed in the pages of the *Western Producer*. In all, Dylan's songs were mention 37 times, with 26 of those concerning Peter, Paul and Mary's version of "Blowing in the Wind;" "Mr. Tambourine Man" was mentioned 4 times; "It Ain't Me, Babe," twice; and each of "All I Really Want to Do," "Don't Think Twice," "Knocking on Heaven's Door," "Lay Lady Lay," and "Positively Fourth Street" was mentioned once.

In comparison, "Georgy Girl" by the Seekers received 92 mentions; Petula Clark's "Downtown" 89 mentions; and "Last Kiss" by

J. Frank Wilson and the Cavaliers 83 mentions. Barry Sadler's "Ballad of the Green Berets" received as many mentions as Dylan's "Blowing in the Wind." Judging by these statistics, prairie adolescents preferred many other performers over Dylan. If such a study were done of east coast u.s. adolescents from the same period, Dylan's songs undoubteadly would be more prominent. The point is that while there is a large pool of popular songs and singers available to North Americans, different groups around the continent choose different subsets from the pool; thus, a specific region or group might be identified by the subset it has chosen.

A similar subset of popular music might be seen in the preference of prairie adolescents in the 1930s for songs specifically related to cowboys and farming, or their preference for topical ballads dealing with Canadian events over American events. For example, "Rescue from the Moose River Gold Mine" was more popular than "Marian Parker." The point is that preference, like syncretism, is a marker of regionalism in popular music.

In this respect, does Canada as a whole represent a region? Do Canadians adopt syncretisms and preferences differently from Americans? One would be hard-pressed to find such a strict dividing line between the two countries. The so-called vertical mosaic of Canadian multiculturalism, as opposed to the melting-pot of the United States, might result in a more pronounced syncretism between Old World and New World musical forms in Canada, but such a conclusion probably works better in the abstract than it does in reality. Despite the pressures for acculturation in the United States, there is a plenitude of fusion music in that country which rivals Canada's ethnic syncretisms.

Canada's identity is tied to regionalism and to group allegiances. As Martin Laba, among many others, has observed, "a singular and impelling concept of a Canadian cultural heritage is historically groundless, and therefore an elusive objective in the many and varied searches for a Canadian sense of nation."[40] A distinct Canadian popular music is also "historically groundless" and the search for such a phenomenon would be frustrating indeed. Just as popular music is "consumed at comparable rate by all social classes," it also diffuses with the utmost ease across national borders.[41] The call, rather, is to study more extensively and carefully the way different groups in Canada – whether regional, ethnic, occupational, or generational – demonstrate their eclecticism, syncretism, and preference for popular music.

12 Our House, Their House: Canadian Cinema's Coming of Age

SETH FELDMAN

Any discussion of American popular culture in Canada is, I believe, in danger of inspiring a spirited round of one-upmanship as scholars compete for the distinction of representing the field most co-opted by the Yankee nemesis. Let me, then, as a student of cinema, stake my ground. Among the popular arts, film is certainly situated in the avant garde of cultural assimilation. It is not just that cinema in Canada has always meant Hollywood cinema; but film, like television, is distinguished by the fact that Canadians not only watch but actually make the American product. We do so literally in productions that highlight American talent and disguise Canada as Anytown, U.S.A. But even in more ostensibly Canadian productions, we do so by subscribing to organizational and artistic practices that work to further secure the definition of the medium as quintessentially American. In both cases we pay dearly for the privilege.

I have a twofold purpose: to examine the history and stylistics of Canadian cinema's cultural surrender and to consider how we might begin to reverse that process. A particularly apt entrée into those subjects is Sandy Wilson's 1985 film *My American Cousin*. I would like to read that film as a useful metaphor for the Canadian ambiguity towards the American presence as a whole and the manner in which that ambiguity expresses itself in cinema. I would also like to view *My American Cousin* in the context of R. Bruce Elder's 1985 manifesto, "The Cinema We Need."[1]

THE OEDIPAL ORCHARD

My American Cousin is centred on Sandy, who as we shall see is a crucial autobiographical reference to the film's director. Its action takes place in the 1950s, when its pre-adolescent protagonist finds herself growing up in the idyllic world of a British Columbia cherry orchard. One night she and her family are paid a surprise visit by her California cousin Butch, a self-styled James Dean lookalike, complete with red Cadillac. The visitor, his music, and his libido quickly upset the tranquillity of the Okanagan Valley. Temptation in the form of indiscreet foreplay and other immoderate behavior rears its ugly head. In the end, though, the threat to the status quo is removed. The secretion of unmentionable hormones diminishes, and all concerned are given one more crack at remaining in the garden.

As even this bare summation of the film indicates, we have here a plot that is rich in subtextual potential. In its setting in the 1950s, for instance, one may detect a complex interplay between a dying British colonial venture and a new American cultural imperialism that has come to replace it. Sandy's father, the owner of the cherry farm, is a retired English officer known throughout the film only as "The Major." While far from being a Colonel Blimp – he is, for instance, still able to assert his military bearing in breaking up bouts of teenage hooliganism – The Major is clearly on the way out. He is tongue-tied when it comes to explaining the facts of sexual life to his newly eroticized daughter, and the prompting of that eroticism is beyond his understanding. More important, though, The Major's cultural milieu, the retirement into landed aristocracy that has shaped English Canada since the Loyalists' arrival, is failing. At the beginning of the film we learn that the financial affairs of the cherry farm are a mess; at the end we are told by the final voice-over that this way of life is a fading dream.

Conversely, the American invasion, which *My American Cousin* depicts as failing, will in the time beyond the film come to replace The Major's world. Indeed, the film owes its quaintness to the fact that its milieu was so decisively smashed. How odd to remember that rock and roll was once available on radio for only a few hours per week and that teenage dances were held in the park bandshell under watchful adult eyes. Odder still is the rustic ideal of the large farm family able to offer an alternative to international culture. But the strangest thought of all is the possibility of cultural isolation, the hubris of believing that any living arrangement could be safe from the onslaught of international culture.

But *My American Cousin* does more than document the substitution of American Canada for British Canada. It also offers a hint about the importance of that process by paralleling it with Sandy's Oedipal struggle. To replace that which is familiar but untenable with that which is alluring and foreign describes both the national and sexual shift.[2] The parallel, like the irony inherent in the film's depiction of victory for The Major's world, also works to mitigate the importance of what we see in the plot. Sandy is disillusioned by the American dream. Yet, as her mother assures her, "Boys are like streetcars; if you miss one, another will come along."

Beyond these understandings of *My American Cousin* is another reading that speaks more directly to our current experience of Canadian nationalism, one that faces the American reality from a mature perspective. That reading comes from the film's rendering of a moment common to most English Canadians, and indeed to most people who grew up outside the borders of the United States. As heartfelt as rock and roll, as deeply repressed as the film's Oedipal encounters, is the trauma of the non-American's realization that he or she is living in the wrong country. The teenage parlance of the 1950s might answer Northrop Frye's inquiry by declaring that "here" is "like nowhere." As all Canadian teenagers know, they are living in the dullest space imaginable. Their only hope is a pilgrimage to virtually anywhere else. And that anywhere else, packaged for facile consumption, is the ubiquitous America.

Not being born in the U.S.A. (a U.S.A. which, as the Springstein song implies, may be as elusive to Americans as it is to foreigners) has thus ensured the predominance of American youth culture in Canada since the Second World War. The effect has been to make us all strangers in our own homes. The teenage rebellion – the first assertion of an adult self – is a pledge of allegiance to American style. Conversely, what keeps us from that American culture is seen as a betrayal of our own adult potential.

My American Cousin is in this regard not so much a youth film as an adult's examination of youth. It wisely defines the adolescent as an American invention that has itself institutionalized the values of American frontier society. Highly individualistic behaviour, unmitigated aggression, and the assertion of a personal right of pre-eminent domain are rewarded by the Americans with the blessing of eternal youth. Of course, eternal youth may limit one's potential to grow beyond the formative years. As we foreigners mature to that realization, we may choose to trade in the self-image of the American adolescent for the self-image of a mature society. But that adult striving never quite cleanses us. The violence of Americans, their phallocentric sexuality, their social injustice, and their militarism are merely pushed to the back of our psychic closet. While our public policy may be able to refrain from the American infatuation with firearms or active persecution of the poor, we do not definitively disassociate ourselves from those impulses. Inevitably, decisions alien to our adult sensibility and way of life mysteriously surface among us.

CANADIAN CINEMA

At this point we might take a detour from this one Canadian film through the evolution of Canadian film per se. For nowhere is the struggle between the adolescent infatuation with American expression and the maturing away from that expression more apparent than in the history and practice of Canadian cinema. For almost a century the very existence of that cinema has waxed and waned around the question of whether or not the medium can be anything other than the embodiment of that eternal American adolescence. The attraction of transforming ourselves into Hollywood North is countered by a repulsion that sees the entire enterprise as just a little bit childish. Hence, the hard decisions become harder. More than one Canadian policy-maker has had to balance the importance of an art form we may not really want against the Americans' determination to maintain an open market for their most consistently successful export. Every Canadian buying a movie ticket weighs (if briefly) the guilt of supporting this alien and slightly demeaning expression against the bother of dealing with the "foreign art house" films made here. And every would-be Canadian filmmaker has had to see cinema either as the solution to being born on the wrong side of the border or as the problem of achieving self-expression without physically or spiritually leaving home.

Can Canadian filmmaking be anything other than commerce with this American regression? Even the Americans, who from the beginning have pulled the financial strings in production and distribution, have been of two minds on the issue. Speaking in Toronto in 1925, D.W. Griffith, the founding genius of American narrative cinema, declared: "You in Canada should not be dependent on either the United States or Great Britain. You should have your own films and exchange them with those of other countries. You can make them just as well in Toronto as in New York."[3] Unfortunately, Lewis Selznick, one of the geniuses of the American film business, reflected a more typical attitude. Three years before Griffith spoke, Selznick said, "If Canadian stories are worthwhile making into films, companies will be sent into Canada to make them."[4]

And so they were. Before 1960 the cinematic image of Canada was almost entirely determined by its integration into Hollywood films and the industry that produced them. Indigenous feature filmmaking in English Canada repeatedly failed, owing to American ownership of theatre chains. "The movies," from the post-First World War period on, came to be defined as the Hollywood hits produced by the theatre chains' parent companies. Recurrent bursts of nationalism fell flat in the face of this hegemony. *Carry On, Sergeant*, an epic insistence on the importance of the Canadian contribution in the First World War, was funded by Canada's most respected citizens. Nevertheless, it was effectively blocked from Canadian screens. A similar burst of patriotic enthusiasm after the Second World War was cut short by the infamous Canadian Co-operation Project. In that deal, Hollywood was assured that the federal government would do nothing to encourage feature film production or discourage American control of movie theatres. In exchange, Hollywood produced a few Canadian travelogues and promised to insert references to Canada in feature film scripts.

There were only two exceptions to this generally dismal picture. The first was cinema in Quebec. A small number of Quebec feature films succeeded in the 1940s and early 1950s by exploiting familiar literary and theatrical sources.[5] Although the re-emergence of the French film industry and the Canadian Co-operation Project ended that wave of production, the interest in feature filmmaking was sustained until the early 1960s, when the technological possibilities of making films in the manner of the French New Wave (low-budget films made on 16-millimetre equipment) inspired a generation of talented individuals whose work continues to this day.

The second exception to American rule was the National Film Board. Founded in 1939 by the British theorist and producer of documentary film John Grierson, the NFB balanced American domination with an aggressive promulgation of a British imperial practice. Grierson imported (in addition to a good deal of British and American talent) the heavy-handed voice-of-God narration, a style well suited to declaiming and often distorting the meaning of each shot.

Grierson's voice-of-God was a manifestation of British documentary films' larger role. The propagandistic "pulpit" of Griersonian documentaries had as its mission the teaching of a fixed notion of geopolitics to an increasingly post-literate world. As imposed on Canada, this mission and its cinematic style represented the technological equivalent of the mother country's asserting its right to name that which it "discovered." What was seen was labelled and, moreover, labelled within a closed, pre-established ideology. This was literally true of the style of the films produced at the NFB during the Second World War. As Ernst Borneman, one of the editors at the wartime board, remembered it,

Since visual, music and effects tracks were running side by side in a highly complex three-part counterpoint, and since the visual by itself constantly skipped from place to place all over the globe, it became doubly important for the commentary to draw the other two tracks and the visual together into a single continuity and this had to be done in such a manner as to make its points through the spectator's subconscious as well as through his conscious. Aside from active verbs and pseudo-quotations ("The experts say that ...") the most important innovation here was the use of metaphors and similes created by a juxtaposition of an incidental aspect of the visual and an incidental aspect of the commentary in such a way that they became meaningfully, though to the spectator imperceptibly, welded together.[6]

Borneman went on to provide examples in which, generally, the object photographed loses its literal identity in favour of a metaphorical meaning conducive to the message of the film (for example, the San Francisco skyline became "a new horizon").

In the late 1940s, with the coming to power of the first generation of Canadians at the board, the authoritarian voice-over documentary gave way to experiments with less assertive and less definitive meaning. Its best work before the early 1960s (including its seminal contributions to the invention of cinema verité) represented a calculated dismembering of the imperial voice in favour of a self-generated and necessarily ambiguous definition of the image. Best exemplified in the work of the board's "Unit B" group, the most important films in this mode included *Paul Tomkowicz: Street Railway Switchman* (Roman Kroiter, 1954), *City of Gold* (Wolf Koenig and Colin Low, 1957), *The Days Before Christmas* (Terrence Macartney-Filgate and Wolf Koenig, 1958), *Back Breaking Leaf* (Terrence Macartney-Filgate, 1959), *Universe* (Roman Kroiter and Colin Low, 1960), and *Lonely Boy* (Roman Kroiter and Wolf Koenig, 1962). All these works insisted upon the vulnerability of cinematic perception and, cumulatively, drew a portrait of the world as open text, free of any geopolitical preconception.

There are two significant and related interpretations of this extremely creative period in the NFB's history. The first, put forth by Peter Harcourt, suggests that Unit B's work was characterized by a meditative open-endedness, a challenge to the codes of cinema itself: "There is something very Canadian in all this, something which my own Canadianness prompts me to attempt to define. There is in all these films a quality of suspended judgement, of something left open at the end, of something undecided ... There is something rather detached from the immediate pressures of existence, something rather apart."[7] Harcourt viewed this aspect of the Unit B documentaries as spilling over into the work of the post-1960 English-Canadian feature filmmakers.[8]

The second interpretation of Unit B's films defined them in terms of an emerging post-colonial experience. In his critique of the Candid Eye movement (an aspect of the Unit B work), R. Bruce Elder defined this post-colonialism as very much a two-edged sword. He admired the style of the films, but he despaired of their endless entrapment in Frantz Fanon's second stage of post-colonial development: "Fanon states that this phase is characterized by an ironic sort of humour. This sense of irony arises from the dialectic inherent in the position of the artist at this stage of development: on the one hand, he is committed to a national culture, while on the other, he views the national culture from a detached, external and hence often amused point of view."[9]

The NFB may be fairly accused, to borrow Neil Postman's otherwise unrelated phrase, of "amusing itself to death" over the last quarter-century. At very least it has stopped well short of Fanon's third stage of post-colonial development, the "fighting phase." Instead it has worked all too hard at an ironic deconstruction of perception, an avoidance of a stance. One of its most highly regarded directors, Michael Rubbo, before his 1985 retirement from the Board, made a career of sorts out of films that focused on his ability (or inability) to respond to the subject or even to complete the film. Elsewhere at the board, films that Jay Scott has labelled "learn along" documentaries have often left us with a director somewhat less perceptive than the ordinary viewer forced to make sense of his or her garbled material.

The NFB's second failure has been its inability to build any kind of bridge between English-Canadian and Quebecois cinema. The wartime board showed little interest in developing the talents of people whose support of the war effort was less than total. That suspicion seems to have continued in the post-war years, years marked by precious few Quebecois productions. It was only with the NFB's own version of the early 1960s Quiet Revolution that a French unit was established. It has since, with some justification, guarded its independence from (and often its hostility to) the priorities and style of

English-Canadian production. If anything, the Quebecois experience at the board has reinforced the concept of cultural separatism, blazing a path through bureaucracy to a curious form of sovereignty-association.

If the NFB has done little to reverse the establishment of two cinematic solitudes in Canada, it has been even less effective in addressing the problematic role of narrative filmmaking. Although its directors showed an interest in narrative virtually from the beginning of the Board's existence, the best of its features – such as *Nobody Waved Goodbye* (Don Owen, 1964), *The Best Damned Fiddler from Calabogie to Kaladar* (Peter Pearson, 1968) – have been made in an uphill battle against shortsighted administrators.[10] Its single greatest work, *Mon Oncle Antoine* (Claude Jutra, 1970), was eventually leased to private concerns because of the legendary incompetence of the board's distribution arm. The big-budget, officially sanctioned features – such as *Running Time* (Mort Ransen, 1974) and *The Wars* (Robin Phillips, 1984) – have fallen flat. The board's current freewheeling Alternative Drama Program has produced documentary – drama hybrids that can be either uniquely whimsical – such as *Ninety Days* (Giles Walker, 1985), *Sitting in Limbo* (John Smith, 1986), *Company of Strangers* (Cynthia Scott, 1990)- or unbelievably vacuous – such as Walker's *The Last Straw* (1987).

PRIVATE PRACTICE

Those in the Canadian feature industry with brains and drive saw very early that their work could be best done somewhere other than the NFB. Let me qualify the phrase "brains and drive." Since 1960 the emergence of a private Canadian feature film industry has merely succeeded in raising the original American question to more expensive heights. Inspired by the success of a number of very low-budget productions, the time was judged ripe in 1966 for the creation of the Canadian Film Development Corporation (now Telefilm Canada) and a number of on-again, off-again tax incentives. The immediate result was new wealth for producers and tax lawyers and some very unpleasant surprises for first-time investors. Most of the features actually produced mimicked American genre film, usually without the talent that made those films viewable.

Several billion dollars later, Canada has created a filmmaking infrastructure: a stockpile of talented individuals and sophisticated facilities that, barring major disincentives (such as an 85-cent dollar), will continue to make American films and television programs in Canada. The curve is almost perfect: the more "international" the story, the easier it is to finance. American talent is smuggled on-screen in package deals that play with the letter of Canadian content provisions while stomping on their spirit. As always, the high profile talents continue to declare film an "international" medium and head south.

Like any good infrastructure, the Canadian film establishment contains some useful loopholes. The arts councils, some government agencies, and occasionally the industry itself will conspire to make low-budget, non-American, even non-narrative productions. Nationalism is, after all, regarded as a sort of tax on real life. As a result, for the Canadian filmmaker interested in making Canadian films, the situation is somewhat more hopeful than it was twenty-five years ago. Nobody can make a living at it, but their films do get shown at festivals, at odd hours on television, and for short theatrical runs in major cities.

The private Canadian filmmaker may be smarter and more productive than his or her colleague at the NFB, but he or she still operates within the context of that grand adolescent fantasy south of the border. From the first post-1960 features, English-Canadian narrative cinema was full of failed adults clinging, along with the sympathetic filmmakers, to some long-lost adolescent realm. As Robert Fothergill documented so thoroughly during the heyday of the "loser" films, these are flawed visions of maturity created by people who are not ready to accept the adult world. In the title of his article, Fothergill succinctly described the protagonists of films like *Paperback Hero* (Peter Pearson, 1973), *The Rowdyman* (Peter Carter, 1972), and *The Hard Part Begins* (Paul Lynch, 1973), as living "The Dream Life of a Younger Brother."[11]

That dream of course, continues to exist, and it is not dreamt only by younger brothers. Its feminization in Patricia Rozema's *I've Heard the Mermaids Singing* retains, more than anything else, the original fear that underlay all that cuteness. Polly, the impossible flake, forecloses the option of professional commitment by working in an art gallery milieu that she and the film conspire to decry as trivial. Her creative work is variously depicted as being either ingenuous or derivative, to the point where the distinction is posited as irrelevant. And Polly's attempt to establish a meaningful friendship is immediately answered with the threat of her friend's lesbian orientation and commitment to another woman.

To her credit, Rozema makes a stab at resolution. The film ends with the adult world's recognizing, and perhaps even valuing, Polly's fear. But it does not end with the kind of narrative closure inherent in the dream life of that adult world. And this too is characteristic of the adolescent escape of English Canadian cinema. The films, like their characters, are designed in a proto-style. The common complaint about English-Canadian films – that so little happens in them – is justified. And that is not just the result of low budgets or a shortage of stuntmen. Rather, it is the adolescent's fear of closure translated into a fear of the finality of narrative. With good reason, English-Canadian cinema is not ready for the assertion of a mature responsibility that comes with the closing of a text. Given Hollywood's hegemony over cinematic narrative, that closure belongs to someone else.

If there is a positive aspect to this, it is the growing awareness that there are alternatives to making the perfectly mimicked American film, the petulant rebellion against that film, or the fear-ridden meandering of an outsider looking in. One such alternative has been proposed by R. Bruce Elder, English Canada's most prolific and vocal experimental filmmaker, in a much discussed manifesto. "The Cinema We Need" condemns narrative film per se as the manifestation of a broader acceptance of technological causality. The structure of American narrative cinema, from corporate producers to the design of a film's shooting and editing, mirrors the values of a culture that habitually narrows its options to meet the dictates of predetermined ends. Certainty becomes the essential value. For narrative cinema, it is the certainty that we are seeing only what we must see at any given instant, that the image we see is entirely relevant to the end towards which we are hurtling, and that the manner in which we present the image points to a single inflexible reading.

There is little doubt that Elder is right in this regard. Certainly the teaching of American narrative cinema in Canadian film schools bears him out. The cumulative lesson of courses in production planning, writing, and shooting is a certain kind of rhetoric, an intuitive bias or what might be called an aesthetic of ellipsis. For American narrative films are made up of what is not there. The history of the development of Hollywood narrative is a history of refining the codification of imagery to eliminate ambiguity. This shorthand permits a character to go cross-country in a single cut, age twenty years in a matter of seconds, or indicate a complex understanding with a glance. D.W. Griffith, his few predecessors, and his many descendants built express trains that travelled in a straight line at breakneck speed – yet gave the illusion of exploring the landscape on either side of the track.

For Elder, the way out is a recognition that Canada need not accept the teleological bias of the American use of technology. Citing Canadians such as Harold Innis, Marshall McLuhan, and George

Grant as humanist alternatives to technological determinism, Elder argues that we deserve better: "The makers of the cinema we need will be those who have the strength to abide with doubt and uncertainty and still open themselves up to unfolding situations, allow themselves even to be remade by experiences the destiny of which they cannot foresee. It is only through this process that truth will arrive."[12]

What Elder proposes, of course, entails a broad re-education of our filmmakers and, over a much longer period, of the culture they serve. The ideal of "Hollywood North," the justification of cinema art as a "cultural industry," even the romantic notion of sturdy independents telling their stories against all odds – all of these clichés are exchanged for a complete reconceptualization of the function of the moving image. That function would be something like a reminder of alternatives, an attack on closure that would, unlike the NFB's simple surrender of responsibility, entail the multifaceted pursuit of an adult perspective.

Elder's remedy may or may not be realistic or even desirable. But "The Cinema We Need" has served to shift the debate from its original Griffith – Selznick dichotomy. The question now is not so much who shall tell Canada's story as it is whether Canada's story is a story at all.

It is in this context that I would like to return at last to *My American Cousin*. For Elder, who is suspicious of any narrative intent, the film is seen as one more manifestation of the American problem. Perhaps he is right. Yet I would argue that there is a step forward that is worth appreciating. For I believe that beyond the interpretations discussed at the beginning of this essay, we may come to find yet another sense to the film. I would like to challenge the dynamic that propelled us through those previous readings: the surface allure of the American dream. I think it is possible to say that the core fantasy of *My American Cousin* is not that of becoming a libidinally released American. Neither is it only the dream of a return to the garden. Instead, the film succeeds by offering an even more attractive fantasy: that of the American's leaving and taking his culture with him. He leaves behind the possibility of making a small and gentle film. Gone are the fast cars, fights, rock and roll, and the imminence of sex. Gone too is the teenage exploitation film. The image of the superkid, a tower of strength in a corrupt universe – went home to James-Dean-land.[13] The Canadian kids go home to mom, dad, and a cherry orchard.

And it is only *a* cherry orchard, not *The Cherry Orchard*. For beneath the core fantasy is an awful and subversive secret: this is really an autobiographical work about a person with no particular claim to our attention. It is shaped by ordinary things that just happen to have happened. As Sandy Wilson describes the making of the film: "The film is autobiographical. I have recreated my family. The film is shot in the house that I grew up in. That was bizarre. It is strange to have one foot in the past and the other in the bizarre reality that is filmmaking. Real life keeps me grounded but I did forget sometimes in my reverie to yell 'cut.'"[14]

Perhaps the most bizarre aspect of the film, though, is that it has been made before. In 1977 Wilson had re-edited her family's home movies into an even more humble film, a film brazenly-entitled *Growing Up in Paradise*. That film introduced the young Sandy, the cherry orchard, The Major, the entire cast of characters, and even the look of *My American Cousin*. Her handicapped brother is the subject of another film, *He Is Not the Walking Kind* (1971). Like the cherry orchard, his handicap serves as a non-allegorical, pre-textual reference.

From one perspective it might be possible to argue that Wilson's documentary background is a continuation of the NFB's documentary tradition. Like the best of the Unit B directors, Wilson is defining herself against the stylistic demands of an imperial voice, a voice that might demand a less subjective, less involved approach to the subject. She differs from the NFB directors, however, through the assertion of a completed self in what she defines as a self-contained and entirely comprehensible world. The documentaries exclude that critical distance that allows them to be either open-ended or ironic. If not bellicose in the sense of Frantz Fanon's "fighting phase," Wilson's personal documentaries demonstrate a culture that will take for granted its right to be heard.

The second difference between Wilson and the NFB documentarian is her ability to work her experience directly into drama. The actual form in which she works matures. Yet through that maturity Wilson maintains a primacy of the pre-textual world, arguing for the importance of the event over the dictates of narrative structure. This is no small transgression when seen in reference to the theoretical underpinnings of her cousin's cinema. For in its presentation of the narrative express train, American cinema offers not just the picture of the perfect adolescent but the adolescent's vision of the perfect adult. He or she (but usually he) is not only strong, graceful, funny, inventive, and sexually victorious but, most important, is in all things seamlessly lucid. And it is to this lucidity, not to some happy accident of the proto-cinematic world, that the American filmmaker owes allegiance.

Wilson, by contrast, explores the landscape while giving the illusion of being on the express train. She makes a film by providing what was there, very much in its own terms. There are many ways of crediting this impulse. As a woman, Wilson has produced a work that values emotional subjectivity over the patriarchal bias for abstract goals and tasks. As a westerner, she displays a sensitivity to nature as a determining factor in characterization and plot development; the beauty of "paradise" overwhelms the human constructs within it. But I suggest that more than anything else *My American Cousin* is a film by an adult whose dream life is framed with the assurance that it was a dream, a set of endlessly intriguing images studied by someone who has survived them. And that study is itself part of our long-lost coming of age.

13 Wives, Whores, and Priests: Gender Relations and Narrative Voices in Two Quebecois Traditions

CHARLINE POIRIER

In 1988 Chantal Hébert suggested one sociological difference between the way burlesque is performed in the United States and the way it is performed in Quebec: "In the U.S., the audience was almost exclusively male ... whereas the audience in Quebec consisted mainly of women. The Quebec texts are also longer ... and put a larger number of actors on stage, and these are mostly women."[1] This characterization is no doubt correct. However, the distinct voices in which the burlesque story is told in each country appear to be more important and consequential to the performances than a merely sociological variation. Indeed, this difference between actors and audience engenders essential formal distinctions between the two traditions of burlesque. It is a form of theatre in which "the art of improvisation plays a key role."[2] Consequently, the actors are the ones who write the text as they act. Quebecois and American actors differ by their sex. This difference, I suggest, is responsible for some of the variations noted by Hébert in the performance of burlesque in Quebec and in the United States.

STORY LINES IN BURLESQUE

Because burlesque is an improvised genre, only the story lines exist for our examination. This is theoretically important: one is reminded of the distinction made by the Russian formalists between story and plot: "the fable (story) is what really happened; the subject (plot) is the manner in which the reader has been informed of what has happened."[3] The absence of written records of performance limits our understanding of the genre. Indeed, a story line offers very little information, and analysis on its basis alone has at least two main shortcomings.

First, identical story lines are found across genres. We have seen, for instance, identical story lines contained in a poem and in a lengthy novel or in a film. And even though one might recognize the similarity of the story lines, one could hardly, on this basis, say anything more about the genres. An extensive literature in folklore studies deals with the problem of identifying and classifying genres.[4] This literature has illuminated the complexity of oral materials. For example, a folklorist reports that in a small fishing community she found a story that half of the community performs in the form of a legend, while the other half executes it as a joke.

Second, the same story and the same plot can carry different meanings as their context of performance changes. A striking example of this phenomenon can be found in Alan Dundes's study of the "wide-mouth frog" joke.[5] Analysing the joke performed in an American context, Dundes shows that this joke is a satire on the anatomy of African Americans. In Quebec, where the joke was also popular at one time, its meaning differs: there it carries a sexual meaning, since the "black reality" is not a social concern in Quebec.

With these limitations in mind, let us consider two general story lines, one found in burlesque performances in Quebec and the other in the United States: "The Québec hero courts a woman in view of marrying her, and her money is of some importance to him; the woman is a 'paying proposition' for the man. Quite to the contrary, the American protagonist courts the woman for the pleasure that she can give him: here, it's the man that becomes the paying proposition."[6]

The limitations generated by the absence of text leaves the analyst little latitude to contrast and compare the two corpuses. Basically, we possess four variables: (1) male character; (2) female character; (3) money; and (4) matrimony or sex. There are two groups of improvising performers, one composed mostly of women and the other composed mostly of men. The relationships between the elements are structurally very different.[7]

The elements, as we will see, are ordered as follows: the tension generator in the Quebecois corpus is matrimony, and the female character becomes the central character; in the u.s. corpus, the tension centres on one's getting sexual favours from someone other than one's wife, and the male character is the central character. One commonality exists in both corpuses: the place and role of money in the narrative dynamics. This common position helps us to contrast the relative position of the other characters. However, though a comparison will highlight some basic differences in the two performances, it will not explain why these performances differ and what causes the differences.

Working with the assumption that the identification of a stereotypical character, as it is presented in oral materials, depends on a recurrence of and stability in its environmental circumstances, we can assume that an intertextual examination of circumstances surrounding characters in other narrative contexts performed orally and traditionally will reveal the tacit knowledge and understanding of characters shared by a narrator and an audience. The stereotypical characteristics of weakly defined characters (as they exist in oral performance) are expected to prevail across genres within the boundaries of popular culture. As Vladimir Propp and others have observed, in popular culture characters remain vague and interchangeable within the boundaries of their stereotypes. The context that determines the characters' identity will proportionately increase the importance of the circumstances and accentuate their rigidity.

On the basis of this assumption, I will demonstrate not only how male and female narrative voices strongly agree over characters' stereotypes, but also how they disagree as to the dynamic tensions between the motifs – that is, how they differ in their thematic interest. This intertextual analysis of voices, I will suggest, explains the differences in story lines between Quebec and u.s. burlesque.

If we place the narrative elements of the two story lines according to their logical relations, we find different patterns, since the value of the elements varies depending on the characters involved.[8] In Quebec, if we look at the woman as the main character, we find that the desired end is "matrimony" and the means to this end is "money." The logical relation of means and ends is as follows:

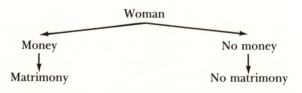

When a woman possesses a certain amount of money, the male character will want to marry her to get her money. Thus, although the woman desires matrimony, she will not be noticed if she has no money. In the case of the male character who desires money and has

to use marriage as his means, the logical relations in the story line
are as follows:

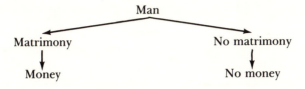

To compare this structure with that represented in the American
corpus, we first have to replace the element "marriage" with the element "sex." For the male character, the desired end is to have a sexual encounter with a woman. His means is "money":

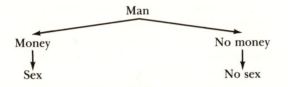

For his female counterpart, the situation is again reversed. She
wants "money" and to get it, she will agree to "sex":

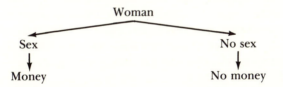

The common denominator between the Quebec and American corpus is "money." A thematic equation between matrimony and sex
would be problematic, since there is no evidence of this equation except in their logical position in relation to "money."

Let us develop a model in which "money" would occupy the same
position in the Quebec corpus and the American corpus. First, we
need a model in which "money" is the means:

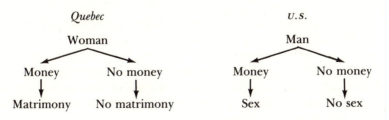

Then we need another model in which "money" is an end:

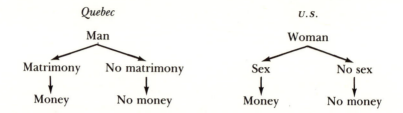

Side by side, the models highlight the national variations: we witness a turnabout of the sex roles, which in turn shows a reversal of the power structure. The American man and the Quebecois woman are the "buyers"; the Quebecois man and the American woman are the "sellers." This interpretation is consistent with contrasting patterns of social and sexual politics. In Quebec women have had a particularly powerful social position, just as men have been traditionally dominant in American society.

This is a first level of interpretation. We will better understand the national differences between the corpuses if we consider the role of male and female voices in constructing narrative meaning. To this end, we will consider the role of voices as a structural force in another oral genre: the traditional legend. Using this avenue of inquiry, we will see that there are important differences in themes, traceable to the voice of the narration; these results help to explain the national variations of the burlesque story lines.

GENDER VOICES IN QUEBEC "PRIEST" LEGENDS

I examined one hundred Quebec legends in which a priest figured as a character.[9] Of this number, 57 per cent were told by women and the remainder by men. In comparing the different voices in which these legends were told, my overall conclusions were as follows:

1 Male and female characters are portrayed as reacting and behaving very differently from one another in legends.
2 There is a tacit agreement between male and female narrators as to the different qualities of male and female characters. That is, there are no marked differences between the representation of men and women in stories told by men and the representation of men and women in stories told by women.

3 The narrative style of the legends itself carries the very characteristics of the male and female characters, thus establishing a clear
distinction between narratives told by men and narratives told by
women. (We will see how this applies in the next section.)

4 Priest characters, who are at the centre of narrative tensions, are
perceived by women to possess the very qualities which they hold,
as revealed both by their storytelling style and by their female
characters, to be feminine qualities. Male tellers describe priests as
possessing qualities characteristic of their own narratives and
their own male characters.[10]

These results, of course, are highly general and schematic. I turn
now to the specifics of narrative voice in this corpus. The characterization of narrative actors in legends is highly tacit: characters are
differentiated only on the basis of the recurrence and stability of
their environment and its relationship to setting, time, roles, action
sequences, and thematic organization.

Although there is a need for specifying the exact geographical setting in which the action takes place (since these legends are believed
to be true stories), men and women accomplish the specification of
setting quite differently. Overall, women are more vague about geographical location. Instead of specifying the locus, they will use a
known personality of the area to orient their audience. For example,
a female narrator will say that this happened to x, who was a parish
priest (this priest is then traceable through church documentation).
Male narrators give a clear geographical orientation. For example:
"This happened during the time of the great 'savane.' When they
built the great 'savane,' here in Ste-Anne."[11]

The characters' travels map the space in legends. These travels
take three main forms: a one-way trip (someone leaves the house
and does not come back, or the devil is chased out, for example);
back and forth between two places (more commonly, the man leaves
his house to bring back the priest); and trajectory, which is a displacement that includes more than two stops (for example, a character goes to fetch a doctor for his wife who is near delivery, but stops
by the presbytery to get the priest's blessing on his trip).

Both groups of tellers describe male characters as mobile and female characters as stationary. In fact, there is a clear division: only
men travel, women stay in the home. "When a woman travels, she is
always accompanied by a man, always her husband; otherwise the
anomaly of her displacement is stressed by the fact that she is escaping (and never returns) or obeying an order of the priest. The mobility of women is always presented in a submissive situation. This

lack of mobility associates her with other characters: the child, the sick, and the dead."[12] Furthermore, there are more displacements in men's legends than in women's. Indeed, as a rule, women's narratives take place in one location: in the home, at the presbytery, or even in the church (the home of the priest); male narrators show their male characters going places and the locus of the actions moving with them. The stability of space is so important to women that often when a character leaves the main locus, he never returns.

Turning to chronology, men tend to report events believed to have taken place between 1830 and 1900 (the most repressive period in the history of the church in Quebec), and usually specify an exact date. In contrast, women's legends are alleged to have taken place more recently and typically involve memorates or fabulates – references to action in which the narrator, or a person known to the narrator, plays a role.[13] As a rule, women do not specify dates. Men use the abstraction of historical time as a narrative device, while women use the field of social relationships.

Internal chronology is more important to women than the external contextual chronology in which the narrative is framed. Women narrators will refer to the time of day, sometimes to the exact hour; for men, the causality of actions is the main frame of temporal organization. The effect of these variations on women's narratives is to make the events seem more familiar and real. In men's narratives, events appear to be more abstract.

The choice of actors also varies according to the voice of the narrator. Specifically, women's stories contain more priests (in this corpus) than men's. In fact, women sometimes cast only priests interacting with each other, or a priest alone. For example, two priests promise each other that the first to die will let the other know about it. One day, one of the priests is sitting at his desk and hears a knock on the door. The other priest walks in and disappears.[14] In men's legends, the priest invariably interacts with parishioners. Thus, men present the priest in terms of his social role, whereas women, by making the priest (or priests) the only character (or social group) of their narratives, make him (or them) more individualistic.[15]

Various names can be used to designate a priest. He might be the parish priest, the priest, the bishop, or the vicar. Women use a larger repertory of names to designate the priest in their stories, possibly because they have a more complex conception of the clergy.[16] Men typically speak only of the parish priest, thus emphasizing the immediacy of his authority.

Furthermore, women often use the family link to identify characters. They will say, for example, that the event happened to their great-grandmother or to an uncle, or that one of the characters is the uncle of another. Men prefer to identify characters through their social roles: the main character will be the butcher or the fireman or some other person situated in historical time. For women, family links and interrelationships are basic to the recognition of individuals, and vague identifications are rare. Men remain vague about their identifications, using social role as the basic means for differentiating characters. Only in the case of female characters will they use the family relationship.

But the greatest difference between men and women as narrators lies in their image of the priest. In women's stories, priests are involved primarily in communication (45 per cent), followed by fighting (22 per cent), and repression (18 per cent). In men's stories these themes are ordered differently: repression comes first (43 per cent), then communication (37 per cent), then fighting (28 per cent).[17] More specifically, women describe priests as possessing extraordinary communicative power (with the dead or with the devil; as well, dead priests communicate with living parishioners). Men pay more attention to the repressive powers of priests: their priests inflict death, handicaps, and loss of property when disobeyed. Thus, for women, communication with the priest is most important; for men, submission and the power of the law dominate.

Even when women exploit the theme of fighting, the priest takes on a protective role and communication appears as a secondary theme. In stories of fire, possession by the devil, or return of the dead, women cast the priest as a protector of the health and physical well-being of the parishioners. In men's stories, however, fighting involves direct confrontation between the priest and the devil or a male character.

Overall, in men's narratives, the priest stands in opposition to men and their desires; he is God's soldier and his work is to maintain the equilibrium of religion and society. To accomplish this, the priest is given some supernatural power over many aspects of the life of his parishioners. His supernatural power becomes the foundation of his authority. The laws of the church in turn support the priest's authority. For women the communicative powers of the priest are at the centre of their concern, and the duty of the priest is to serve as a bridge between the living and the dead, between the natural life, the religious life, and the eternal life, between the human and her God.

In fact, the themes of communication and repression are two facets of one reality: the powerful authority of the priest in Quebec. Women render this authority concrete by showing the priest as a liaison, while men show this power by looking at the priest as a ruler. Thus, on the one hand, priests become a bridge between all the forces of nature, society, and eternal life. On the other hand, the priest is the key element of social coherence. Men essentially describe the priest's efficiency and success: women insist on his superior communicative powers. For men, the priest has a transformational active power; for women, the priest possesses a power that affects the existential quality of life. We might say that the priest, in the feminine voice, *is*; in the masculine voice, the priest *can do*.[18]

PSYCHOLOGY AND PERFORMANCE

In her book on women's psychology, *In a Different Voice*, Carol Gilligan wrote: "The images of hierarchy and web, drawn from the texts of men's and women's fantasies and thoughts, convey different ways of structuring relationships and are associated with different views of morality and self." She added that both male and female "children thus recognize the need for agreement but see it as mediated in different ways – he impersonally through systems of logic and law, she personally through communication in relationship. Just as he relies on the conventions of logic to deduce the solution ... assuming these conventions to be shared, so she relies on a process of communication, assuming connection and believing that her voice will be heard."[19] Gilligan obtained these results through interviews with young men and women. She posed a moral dilemma and examined the responses given by both sexes. Our observations here are very similar to hers. Indeed, I have stressed the fact that in legends women organize the world around relationships, while men organize the world around antagonistic forces regulated by the law of the church.

If we further examine the legends as tensions between narrative forces, we again reach the same conclusions as Gilligan. She found that "if aggression is tied, as women perceive, to the fracture of human connection, then the activities of care, as their fantasies suggest, are the activities that make the social world safe, by avoiding isolation and preventing aggression rather than by seeking rules to limit its extent." The study of voices in legends shows that women view communication as a generator of tensions and conflicts; consequently, their perception of priests comes through the image of the extraordinary communicator. (We should also remember that in legends in which fighting is the theme, the priest is always a protector.) When men become narrators, however, the generator of tensions changes. Gilligan found that "the prevalence of violence in men's fantasies, denoting a world where danger is everywhere seen, signifies a problem in making connection, causing relationships to erupt." In men's legends repression is the vehicle for tensions, and thus disobedience is the means of breaking links with the community. In this context, the priest is the extraordinarily powerful ruler. Gilligan wrote that "rule-bound competitive achievement situations, which for women threaten the web of connection, for men provide a mode of connection that establishes clear boundaries and limits aggression, and thus appears comparatively safe."[20]

Thus, in their image of violence, women see the lack of communication, which will be remedied by the priest, as the main threat, while the image of violence in men's stories is one of confrontation between individual desire and the law of the church. Consequently, there are often violent conclusions to male tellers' legends, whereas in female tellers' legends the breach of communication will often be mended. These observations imply that we should expect significant changes in the story lines when the voice of the narrator changes.[21]

To return to burlesque: recall that in the Quebec and u.s. traditions "money" occupied the same position. We have also seen that in Quebec burlesque "matrimony" has replaced "sex." In turn, these differences affect the position of the sex roles. Let us compare these in more detail.

The first distinction between the Quebecois story line and the American story line is the location of the action. In the priest legends, Quebecois woman accentuates relations. She relates her narration either to people of her environment or to recent times; she connects her characters to each other through family links; and she stabilizes the environment by limiting the displacement of the characters to a minimum. From this, and given the main elements of the burlesque story line, we might predict that the home is likely to be the focus of the story line in Quebec burlesque.

The male narrator, however, sees the world as a social organization based on individual functions, recognizes characters according to their social roles, and diversifies the environment through travel. For such a narrator, and (again) given the main elements of the burlesque story line, the locus of action is likely to be out of the home, somewhere in the social world. Thus, when the female narrator views the home as the locus of humour, the male narrator sends his characters into the social setting in which each possesses a specific function.

Burlesque stories exploit tensions between characters just as the priest legends did, but the tensions and oppositions are framed differently. Women who perceive the world as a "web of connections" are likely to find in the setting of a new permanent relation (a marriage) the seeds for humorous developments (just as they see tension in communication in their legends).[22] Men favour the theme of repression in legends. Similarly, in burlesque they describe antagonistic forces: the tension between wife and prostitute: "He pays his wife to keep his peace and a prostitute for the time she devotes to him."[23] As well, male narrators explore the rules and laws of marriage and oppose, as they did with their priest legends, sexual desire with sexual duty.

As the home becomes the centre of the events in female story lines and the accent on family relations is stressed, the sexual satisfaction that takes place outside the home loses its humorous quality. Thus the prostitute would be too controversial or delicate a subject to be cast in Quebecois burlesque if her presence (even in thoughts) entered the family home.

The male narrator, however, sees the world as a place of tension between antagonistic forces, which he finds outside the home. In the home, traditionally, he should find submission to his authority. Thus a challenge to this authority in the home would be no more a laughing matter than the presence of the prostitute for women narrators. In a way, we can say that male characters connect the family to the external social reality (by their travels and by their sense of historical time, for example). There is no particular bar to finding the social role of the prostitute humorous.

In the burlesque of both countries money occupies the same logical position. There are more similarities, however. In both story lines money is connected with the family: in the American burlesque, the money is the man's and his wife's; in the Quebecois burlesque, the money is the woman's and her family's. Because of this, the sex roles are reversed.

We have seen that in the Quebecois corpus of legends there is an opposition created between social and familial roles. A character will take either one or the other role: in the female voice it will more often be a familial role, while in the male voice it will be a social role. In burlesque, "money" plays the role of opposing the social with the familial. For both men and women in the Quebecois corpus of legends, the man is the social figure and the woman represents the familial figure; therefore, we are not surprised that the sex roles should be reversed and an equation drawn between the American prostitute (which, I repeat, is a social role) and the courting young male.

In short, performance is given meaning through the voices in which it is articulated and the audiences to which it plays. Whether on stage or in storytelling, the different voices of men and women provide a useful key for understanding crucial differences between U.S. and Quebecois entertainment traditions. When the voice of the narrator changes, it is the logic of performance that changes.

Merchandising Culture

Part Four returns to a continuing theme of this volume, the meaning
of the persistent merchandising of American culture in Canada.
Michael Ames, an anthropologist and the director of the well-known
Museum of Anthropology at the University of British Columbia,
treats Expo 86, the world's fair in Vancouver, as an essentially
American event occurring in Canada. The process began with
a significant number of Americans and American companies being
hired to create the fair itself and to make it work. But, Ames
argues, Expo 86 became distinctively Canadian in style, and "American popular themes and institutions were taken over, Canadianized, and sold back to the Americans as something new. This,
in fact, is what Canadians do all the time to American popular
cultural forms – we borrow from the United States, reconstitute the
materials, and then re-export the modifications to American
consumers." Ames suggests that a Canadian style was visible particularly in certain interconnected aspects of Expo 86 – the
Canadian self-image that was projected through pavilion exhibits
("a celebration of pioneer individualism, of great men who heroically overcame the inanimate and often hostile obstacles of time,
distance, and nature"); the presentation of the fair site, and by
implication the country as a whole, as a "neutral space" for foreign
powers to display their wares and to promote their interests;
and the promotion of the Canadian version of state capitalism as
a way of life (the government provided entrepreneurs with an
opportunity to make money). Ames shows how in various ways these

themes diverge from the u.s. cultural model and can be "taken to constitute a formula for the construction of popular culture in Canada."

Geoffrey Wall, a geographer and specialist in the understanding of tourism, explores the importance of u.s. tourists in Canada and their influence on tourism and recreation. He briefly reviews the American market for high culture in Canada, Canadian and American purchases of souvenirs, and the marketing of cultural groups as tourist attractions. For cultural institutions like the Art Gallery of Ontario or theatre festivals in places like Stratford and Niagara-on-the-Lake, the patronage of u.s. visitors is financially important. However, Americans are not especially attracted to amusements such as Canada's Wonderland (perhaps failing to appreciate from the name that it is a u.s.-style theme park). Wall compares the marketing as cultural attractions of the Old Order Mennonites of Waterloo, Ontario, and the Old Order Amish of Lancaster County, Pennsylvania, and finds that the local culture is exploited to a greater degree and in more commercial ways in Lancaster County than in Waterloo. But perhaps Canadian tourist marketing is simply lagging behind u.s. efforts in this area. Wall concludes with a discussion of how the marketing of Canada to u.s. tourists has changed in recent years from an early emphasis on Mounties and the great outdoors to a promotion of vibrant, clean, safe Canadian cities with good shopping and ample nightlife. This suggests that American tourists, like their counterparts in other locales, will continue to be struck by the gap between what is advertised and what is delivered.

14 The Canadianization of an American Fair: The Case of Expo 86

MICHAEL M. AMES

Vancouver's Expo 86 was described by a reporter as "the largest American fair ever held outside the United States"; only the address was Canadian.[1] Fears about the Americanization of Expo 86 were expressed early when a u.s. theme park expert, Michael Bartlett, was appointed the fair's president. The trouble with Bartlett, complained the *Vancouver Sun* columnist Marjorie Nichols, was that he was "a transplanted American with carnival credentials" who was, heaven help us, "hell bent on turning Expo 86 into a doppelganger for Disneyland."[2] Bartlett was quoted as saying that the philosophy of running fairs was quite simple: "You get 'em on the site, you feed 'em, you make 'em dizzy, and you scare the shit out of 'em."[3] He was subsequently fired by the chairman of the Expo Corporation, Jimmy Pattison, for not being responsive enough to local business and political interests (though he was also credited with cleaning up an inefficient organization in order to produce a fair "on time and on budget").[4]

An American was also hired to stage the $600,000 opening ceremonies; a number of Canadian pavilions, including those of British Columbia, Telecom Canada, and General Motors of Canada, hired American design firms to create their exhibits and films; and the largest "art" commission, "Highway 86," worth $4.5 million, was awarded to a New York firm. ("Highway 86" was an outdoor installation of cars, trucks, and bikes set on an undulating road, each with a coating of concrete. People argued over whether it was art or popular entertainment.) The Los Angeles Olympics had a major influence on the design of Expo 86. Space exploration, which was the theme of the U.S. pavilion, provided the metaphor for much else, ranging from hot-dog-stand architecture through street graphics to the exhibits in the Canada and B.C. pavilions. American computer technology, courtesy of IBM, was used to direct people around the site. Expo 86 awarded its largest contract, an estimated $75 million worth of souvenir sales, including the rights to the Canadian maple leaf and the word "Canada," to an American novelty firm, forcing the federal government to negotiate the return of the rights to the national emblem.[5] Finally, the Expo Corporation went all out to attract American participation and interest in the fair; besides the U.S. exhibit, state pavilions represented Washington, Oregon, and California – added enticements in a $12 million "bazooka" marketing campaign to attract visitors, 35 per cent of whom were expected to be American.[6]

McDonald's, the U.S. fast-food giant, installed five restaurants on the fair grounds, including one floating barge, and was soon feeding one-third of all Expo visitors. By the middle of the summer they had become the busiest outlets in the 9,500-restaurant worldwide McDonald chain. McDonald's even installed the world's first walk-through service, allowing customers to pre-order at the door and pick up their food by the time they reached the cash register.[7]

The criterion Expo officials used to plan for success was quintessentially American: will it sell? Success was defined in terms of numbers: numbers of pavilions, numbers of people served, numbers of happy customers, and numbers of dollars saved or earned. It was an "unseemly drive to make money," complained Ted Allan, the commissioner general of the Britain pavilion and the representative of the International Bureau of Expositions, but even he had to praise the Expo Corporation for planning and operating such a successful enterprise.[8]

The ethic of the marketplace is, of course, common to all consumer-oriented societies, of which the United States is the prime example. The idea that the market is the most effective measure of what is good and proper was in this case extended beyond the marketplace itself to encompass social and cultural affairs. For Expo 86 artistic success meant market success, the number of people through the gate (and preferably single-visit customers, since Expo did not earn as much money from those who purchased season passes).

In many respects, therefore, Expo 86 was as American as apple pie, and people loved every piece of it. Underlying the surface appearance, however, was an infrastructure that was distinctively Canadian both in character and in organization. Although Canadian pavilions used the metaphor of space technology, the message was about the Great White North. Expo 86 could boast of greater American participation than any other non-American fair, but it also managed to have a greater international "flavour" than any American fair. And although Expo 86 planners studied carefully the successes and failures of U.S. fairs and the Los Angeles Olympics, the spectacle they finally organized was distinctively Canadian.

Expo 86 may have been American in appearance, but it was Canadian in style. American popular themes and institutions were taken over, Canadianized, and sold back to the Americans as something new. This, in fact, is what Canadians do all the time to American popular cultural forms – we borrow from the United States, reconstitute the materials, and then re-export the modifications to American consumers. The Canadian style of Expo 86 was seen particularly in the Canadian self-image that was projected through pavilion exhibits; the presentation of the fair site, and by implication the country as a whole, as a "neutral space" for foreign powers; and the promotion of Canadian state welfare capitalism as a way of life.

THE CANADIAN IMAGE: ITS HISTORY AND NATURE

How a society deals with its past says much about what that society tries to be in its present form.[9] In their attempts to reconstruct their history, people reconstitute themselves according to current values and beliefs, and world fairs provide an opportunity to observe how they do this. At Expo 86, for example, the Asian and African nations constructed exhibits that connected their present circumstances to their histories, while the North American pavilions were more interested in demonstrating how they had transcended their pasts through high technology. In the Japan pavilion, for example, respect was paid to the "courage and intelligence of the ancestors." The display in the Pakistan pavilion began with a reference to the five-thousand-year-old Mohenjodaro civilization and the thousand years of Islam to show how history and religion provided the foundation for the modern state. In the Kenya pavilion the legend accompanying the first exhibit read, "Kenya, a modern nation, still values the multitude of traditional ways of life and vast areas of unspoiled scenery it possesses." In the final gallery of the Indonesia pavilion the figure of the ancient Hindu monkey-god Hanoman was shown flying through space holding an Indonesian satellite in his outstretched arms. The legend read, "In Hindu mythology,

Hanoman, or the Monkey God, could snare the moon with his tail while staying firmly on the ground. Able to cover vast distances in a single leap, Hanoman symbolizes the ties between yesterday, today and tomorrow. Here he is holding Palapa, the Indonesian satellite that also connects yesterday with tomorrow in modern-day Indonesia."

Compare these approaches with the treatment of history by the Canada pavilion at Expo 86. In a design brief prepared for the exhibitions, designers were advised to emphasize the individual's confrontation with nature and technology.[10] History was to be presented in "a witty and humorous" manner, celebrating heroes who "used their creativity to create unique solutions to domestic problems" and whose achievements in transportation and communication "symbolize great moments in Canadian history." Northern bush-pilots were presented as the exemplars of heroic Canadian adventurers. "Their exploits," the introductory legend to this section of the Great Hall stated, "are remarkable stories of human achievement and perseverance in the face of great odds." The adventures of individual pilots were then described.

Canadian history was seen as a set of discrete problems or tasks to be transcended or overcome by creative individuals; their exploits were described in a whimsical or romantic manner. History was thus presented as a celebration of pioneer individualism, of great men who heroically overcame the inanimate and often hostile obstacles of time, distance, and nature. The contributions of institutions, collectivities, or social, political, and religious policies were scarcely noted. History is governed by the genius of individuals (typically men).[11]

Asian and African nations, by contrast, spoke of continuous histories stretching back for thousands of years and incorporating both indigenous peoples and a long series of immigrant groups. They all became part of one historical amalgam, their achievements the common inheritance of those living today. In Canada we tend to separate the past from the present, and then to separate ourselves from the past because we were not present for most of it. There were "only" Natives and Inuit "then," along with other wildlife; and just as we find it difficult to embrace indigenous peoples as equals today, unless they assimilate white culture, we are uncomfortable about embracing their past as ours.

Attitudes towards nature also reveal much about what is thought to be the basis of a good society. Though all nations must come to terms with their environments, and all wish to maximize the benefits to be derived from natural resources, they nevertheless express different attitudes towards natural phenomena. For Canadians, nature may be beautiful and bountiful, a resource bank to be exploited, but it is also threatening, hostile, rugged, something to be mastered or dominated. In the Great Hall of the Canada pavilion, for example, the following introduction to exhibits of "micro environments" appeared: "*Survival.* Canada's multiple environments, its extreme northern climate, and [its] varied terrains test the endurance of the human body. Equipped with technology's skins, eyes, ears, hands, and feet, we go where we have never been before."

The theme was repeated at the British Columbia pavilion: our country is a supernatural wilderness that has only gradually been tamed, controlled, and exploited. Nature is to be mastered and processed as a commodity or used as a recreational "supernature." At Expo 86 a small forest with a running stream was constructed at the entrance to the B.C. Discovery pavilion, an elegant tribute to nature. Upon exiting from either side of this pavilion, however, one was greeted by arenas where brawny men demonstrated the arts of turning trees into timber, called "logging sports" and "boom boat ballet." (Boom boats are used to herd logs into log-booms.)

Exhibit guidelines prepared for the Canada pavilion expressed a similar attitude: "From icebreakers to snowmobiles, fast trains to urban buses, invisible communications networks to fiber optic cables, the Canadian landscape is characterized and identified by the unique patterns that humans have *imposed* upon the natural patterns of the landscape." Further, "Man's increasing ability to work *in hostile environments* has led to the development of sophisticated remote manipulating devices, which are the latest generation of robotic technology."[12]

The American pavilions (United States, California, Oregon, and Washington State) also gave only passing attention to history and focused upon present technological achievements and future possibilities.[13] The U.S. pavilion was entirely devoted to space exploration. California, with the theme "California, Creating the Future," presented itself as "a laboratory for new modes of thought and new styles of living," noting that "today, the state leads the world in aerospace technology." Oregon used a tunnel built to resemble a twenty-first-century covered wagon to take visitors on a time trip from the past to the future. Washington presented its "spectacular beauty" while noting it was also "the leading manufacturer of jet aircraft." For the Americans, nature was scenery, recreational opportunities, backdrops for hydroplane and hot-air balloon races, and laboratories for industrial and technological developments. There were no wide-open spaces left to conquer; nature was there to be enjoyed and used.

CANADA AS A NEUTRAL SPACE

Expo 86 was truly an international fair: more than fifty nations were represented there. It was also the first North American fair to bring mainland China, the Soviet Union, and the United States together in one place; the China pavilion was at the eastern edge of the site, the United States was at the western end, and the Soviet Union was halfway between. The three pavilions were linked by monorail and ferry. There were multicultural displays of food, souvenirs, and performances to complement the national pavilions. This was in direct contrast to u.s. world fairs, which for the most part have been national affairs emphasizing American states, corporations, and technology.

Just as Canada has offered neutral space for wave upon wave of immigrants (railways, militia, and police forces preceded or supported most large immigrant settlements on Canada's western frontier), so Expo 86 provided neutral space in which nations could display their wares and promote their interests. According to an Expo 86 commissioner general, Patrick Reid, who was responsible for signing up most of the exhibiting nations, Canada's international reputation as a host was one of the main reasons for this high level of international participation.[14]

Neutral space, like a playing-field, allows for competition between nations. "The superpowers are fighting it out at Expo 86," a *Vancouver Province* reporter proclaimed before the fair opened.[15] "The space race between the global superpowers has been renewed on the British Columbia shore at the 1986 world's fair," said the *Globe and Mail*.[16] The fair was defined as a friendly competition, of course, by which is meant that the participants pretended they are not competing. The Chinese mounted a space rocket and a communication satellite, the Americans presented Mercury rocket capsules and a model of a proposed space station, and the Soviets exhibited a thirty-five-ton spaceship. Not to be outdone, Sri Lanka mounted a larger-than-life photograph of the science fiction writer Arthur C. Clarke a Colombo resident and a citizen of Sri Lanka, who used his portable computer to communicate with the western world via satellite.

"Ours is the biggest but we are not having a competition," a Soviet representative was quoted as saying just before the fair opened.[17] "The spirit is not competitive," the director of the u.s. pavilion said, noting, however, that the u.s. presence was larger than the Soviet if you counted the three state pavilions as well as the national one. The Canada pavilion was actually larger than any of the superpowers' and in fact was said to be the largest pavilion ever built for a world's fair.[18] In one of its theatres the Canada pavilion featured a Canadarm attached to a u.s. satellite, so perhaps it was counted as part of the American presence.

Expo 86 provided a safe and friendly site for nations to come together, creating the opportunity for people to consume other people's cultural productions. Indeed, that is what a marketing survey showed Canadians and Americans most wanted to see at the fair: international events and displays. Perhaps in this way Expo 86 served as a metaphor for one of the great myths of Canadian society: that it is a playing-field always open to outside influences, a neutral space that allows for cultural diversity. (This same ideology of neutrality also serves to inhibit the development of a unified dominant culture – with the exception of French-speaking Quebec). Canada, it is often proclaimed, is a vast space neutralized by law, order, and technology (serving as the hidden instruments of a "free market"), waiting for visitors to lay their tracks and for popular cultural forms to flow across its borders. "One of the great virtues of Canada," the Vancouver critic Max Wyman observed six years after the fair, "has always been its undemanding receptiveness. Newcomers are encouraged to retain their own identities within the framework of this new society. No one's beliefs are turned away; beyond the normal limitations of law, conformity is not enforced. It is a welcoming place."[19] While there may have been no "melting-pot" ideology imposed on immigrants, it is nevertheless true that the actual experience of neutrality has varied according to how closely immigrants approximate Canada's western European norm.

THE ORGANIZATIONAL STYLE OF EXPO 86

Another feature of Expo 86 that distinguished it from previous American fairs was the distinctively Canadian style of business organization, a form of state-sponsored mass merchandising. This was perhaps best illustrated by the numerous fast-food outlets – Boston Pizza, McDonald's, taco stands, hot-dog stands – and souvenir outlets that dotted the four-kilometre length of the fair like a series of friendly welcome beacons. When McDonald's signed a contract to operate five restaurants on the site, Pattison announced to the press that "McDonald's stands for everything that Expo stands for – quality, service, and cleanliness."[20] He was enunciating a basic populist ideological position.

Expo 86 was presented as a people's fair, something promised for everyone, brought to us through the initiative and financial support of the government working with private enterprise and the manual skills of the labour force. It was the "IKEA of world's fairs," *Sun* columnist Pete McMartin observed shortly after the fair opened, "marketed to appeal to a common denominator in tastes. McDonald's and the Boston Pizzas and the execrable Expo Ernie [the Expo robot] are there because people like them."[21] The objective of the Expo Corporation was not to be crass, as some intellectuals suggested, but to be popular by "giving the best value for the dollar." This objective was largely achieved. In a newspaper survey of one thousand visitors to the fair, only 7 per cent expressed disappointment; 92 per cent said they would recommend Expo 86 to others.[22]

Expo 86 was a monumental example of the Canadian version of state capitalism at work. The government, through its borrowing power, creates business opportunities for a competitive private sector, and success is assigned to the individual efforts of entrepreneurs. After the government-financed Expo Corporation established a number of food and merchandise concessions on site, for example, they were turned over to the private sector to operate. "The policy of the Corporation," Pattison announced, "is based on the belief that the private system will be more efficient and there is also less risk for the Corporation."[23] He did not mention that the government corporation was enabling entrepreneurs to go into business without bearing major capitalization costs.

Pattison, who continued to oversee his personal empire while managing Expo, and who remained chairman of the board when he took over the presidency after firing the American Michael Bartlett, became the exemplar of this philosophy. He applied his talents as a successful frontier entrepreneur to the management of public affairs. His management style thus provided the model for public business. "In B.C.," the political scientist Paul Tennant remarked, "private business success stories are seen as the model for public business ... And while Pattison may be too flashy for Eastern Canadian attitudes, he's somewhat of a local treasure here because he's made so many millions."[24]

The government's policy of providing, at public expense, opportunities for private entrepreneurs to make profits has characterized the development of Canada since the first Europeans came in search of codfish and beaver pelts. Organized government, multinational companies, the military and police, and publicly funded railway companies preceded the settlement of western Canada. This contrasts with the American experience, where individual initiative and free enterprise reigned more freely. "Historically, where state activity is concerned, Canada has been situated somewhere between the

American and West European norms," Philip Resnick has noted. "There has been a greater tendency to use the state as an instrument of infrastructual development than in the United States ... In sum, capitalism in Canada was fostered far more within the bosom of the state than was true south of the border."[25]

The recent U.S. fairs and the Los Angeles Olympics were primarily creations of the private sector. Expo 86, backed and bankrolled by the provincial and federal governments, outgunned them all, even in the area of private sector contributions. Corporate support for Expo 86 reached a value of $157 million, greater than the combined support of the last four American world's fairs that occurred prior to the Los Angeles Olympics and more even than the $150 million in corporate support (excluding television rights) raised for the Los Angeles Olympics.[26]

According to a British Columbia government brochure, Expo 86 was "a perfect marriage of public and private enterprise." The implication is that the common good is best served by using public funds and resources to facilitate the making of private profit. Thus, the heroic individual successfully struggling to master a rugged wilderness in the interests of scientific progress serves as Expo's metaphor for the triumph of competitive individualism in a state-sponsored "free market" society.

In March 1988 the Ontario mining magnate and multimillionaire Stephen B. Roman died of a heart attack. His funeral, attended by more than 1,600 mourners, including senior representatives of the Canadian government, had the markings of a state ceremony.[27] The eulogy described Roman's rags-to-riches rise from a penniless immigrant to the president of a $2 billion corporate empire. Robert C. Coates, MP, wrote to the editor of the *Globe and Mail*, "Mr. Roman may have had a humble beginning, but through dedication and perseverance, not to mention hard work, he was able to develop a unique status in our nation."[28] But Roman did not make it on his own. The *Globe and Mail*'s business reporter, Paul McKay, pointed out that it took more than $2 billion in public subsidies, interest-free loans, and guaranteed government purchases, including a thirty-year cost-plus, multibillion-dollar contract to provide a uranium stockpile for Ontario Hydro, to help Roman build his $2 billion empire. And as a legacy of the Roman deal, Ontario Hydro was now paying "three times the world market price for the privilege of obtaining uranium mined in Ontario."[29]

The Hibernia offshore oil development proposed for Newfoundland might serve as another example. The federal government promised a $1 billion grant and $1.66 billion in loan guarantees to an oil consortium in order to create about ten thousand worker years of employment, with no guarantees of tax returns to the government; that amounted to an annual price tag of $100,000 for each job.[30] Our Canadian system of welfare capitalism, which makes public resources available for private profit while cloaking the arrangement within the popular imagery of individual achievement and transcendence over natural obstacles, continues to flourish. The organization of Expo 86 was a national celebration of this ideology.

Despite the surface glamour of an American-style fair, the infrastructure of Expo 86 reflected a distinctively Canadian style. I cited three examples that could be taken to constitute a formula for the construction of popular culture in Canada: our country represented as a Great White North tamed through the application of technology by heroic individuals; its transformation into neutral space in which newcomers could seek their fortunes; and the use of the state apparatus and public resources to promote private enterprise. Much of our popular culture, whether locally produced or imported, is constructed and reconstructed according to the formula; its role, in turn, is to transform the underlying ideological principles into common sense through repetition and popularization. Expo 86 was as American as an apple pie baked in Canada and shared with the world.

15 Culture for Sale: American Dollars Preferred

GEOFFREY WALL

The border between Canada and the United States is a permeable barrier. Residents of one country can pass to the other with a minimum of formality, and many do so. Most such travellers, numbering in the millions in both directions, are tourists drawn by the attractions on the other side of the fence. Florida, for example, attracts both English- and French-speaking Canadians, particularly in the winter, but the two groups head for different locations. Arizona also hosts large numbers of elderly Canadian snowbirds. Myrtle Beach has its "Canadian week," and some ski resorts in New England accept Canadian currency at par. The imposition of the goods and services tax (GST) in Canada has prompted many Canadians to travel across the border in search of shopping bargains, and the number of short visits by Canadians to the United States has increased substantially in recent years. The experience of visiting there is so common for many Canadians, most of whom live in close proximity to the border, that even though trips are made to another country, it can be argued that they are part of the experience of many Canadians and therefore part of the Canadian experience.

However, movements of Canadians to the United States are not the major concern of this essay. Rather, I wish to focus on the flow of Americans to Canada. Canadians exhibit a love-hate relationship in their attitudes towards Americans. Millions of dollars are spent on sophisticated advertising to persuade Americans to come to Canada, yet we complain when they do. We want them to buy our gold-plated maple leaves, plastic CN Towers, and Eskimo carvings, but we are upset when they ask what the price is in "real" money. Americans are stereotyped as "ugly," stomachs protruding through their multicoloured Hawaiian shirts, draped with cameras, cigars smouldering beneath sun-visors, always in search of iced tea. Canadians poke fun at those who arrive with skis during the summer. (I once met a couple from Baltimore in Iqaluit, Baffin Island. They wore sandals, shorts, and T-shirts, and could not wait to escape from Iqaluit to Pangnirtung, which at least had a park.) At the same time we find it necessary to wear miniature Canadian flags in our lapels when travelling abroad, not so much to assert our identity as to ensure that our origin is not misconstrued. That Canadians and Americans can be so much alike is disconcerting: in the words of former Prime Minister Lester Pearson, "If you're supposed to be anti someone you resemble so much, it makes for a kind of schizophrenia." [1]

The influence of American culture on tourism and recreation in Canada is an extremely broad topic that has yet to be explored in all its ramifications. Elsewhere I have discussed how the history of the Canadian National Exhibition has reflected changes in Canadian life, and how American influences have displaced most of the earlier British content over time. [2] Relations between outdoor recreation and the Canadian identity have received cursory discussion; I have pointed out, for example, that the United States is often employed as a standard of comparison whether one is arguing the existence of differences or of similarities. [3] Consider the aphorism "Americans go to war at the drop of a hat; Canadians go to war at the drop of a puck," or the American joke that asks for the difference between a Canadian and a canoe (the answer is that one tips and the other does not).

Other contributors to this volume have examined professional sport, particularly football and baseball, but a definitive framework that can embrace the various findings has yet to be found. The aims of this essay are modest. The presentation of some data on the number and significance of American visitors to Canada will be followed by a brief consideration of three topics: the American market for high culture in Canada; a comparison of Canadian and American purchases of souvenirs; and a discussion of the marketing of cultural groups as tourist attractions. The essay concludes with a discussion of current strategies to market Canada to potential American tourists.

THE SIGNIFICANCE OF AMERICAN VISITORS TO CANADA

When I first became interested in tourism and recreation as a research area approximately twenty years ago, my responses to ques-

Canada in International Tourism

	1986	1987	1988	1989	1990
AS A DESTINATION					
Arrivals (millions)	15.6	15.0	15.5	15.1	15.3
World share (percentage)	4.6	4.2	4.1	3.6	3.5
Receipts (US$ billion)	3.9	4.0	4.6	5.0	6.4
World share (percentage)	3.0	2.3	2.3	2.4	2.5
Origin (percentage)					
USA	87.0	84.9	82.4	80.6	80.4
Other	13.0	15.1	17.6	19.4	19.6
AS A GENERATOR					
Departures (millions)	13.1	14.9	16.5	18.3	20.5
World share (percentage)	3.8	4.2	4.3	4.4	4.6
Expenditures (US$ billion)	4.3	5.3	6.3	7.4	8.4
World share (percentage)	3.3	3.1	3.2	3.5	3.3
Destination (percentage)					
USA	84.0	82.2	83.0	83.6	84.7
Other	16.0	17.8	17.0	16.4	15.3

Source: Compiled from data provided by the World Tourism Organization, Madrid.

tions concerning my research interests were greeted with mild amusement: "That must be fun!" Evidently tourism did not appear to be a topic worthy of scholarly attention. That situation has changed considerably. However, the importance of tourism still has not received the recognition it deserves. For example, the widely acclaimed report of the Brundtland Commission on sustainable development does not even mention the word.[4] It is appropriate, therefore, to provide some background information on the importance of tourism to Canada and, in particular, the importance of American visitors.

Some recent statistics on Canadian tourism are presented in the accompanying table. It shows that in 1986 the number of people travelling to Canada exceeded the number of Canadians travelling elsewhere; by 1990 the reverse was true. The relatively large number of arrivals in 1986 was the result of Expo 86 in Vancouver, the comparatively low value of the Canadian dollar, world terrorism (which encouraged many North Americans to vacation on this continent), and the adoption of a new tourism marketing strategy. There has been an absolute decline in the number of Americans visiting Canada. Canadians spend more abroad than foreign visitors spend in Canada – that is, there is a deficit in the tourism balance of payments. Some immediately jump to the conclusion that this is a reflection of poor performance by the tourist industry, but that is not necessarily the case. The comparison of arrivals and departures is akin to comparing apples and oranges: we do not expect to balance wheat or banana exports and imports.

In spite of the reduced number of American visitors, more than four of every five foreign visitors to Canada are residents of the United States. American companies are also extremely important in all aspects of tourism, including transportation and accommodation. Canada's Wonderland, an amusement park on the outskirts of Toronto, is owned by an American company and was developed by Taft Broadcasting partly because of the site's accessibility to the American market. In spite of the park's name, the Canadian theme area has yet to be completed.

Americans do not constitute the majority of tourists in Canada, however: approximately three out of four pleasure trips to Canadian destinations are taken by Canadians. At most sites, Americans will be in the minority. However, the distribution of American visitors is not even. There is a tendency for them to be concentrated near access points in close proximity to the border. Nonetheless, approximately two-thirds of the customers of Ontario outfitters of fishermen and hunters are Americans, and the proportion of Americans increases with the distance from Toronto and southwest Ontario. In northwest Ontario, the prairies, British Columbia, and the far north, American patronage approaches 100 per cent. Thus, the distribution of American tourists – and, by extension, their influence – is complex.

THE AMERICAN MARKET
FOR HIGH CULTURE

I have written elsewhere on the arts, their clientele, their economic impact, and their links with tourism. My interest in this topic began with a study of a number of recreational and cultural facilities in Toronto.[5] While working at the Art Gallery of Ontario, I became aware of the impending Tutankhamun exhibition.[6] It was staged in seven locations in the United States between 1976 and 1979 before its arrival in Toronto in 1979. The Art Gallery of Ontario approached the provincial ministry of tourism for assistance in marketing the exhibition. The initial discussions immediately revealed a divergence of priorities. The ministry saw the opportunity to attract American tourists and dollars and wanted to advertise in the United States. The Art Gallery of Ontario saw its major responsibility as serving the Ontario public, particularly since Americans had already had ample opportunity see the treasures. The result was that there was little cooperation between the two in marketing. As it happened, the exhibition became a media event, and the art gallery received a great deal of free advertising in the form of newspaper and television feature stories. However, only 10.7 per cent of visitors to the Toronto exhibit were American.

Some months later the Art Gallery of Ontario mounted an exhibit entitled "Van Gogh and the Birth of Cloisonnisme." While the show was a major artistic event, it received less media coverage than the Tutankhamun exhibition. The Van Gogh exhibition did not travel to the United States, and admission was much more readily available than for the Tutankhamun exhibition. Nevertheless, more than 90 per cent of the visitors to the exhibition were Canadian.[7] Thus, both exhibitions drew about 10 per cent of their visitors from the United States.

The proportion of American visitors varies greatly by attraction and by season, and this knowledge can be useful for marketing purposes. For example, approximately 40 per cent of visitors to the Ontario Science Centre during the summer are from the United States. In preparation for the Chinese exhibition in 1982, the centre decided to advertise extensively in the American border cities to attract summer tourists but to limit advertising in the local market. It was hoped that Toronto residents might be encouraged to visit in the fall, thus leading to a more even flow of visitors.

Theatrical festivals are popular tourist attractions in Ontario, and the American market is important to them.[8] Again, the proportion of Americans varies considerably between sites. Surveys undertaken in 1985 revealed that 44.3 per cent of visitors to the Stratford Shakespearean Festival were Americans; the figures for the Shaw Festival in Niagara-on-the-Lake and for Blyth (Ontario) were 32.4 per cent and 1.6 per cent respectively. With the exception of Blyth, which specializes in Canadian plays set in rural and small-town settings, original works by Canadians are seldom performed. Distance from the border is a contributing factor in the small proportion of Americans at Blyth, but it is not the only factor. The evidence suggests that as a festival gains recognition it tends to attract people from further afield. They tend to have high incomes and educations and, because they have come a long way, they must stay overnight. In consequence, their expenditures on accommodation and food tend to be large. Such people, many of whom are Americans in the cases of Stratford and Niagara-on-the-Lake, are highly desirable customers from the perspective of the local business community.

PURCHASES OF SOUVENIRS

In addition to the costs of travel, accommodation, and food, most tourists make expenditures that are often collected by analysts into an "other" category. Such items are important because of their contribution to local economies. The items purchased may also provide a clue to the perception of place. During the summer of 1986 Canadian and American travellers were interviewed on the north shore of Lake Superior concerning the purchases they had made and the factors that influenced their shopping decisions.[9] A larger proportion of Americans (57 per cent) than Canadians (45 per cent) purchased souvenirs and, on average, Americans spent more than Canadians. Americans constituted 40 per cent of those interviewed; they represent a large and comparatively free-spending market segment. However, no major differences were found in the criteria used to select souvenirs – price, originality, beauty, and workmanship. An important but not surprising difference between the two groups was that Americans were more likely than Canadians to purchase souvenirs derived from or based upon native cultures. Proprietors of sales outlets verified in interviews that such items were particularly popular among American visitors.

A full interpretation of these results awaits more detailed analyses, because Canadian tourists also differed from Americans in ways other than nationality and purchases. For example, American travellers, on average, were considerably older, more likely to be visiting the area for the first time (66 per cent as compared with 28 per cent of Canadians) and less likely to be on a business trip (2 per cent as compared with 14 per cent).

CULTURAL GROUPS AS TOURIST
ATTRACTIONS

In much the same way that tourism has developed in warm climates, stunning topography, and places of historical or religious significance, so also has it been based upon a culture or a way of life. Human beings display a natural curiosity about people who are different from themselves. The people who are objects of interest may lead simple, mundane lives but may, nevertheless, appear exotic in the eyes of the tourist. Indeed, the very existence of an ethnic distinction may create a tourist attraction.[10] The natives of the southwestern United States and of the Canadian west coast and Arctic are examples of people who have become tourist attractions.

The marketing of a culture for tourism inevitably changes the culture. The local citizens may choose to become involved in the tourist industry by catering to tourists' desires. For example, they may set up roadside stands selling arts and crafts or sell tickets to view or take part in a traditional cultural event. At the same time they may become resentful of the tourists and the problems associated with large numbers of visitors.

The Old Order Mennonites of the Waterloo, Ontario, region and the Old Order Amish of Lancaster County, Pennsylvania, provide good examples of culture as a tourist attraction. Both groups place great importance on remaining separate from society: they wear a sixteenth-century mode of dress, use horses and buggies for transportation, and reject the use of telephones and electricity. Nostalgia for the quaint, peaceful, and often idealized lifestyles of the Amish and Mennonites provokes curiosity among many North Americans, and entrepreneurs promote the groups as tourist attractions.

A comparison of tourism in the Waterloo region and Lancaster County has the potential to reveal similarities and differences in American and Canadian development of cultural groups for tourism. An analysis of attractions, tours, accommodations, restaurants, shopping, and interpretive centres reveals that the exploitation of cultural themes is much more frequent and more extreme in Lancaster County than in the Waterloo region.[11] Pictures of the Amish and references to their lifestyles are much more common in promotional materials and in roadside advertisements than similar references to the Mennonites. Furthermore, larger-than-life statues of Amish men and contrived attractions (such as the Dutch Wonderland and Water Buggy entertainment complexes) which, in spite of their names, have little basis in the local culture are found much more often in Lancaster County than in the Waterloo region. The inescapable conclusion is that the local culture is exploited to a greater degree and in more commercial ways in Lancaster County. This is not to imply that signs of movement in the same direction are absent in the latter case. Could it be that Waterloo is some years behind Lancaster but headed in the same direction, or do Canadians tend to be less extreme in many ways than their American counterparts? Either way the interpretation fits commonly held notions of the differences between Canadians and Americans.

THE MARKETING OF CANADA

In this essay I have stressed the importance of tourism, especially American tourism, to Canada. The importance of American tourists lies both in their numbers and in their expenditures while in Canada. As foreign tourists, Americans spend more money, on average, than Canadian vacationers. The importance of an American clientele has been documented with respect to cultural events and, to a lesser extent, the purchase of souvenirs. A comparison of tourism in

Waterloo, Ontario, and Lancaster County, Pennsylvania, suggests that cultural groups may be exploited for tourism in a more commercial manner in the United States than in Canada.

Given the proximity of the United States and its large population, it is not surprising that major proportions of marketing budgets, both at national and provincial levels, are spent to activate the u.s. market. While Americans constitute a large proportion of foreign visitors to Canada, less than 5 per cent of all trips taken by Americans, including domestic trips, are to Canada. Thus there is plenty of scope for increased market penetration.

For many years the message directed at potential American visitors was "moose, mountains, and Mounties." The rugged fisherman clad in a plaid shirt, sitting in a canoe in the middle of a picturesque mountain lake, was almost always a part of the publicity. Natural environments and magnificent scenery were stressed. Mounties constituted a Canadian symbol that Hollywood has glamourized, and their images were widely employed in tourism advertising.[12] However, to avoid disappointment among visitors, what is advertised must also be made available. The implication was that no foreign visitors' trips to Canada would be complete until they had their photographs taken with a Mountie. Unfortunately, while there is a lot of scenery in Canada, there are insufficient Mounties to cover the ground. Small numbers are stationed in visible locations (for example, outside the parliament buildings) so that tourists' expectations can be met. Also, additional help must be hired for the summer to change the guard. Reality is moulded to make it congruent with an image.

A 1986 study conducted by Longwoods Research Group Inc. for Tourism Canada resulted in major changes in marketing strategies. To the surprise of many Canadians, Americans believe that their own outdoors is just as attractive as Canada's. Canada does not have a comparative advantage in wilderness, as was previously thought, since the United States has areas which are just as great, just as white, and just as far north. Although Canada continues to market its outdoors, this tactic is now supplemented with images of vibrant, clean, safe cities with good shopping and ample nightlife. One journalist described the new strategy as a "cross between Las Vegas naughtiness and a bracing summer camp, with a dollop of European quaintness from vieux Quebec tossed in for good measure."[13] "The World Next Door" became the new slogan as an attempt was made (at a cost of $20 million in 1986) to employ ethnic diversity and cultural attractions to demonstrate that Canada can be a foreign destination at the end of a day's car ride rather than an ocean crossing. Is this an appropriate image for Canada? It certainly reflects a greater emphasis in tourist marketing on some expressions of Canadian culture as opposed to natural attractions.

What is an authentic Canadian experience? The question is all the more difficult to answer when it is acknowledged that most tourists spend much of their time in environments that are purpose-built to cater to their perceived needs and desires. However, there is more at stake than image: what is advertised must also be made available if visitors' expectations are to be met. The biblical dictum for life is particularly appropriate to tourism: that which ye sow, that shall ye also reap.

PART FIVE

Reflections

Since many of the essays in this volume deal with specific topics, readers are fortunate that this concluding part is a series of reflections that try to bring together some of the broad themes outlined in the preface and introduction. In the first essay Paul Rutherford, a leading historian of Canadian culture, reflects upon Canada's experience with mass culture during the past hundred years or so. Along the way he seeks to dispel several myths, especially nationalist ones. His focus is "the products, services, and practices manufactured by the communications, advertising, education, sports, leisure, and recreation industries to serve a huge market of consumers." However, he wisely warns readers that large chunks of the history of mass culture in this country have not been explored in sufficient detail. Rutherford notes that at the time of Confederation the United States was viewed as corrupt, disorderly, and money-oriented, which inspired various forms of moral protectionism to insulate those north of the border from such taint. Yet the developing mass culture of the United States gradually seeped northward through tourism, newspapers, magazines, books, and sports. In the 1920s, Rutherford argues, urban Canadians in particular "became wedded to the idea that a continuous supply of American entertainment and sports was their birthright." The old and new media of mass communications – magazines, movies, and radio – were the most important agencies of Americanization. Critics, including moralists, nationalists, and highbrows, bemoaned the onslaught of mass culture and the loss of cultural sovereignty. Thus state agencies of culture such as the CBC and the National Film Board made their appearance. Although cultural nationalists received additional support from the Massey report of 1951, mass culture continued to grow in popularity in the 1950s and 1960s, especially with the advent of television and then cable TV. Rutherford argues that Canadian mass culture is part of a continental popular culture in which the 49th parallel has only slight significance, something that only élite cultural nationalists continue to resist and reject.

In her commentary on American popular culture in Canada, Thelma McCormack, a sociologist, begins by defining popular culture broadly as "both an art form and a record, a source of pleasure and a way of learning about a people." In scholarly terms, the study of popular culture remains diffuse, diverse, and lacking in coherent theory. Research on popular culture has itself become a form of popular culture. She illustrates her discussion of various theories and models of mass society, leisure, and cultural hegemony by showing how the contributors to this volume can be identified with the several traditions. She concludes that it may be time for a "different paradigm based on theories of social control." McCormack reflects on a series of recent developments that have affected the current state of concern over identity and cultural nationalism in Canada. Given the advent of the Charter of Rights and Freedoms, the North American free trade agreements, and cultural bureaucracies, McCormack insists that the search for a national identity in Canada has to examine the role of the state, especially with respect to the critical edge of the relationship between state and culture, the issue of pornography and censorship. McCormack regards efforts to regulate pornography as a good example of the recent conservative cultural environment in English-speaking countries and as "part of a more general policy of decontrolling the economy and controlling morality." She identifies pornography as a highly popular form of mass culture, often imported from the United States. In her judgment, students of popular culture and civil libertarians had an obligation to defend the unfettered distribution of pornography to adults when the practice was attacked in the 1980s. She views government efforts to censor pornography as "a threat to all creativity, to all popular culture" and as a form of "cultural oppression."

The final essay is by Andrew Wernick, a cultural theorist, who emphasizes the national and socioeconomic determinants of American dominance of Canadian popular culture. His judgment is

that "from TV and pop music to fast food and fashion, the homogenized style of mass consumption we think of as American popular culture is all-pervasive, its continuous penetration of Canadians'
symbolic life not just imposed but gladly welcomed." In fact,
those living in the hinterlands feel deprived of adequate access. The
seductive appeal of U.S. popular culture continues to raise
serious issues of national autonomy, even as the "history of shared
origins and mutual borrowings ... makes problematic the very
distinction between what is Canadian and what is American." Yet
at the same time the penetration, domination, and homogenizing effect of U.S. mass culture is an international phenomenon of
"commodification."

16 Made in America: The Problem of Mass Culture in Canada

PAUL RUTHERFORD

> A nation needs a literature – including some anonymous sage from bygone days and a gallery of talented writers in more recent times.
> K.R. Minogue,
> *Nationalism* (1967)

The doctrine of nationalism has bedevilled intellectual discourse in Canada.[1] The country has never fit the ideal model: there has always loomed some outside empire, whether centred in London, the Vatican, or Washington, to restrict the country's sovereignty; the persistence of the "two solitudes," French and English, has made a mockery of efforts to build a pan-Canadian nationality; and the derivative or dependent character of our social or literary or even audio-visual life has been a bitter pill for any devout nationalist to swallow. Unfortunately, nationalist thinking has usually prevailed in debates about culture. My purpose here is to reflect upon the cultural experience of Canada during the past hundred years or so and, along the way, to dispel several myths about what it all means.

I am most interested in the phenomenon of mass culture, which refers to the products, services, and practices manufactured by the communications, advertising, education, sports, leisure, and recreation industries to serve a huge market of consumers. Note that we are dealing with industrial products, whether the creator and/or distributor is a private company (Canada's Wonderland), a public corporation (the Canadian Broadcasting Corporation), or even a voluntary association (a parent-teacher association). Thus mass culture incorporates such phenomena as advertising, tourism, televangelism, schooling, shopping, and teen dances. It has shaped the passion for news as well as the search for diversion. The chief characteristic of this culture is that its products are accessible to very large numbers of people, unlike opera, much scholarship, and even folk art. Entertainment, sports, news and views, and advertising are among the most important things that a people can share; they foster that community of discourse and interest necessary, according to Karl Deutsch and other theorists, to support a separate national existence.[2]

Much of the argument that follows can be described as tentative and sometimes speculative, since there are large chunks of Canada's cultural history (notably its popular culture) that have not been explored in detail.[3] In such circumstances a survey of the kind attempted here is likely to miss, if not misconstrue, some important dimensions of what happened. The risk seems worthwhile to bring some order to the field.

Underpinning the political nationality launched in 1867 was a social ideology that expressed the values of the bourgeois mainstream in British North America. "Our scheme is to establish a government," said George Brown during the Confederation debates, "that will endeavour to maintain liberty, justice, and christianity [sic] throughout the land."[4] That reference to Christianity, "la principe de notre force" and "the chief cornerstone" of our civilization, would have sparked in contemporaries a recognition of a much wider range of presumptions about the proper society, presumptions that might best be described as the Victorian ethos.[5] Before and after Confederation, both francophone and anglophone newspapers urged the virtues of a community organized around a series of moral authorities and disciplines: the churches and religion, the family and marriage, the workplace and the work ethic, the school and education, the courts and the rule of law, political parties and partisan loyalties.[6] People were expected to abide by an increasingly rigid code of behaviour which segregated the sexes, emphasized self-improvement and class harmony, and embodied a puritanical distrust of pleasure.[7] Although such dreams were never altogether realized in practice – late nineteenth-century Canada was in many ways an "Un-Victorian society" – the ethos imparted to Canada an image as a purer and better country (often portrayed as a young if rather stern maiden) than its big neighbour to south (which was depicted as an older, leaner, slightly seedy male).[8] Indeed what struck many Canadians when they looked at American society was its disorder, its corruption, its worship of Mammon – in a word, its lack of an effective moral authority.[9]

The ideology was sufficient to justify efforts to protect Canada against the ill effects of the American example and American ideas.

One reason that Egerton Ryerson, Ontario's long-time schoolmaster, insisted on taking control of Ontario's textbooks and library books was to rid the state's chief cultural agency, the public schools, of American reading material.[10] A section of the Customs Act, reaffirmed in the famous National Policy Tariff of 1879, prohibited the entry of indecent and treasonous matter, and over time the Customs Department would create what amounted to a Canadian index of forbidden works.[11] A prohibition on the importation, sale, or possession of alcohol in the Northwest Territories was imposed in 1875 to prevent the arrival of the American whisky-trader and, more generally, the lifestyle of the American west.[12] A purpose of the many sabbatarian laws, which culminated in the Lord's Day Act of 1906, was to block the emergence of something journalists liked to call "the American Sunday," apparently a day of unhindered licence when bars and theatres stayed open, sporting events were scheduled, streetcars operated, and commerce thrived.

None of this moral protectionism, however, served to prevent the northward spread of the developing mass culture of the United States. Indeed, Canadian élites sometimes welcomed aspects of that culture. Consider the case of tourism: the respected citizens who promoted Quebec City's first winter carnival in 1894 were intent on attracting American visitors by presenting their community as the home of a happy family, set in a pre-industrial past, where people could escape their daily cares.[13] Likewise, the CPR and other entrepreneurs marketed the country's unspoiled wilderness, its majestic mountains, the awesome Niagara Falls, and beautiful lakes and streams for the pleasure of the sportsman and the tourist alike.[14] Even before the close of the century, then, tourism and travel literature were applying particular images to Canadian places and scenes, if not to the country as a whole.[15]

The most powerful agent of Americanization was the daily press – which was something of a paradox, since it was the workings of the press that created a community of discourse across Canada. The self-styled people's journals that appeared in the late nineteenth century, dailies like the Montreal *Star*, the Toronto *Telegram*, or later Montreal's *La Presse*, were modelled upon the American journals of sensation, human interest, and crusades like James Bennett's *Herald* or Joseph Pulitzer's *World* in New York, although the Canadian version of yellow journalism remained comparatively mild by American standards.[16] By the 1880s and 1890s, newspapers were full of ads for American patent medicines and brand-name goods; just as important, the advertising copy for Canadian products or department stores employed the same style of "Tall Talk" and reason-why argument prevalent in American cities.[17]

Nearly all dailies, even high-quality papers like the Toronto *Globe* or the Montreal *Gazette*, took much of their world news from American papers or news agencies and often subscribed to American syndication services which supplied feature material, humour and fiction, even sermons. According to a survey taken in 1895, thirty-three papers subscribed to the United Press Service and fourteen to the rival Associated Press.[18] The result, said an unhappy *Le Monde* in 1892, was that "le plus petit incident" occurring in the United States was telegraphed across the dominion while important news from Europe was always slighted.[19] Such a concern led the Toronto *Telegram* and the Montreal *Star*, assisted by a modest grant from the federal government, to organize a Canadian Associated Press in 1903 to furnish a summary of news from London directly to Canadian clients. Yet when the Canadian Press news agency was organized after 1907, its chief role was initially to act as a holding company for the Canadian rights to the Associated Press's world copy.[20]

The situation was no less complicated when attention shifted to other kinds of leisure and literary material. There was no tradition of Canadian play-writing to speak of, and most theatres depended on foreign touring companies, mostly American. British and American magazines had always found a ready audience in middle-class homes in English Canada, so when home-grown periodicals like the *Canadian Magazine* or *Maclean's* entered the picture they found that outsiders already occupied their market; in 1912 it was estimated that sales of British magazines and newspapers stood at $77,000, and sales of their American rivals at $880,000.[21] Book publishers made their money by offering British and American reprints rather than original Canadian works, because that practice suited bourgeois tastes.[22] A survey of lists of two hundred bestsellers in English between 1899 and 1919 counted 44 per cent by American authors, 36 per cent by Britishers, and 21 per cent by Canadians.[23] A number of English-Canadian authors like Charles Gordon (writing as Ralph Connor), Gilbert Parker, Stephen Leacock, and Margaret Saunders won large Canadian audiences and some international fame by writing moralistic adventures, historical romances, humour, and animal stories.[24] Their reputation in Britain and the United States was the first evidence of a successful adaptation by a group of Canadians to the tastes of anglophone readers elsewhere.

Similarly, in the novel realm of organized sports, imported and indigenous games competed for public favour. Ice-hockey began to develop as Canada's winter sport after 1890, reaching across the country by 1905, although its appeal as a participation sport was apparently limited largely to the middle class. British games like cricket and above all soccer survived because successive groups of immigrants from the old country kept them alive. A lacrosse league with teams based in Vancouver, Toronto, and Montreal had appeared by 1907, although the sport never fulfilled its boast of becoming Canada's national game. That accolade better suited baseball, which was played and watched in cities and towns across the land by all kinds of people. "When the Eastern League for 1905 opened in Toronto," noted Samuel Moffett, "the Ontario Legislature cut short its session for the game and the Prime Minister pitched the first ball."[25] Baseball was also the most professional and commercial of sports, characteristics which the athletic purist correctly identified as American, since it was in the United States that entrepreneurs pioneered spectator sports as a commodity to satisfy the mass demand for leisure pursuits. The assorted leaders of amateur sports in Canada, mostly drawn from the upper echelons of society, fought a vigorous rearguard action to prevent the professionalization of their games, part of a general effort to preserve the status of organized sport as a pastime of the gentleman.[26]

What was especially striking, in sports and much else, was that the taste for things American was greatest among the young and the masses. Many an editor over the years worried about the impact upon impressionable young minds of "pernicious literature" – dime novels, adventure and humour stories, illustrated magazines, all from down south. The American-style people's journals caught on first with clerks, factory workers, domestics, and the like, some of whom had never before been regular newspaper readers. The records of mechanic's institutes and public libraries (many of which were assisted by the generosity of the American millionaire Andrew Carnegie) indicated a definite popular taste for escapist novels, much to the disgust of moralists. What appealed to ordinary folks were professional leagues and professional stars, one of the first being Toronto's Ned Hanlan, the world's best sculler between 1880 and 1884. For most people live performances meant American vaudeville, melodrama, and circuses: it was, for example, American troupes who brought burlesque shows to Montreal and Quebec city in the pre-war years.[27]

In short, the building of a Victorian Canada was very much an élite cause, though undeniably the ethos had many champions among urban professionals and businessmen as well as in the farm homes of rural Canada. The rougher elements of society preferred an entertainment that was imported from the United States or that imitated American ways.

"The conclusion to which all the converging lines of evidence unmistakably point is that the Americans and the English-speaking Canadians have been welded into one people," wrote the American Samuel E. Moffett in 1907, in a PH.D. thesis first entitled *The Emancipation of Canada*, later *The Americanization of Canada*. "The English-speaking Canadians protest that they will never become Americans – they are already Americans without knowing it."[28] Moffett was right, up to a point: a continental outlook was in the making. The mythology of individualism, the belief in "home, sweet home," the image of the evil city – these and many other notions were shared by people living on both sides of the border.[29] Yet even he recognized that Canadian leaders and newspapers were devoted to their British dominion and hostile to absorption into the flawed republic. Besides, in French Canada the persistence of a traditional cast of mind and the powerful influence of Catholicism buttressed a separate and distinct sense of nationality. Nearly as important, at least in English Canada, was the presence of the British counterweight: in 1905–6 J.A. Hobson found that British books and magazines were commonplace.[30] It was not surprising that the Conservative opposition won a spectacular victory in 1911, in part by warning voters that the reciprocity agreement sponsored by Sir Wilfrid Laurier's Liberals would swiftly lead to the absorption of Canada by the United States. This merely reaffirmed the fact that Canadians were the other Americans.

In retrospect, the 1920s were a turning-point in cultural history. Especially in the cities, Canadians became wedded to the idea that a continuous supply of American entertainment and sports was their birthright. In part that was because of the decline or disappearance of any countervailing forces to American influences. But the chief cause was actually Canada's porous border: there was an extraordinary increase in the pace and scope of that American penetration which had always been an aspect of the Canadian experience. Provincial governments speeded the arrival of the so-called car culture by pouring money into highway development to attract the Yankee tourist, even though rural voters were none too pleased by the invasion of the automobile – two to four million American cars were coming each year by the end of the 1920s.[31]

The small doings of America's professional sports world dominated the pages of daily newspapers, and sportswriters turned players like baseball's Babe Ruth and boxing's Jack Dempsey into national heroes.[32] Lacrosse soon became virtually extinct as an organized sport. Hockey was transformed, and perhaps saved, by an American takeover in the mid-1920s, which turned the so-called National Hockey League into a commercial and professional sport along American lines. Still, if most of the franchises were now in the United States, most of the players remained Canadian.[33] By contrast, Canadian football was troubled by the spectre of too many American "imports" coaching and playing, though the acceptance of the forward pass in 1931 indicated that the process of Americanization would continue largely unchecked.[34] In any case, the 1920s were the first years in which Canadians generally, like Americans, were caught up in sports madness as fans and spectators.[35]

The most important agencies of Americanization, however, were the old and new media of mass communications. In 1928 another British visitor to Canada lamented the fact that British publications had virtually disappeared from sight, to be replaced with American products.[36] The circulation of American magazines had reached some 50 million copies by 1926: four years later *Pictorial Review*, *McCall's*, *True Story*, and *Saturday Evening Post* (which called itself, with some exaggeration, "Canada's leading magazine") had over 100,000 Canadian sales per issue.[37] But while some Canadian magazines survived, a Canadian movie industry did not. When the Hollywood moguls took control of production, distribution, and exhibition right after the war, the few Canadian interests, such as the producer Ernest Shipman or the Allen chain of cinemas, were replaced or swallowed up, as were independents throughout the continent.[38] People in ever-increasing numbers watched the Hollywood product: there were over 100 million paid admissions by 1930, making movie stars like Mary Pickford, Douglas Fairbanks, or Tom Mix Canada's stars as well (Pickford, America's sweetheart, happened to be Toronto-born).

And it appeared that radio, the most recent of the new media, would go the same way, since the development of private radio was extremely slow by comparison with the explosive growth in the United States, where the NBC and CBS networks were already supplying enriched programming. It was estimated that 80 per cent of the programs Canadians listened to at the end of the 1920s were American.[39] Three of the country's most important radio stations – CKAC (Montreal), CFRB (Toronto), and CKGW (Toronto) – became affiliates of American networks in 1929.[40] That enabled CKGW to bring in NBC's highly successful *Amos 'n' Andy*, which had already proved as popular with Canadian audiences as with American. All of this foreshadowed an American takeover of the airwaves.

The onslaught coincided with the popularity of one particular image of Canada as a land of empty spaces, of wilderness, of Nature, an image that ironically suggested a Canada untouched by urban ways or mass culture. Such imagery had enjoyed some currency in intellectual and literary circles for many years, where the ideal of "the true north, strong and free" appealed as a way of identifying Canada's distinctiveness in a fashion that avoided the consequences of racial diversity.[41] But this image was established as a leitmotif in mainstream thinking about the country by the actions of a mix of Canadian and American agents. One genre of popular literature in which Canadian authors had come to excel was nature writing, whether that meant natural history, outdoors books, or animal biographies: perhaps the most famous Canadian writer of the 1930s was the bogus Indian, Grey Owl, who wrote about the romance of the Canadian wilderness and the fascinating ways of wildlife.[42] Even more important, though, was the Group of Seven, whose special vision of Canada as a land of harsh and noble grandeur was greeted with rave reviews inside and outside the country and swiftly popularized among the masses: the artists became "cultural heroes" and their work "national icons."[43]

The chief American agency was Hollywood, which during the 1920s marketed a large number of "northerns," portraying Canada as a great, often snowy wilderness, where wolves, halfbreeds, whites, and Mounties fought each other and nature, where the unspoiled environment held out the hope of moral regeneration.[44] Even the state played its part, through tourist advertisements, scenic films, and promotions designed to attract resource capital. It was fitting that the Canada pavilion at the famous "World of Tomorrow" World's Fair in New York in 1939 presented an impression of Canada as a largely unpopulated place full of scenic wonders and infinite resources.[45] It all suggested a land without a past, but with a glorious future.

That kind of imagery may have disturbed some observers. Much more worrisome, though, was the fact that the mass culture of America posed a severe challenge to the Victorian ethos which gave an additional definition to the dominion. The messages of advertising, entertainment, and sports represented a revolt against America's own Victorian past. Simply put, mass culture rejected some of its core values (like self-restraint), transmuted others (like home, sweet home), and incorporated another group (like femininity or individualism). And it absorbed elements of pre-existing subcultures that had been outside the mainstream, whether regional (southern country music), ethnic (black ragtime), proletarian (rough sports), or youth (experimentation) to fashion a new, ersatz brew that appealed to everyman and everywoman, and most especially to the middle classes.[46]

Two examples will suffice. Except for a brief period in the late 1910s, Hollywood did not directly confront the Victorian credo of puritanism. Rather, its westerns, romances, comedies, and the like worked so well because, among other things, they offered a series of dream worlds in which the peoples and the sexes mixed, in which fantasies about sex and violence could be played out, in which goods as well as people were on display, where private fulfilment was emphasized, even if the moral resolution of the plot might hark back to Victorian days.[47] This message neatly fitted the gospel of conspicuous consumption which the triumphant advertisers were preaching in print and over the airwaves. They were heralds of modernity, showing people how to realize themselves and fulfil their fantasies through the purchase of goods: a car to demonstrate status, a mouthwash to bring social success, bath towels to beautify the home, and a washing-machine to ease the burden of housework.[48] Altogether this amounted to a message of liberation from the old-fashioned rigours that had conditioned the life of the previous generation, and in some measure it became a celebration of hedonism.

Little wonder that the onslaught of mass culture upset moralists, nationalists, and those who would soon be called highbrows in Canada. Indeed, many a critic belonged to all of these camps. The hold of traditionalism on the country's intelligentsia was extraordinary, not just in the 1920s but for the next generation as well, and their views were often echoed by church and women's groups, in the daily press, and by home-grown magazines. "How can a generation fed on movies and bred on motors understand Wordsworth?" asked the academic Archibald MacMechan.[49]

Admittedly, few critics were quite so extreme as Abbé Lionel Groulx and Action Française, the dominant circle of Quebec nationalists in the 1920s, who condemned such assorted American agents as the yellow press, the cinema, vaudeville, fashion and advertising columns, and dance halls for spewing forth a mental and moral poison that imperiled the health of the French-Canadian community.[50] But the animus, the fear of contamination, was enough to legitimate new efforts to protect the Canadian hearth and home against foreign books, magazines, and above all movies. The provincial governments employed boards of censors to ban offensive movies (101 features in 1932) and to cut offensive scenes (apparently, sexual innuendo was removed from *Gone with the Wind* in Quebec). The definition of what was offensive was very broad: "pictures of crime," "pictures of horror," "excessive drinking," "loose conduct between men and women," religious or racial ridicule, even undemocratic opinions.[51]

Increasingly, critics had begun to wrap themselves in the flag and argue the merits of cultural sovereignty. The danger for Canada no longer lay in annexation, Archibald MacMechan warned in 1920, but "in a spiritual bondage – the subjection of the Canadian nation's mind and soul to the mind and soul of the United States."[52] Avoiding this imminent peril required that the state either privilege or establish media that would express and nourish Canada's soul. That was not easy to do. Proposals for a yearly quota requiring that perhaps 20 per cent of the films displayed should be British were impractical, partly because of industry opposition but also because there were not enough British movies and those that were available often did not appeal to audiences. In 1931 the Conservative government imposed special duties on American magazines with many ads or full of fiction or comics (in a word, lowbrow). Circulation figures published some years later indicated that leading Canadian periodicals gained while their American rivals lost; even so, the duties disappeared after the Liberals returned to power in 1935.[53] The lasting achievements were the establishment of public radio in 1932, the Canadian Broadcasting Corporation in 1936, and the National Film Board in 1939, which gave the state the tools to realize some of the goals of cultural nationalism.

In fact, the record of these state agencies of culture was mixed. Under the masterly direction of John Grierson, the British documentary filmmaker, the NFB excelled as a source of wartime propaganda which reached millions because it was able to use regular cinemas and to establish non-theatrical circuits to show the product. But that did not threaten the dominance of Hollywood, and after the war the significance of the NFB quickly waned.[54]

The CBC, by contrast, did become an instrument of mass entertainment, or rather two different kinds of entertainment, because it was divided into French and English services, which prevented public radio from ever realizing early hopes that it would build a pan-Canadian consciousness. The French service managed to exploit the existing tradition of popular literature in Quebec to produce some extraordinarily successful radioromans about life in Quebec's past and present. The English service had more success with its hockey broadcasts, which finally made hockey Canada's national sport and the announcer Foster Hewitt a household name, and with its radio plays, notably Andrew Allan's *Stage* series, which featured adapted and original plays by Canadians and won a large enough audience to become the national theatre of English Canada. Yet often the biggest draws on the CBC schedule were the American imports, carried to please listeners and wean them away from American stations. Thus in the February 1950 ratings sweepstakes the top two radio programs on CBL-Toronto were *The Bob Hope Show* and *Fibber McGee and Molly*, followed at some distance by a similar Canadian offering, *The Wayne and Shuster Show*.[55] The CBC's importance in radio also waned after the war because independent private stations grew in number and power, and so in reach; they offered Canadians a steady diet of recorded American music as well as comedy and drama. But the CBC excelled as a producer of educational broadcasts, opinion forums, and high-quality programming (notably *Wednesday Night*), which earned it kudos from highbrows, though these offerings hardly constituted a counterweight to American imports.

The reality was that Canadian audiences, and especially anglophone audiences, by and large preferred the imported American entertainment even to home-grown imitations, never mind to high-quality material. That did not make them into Americans, however. A survey of opinion carried out by H.F. Angus and other researchers during the mid-1930s indicated that the images of American life flooding Canada often upset Canadians and convinced them of the superiority of their own country. Americans were seen as excitable, even "childlike," "money-mad," lawless, "more corrupt" and "less moral," boastful, and "less cultured," although they were given credit for being "daring and enterprising" or generous. By contrast, Canadians appeared more honourable, law-abiding, and conservative, and their society "quieter, slower in tempo and saner in quality."[56] Public opinion polls during and after the war indicated a similar desire to remain separate: true, in 1943 21 per cent of respondents did feel Canada ought to join the United States, but that figure had fallen to 10 per cent in 1952, where it would remain throughout the 1950s.[57] Put another way, the onslaught of mass culture had not yet destroyed the Victorian imprint on the Canadian identity.

No one should have been surprised that the famous post-war "culture probe," the Massey Commission, worried about "the very present danger of permanent dependence" on "a single alien source."[58] Nor that it espoused an élitist definition of culture ("that part of education which enriches the mind and refines the taste") and evinced a disdain for the vulgarity and the materialism it found all too common on the air and in print.[59] The Massey Commission was born out of "the revolt of the highbrows" against the rule of commerce and the influence of mass culture. A loose coalition of arts, letters, musical, and academic groups took up a crusade to civilize Canada and, in the process, to assert their own significance as a cultural élite.[60] Vincent Massey, the man chosen to head the commission, had already published a tract entitled *On Being Canadian* (1948), wherein he proclaimed the need for the Canadian people to recognize the claims of the arts and crafts, high culture, and the academy, and for the state to sponsor the growth of high culture. He was joined by three academics and one lonely engineer, placing the ivory tower in command. Their 1951 report, both lengthy (517 pages) and literate (opening with a quote from St. Augustine), became the new bible for the cultural nationalists.

Things would change, though not always as the commissioners had hoped. The next fifteen years witnessed the apparent victory of a mature and homogeneous mass culture over the separate identities of class, region, and rural life across the whole of North America. Sports, advertising, and above all entertainment offered a much needed solace to North Americans in a world of insecurity and complexity by propagating, as Roland Marchand has chronicled, "compensating, vicarious adventures in potency and dominion" for a mass of anxious consumers.[61] Canada was no exception: more leisure and more money broke down the old barriers to permissiveness, though it did take time.[62] Beginning in the early 1950s, liquor laws slowly eased across English Canada, Sunday sports and Sunday newspapers became common, and the courts, the customs officials, and the movie censors proved increasingly lenient in their standards of acceptability. The discovery of teenagers set loose a youth cult with its own music, style of dress, codes of behaviour, products, and heroes: when *Love Me Tender*, Elvis Presley's first film, opened in Toronto in 1956, adolescents broke through the cinema's doors, knocked over police and ushers, smashed two mirrors, tore down Elvis posters, and "used lipstick to scribble 'I Love You' on his publicity stills."[63] A shopping madness swept over the land: total retail sales rose from $5.8 billion in 1946 to $16.5 billion in 1960, which brought into being that new focus of urban life, the shopping plaza – and, briefly in 1968, a venue for a "pop" style of politics because of the newcomer Trudeau, dubbed Pierre de la Plaza.[64]

Teachers and churchmen in the 1960s grew less concerned with upholding old standards, and more worried about their own relevance. In June 1968 there appeared Ontario's famous Hall-Dennis report, *Living and Learning*, which embodied "a concept of education that was romantic, humanitarian, inspiringly idealistic and, most important, directly relevant to contemporary and future society," in the words of one enthusiast.[65] Even in French Canada, tradition gave way to modernity during the course of the Quiet Revolution as

French Canadians rushed to take up all the trappings of North American life. The point was that many of the structures, institutions, and conventions that once had embodied different values and assumptions seemed to be overwhelmed or transformed in the new era of affluence, largely because of the effects of television, that enormously potent instrument of mass culture. It was enough to make one conservative, George Grant, write his lament for a Canada that had passed away, though he blamed everything from Liberal shortsightedness to the Forces of History for the country's sad fate.[66]

The victory of the mass culture soon proved illusory. Even in the United States the waning enthusiasm for television, the birth of the counterculture, the feminist assault on advertising and entertainment, and eventually a neo-conservative reaffirmation of "old values" represented something of a reaction against the images and authority of mass culture. In Canada the sense of the country as a distinct public entity, with its own brand of law, politics, and governance and a civic ethic, had survived the new wave of Americanization. Indeed, at the end of the 1960s the country seemed afire with competing brands of nationalisms: Pierre Trudeau's biculturalism, René Lévesque's separatism, the anti-Americanism of the leftist Waffle element in the NDP, a renewed cultural chauvinism, plus a variety of amalgams and variations. So far had the passion spread that one Canadian advertising executive, Jerry Goodis, grew indignant over what he saw as the rapid takeover of Canadian advertising by American agencies.[67]

The crucial fact was that a Canadian tradition of the "public arts" flourished in print and on the air, even if a closer look would reveal that it was influenced by American news and ways (the best evidence being the emerging popularity of the idea of adversary journalism after 1960). After the mid-1960s, CBC radio came to excel as a medium of information about the affairs and life of the country (among the best of the new shows were *This Country in the Morning* [later *Morningside*] and *As It Happens*), albeit for a small audience of mostly upscale listeners. One can debate whether the competition of television hurt print by stealing away readers or by fostering the notion of news-as-entertainment, though even the overly critical Kent report of 1981 claimed that newspapers remained "the medium of record" and "the main originators, gatherers and summarizers of news."[68] But prime-time television, especially the version supplied by CBC-TV, did cater to the assumption that Canadians were, in the words of Knowlton Nash, a nation of "infomaniacs," just as willing to "engage" as to "escape" the day's happenings, even in the evening hours.[69] Witness those successes of the past, *Point de Mire* or *This Hour Has Seven Days*, as well as the *National / Journal* – the Caplan-Sauvageau task force on broadcasting rightly called news and public affairs "the great Canadian TV success story" because of its supply and its popularity.[70]

One of the signs of a distinct civic ethic was the emergence of the politics of culture as an important dimension of public life, much more vital in Canada than in the United States. The Massey report legitimized the belief that the state must become a major player in the cultural life of the country.[71] Over the course of the next generation the federal government steadily expanded its activities into more and more realms of mass communication, sports, recreation, and leisure activities. It endeavoured to mastermind the development of television (a striking contrast with the neglect of radio in the 1920s), initially relying upon CBC-TV, but after 1958 creating a complicated mix of private and public services purportedly wedded to a common purpose through the workings of the Canadian content regulations and a semi-autonomous regulatory agency.[72]

The CBC remained the government's main cultural instrument. Its expenditures grew from $10 million a year in 1949–50 to almost $1.4 billion in 1990/91 (of which the government contributed nearly $1 billion).[73] The government established the Canada Council in 1957 to fund "the production of works in the arts, humanities, and social sciences"; the council and other special programs and related agencies became central to the continued health and welfare of the arts and academe in Canada.[74] In the early 1960s the state moved forcefully into amateur sports, motivated by a cult of fitness as well as the pursuit of national unity and glory, for world sports had become a new arena of national competition.[75] In 1965 it amended the Income Tax Act to block foreign ownership of newspapers and periodicals. Similar restrictions extended in 1976 to broadcasting, although the government stayed away from regulating the content of print, evidence of the continued homage paid to the notion of a free press.[76]

In 1968 the government created the Canadian Film Development Corporation (now Telefilm Canada) to promote a feature film industry that might finally challenge Hollywood's control. In 1970 the Canadian Radio-television Commission, as it was then known, required that 30 per cent of all music played on AM radio be Canadian; the intention was to promote a record industry and a home-grown style of popular music. The provinces (and even well-off municipalities) soon got into the act, with the establishment of arts councils, educational TV, publishing grants, and the like. In

short, the scope of the state's cultural policies far exceeded the wild-
est dreams of the Massey Commission by the time activity slowed
down in the mid-1970s.[77]

What has all this state activity actually achieved? Fortunately, the
new interest of the state coincided with a burgeoning arts movement. Massey's goal of civilizing the country was realized, and one
should thank the Canada Council (along with business patrons) for
acting as "midwife" to "the upsurge of the arts" that occurred after
1960.[78] Further, the state worked to nourish a cultural élite of authors, artists, performers, producers, and the like, centred in Montreal and Toronto, who took on the neverending task of interpreting
and defending the Canadian experience. The flowering of the novel
in English Canada, the excitement of the Quebec theatre, and the
booming interest in native and Inuit art are evidence that not all of
the doleful effects of mass culture have been realized: the "bad" does
not necessarily drive out the "good." Canada does have a "literature," or maybe two "literatures," to use Minogue's terminology, to
give substance to its national identities.[79] In fact, if one can believe
apologists like Gaile McGregor, Canada has a literature that is radically different in style and character from its American counterpart.[80] However distinct, this literature by and large falls into the
category of élite culture, consumed much more by the highly literate
than by ordinary people.

The achievements in the realm of the popular arts were not as
spectacular because they were already overwhelmingly American,
especially in English-speaking Canada. In the 1950s and 1960s managers and producers at CBC-TV hoped that they would be able to
offer a complete service, including "something distinctive in the entertainment field" to Canadian viewers.[81] The age-old disdain for
the popular arts had finally lost its force. In 1960 the president of
the CBC, Alphonse Ouimet, declared that "Canadian culture embraces everything from sled-dog races to symphony orchestras, from
comedy to opera, from good talks to jazz."[82]

Yet in reality only Radio-Canada, as before, had much permanent
success in this endeavour: it was able to design a collection of
téléromans, the first being the famous La Famille Plouffe, which drew
upon the distinctive traditions and stereotypes in the popular culture of Quebec.[83] In Toronto, by contrast, the TV experiment soon
floundered, after some brief success with variety programming, because of limited talent and resources. Many an Anglo-Canadian artist left the country once his or her accomplishments brought job
offers from elsewhere: the film director and producer Norman
Jewison was only one in a long line of CBC producers who found

"happiness" in Hollywood.[84] In addition, CBC-TV had to carry American imports in choice locations on the prime-time schedule, and in greater numbers than in the radio days, to satisfy viewers and to generate the advertising revenues necessary to finance its home-grown programming. The launching of independent private television in 1960 did not bring about the promised development of a made-in-Canada entertainment; instead, it merely increased the amount of air time given over to American imports in order to guarantee profits. That was what viewers wanted, even in Quebec, where the independent Channel 10 was able to capture Montrealers by offering dubbed American series.[85]

To put it another way, Canadians generally preferred to watch Hollywood film and TV drama, to listen to imported rock and roll, or to read American genre fiction as their chief source of relaxation. From the late 1960s Canadian homes eagerly embraced cable television because it promised them, in addition to better signal reception, access to a wider range of American programming. The Caplan-Sauvageau task force on broadcasting was disturbed by evidence that even in French Canada audiences, especially young people, were consuming more and more American products (dubbed, imported, or direct) than ever before.[86]

Canada's culture critics have nonetheless managed to detect a special flavour, a different mood or tone, even a distinctive tradition in the few examples of the popular arts that Canadians have produced.[87] One of the most venerable of these findings is that Canadian artists have consciously adopted a greater realism than their American counterparts, which might be best described as a borrowing from the tradition of the public arts.[88] The merit of this view is evident when one considers the wealth of historical docudramas produced by the CBC and the NFB, though its proponents usually fail to recognize just how diverse the American product is and to exaggerate the uniqueness of made-in-Canada material.[89] Many of CBC-TV Toronto's successful productions, whether *Front Page Challenge*, *Wayne and Shuster*, *Wojeck*, or *King of Kensington*, were variations on types of programming pioneered in the United States. At least from the nationalist perspective, however, the more serious difficulty is that, as Morris Wolfe pointed out, "the Canadian documentary tradition has never been particularly popular with Canadians themselves."[90]

The greatest defenders of home-grown entertainment have always been the cultural élite, who have persuaded themselves that Anglo-Canadians would consume more if more was only available. That assertion remains dubious: even if production values in Toronto matched those of Hollywood (and it is amazing how often people claim they can "tell" a Canadian show by its look and feel), the fact that the artistic producers will avoid the clichés and the conventions of Hollywood actually makes their work more difficult and less accessible to an audience in search of relaxation. The taste for Canadian entertainment remains particular – except for the occasional *Anne of Green Gables*, which strikes the fancy of the masses. No wonder assertions that the Canada-u.s. free trade agreement posed a threat to Canada's apparently fragile culture did not provoke much response from the public.[91]

Still, the efforts of Canadian television at home were and are a cause for lamentation only among those people who believed in the impossible: that television really could give birth to a Canadian Pop-Cult. cbc-tv has a credible record as an agency that maintains a Canadian voice on the airwaves, much as home-grown newspapers, magazines, and books have done in the realm of print. The record was much less respectable when the context changed from Canada to the world at large: made-in-Canada programming won a domestic audience, but not much in the way of an international reputation. Those superb clowns, Johnny Wayne and Frank Shuster, showed it was not impossible; they appeared sixty-seven times on the Ed Sullivan show, far more than any other comedians, for their special brand of satire and farce pleased American audiences at least as much as Canadian.[92]

Part of the explanation for the cbc's failure lies in the economics of culture: it is very difficult to find money to produce any show that might hope to become an international hit. Ironically, when an independent producer had a modest success with a made-in-Toronto police drama, *Night Heat*, shown on ctv in the late 1980s, it merely earned the disdain of the cultural élite, since the show was so obviously American in style and tone, stripped of all honoured "Canadian" qualities. The rest of the answer lies in the presumptions of the cbc itself, which rarely set its sights beyond the bounds of Canada. The corporation, especially its English-speaking service, has reflected one of the predominant traits of Canada's cultural industries, namely, a hankering for protectionism and a fear of free trade. Its leaders have never recognized that America's mass culture is also Canada's. Rather, they have at times looked upon the American product as something of an enemy, a view embodied in the famous "Touchstone for the cbc" issued by cbc President Al Johnson in 1977. Therefore, the public network and the government fought to combat the invasion – however paradoxical that stance might seem, given the cbc's carriage of American signals. This attitude in turn has bred a defensive posture, preventing the development of a strategy that might have converted the CBC into a much more aggressive player on the global scene, one that could compete, if modestly, with Hollywood for the attention of viewers. The "failure" of Canadian television, in short, has been in the wider cultural marketplace, not at home.

There is a deeper and perhaps unpalatable truth that the CBC, the CRTC, and cultural nationalists must recognize. The fact is that the continental outlook Samuel Moffett first discovered at the turn of the century has won the day: North America boasts a common range of cultures, a fact that sometimes seems more obvious to observers in Europe than in Canada. Not that this unity has reduced a pluralistic North America into one homogeneous mass: some years ago Joel Garreau pointed out that there were really "nine nations" on the continent, a division that had little to do with political boundaries.[93] The crucial point is that the forty-ninth parallel has only slight cultural significance nowadays. That is true not only because Canadians consume American culture; it is also evidenced by the raft of ex-Canadians active in New York's world of news and advertising and Hollywood's world of entertainment; the common sound of country music everywhere, be it performed by Hank Snow or Tommy Hunter; the sudden spread of hockey across the continent after 1968, so that a Wayne Gretzky can be a hero in Edmonton and in Los Angeles; and the reputation of a Margaret Atwood or a Robertson Davies in the United States.[94]

The strategy of resistance urged by Canada's nationalists is, at bottom, another example of the highbrow disdain for mass culture, reflecting presumptions about television, movies, and literature that would be readily accepted in the homes of American intellectuals and academics. Compare, for instance, Morris Wolfe's complaints about American television with the erudite diatribe of Neil Postman.[95] The rather chilling notion of a "Fortress Canada" which seems to attract some members of the cultural élite does not fit the reality of what has happened, especially since the advent of television: it amounts to a retreat into a past that never was to suit the ambitions and tastes of a small minority of writers and artists.[96]

"My fundamental thesis is that the Canadian public experience of polyethnicity on the one hand and of ambivalence towards a richer and more powerful neighbor on the other is shared with most the rest of the world through recorded history," declared the world historian William H. McNeill in his introduction to the Creighton Lectures in 1985. "Marginality and pluralism were and are the norm of civilized existence. Metropolitan centers were and are necessarily exceptional ."[97] This means that a Canadian nationality in any typical sense of the word is an impossibility. Most Canadian intellectuals, not least the ghost of Donald Creighton, would not agree with so radical a thesis.

Three images of Canada have occurred time and again in our past and retain their force among the intelligentsia and the public even today. The first of these portrays Canada as a peaceable kingdom, devoted to the hallowed goals of peace, order, and good government, a haven of sanity and tolerance in a disturbed world, a country that is less aggressive and more humane than its American neighbour. That image harks back, of course, to the Victorian and British past, although nowadays its apologists usually perceive the country's experience from the perspective of politics: Canadian history becomes a story of prime ministers and premiers, careful compromises, judicial and constitutional wrangles, a benevolent state, and occasionally British regulars and the RCMP to add a bit of spice. Enthusiasts can look forward to a future in which Canada may "serve as a guide to other peoples who are seeking a pathway to the peaceable kingdom!"[98] What is emphasized here is the ideal of citizenship, the loyalty to a particular polity. The sense of self this image propagates has a good deal of residual strength among Canadians: it is worth remembering that the federal election campaign in 1988 was upset when challenger John Turner managed to persuade a number of people that the Canada-U.S. free trade agreement imperilled our social programs and our political sovereignty.

The second image is "Canada as Nature," an inexact phrase that can incorporate related images of the Great North, the land of empty spaces, or wilderness Canada. When it figures at all, the past becomes a story of individuals and groups who have usually conquered or exploited the land. More attention is generally paid to some golden future: the imagery can accommodate the fetish of technology, whereby man has or will overcome nature, as well as the newer dream of ecology, wherein man lives in harmony with nature.[99] Evidence of its appeal is found in various kinds of advertising, notably tourist ads, as well as in public celebrations, particularly Vancouver's Expo 86.[100]

These two images are in many ways complimentary. The literature about the Niagara region available for sale to the tourist, for example, evidences the two mythologies about Canada. Some English-speaking historians of a conservative persuasion have written chronicles of Canada which incorporate elements of both, notably W.L. Morton in *The Canadian Identity*.[101] Each can accommodate the metaphor of the mosaic or the slogan "unity in diversity" (or Joe Clark's "community of communities") in which Canada becomes a home for many different peoples and cultures.[102] The popularity of multiculturalism in official circles has given this metaphor a good deal of currency, particularly in the schools. Perhaps most important, though, the notions of the peaceable kingdom and Canada as Nature present Canada as very un-American or other-American.[103] In this scheme of things the United States becomes a melting-pot, an industrial dynamo, a land of liberty and licence, an imperial power beset by troubles or sins that can induce a certain smugness in Canadians.

The last image, by contrast, is bleak: Canada appears as a victim, a vassal state, a perpetual colony, an imaginary nation or a non-nation. It has a special attraction for the cultural élite: Robert Fulford (himself a member of this élite) has shaken his head over the pessimism of his fellows, over their "distinct sense of failure, expressed as often as possible in the most alarming terms," whatever the proof to the contrary.[104] The dismal mythology of dependence was first constructed by conservatives like Harold Adams Innis, and later picked up by radicals like Dallas Smythe, to justify their hostility towards American influences, especially economic and cultural imperialism.[105] In its milder expressions, such as that articulated by Margaret Atwood some years ago, the image of the victim highlights the theme of survival in Canadian life.[106] At its most extreme, dependency theory leads to the assumption that Canada's national identity is "purely fictional," in the words of Tony Wilden – designed to hide the fact that "we are colonized – historically, economically, socially, politically, and personally."[107] Both versions, though, amount to a call to arms, a demand that Canadians resist a culture made in America and seek their own destiny.

The image of victim or colony, then, is the most logical expression of cultural nationalism on the intellectual scene in Canada. But it is also the least popular of the three images, since it requires Canadians to deny what has long been part of their symbolic and ideological heritage – namely, the popular arts of the United States – if not to treat everything American as an implacable enemy.

Of all of these images and identities, I think that history is on the side of the mythology of the peaceable kingdom, always allowing for the fact that its most enthusiastic apologists substitute wish for reality. That is because the mythology admits, if only by implication, the importance of the public arts and a distinct political culture as the source of lasting definition in Canada. Frank Sinatra and Michael

Jackson, Louis L'Amour and Roger Zelazny, *Miami Vice* and *The Cosby Show*, *Fatal Attraction* and *Nightmare on Elm Street*, *Monday Night Football* and Budweiser ads and even Jimmy Swaggart become merely commodities, something we consume the way we do Coke and hot dogs. These commodities have an impact: I recall hearing on *The Journal* some years ago a Montreal policeman declare that many of his colleagues were attracted into the service by images of fast cars and an exciting life served up in Hollywood's crime shows.[108] But mass culture in itself does not pose, and never has posed, a direct threat to the Canadian identity, because consumers have "read" its messages through a special lens made in Canada. Canada is living proof that the doctrine of nationalism does not really explain how things work.

17 American Popular Culture and the Canadian State: The Case of Pornography

THELMA McCORMACK

> Great nations write their autobiographies in three manuscripts. The book of their deeds, the book of their words, and the book of their art. Not one of these books can be understood unless we read the other two. But of the three, the only quite trustworthy is the last. The acts of a nation may be triumphant by its good fortune, and its words might be the genius of a few of its children, but its art only by the general gifts and common sympathies of the race.
>
> John Ruskin,
> *St. Mark's Rest* (1877)

It is a long way from John Ruskin to Andy Warhol's cookie jars or burlesque in Quebec. Nevertheless, Ruskin's words convey today, as they did when he wrote them, that the record of a culture lies in its arts – not necessarily in the masterpieces or the Pulitzer prizes or the governor general's awards, but in the everyday forms that are the expression of the widest possible base of the society or the "common sympathies of the race."

Popular culture, then, is both an art form and a record, a source of pleasure and a way of learning about a people. Its virtue is that we can enjoy it while studying it. But it is not a sufficient way of understanding complex societies, and there is some possibility that it can mislead us. We need to be reminded that we are often looking at the bumper-stickers of a society. Nevertheless, it will tell us something about the values we share regardless of our many cultural, class, age, and ethnic differences, and about those we do not share despite our demographic similarities. The explicit content, the latent structures, the forms, and the deviations from forms, are all ways of understanding our own social and psychological histories.

Yet we have no agenda. Much of our discussion about the many meanings of "culture" and of the place of history in our approach is symptomatic of a discipline that is not quite sure of itself, a discipline that has been working in the dark. I know of no other discipline that is so unstructured. The diversity of the essays in this volume is indicative of how casual our work is; it does not build; it does not add up. We are a product of chance. Nevertheless, we can see some continuities.

THREE PARADIGMS

Mass society theory has been a major influence on interpretations of popular culture since the 1940s. The major thinkers were Europeans who had fled German Nazism but who often detested the cultural democracy of the United States. They read into our popular culture the debasing of taste, the commodification of art, and a political scenario of passivity and alienation which could only lead to a similar fate for American society. Theodor Adorno was one of the major thinkers in this tradition.

Many listened but few heeded the warning of the mass society theorists. American society might be the prototype of mass society, but the political outcomes were not what was predicted. The affluent and booming 1950s gave us on orientation based on leisure. Popular culture could be understood simply as entertainment, as pleasure, as ludic games, escapism from the boredom and monotony of most forms of work. The fate of democracy did not depend on it. And if entertainment was escapist, so what? It did no harm. It was "the greening of America," and in this period we began to include studies of sports and recreation in the overarching discipline of popular culture. Robert Stebbins on football, Robert Barney on baseball, and Geoffrey Wall on tourism belong to this period and its dominant framework. Leisure theory had its serious side, too, for it was assumed by many of the most advanced theorists that a future society would be a leisure society, and that our work-oriented psyches were not prepared for the shock. What concerned leisure theorists about popular culture was the passivity of its audiences; hence, the need to develop more participatory forms of popular culture (interactive TV was one of the hoped-for innovations).

The dominance of American culture was not seen as problematic either by the mass society theorists, who were more concerned with its populist aesthetics and message, or by leisure theorists, who had taken from social anthropology a model of cultural diffusion in which cultures borrowed selectively from each other. Michael Ames's essay on Expo 86 demonstrates this blending, and it can be seen too in Andrew Lyons and Harriet Lyons's essay on televangelism in Canada and the United States. The manifest symbols of American culture are incorporated into a deeper Canadian mythos. The similarities between the two cultures made the process easier and less traumatic, but the fears of a Canadian culture's being destroyed by this American influence were not justified.

Dominance, however, is the crux of the third paradigm based on theories of cultural hegemony. Do cultures borrow from each other selectively, or does one culture impose its values and style on the weaker and more dependent partner who, over time, becomes even more dependent on the hegemonic power? Reid Gilbert's essay in this volume reverses Ames's theme. Gilbert sees Canadian symbols imposed on an American template. Paul Rutherford, by contrast, contests the idea of dominance. In his opinion, Canadian popular culture, and particularly television, is a regional culture in a larger North American area the centre of which is Hollywood. Discussions of dominance are consequently irrelevant.

These three paradigms – mass society theory, leisure, and cultural hegemony – have framed our scholarship, and, as I have suggested, they still do. They overlap, yet each corresponds to a period: the 1940s with its agony of Europe, the post-war economy of the 1950s, and the politics of identity in the 1960s. I want to suggest that these theoretical models are no longer as heuristically powerful as they once were. In the 1990s and thereafter we need a different paradigm based on theories of social control.

On a more practical policy level, Canadians have been concerned with protecting and encouraging Canadian culture. The 1951 Massey Commission, without benefit of Marxist or neo-Marxist theories, addressed the issue of Americanization and the loss of Canadian folk culture that Canadians sensed.[1] Canadian intellectuals were less interested in saving our genuine folk culture, except as a museum record, than in developing a modern Canadian culture and a modern Canadian (non-British, non-French, and non-u.s.) identity. This new pride in Canadianization was the aftermath of the Second World War, when, for the first time, Canadians saw themselves as strong and independent players.

The struggle to find, create, and repatriate an identity as a nation is the contemporary history of Canadian culture. It coincides with a period of great economic growth, large increases in population as a result of immigration, and a new political independence. We see the same pattern today in many Third World countries as they too become more economically sufficient and less politically dependent. A new post-war Canada needed more than a flag; it needed a collective identity. Who were we?

IDENTITY AND THE ROLE OF THE STATE

The history of the struggle to find an identity is as interesting as the result, for it is as much a story of the state as it is of the arts. And I want to discuss the state.

There are several reasons for this focus. First, we now have the Charter of Rights and Freedoms; the way it is interpreted – especially section 2(b), which guarantees freedom of expression – has a great deal to do with our own creative lives and the future. If the Supreme Court of Canada was a narrow, inward-looking court, our popular culture could shrivel into something pale, innocuous, and sanctimonious – reruns of *The Waltons*. If the Supreme Court made its decisions on the basis of the desirability of laissez-faire, our popular culture might turn into an intense competition within a narrow band of choice. But the members of the court are also members of our society who have a particular level of cultural education and taste, who have their own style of relaxation, and who are influenced by our cultural pasts. Their decisions, therefore, may not be a clear-cut choice between these two alternatives.

The second reason to look at the state is that the relationship between culture and state has changed. Indeed, I want to emphasize the critical edge of the relationship, the issue of pornography and censorship. Canadians may never have been as committed to civil liberties as their U.S. counterparts, yet we have enjoyed an atmosphere of cultural tolerance, of liberal live-and-let-live attitudes, which accompanied modernization and the transformation of Canadian society from a rural to an urban ethos. During the 1980s we turned in a different direction, away from this model of modernization yet not back to an older form of intolerance. This emerges in the pornography debate.

Finally, there is the question of free trade with the United States, where, despite assurances to the contrary, culture is, "on the table." In any case there is no such thing as a "level playing-field" in culture. Indeed, the metaphor itself is inappropriate in the same way as arts economists' talk about works of art as "market failures."

Those are the practical reasons for looking at the state: the Charter, the new law-and-order politics, and the existence of a government-initiated free trade agreement. On a theoretical level, we can begin to construct a more coherent theory of popular cultures by examining instances where there is a clash between the institutions and our definitions of culture. To put it another way, people in this field have spent a great deal of time trying to differentiate popular culture from high culture or folk culture; we need to examine popular culture along a different and more political continuum.

First, a few observations about the context of changes taking place in the culture – state relationship since the Massey Commission and partly as a result of it. The first trend is the decline in our anxiety about cultural hegemony and the need for a distinctive Canadian identity, which existed in the early 1960s. The kind of Canadian nationalism represented in the angry outbursts about u.s. professors taking over Canadian universities has largely subsided. Instead there is a growing concern with the price of success; that is, of arts bureaucracies as an obstacle to creativity. In addition, more attention is given to the impact of policies (like free trade) on the careers of artists. In the 1950s there were no arts bureaucracies, and the major preoccupation was with the aesthetic of Canadian art as it emerged and as the years of colonialism were stripped away. Marshall McLuhan was engrossed with communications technology; he had nothing to say about artists.

This situation has changed; there is a shift away from persuading governments to subsidize the arts and towards administration, and from the aesthetics of art to the careers of artists. Both trends are reflected in the Applebaum-Hébert and the Caplan-Sauvageau reports.[2]

A third trend is the decline of nationalism. Seth Feldman's essay on film suggests to me that the social history of the narrative film may also depend on the rise and fall of nationalism. If we look at the sources of energy in Canadian society today, they are to be found in the formation of new social movements: feminism, environmentalism, the peace and disarmament movements. That is where the avant-garde is, where one can find the intelligentsia and last year's cultural nationalists. What is different about these groups is that their frames of reference are *international*. Canadian environmentalists look at air, water, and wildlife, and do not stop at national borders. Canadian peace activists base their Canadian agenda on a larger one, which they share with disarmament movements in Europe. Feminists similarly belong to a worldwide movement for gender equality and are as much concerned with sexual abuse in Egypt as they are with pay equity in Canada.

The feminist movement is of special interest because it has developed a particular critique of popular culture and it has been instrumental in the formation of censorship policies. This volume lacks an informed representation of feminist research and feminist thinking about popular culture. This type of research ranges from the most conventional kind of content analysis to some very sophisticated analyses of film based on Lacanian psychoanalysis. It is both critical and analytic; the very best of it is developing new paradigms about popular culture.

Finally, there is the new conservatism. Lyons and Lyons's essay on televangelism is revealing of this new ambience. The pornography issue is, I believe, a good example of the cultural environment of the 1980s (Reagan, Thatcher, Mulroney); it is part of a general policy of decontrolling the economy and controlling morality. The more liberal policies of the post-industrial state were just the reverse: greater controls over the economy and fewer over our social norms. Bill c-54, the censorship bill that was before parliament in 1987–88, was symbolic of a side of Canadian character-structure, and constituted a very real threat to a revitalized popular culture.

The Supreme Court's decision in February 1992 in *Butler* v. *The Queen*[3] is a marker signalling the end of a liberal era in which popular culture was more or less protected as freedom of expression. From now on, all culture and entertainment, highbrow or lowbrow, will be subject to a morality test. The intention of the decision was to protect women (from what?), but the first victim of this new hard line was a book store that primarily serves the gay community in Toronto. Our new agenda, then, starts with a concern about creativity rather than Canadian culture, about the artists more than their work, about different patterns of identity, and a new cultural intolerance.

Bruce Feldthusen's essay is consistent with this new perspective, for he recommends the American pattern of a strong, economically viable private sector of broadcasting along with a small élitist public sector. Anyone who watches PBS knows how that dream deteriorated into British imports and very little for the mind. Feldthusen offers us the economics of the Applebaum-Hébert report. But the report was not about Canadian content regulations; it was about the dead hand of both private and public bureaucracies. And its recommendations (which were in my opinion naive) were based not on criteria of administrative efficiency or economic viability, but on guaranteeing the best possible conditions for our young talent to be fulfilled.

Cultural bureaucracies are new to us and they are the result of policies of the federal and provincial governments. But could a Bruce Elder make the kind of experimental film that Seth Feldman envisions within our arts bureaucracies? Would it make a difference if CBC-2, which Feldthusen regards as "extravagant, unrealistic, and unnecessary," was set aside as an experimental studio? How far could the experiments go before censorship was invoked? Does the fact of censorship have a "chilling effect?"

Our concerns about bureaucracies have replaced our older ones about cultural hegemony. Nowadays Canadians talk about the impact of American cultural imperialism on Latin American countries as if it were no longer a Canadian issue. And to judge from some of the essays in this volume, it is not. We take the presence of American culture in Canada as a given, something that is not better or worse but different. Having it here is a way of sharpening our own sense of what is distinctively Canadian. Mary Jane Miller's essay comparing *Street Legal* and *L.A. Law* is a good example. *Street Legal*, which deals with issues like surrogate parenting, is in the tradition of Canadian excellence in documentaries: *The Nature of Things, Fifth Estate, The Journal, As It Happens, W5, Morningside, Marketplace* – all of these and others demonstrate(d) a kind of communication I have seldom seen elsewhere. My one regret is that Miller did not include *Rumpole of the Bailey* and *Perry Mason* in her discussion. Rumpole, a quintessential Dickensian character, is a mild reproach to the British class system, while Perry Mason is the early solo lawyer, one step removed from the frontier. Perry's relationship with Della is courtly, while Arnie and Rock's in *L.A. Law* is masochistic. In any case, Miller's essay illustrates how far we have travelled from those polemics of the 1960s based on the politics of identity.

However, we need to maintain some vigilance in the area of news. Despite Canadian ownership of the Canadian press and despite the CBC, there is a tendency to view Canadian politics through American eyes, to interpret Canadian politics as a two-party system, and to use research methods developed in the United States (where there is a two-party system) to study the media. We cannot put this issue of Americanization entirely behind us, as Paul Rutherford suggests. Although Canadian nationalism is not at the top of our agenda, it is not at the bottom. All complex cultures in the modern world have identity crises, and that has become a permanent part of Canadian lives.

PORNOGRAPHY AND THEORIES OF SOCIAL CONTROL

Pornography is a popular form of popular culture and one which is typically imported from the United States. In the censorship scenario, the country of origin is important. Pornography is seen as a phenomenon of others, of people with less moral fortitude, who are flooding our country with their filth, corrupting our children, and undermining our culture. We are not displaying anti-Americanism here but rather xenophobia.

Pornography deals with our sexual taboos and treats them in a particularly indifferent way. It assumes that they are not taboos; no matter how gross or profane, pornography treats the taboos as if they were normal, typical, everyday behaviour. And that is what produces the shock. Pornography that did not unnerve us would be like ghost stories that did not scare us. It is a special genre. Hard-core pornography shocks us more than soft-core, and the line between the two keeps shifting.

Pornography has a long history and is interesting to study as a subset of social history. During the Reformation pornographic works dealt with the church; in the eighteenth century, with the court; and in the nineteenth century, the new capitalist entrepreneur. In the twentieth century they feature the new middle class — airline attendants, psychiatrists, lawyers, teachers, and suburbanites. But wherever the line is drawn, and no matter in what historical context, pornography is a form of the profane. It mocks us, it laughs at our sexual hypocrisies, it subverts without being political. Pornography is not dissent; it is transgression.

There are many theories about the appeal of pornography, but not many data to support any of them. But in the liberal period from roughly 1920 to 1960, pornography was seen as harmless, a victimless crime. Freudian psychology in particular shifted the criticism to the censors. What is the pathology of the mind of those who crusade for decency?

For a short period in the late 1960s, pornography was thought to have a revolutionary impact similar to that attributed to rock and roll. The sexual revolution must precede the social and economic revolution if we were to avoid a socialism of Stalinism. But Herbert Marcuse made a distinction between sexual liberation and the pseudo-liberation of the sexual revolution: he and his followers looked upon pornography as sexual commodification and as a form of "false consciousness."

The women's movement regarded pornography as the most extreme version of misogyny. Robin Morgan declared that "pornography is the theory, rape is the practice," while Gloria Steinem, the former editor of *Ms.*, compared it to "hate" literature.[4] The Morgan dictum led to an extensive body of experimental research which has been cited as proving that men's exposure to pornography contributes to the possibility of sexual assault.

Where were the Canadian experts on popular culture when the House of Commons Committee on Culture inquired into what pornography was and how it should be understood? Where were the scholars of marginal and deviant cultures when the Fraser Committee on Pornography and Prostitution invited briefs? When the Metropolitan Toronto Task Force on Violence Against Women issued its report on pornography in 1983? When the pressure groups promoted the idea that pornography was an American import that would undermine the values of Canadian society?[5] The silence among cultural theorists both here and in the United States, where the Meese Commission was conducting its inquiry, was deafening, and in my opinion reflects badly on the professional community.

The research on pornography was not done by people with a background in cultural theory. And there was no protest from the cultural theorists who knew better than anyone about the limitations of a positivist model of research and about the shortcomings of a behaviourist approach to pornography. The research was conducted by behaviourists using the most conventional experimental lab models. The investigators, all psychologists, explained what the "message" of the pornographic text was. I did not hear anyone say that the message of *any* text is complex, depending on whether you read Northrop Frye, Horace Newcomb, Michel Foucault, or Roland Barthes. I have read miles of papers by graduate students on deconstructionism, but where were the deconstructionist theorists to talk about pornography as a text?

Research on pornography in itself is a form of popular culture. It is based on exactly the same assumptions about human nature and social behaviour as pornography is. It assumes that we are completely motivated externally, that we have no values, that our inhibitions against any antisocial act can be conditioned so as to permit us to engage in behaviour that otherwise would have been repugnant to us. Pornography makes the same assumptions, and there is work to be done comparing the pornography text with the research assumptions, treating both as popular culture.

The findings of the experimental research do not justify the policies proposed. Here, too, where were the communications research people to object to the interpretations being put on the research? When, at last, the Canadian Civil Liberties Association presented its brief, it drew on the services of an eminent psychologist at the University of Toronto. I have waited in vain for letters to the *Globe and*

Mail from other social psychologists and communications experts, who retreated into the groves of academe while this pseudo-science was being advanced.

Then we reach the criminal code and censorship. Among the people I talked to who were university graduates and more, very few had the vaguest understanding of civil liberties. The cornerstone of a free society is that we control and regulate behaviour, not the mind or imagination. Yet a pro-censorship activist told me that if the government could control weights and standards, it could control this kind of material. Ironically, she and others in the women's movement were advocating the removal of prostitution from the criminal code and the addition of pornography; thought might be controlled, but not behaviour.

The Fraser report dismissed the experimental research as unsatisfactory and inconclusive. Instead, the committee argued that pornography interferes with the realization of gender equality guaranteed by section 15 of the Charter. If there is a conflict between section 2(b) (freedom of expression) and section 15 (equality rights), section 15 should prevail. The committee then went on to outline a three-tier system of censorship that took jurisprudence back to the Victorian era.[6] Where were the editors and reporters, the deans and professors of journalism, who might have questioned whether there is a conflict between sections 2(b) and 15, who might have described the Orwellian lifestyle we would have if section 15 existed but not section 2(b)? The two groups who protested Bill c-54 most vigorously were librarians and artists – writers, video and film-makers, actors, photographers – not the academics, not the critics, not the scholars. Why?

We trivialize our scholarship on popular culture if we restrict it to the easy things; we trivialize popular culture itself if we do not recognize that it has a dangerous zone. We fail to understand what the future holds if we do not recognize that we are in an age of conservative politics and economics, which means a conservative culture. Studying pornography is one way of not being co-opted by that culture.

I suspect one reason that many people stand on the sidelines is a certain discomfort with traditional civil libertarian philosophy. If pornography is a form of "hate" literature, what should we do about it? We need to rethink our traditional understanding of civil liberties. That understanding began in the great struggles of the seventeenth century for the protection of religious dissent and continued into the eighteenth-century struggle for the protection of political dissent. We have inherited this tradition, but we have never been convinced that it applies to cultural phenomena as it does to politics and religion. Pornography and racist "hate" literature pose an even more difficult problem. Strictly speaking, they are not a form of dissent. Feminist critics are right when they say that pornography is an extension of the misogyny of the culture; similarly, "hate" literature is a form of prejudice. Neither of them challenges, as dissent does, the power structure of the society. Neither of them tests the freedom of the state.

But the texts of transgression, pornography, and "hate" literature test the tolerance of the society. And in contemporary political sociology, it is that relationship between state and society, freedom and tolerance, that constitutes a central issue. Cultural censorship, then, is a danger not to the freedom of the state but to the tolerance of the society. For cultural theorists, that is one point for developing a theory of popular culture with meaning in a wider theoretical framework.

CONCLUSIONS

In summary, we have never had a genuine theoretical grounding that could lead to careful systematic research on popular culture. We have been influenced by different perspectives: mass society theory, leisure theory, hegemonic theory, and, more recently, postmodern deconstructionist theory. Is it too much to expect that we can integrate them?

We need a theory that recognizes the changes that have taken place since the Massey report was issued in mid-century. I have discussed some of them: the growth of cultural bureaucracies; an increase in the number of people for whom work in the arts is a full-time career; the emergence of new types of social movements in which the identification is international; and the law-and-order mentality of conservative governments, not just in Ottawa, but in Washington and London.

I have used pornography as a kind of test case for looking at our understanding of popular culture. And I have suggested that Bill c-54 was a threat to all creativity, to all popular culture: it represented cultural oppression. As a feminist, I have been in the eye of the pornography – censorship controversy. And I have been profoundly disturbed by the passivity of most academics, particularly the group most knowledgeable about popular culture. When we study contemporary popular culture, we are not looking at ancient cave drawings. (Some of them might be classified as pornographic by the proposed legislation.) I want to suggest too that we begin to look at some of the research that is carried on as popular culture. That may sound like heresy, but research on pornography is a good place to start.

Cultural studies will continue to be a multidisciplinary enterprise, and in a period of university budget cutbacks we will have to fight for scarce resources. Nevertheless, we have made an impressive beginning in Canadian universities, and this volume adds not only to the credibility of what we do but to its distinction.

18 American Popular Culture in Canada: Trends and Reflections

ANDREW WERNICK

I am told by a friend who likes to spend his summers in Prince Edward Island that a couple from "away" recently tried to launch a new eating establishment in the north shore town of Morell (population 600). Named "The French Café," it specialized in quiche and salads. Since the café opened in February, it was at the mercy of an exclusively local market and was gone long before the tourists arrived. Its rapid slide into bankruptcy was attributed locally to the fact that "its burgers were no good" and that it failed to serve either french fries or brand-name pop.

The incident is reported not to scoff but simply as an index of a stark and obvious fact: from TV and pop music to fast food and fashion, the homogenized style of mass consumption we think of as American popular culture is all-pervasive, its continuous penetration of Canadians' symbolic life not just imposed but gladly welcomed. Moreover, despite what romantic urbanites might imagine about the persistence of earlier traditions in rural areas, a belief that is itself part of a continentally diffused code of class-cultural ("yuppie") values, nowhere is the welcome warmer than in hinterland communities: communities whose young, especially, have increasingly come to measure their deprivation in terms of inadequate access to media-relayed patterns of consumer culture from the cities that dominate them. No wonder that the McDonald's chain, in a surge of reciprocity, felt moved to announce on a sign that for years greeted motorists leaving Charlottetown on Highway 2: "McDonald's Loves the Island."

The question of American cultural domination has inevitably been an important subtext in a volume devoted to American popular culture in Canada. Few herein are nationalists, yet fewer still would contest the view that the seductive embrace of American entertainment, sport, and advertising raises serious issues of national autonomy, for what that is worth, vis-à-vis the United States. This is not a uniquely Canadian worry. The Academie Française stands linguistic guard against the import of Americanisms; through UNESCO, third world countries have pressed for a "new world information order"; and for three decades Radio Free Europe broadcast American pop music as part of its propaganda barrage to the east. But Canada is next door, and the doleful conclusion drawn by Harold Innis in the wake of the 1951 Massey report on national development in the arts, letters, and sciences has retained its currency: "We can only survive by taking persistent action at strategic points against American imperialism in all its attractive guises."[1]

In what follows I want to offer some summary reflections about how, on the evidence of the essays in this volume, the issue of American cultural domination is now being discussed, and more particularly about how the terms of that discussion seem to have shifted since the revival of English-Canadian nationalism in the 1960s and 1970s again placed it firmly on the agenda.

Noteworthy, first, is the extent to which a simple domination model of the cultural relation between Canada and the United States has given way to a more ambiguous picture that takes into account the fuller web of interactions, on and off the continent, within which that relation is set. Several contributors to this volume, for example, have highlighted a history of shared origins and mutual borrowings that makes problematic the very distinction between what is Canadian and what is American. Thus, in the tribally important sphere of spectator sport, Robert Barney disabuses us of the myth that baseball is a recent American import that spread to Canada only with the entry of the Montreal Expos and the Toronto Blue Jays into the major leagues, while Robert Stebbins connects the tribulations of Canadian football to the ambivalent relation it has long had with the American version of British rugby. Other essays remind us that origins are not everything. If, in production, Canadian popular culture continually appropriates American forms, that appropriation, as in Quebec burlesque or in CBC's renditions of the western, can crucially modify their ideological and aesthetic character.

Beyond this, the problematic character of dependency has itself been overtaken by a realization that the Canadian problem of continental integration is in any case not unique. In the world of the transnationals, capital pools overflow national boundaries, and this has homogenizing effects everywhere. Thus Canada's is not the only national culture (if the term retains meaning) to be submerged.

Even in Canada, moreover, the phenomenon is wider than Coca-Colonization, since more than just American commodities and capital are involved. When Prime Minister Brian Mulroney abolished the Foreign Investment Review Agency (FIRA) in the mid-1980s and declared that Canada was "open for business," the welcome was extended, whatever the special openness implied by continental free trade, to Asia and Europe as well. Expo 86, observes Michael Ames, even built this message into its site layout: "The fair site, and by implication the country as a whole" was presented "as a neutral space for foreign powers." It need hardly be pointed out that the flow of capital is also two-way. If Hollywood dominates Canadian screens, Canadian capital (through Cineplex Odeon) is a major player in film distribution in the United States. The international media adventures of Kenneth Thomson, Garth Drabinsky, Conrad Black, and others give a new meaning to Canadianization, and would be worth a study in themselves.

We are thus drawn to recognize two things. First, any statement about the historical domination of Canadian by American popular culture can only be regarded as a first approximation, since it has been complicated by elements of economic and, on another level, cultural interpenetration that must also be taken into account. Second, there is a process of global assimilation associated with international capitalist development that operates over and above the hegemony of any particular region. Paul Rutherford put the point succinctly at our 1988 conference at the University of Western Ontario: "The Canadian imagination may have been thoroughly 'colonized' by Hollywood and New York, but then so has the mind of the American south ... The messages of Hollywood and New York are part of our heritage as North Americans." This statement will doubtless infuriate nationalists, but perhaps Rutherford does not go far enough. From pop music to architecture, the cultural space that Canadians inhabit is continuous not just with the rest of the continent but with the whole "advanced" world. The global character of contemporary capitalism and the ubiquity of its cultural forms made increasingly problematic a nationalist reading of even such "American" phenomena as the ones with which these remarks began.

None of this is to deny that Canada, in Innis's evocative phrase, has moved from "colony to nation to colony." But the fundamental question of what inhibits or vitiates our organic cultural development – posed long ago and in more general terms by the classical sociologists of imperial Europe – is not fully answerable thereby, even where, as in Canada, modern capitalism's inexorable flattening of the cultural landscape has a national dimension. In other words, the issue of Canada's Americanization has to be disentangled from that of its commodification, and this again from the question of the diffusion, whether through American or other channels, of what we might call an international commodity style. The tentacular spread of the shopping-mall, which combines all three processes, may be taken as emblematic of the difficulty.

Above all, in the teeth of both Canadian and American national mythology, what must be resisted is any facile identification of the market and its culture with the defining essence of the United States. To which there is a corollary: if the dominant media and consumer culture cannot properly be called "American" because its origin is more diverse and its commercial and promotional form more universal, then neither can the related issue of Canadian identity (what is it? has "it" been obliterated?) be posed solely in terms of a problematic of colonization.

And this brings me to a second level at which, on the evidence of this volume, a shift in the Canada/America discussion has begun to occur: the question of whether, and in what respect, Canadian popular culture manifests any specific national difference. I say begun, because the old essentialism, according to which each sovereign society expresses itself (or ought to) in a unique national identity, remains a ghost in the discussion. It appears, for example, in Bruce Feldthusen's selection of a "way of life" definition of culture as a starting-point for considering strategies to preserve the independence of Canadian television. The problem with such a definition – Johann Herder's *Volksgeist* rendered into anthropologese – is that it embraces too much, and in so doing tends to imply that the shape and development of key institutions, even the economic, somehow reflects the general will. This is perhaps unobjectionable when formulated simply as a take-it-or-leave-it assumption for policy. But real mystification occurs when it is linked to a search for the holy grail of Canada's (suppressed) national identity.

What has particularly bedevilled that search, from George Grant's *Lament for a Nation* (1965) to Gaile McGregor's *The Wacousta Syndrome* (1985), is that "the" Canadian difference has tended to be defined in terms of quasi-logical contrarieties vis-à-vis the United States. Leaving aside its essentialism, such a procedure is suspect because the map on which it is based tends to presuppose rather than critically reflect upon the binary givens of the dominant ideological field. Especially tenacious has been a romantically tinged dichotomy that counterposes America as a symbol for city, industry, and automobile to Canada as a figure for escape and the untamed land.

More subtle is the nationally divergent approach to Nature depicted by Northrop Frye (*The Bush Garden*, 1971) and Gaile McGregor. On this reading, the American myth of wilderness is anthropocentric and paradisiacal – Nature as cooked – whereas the Canadian myth is defensive and agonic – Nature as raw. Others have stressed the Canadian emphasis on tradition and collectivity in contrast with the American stress on present-mindedness and the individual. And parallel with this have been home-grown images of Canada as a community of communities, a mixing-bowl, as against the American melting-pot: one people under God.

While these ghosts continue to flap around, in several respects the essays in this volume register an important advance. First, from Andrew Lyons and Harriet Lyons's comparison of American and Canadian televangelism to Stebbins's discussion of football, differences between equivalent Canadian and American forms are referred to the specifics of social and historical context rather than reduced to matters of an identitarian and differential national subjectivity. Second, where attempts are made to depict Canadian and American differences in the model of a full-blooded cultural contrast – for example, in Reid Gilbert's and Seth Feldman's essays – the essentialist move is checked by the deconstructive way it is done. That is, Canadian culture is defined as essentially heterogeneous, and specific only in terms of its particular regional mixture of modified borrowings.

To begin with, Canadian consciousness is depicted as an ironic duality that borrows the clothes but not the spirit of American razzle-dazzle, and self-deprecatingly knows itself to be rooted in the dull daily experience of living in a peripheralized region in which nothing really happens. For Gilbert it is the very play of this ambivalence – reflected, as several contributors note, in the preference of Canadian TV viewers for American entertainment and Canadian news – that is the key to the Canadian difference. Feldman's argument has a similar ring. In support of Bruce Elder's manifesto for anti-narrative film, he observes that "the question now is not so much who shall tell Canada's story as whether Canada's story is a story at all."

With this step, the essentialist dichotomy reaches an outer limit. America, the incarnation of centralizing and homogenizing industrial progress, is still *modernity*. But Canada, a dispersed society of margins without a centre, now becomes a figure for *post-modernity*.

Even with its hint of national self-flattery, the result is intriguing. It is as if, through a paradox of its cultural absorption, Canada, not the United States, is the most contemporary – that is, the most post-modern – of nations; and this because, precisely in that subordinated context, its national identity is founded in the determined absence of any such thing.

A number of essays, among them Geoffrey Wall's, also touch on a fundamental point: the transformation of countries into mythic signifiers is not just ideological, but is itself in part a promotional side-effect of capitalist development. Both as a commodity in its own right (through tourism) and as a value-laden symbol with which to promote other commodities (such as beer), the concept of "Canada" has been subject to the same process of commercially driven stereotyping as everything else.

In Canada's case the mythification process is more than ordinarily opaque. The imaged Canada that circulates at home combines a cluster of images fashioned for the domestic market with others that are generated externally and, then, through American media, reimported. That reimportation, as Gilbert notes with regard to the depiction of Quebec City in a 1987 episode of *Murder, She Wrote*, can be excruciatingly offbase. But the former, too, are mythic. Indeed, to round out the picture, it would be instructive to compare the "Canada" of American media not only with the one that appears in Canadian-targeted commercial iconography but also with the "Canada" that Canadian companies (for example, in British and American ads for Molson's and Labatt's beer) themselves project abroad.

It is worth underlining, finally, what the publication of this volume signals: namely, that while patterns of ownership and control remain contentious, and the old equation of economic and cultural control still holds force, the focus of concern among those interested in the Canadian–American relationship has switched from questions of primary and secondary production to ones of culture and communication.

In part this represents a recognition of the way in which the production, distribution, and consumption of culture has become a commercial and industrial process in its own right, and indeed one of great importance to the economy as a whole. Hence, from Paul Audley's *Canada's Cultural Industries* (1983) to the Caplan-Sauvageau report (1982), a plethora of studies examining Canada's "cultural industries" has appeared over the past decade, linked to a policy debate about how much protection, subsidization, etc. is needed to help those industries compete and grow.[2] Similar examples of such an approach in this volume are Feldthusen's examination of the con-

tent regulations of the Canadian Radio-television and Telecommunications Commission, and, less directly, Wall's discussion of
strategies aimed at marketing Canada to potential American tourists. It was with that understanding that the 1982 Applebaum-
Hébert report sought to end a thirty-year emphasis on public sector
support and high culture by de-bureaucratizing cultural management and placing new emphasis on the development of the more
popular "cultural industries."[3] "The 'failure' of Canadian television,"
notes Paul Rutherford, "has been in the wider cultural marketplace,
not at home."

But the turn to culture has also been paradigmatic. In Canada, as
elsewhere in the past two decades, it has reflected a broader intellectual development to which there have been main three main components: among critical social scientists, a shift from (Marxist-inflected)
issues of political economy to (post-Marxist) issues of discourse, symbolism and media; among literary theorists and philosophers, a
growing focus on textuality and on the problematic relation of
thought and consciousness to language; among communications
specialists, growing attention to the overall characteristics of a culture mediated by media. The main academic expression has been
the rise of cultural studies as a new interdisciplinary venture. An
overall result has been that the study of popular culture itself, once
at the despised margins, has been made central to an understanding
of the symbolic constitution of the contemporary world.

As Thelma McCormack notes, the imprint of "cultural studies"
can be seen throughout this volume. While generally welcoming it,
she nevertheless expresses alarm at the eclecticism to which such an
approach, or approaches, to the study of Canadian popular culture
can lead. "I know of no other discipline that is so unstructured. The
diversity of the essays in this volume is indicative of how casual our
work is; it does not build; it does not add up." The description is
fair, but a distinction is worth making that might remove its sting.
The diversity she complains of is endemic to the field – not surprisingly, considering that it represents the confluence of such disparate
currents as Marxism, semiology, psychoanalysis, and feminism, not
to mention various schools of classical sociology and cultural anthropology, and what Dick Hebdidge has called "the posts."[4]

Those who advocate multiple perspectives, of course, might query
the value of greater coherence. And it is not clear, outside an empir-
icist discourse, what it might mean for knowledge to "build." But
there are also special reasons, not unconnected to the theme of this
volume, why Canadian developments in cultural studies have been
particularly scattered and inchoate. Canadian universities are is-

lands in an international sea. With the exception of occasional opportunities like this volume, there has been too little lateral communication between them to create, even among those for whom this might be desirable, a national context within which a sustained and distinctively Canadian development of cultural studies could take place. Moreover, the amalgam of traditions this new area has brought together is not only imported. It derives from countries – mainly England, France, and the United States – whose intelligentsia have been able to read their local urban cultures as straightforwardly exemplifying global developments, without needing to think about the specific relation of those developments to their national context. Jean Baudrillard looks at the Pompidou Centre, or Frederic Jameson at Andy Warhol, and sees advanced capitalist culture in its post-modern form.[5] Ames looks at Expo 86 in Vancouver, and (rightly) considers whether and in what sense something foreign has been imposed.

This is not to dismiss the relevance of post-structural semiology and all the rest to an understanding, for instance, of closure in Canadian TV shows about lawyers (Mary Jane Miller) or of realist narrative in Canadian film (Feldman). It is simply to emphasize that the process of incorporating these new perspectives has been complicated in Canada by the continual need to highlight an additional set of considerations concerning national domination and cultural identity, which, to compound matters, can only be theorized from some other point of view.

Nor in the specifically Canadian reception of cultural studies is this the only problem to overcome. As yet unassimilated into the mix is a powerful tradition of cultural thought indigenous to Canada itself. Centred on the figures of Eric Havelock, Harold Innis, George Grant, and Marshall McLuhan, its thematic focus is the interplay between cultural sensibility and technological environment, particularly as fashioned by the media. To a large degree the recent influx of European theory has pushed this tradition to one side. In that context, the fact that none of the essays in this volume integrates any of its thinking into their own framework of analysis is only symptomatic of a wider disregard. But the displacement has not been total. The Innis – McLuhan tradition continues to exercise attraction – for example, in the work of Arthur Kroker, John Fekete, Paul Heyer, and Donald Theall – and so survives as a further piece of incoherence in the Canadian intellectual field.[6] What this points to, more positively, is a task of theoretical bridging that might not only yield substantive insight about Canada but would also, at the international level, enrich cultural studies itself.

I would like to conclude by mentioning two aspects of the relation between Canada and American popular culture which these comments (in common with this volume itself) have left in the shade. The first concerns the place of Quebec. That this topic is often omitted from the discussion is due in part, one suspects, to a continuing assumption by progressive opinion in English-speaking Canada that the maintenance of linguistic difference is (or should be) sufficient to prevent a similar process of continental cultural integration from taking place there. A moment's reflection on the importance of audio-visual media is enough to dissipate such an illusion, which, despite Quebec nationalism's preoccupation with English Canadian rather than American domination, has not gone without challenge in Quebec itself. One might cite, for example, the *Elvis Gratton* movies, which brilliantly satirized the abject Americophilia of Quebec's small-town working class. And it is surely not without a hint of similar self-mockery that sophisticated Montreal anglophones, during the cola wars of the 1970s and 1980s, derisively referred to their francophone counterparts as "les Pepsis." For what does this make the deriders themselves, if not "the real thing"? What is needed, at any rate, is more comparative work on the similarities and differences in the ways American popular culture is received and appropriated on both sides of Canada's internal divide.

Second, the recent replacement of the term "mass culture" with "popular culture" (a style followed here, as well as throughout the volume) has the virtue of valorizing (or at least conveying a more complex attitude towards) tastes and genres that the Frankfurt School (most notoriously Theodor Adorno) dismissed as manipulative pap. The new term emphasizes popular culture's creative and active side. But just as the Frankfurt School's critique of "mass culture" tended to emphasize its top-down and ideological character at the expense of what people actually make of it, the new term "popular culture" is associated with approaches that can one-sidedly do the reverse. Either way, what is easily hidden is the uneven and contradictory interaction between what emerges organically as collective self-expression and what is commercially dished out. Ultimately, perhaps, these may be said to merge.

Lived culture derives its everyday material from the cultural industries, just as cultural industries appropriate from the lived culture whatever is marketable. However, the relation varies considerably from medium to medium. Television, for example, provides the frame, symbols, and subject matter for much face-to-face interaction; but it only feeds back passively, through revealed consumer choice, into production itself. With music, by contrast, which is a live as well as a recorded medium, the receiving audience can develop a musical voice of its own. And the same is true of locally produced and performed drama and poetry.

In Canada, to be sure, the monopolization of distribution by American-based multinationals and their orientation to a larger market prevents such cultural expressions from becoming fully autonomous, or even from extending their communicative reach. But in line with a time-honoured Canadian tradition of emphasizing the strategic importance of the oral and the face-to-face, it is also worth considering whether, despite everything, there is a basis in such locally generated culture as flourishes in some bars, performance halls, and art galleries for at least imagining a more radical possibility: that from these interstitial developments there might some day emerge, as part of a wider process of renewal, an authentic popular culture strong enough to displace, and indeed to replace, the commercially administered one with which we are currently saddled.

Notes

CHAPTER 1   REVERSIBLE RESISTANCE

1 A 1989 Gallup poll found that 60 per cent of Canadians believe that
   their way of life is influenced too much by the United States – a
   higher percentage than at any time since 1956, when the question was
   first asked. The poll was reported in the *Toronto Star*, 7 August 1989.
2 Quoted by Robert Fulford, *Best Seat in the House* (Toronto 1988), 188.
3 See Margaret Atwood, *Survival: A Thematic Guide to Canadian Literature*
   (Toronto 1972).
4 Gregory Bateson, "A Theory of Play and Fantasy," in Richard
   Schechner and Molly Schuman, eds., *Ritual, Play, and Performance*
   (New York 1976), 69.
5 In the United States the study of popular culture has been associated
   chiefly with the vast teaching, research, and publication program
   that developed at Bowling Green University in Ohio in the 1960s. The
   program includes the publication of the *Journal of Popular Culture*
   and is the focal point of two scholarly societies, the Popular Culture
   Association and the American Culture Association. In Britain, popular culture has been given notable and systematic attention at the University of Birmingham's Centre for Contemporary Cultural Studies,
   which also emerged in the 1960s. British studies, however, have in general been more narrowly defined than their American counterpart
   and oriented theoretically towards cultural criticism and neo-Marxist
   social analysis. Popular culture studies have recently attracted considerable scholarly interest in Japan, and, to a lesser extent, in Russia

and the People's Republic of China. With respect to the Third World, John Lent has edited a comprehensive volume entitled *Caribbean Popular Culture* (Bowling Green 1990). For a similar examination of Latin American popular culture, see Harold F. Hinds and Charles Tatum, eds., *Handbook of Latin American Popular Culture* (Westport, Conn. 1985). There is also an emergent interest in popular culture studies in India. A selective and highly personalized history of the U.S. popular culture studies movement and its impact on other countries is Ray Browne, *Against Academia* (Bowling Green 1989).

6 There are no university departments in Canada devoted to popular culture studies, and in only one program, at Trent University, is there a curriculum that gives the subject focused attention. The Trent program, however, has placed more emphasis on general theoretical issues than on the ethnography of Canadian culture. An attempt to form a Popular Culture Association of Canada was made (by American scholars) in 1984, and such an organization was actually established in 1987 at the annual meeting of the (U.s.-based) Popular Culture Association, held in Montreal. Interest quickly waned, however, and the group never formally met on its own. For a discussion of this episode, see Browne, *Against Academia*, 74–5.

7 For a comprehensive and balanced discussion of the Meech Lake accord, see Michael Behiels, ed., *The Meech Lake Primer: Conflicting Views of the 1987 Constitutional Accord* (Ottawa 1989).

8 Bernard Ostry, *The Cultural Connection* (Toronto 1978).

9 The notion of a Canadian "civil religion" is advanced guardedly. In many respects, and as many scholars have argued, including contributors to this volume, it is the *absence* of a civil religion that distinguishes Canada from the United States. Nonetheless, within the past two decades multiculturalism has clearly become, in English-speaking Canada, a politically unassailable basis of public policy and a dominant symbol of the rhetoric of social identity.

10 The anthropological literature on cargo cults is extensive and by no means uniform in its conclusions. Representative classic studies include Peter Worsley, *The Trumpet Shall Sound* (London 1957) and Kenelm Burridge, *New Heaven, New Earth* (Oxford 1969).

11 The best depiction of the combined playful and political nature of cargo cults is seen in *Trobriand Cricket*, a film produced by the anthropologist Jerry Leach. The film deals with how the Trobriand Islanders transform the game of cricket and recontextualize it in a field of native "traditions," some authentic and others deliberately contrived in response to current political circumstances.

12 Clayton Ruby, "Who Would You Want in *Your* Corner?" *T.V. Guide*, 18 April 1988.

13 Robert Merton, *Social Theory and Social Structure* (Glencoe, Ill. 1957), 439. For a comprehensive sociological study of American media research, see Charles Wright, *Mass Communication: A Sociological Perspective* (New York 1969). For a dated but insightful critique of American mass communications research, see James Peacock, "Religion, Communications, and Modernization: a Weberian Critique of Some Recent Views," *Human Organization* 28:1 (1969), 35–41.

14 See Morris Dalla Costa, "Baseball, Eh?" *London Free Press Magazine*, 4 June 1988.

15 C.L.R. James, *Beyond a Boundary* (London 1963), 97.

16 Victor Turner, *From Ritual to Theater: The Human Seriousness of Play* (New York 1982), 41.

17 Natalie Zemon Davis, "Women on Top: Symbolic Sexual Inversion in Early Modern Europe," in Barbara Babcock, ed., *The Reversible World: Symbolic Inversion in Art and Society* (Ithaca 1978), 147–90.

18 This is a recurrent theme in Burke's seminal contribution to the literary study of symbolic forms and social processes. See especially Kenneth Burke, *Language as Symbolic Action: Essays in Life, Literature, and Method* (Berkeley and Los Angeles 1966).

19 For an insightful discussion of the Calgary Stampede as a fictive historical performance, see Herman Konrad, "Barren Bulls and Charging Cows: Cowboy Celebrations in Copal and Calgary," in Frank E. Manning, ed., *The Celebration of Society: Perspectives on Contemporary Cultural Performance* (London, Ont. 1983), 145–64.

20 Dean MacCannell, *The Tourist: A New Theory of the Leisure Class* (New York 1976), 1–16. MacCannell develops this perspective in the context of working towards a paradigm of the touristic practice of sightseeing.

21 Seymour Martin Lipset, *Continental Divide: The Values and Institutions of the United States and Canada* (New York 1990). A limited edition of the book was published in October 1989 by the C.D. Howe Institute, Toronto, and the National Planning Association, Washington, DC.

22 Lipset, *Continental Divide*, 1. All references to this book pertain to the 1989 edition cited above.

23 The complexities of this apparent contradiction are a central problem in Schechner's recent work. See especially Richard Schechner, *Between Theater and Anthropology* (Philadelphia 1985).

24 For a review of this analogy in anthropological and feminist literature, see Sherry Ortner, "Is Female to Male as Nature to Culture?" in Michelle Rosaldo and Louise Camphere, eds., *Woman, Culture, and Society* (Stanford 1974), 67–87.

25 See, for example, Richard Swiderski, *Voices: An Anthropologist's Dialogue with an Italian-American Festival* (London, Ont. 1986), xii.

CHAPTER 2   AMERICAN CULTURE
IN A CHANGING WORLD

1 Bruce Russett, "The Mysterious Case of Vanishing Hegemony; or, Is Mark Twain Really Dead?" *International Organization* 39, no. 2 (1985), 229, 230.

2 Department of Communications, *Vital Links: Canadian Cultural Industries* (Ottawa, April 1987), 21, 61–2.

3 U.S. House of Representatives, Committee on Government Operations, *International Information Flow: Forging a New Framework*, Thirty-second Report, 96th Congress, 2d session, HR No. 96–1535 (Washington 1980), 23.

4 Department of Communications, *Vital Links*, introduction.

CHAPTER 3   AWAKENING FROM THE NATIONAL
BROADCASTING DREAM

I would like to thank the Faculty of Law, University of Western Ontario, and the Ontario Law Foundation for financial assistance, and R. Jeff Anderson for research assistance.

1 "Culture" is used here in its anthropological sense: "Culture consists of patterns, explicit and implicit, of and for behavior acquired and transmitted by symbols constituting the distinctive achievement of human groups, including their embodiment in artifacts; the essential core of culture consists of traditional (i.e. historically derived and selected) ideas and especially their attached values; culture systems may, on the one hand, be considered as products of action, on the other as conditioning elements of further action." Alfred L. Kroeber and Clyde Kluckhohn, *Culture – A Critical Review of Concepts and Definitions* (New York 1963), 357. Nothing in this essay is intended directly to address the merits of arts policy, which also has a legitimate claim to the word "culture."

2 Two distinct cultures exist in Canada, one English-speaking and one French-speaking. This is reflected clearly in television broadcasting and the legal regulation thereof. Although many of the trends, observations, and criticisms described here are relevant to a certain degree to the French-speaking television environment, I do not purport to give that environment the individual attention it deserves. Both the existence of the two different milieus and my failure to deal seriously with them here constitute important aspects of unique Canadian culture.

3 To speak of culture is to speak of the culture of a particular group. It is legitimate and often useful to analyse local cultures, regional

cultures, ethnic cultures, or religious cultures, for example. However, national cultures are generally regarded as conceptually different in that they constitute total cultural systems. "[T]he tribe and the nation are ... the only significant cultural systems in human history." From the external point of view, the institutions associated with nation-states, most obviously the political and legal, permeate every other aspect of the national culture. From the internal point of view, national patriotism constitutes the most powerful bond known to modern human beings. This suggests that the Canadian national culture, like any national culture, is a significant one for the nation's citizens, and that the differences between it and the American national culture may be greater than some suppose. The degree of significance and difference are matters for legitimate debate, not their existence. See Leslie A. White, *The Concept of Cultural Systems: The Key to Understanding Tribes and Nations* (New York 1975), 3, 17, 173, and 174. This does not deny the significance of other cultures within the nation. The concept of national culture refers to what is common within a nation, but does not entail necessarily that all or even most cultural patterns within the nation are common. Herschel Hardin, in *A Nation Unaware: A Canadian Economic Culture* (Vancouver 1974), 12, says: "What are the basic contradictions of the Canadian experience? There are three of them: (1) French Canada as against English Canada; (2) the regions as against the federal centre; and (3) Canada as against the United States ... That these three contradictions are at the centre of the Canadian experience, that they have been the forcing ground of our identity, is obvious."

4 The complexity of the concept makes it difficult to analyse national cultural policy in traditional market failure terms, using familiar empirical techniques. The question whether Canadian national culture is "worth" preserving suggests a cost-benefit analysis. The cost of cultural policy can be estimated; the impact of particular policy initiatives on national culture cannot. Nor can the benefits of national culture be measured and revealed by empirical data, as some would wish. Except for particular patterns and for specific purposes, it is meaningless to speak of cultural patterns, let alone entire national cultural systems, as right or wrong, good or bad, valuable or worthless. Culture is a thing sui generis; the function of culture is culture; the value of distinctive national culture is distinctive culture; the value of Canadian national culture to Canadians is largely that it is their culture. The strength of nations, the bonds of patriotism, and the comforts of familiarity are such that the majority of citizens are likely to favour policies that promote national culture. In this sense, national culture is its own justification. It is both understandable

and legitimate that some citizens will not find such a case compelling, particularly if the cost of cultural policy is regarded as too steep and the effects of cultural policy as too uncertain. This essay proceeds from the opposite point of view. It accepts that national culture is worth preserving and that it is possible to make meaningful policy choices, even if the outcomes cannot be measured precisely.

5 See generally John Meisel, "Escaping Extinction: Cultural Defence of an Undefended Border," in David H. Flaherty and William R. McKercher, eds., *Southern Exposure: Canadian Perspectives on the United States* (Toronto 1986), 152–68. Meisel supports many of the arguments made throughout this essay. See also Abraham Rotstein, "The Use and Misuse of Economics in Cultural and Broadcasting Policy," research report prepared for the Task Force on Broadcasting Policy, Department of Communications (Ottawa 1986).

6 Critics of cultural regulatory policy in Canada acknowledge the overwhelming difficulty of attempting to address this question with traditional social science methodology. They are too readily able to resolve this difficulty to their own satisfaction by declaring by fiat that the burden of proof on issues of cultural intervention rests with proponents of cultural regulation. For an example of this general view, see Steven Globerman, *Cultural Regulation in Canada* (Montreal 1983), 31, 61. Such an a priori fiat against regulation is unwarranted either rationally or as a matter of national cultural experience. "There is a unique public enterprise style, or aspect, to Canadian life. This shows up in the economic culture, if we look for it, and in communications which are linked to the economic culture. But beyond that, it inheres in our psyche." Hardin, *A Nation Unaware*, 136–7. "It is not difficult to understand the cultural nationalist's conviction that state intervention, direction, and even ownership must be seen as fundamental ... It is not merely that the state alone has the resources necessary to finance cultural survival ... it is also that a statist or socialist approach to culture would in itself be evidence that Canadian culture is different from the free enterprise culture of the u.s.": Ramsay Cook, "Cultural Nationalism in Canada: An Historical Perspective" in Janice L. Murray, ed., *Canadian Cultural Nationalism* (New York 1977), 17.

7 For example, the FCC has authorized u.s. penetration by satellite, citing interest in the Canadian export market, additional revenues for u.s. programmers and carriers, and increased hardware and program sales. See Stephen Clarkson, *Canada and the Reagan Challenge* (Toronto 1982), 227.

8 "Four of five Canadians think they should be allowed access to any u.s. television stations they wish.": *Globe and Mail*, 22 May 1984.

9 *Report of the Task Force on Broadcasting Policy* (Ottawa 1986) (cited as the Caplan-Sauvageau report), 90. The chairpersons were Gerald L. Caplan and Florion Sauvageau. See also *Report of the Federal Cultural Policy Review Committee* (Ottawa 1982) (cited as the Applebaum-Hébert report), 180. The chairpersons were Louis Applebaum and Jacques Hébert. *Canadian Broadcasting Corporation Annual Report 1987–8* (Ottawa 1988), 9, reported the u.s. audience share at 31.9 percent. The Canadian program share of English television viewing is even less encouraging. It rose from 26.7 per cent to 31.6 per cent between 1984 and 1989. In 1990 it dropped back to 26 per cent. See cbc, *Annual Report 1989–1990* (Ottawa 1990), 21; and Statistics Canada, *Viewing 1990 Culture Statistics* (Ottawa 1992), 7.

10 Canada, *Canadian Broadcasting and Telecommunications: Past Experience, Future Options* (Ottawa 1980), 23; Caplan-Sauvageau report, 105. The Canadian program share of French-language viewing rose from 66.8 per cent to 76.4 per cent from 1984 to 1989. See cbc, *Annual Report 1989–1990*, 21.

11 ctv increased its share from 25 to 30 per cent. tva increased its share from 48 to 53 per cent. The cbc English-language network's share fell from 35 to 18 per cent, its affiliate share from 12 to 5 per cent. French-language cbc owned stations increased their share from 40 to 42 per cent; their affiliates decreased from 12 to 3 per cent: Caplan-Sauvageau report.

12 "matv" refers to master antenna receiving equipment, which is popular in hotels, bars, and apartment complexes. "tvro" refers to direct-to-home receiving equipment for receiving satellite signals, known as "television receive only antennas" or satellite dishes. Early attempts to regulate individual use of tvros were abandoned in 1983. For further discussion of the so-called Death Stars, see David Ellis, *Split Screen: Home Entertainment and the New Technologies* (Toronto 1992), 160–70.

13 In 1928 Canada struck the first federal royal commission, the Aird Commission, to recommend a national broadcasting policy. See *Report of the Royal Commission on Radio Broadcasting* (Ottawa 1929). The chairman was Sir John Aird. Even then there were many more u.s. stations available to Canadians than domestic. The u.s. stations were more powerful, interfering with Canadian stations in some markets, and providing the only radio service available to a substantial number of Canadians living outside the lucrative urban markets. In 1924 *Maclean's* magazine reported that "nine-tenths of the radio fans in the Dominion hear 3 to 4 times as many United States stations as Canadian." American radio programming, like television programming today, was both readily available and extremely

popular. See Margaret Prang, "The Origins of Public Broadcasting in Canada," *Canadian Historical Review* 46 (1965), 1, 3–4; and Susan Crean, *Who's Afraid of Canadian Culture* (Don Mills, Ont. 1976), 28–9.

14 In 1977 62 per cent of English-speaking Canadians had access to four U.S. channels; 46 per cent to four Canadian channels (*Canadian Broadcasting and Telecommunications: Past Experience, Future Options*) 23.

15 Canadian Radio-television and Telecommunications Commission (hereinafter CRTC), *The Year in Review, 1990–1991* (Ottawa 1991), 71. See also Applebaum-Hébert report, 283.

16 PBS regularly attracts approximately a 5 per cent audience share in the United States. See Richard S. Katz, "Public Broadcasting and the Arts in Britain and the United States," in Kevin Mulcahy and C. Richard Swaim, eds., *Public Policy and the Arts* (Boulder 1982), 263.

17 It is generally agreed that transmission, learning, and sharing are the three key features of cultural study. See Mary Ellen Goodman, *The Individual and Culture* (Homewood, Ill. 1967), 60.

18 Herbert I. Schiller, *Communication and Cultural Domination* (White Plains, NY 1976), 21.

19 Harry Boyle, the former CRTC chairperson, in a speech delivered in San Francisco, 29 December 1969.

20 James D. Halloran, *The Effects of Television* (London 1970), 30.

21 Peter A. Herrndorf, lecture presented at the Stratford Festival Lecture Series, 19 August 1984.

22 Globerman, *Cultural Regulation in Canada*, 44–5.

23 Globerman, ibid., uses the example of *All in the Family* as a useful commentary on bigotry. Bigotry is probably a cultural universal. A character in English Canada complaining about French copy on a cereal box would have far more to say than Archie Bunker about the manner in which bigotry is practiced in Canada. Significant cultural differences do not manifest themselves generally in abstract social issues. Nor is the complexity of national culture captured by a focus on an issue; it entails the interrelationship between various issues, the values that are expressed on those issues, and the relationships between and among them.

24 Globerman, ibid., dismisses the differences because they are marginal. This is a strange statement in an unabashedly economic analysis. Marginal differences are not necessarily small or insignificant. They lie at the heart of all economic analysis. They also lie at the heart of concern for national cultural policy.

25 See Conrad Winn, "Mass Communication," in Conrad Winn and John McMenemy, eds., *Political Parties in Canada* (Toronto 1976), 142–6.

26 Herrndorf, lecture, 19 August 1984.

27 Globerman, *Cultural Regulation in Canada*, 44–5.

28 See T.L. McPhail and George A. Barnett, *Broadcasting – Culture and Self: A Multi-Dimensional Pilot Study* (Ottawa 1977), 26–9; Walter Benjamin, "The Work of Art in an Age of Mechanical Reproduction," in Walter Benjamin, *Illumination* (New York 1968), 217; Mark Frieman, "Canadian Content in Private Television: An Innisian Analysis," *University of Toronto Faculty of Law Review* 41 (1983), 19, 23. "People watch television only about half the time their sets are on, and spend the rest of the time talking, eating, ironing, dressing their children, playing the flute, or cuddling on the couch, according to an Oxford University study." Oceanside, Calif. *Blade-Tribune*, 21 May 1986.

29 Herrndorf, lecture, 19 August 1984. The figure is 50 per cent for French-speaking children.

30 See generally Herbert I. Schiller, *Mass Communications and American Empire* (New York 1970); Schiller, *Communication and Cultural Domination*; and Raymond Williams, *Television: Technology and Cultural Form* (London 1974).

31 Schiller, *Communication and Cultural Domination*, 24 and, generally, 7–23.

32 See the Caplan-Sauvageau report, 104–5.

33 See Roger F. Swanson, "Canadian Cultural Nationalism and the U.S. Public Interest," in Murray, ed., *Canadian Cultural Nationalism*, 69; and Crean, *Who's Afraid of Canadian Culture?* 60.

34 See the Applebaum-Hébert report, 283.

35 Joyce Nelson, "Global Pillage: The Economics of Commercial Television," in David Helwig, ed., *Love and Money: The Politics of Culture* (Ottawa 1980), 22.

36 Applebaum-Hébert report, 282.

37 In 1987 the commission affirmed that it had no intention of regulating the Canadian content of commercial messages, and abandoned an earlier policy of requiring their registration. Public Notice, CRTC, 9 January 1987, s. V.

38 CRTC, *Year in Review, 1990–1991*, 68.

39 Caplan-Sauvageau report, 99; Applebaum-Hébert report, 280.

40 CBC, *Annual Report, 1986–7* (Ottawa 1987), 13. The Caplan-Sauvageau report, 99, reported a 48 per cent share.

41 CBC, *Annual Report 1988–1989*, 9–11. See also Caplan-Sauvageau report.

42 CBC, *Annual Report 1990–1991*, 32, suggests the figure is in excess of 20 per cent.

43 Ibid.

44 Katz, "Public Broadcasting," 241.

45 See Schiller, *Mass Communications*, 107–11, and, generally, 88–9.

46 "The Canadian Broadcasting System: An Objective Unfulfilled," in *The Canadian Identity* (March 1981), 10, submitted by the CBC to the CRTC, Cultural Policy Review Committee; A.W. Johnson, "Touchstone for the CBC" (June 1977), statement by the CBC president, 76–7.

47 Clarkson, *Canada and the Reagan Challenge*, 224. Ten hours of the Canadian series *Chasing Rainbows* cost approximately $11,000,000. A rule of thumb in the industry, according to Stan Thomas of CKND-TV, Winnipeg, is that it costs ten times as much to produce a program as to buy one.

48 *The Canadian Identity*, 10.

49 Crean, *Who's Afraid of Canadian Culture*, 49. These examples are dated, but their message remains true today. See Ellis, *Split Screen*, 136.

50 See Frieman, "Canadian Content," 24.

51 Crean, *Who's Afraid of Canadian Culture*, 44.

52 See Oceanside, Calif. *Blade-Tribune*, 21 May 1986.

53 On the program content control of advertisers, see generally Winn, "Mass Communication," 131. "Chrysler Motors Corp., which was to have been one of the biggest commercial sponsors of ABC's *Amerika* mini-series next month, said Tuesday it wants to pull its ads from the program after reviewing part of the program ... Chrysler says it has 'no personal quarrel' with what it saw and was convinced the program will attract a huge audience. But the company said 'the subject matter' and its portrayal are so intense and emotional that our upbeat product commercials would be both inappropriate and of diminished effectiveness in that environment." *London Free Press*, 28 January 1987.

54 Winn, "Mass Communication," 142–5.

55 See Schiller, *Mass Communications*, 100–3, 118–19.

56 Frieman, "Canadian Content," 25–7. The quotation is taken from CRTC, *Symposium on Television Violence* (Kingston, Ont. 1975).

57 Graham Spry, "The Decline and Fall of Canadian Broadcasting," *Queen's Quarterly* 68 (1961), 213, 225. See generally Prang, "Origins of Public Broadcasting," 134.

58 Spry, "Decline and Fall," 221–3 and 140.

59 *Report of the Royal Commission on Radio Broadcasting* (1929).

60 Ibid., 6–7, 9–10.

61 See A.J. Beke, "Government Regulation of Broadcasting in Canada," *Canadian Commercial Law Review* 2 (1970), 105, 114.

62 Broadcasting Act, SC, 1958, c. 22.

63 The reference to public ownership reappeared in the Broadcasting Act, RSC, 1970, C. B-11, S. 3(a).

64 Applebaum-Hébert report, 311.

65 RSC, 1970, c. B-11.

66 See generally Crean, *Who's Afraid of Canadian Culture*, 28–9; and Prang, "Origins of Public Broadcasting."

67 See John A. Porter, *The Vertical Mosaic: An Analysis of Social Class and Power in Canada* (Toronto 1965), chapter 15.

68 See Williams, *Television*, 41.

69 Ibid., 42 and 39.

70 Ibid., 39–43; Schiller, *Mass Communications*, 79–87; and Schiller, *Communication and Cultural Domination*, 11, 20–1.

71 Schiller, *Communication and Cultural Domination*, 95.

72 Ibid., chapter 9, and 101–7. This has been most obvious in western Europe. In addition, commercial broadcasting now penetrates Russia through Finland.

73 Macdonald, "Sky Channel and the Coca-Cola Bird," *Broadcaster*, March 1985. See generally Ralph M. Negrine and Stylianos Papathans-sopoulos, *The Internationalization of Television* (London 1990), especially 1588.

74 See Robert E. Babe, "Regulation of Private Television Broadcasting by the Canadian Radio-Television Commission: A Critique of End and Means," *Canadian Public Administration* 19 (1976), 552, 555.

75 Radio (TV) Broadcasting Regulations SOR/59-456, *Canada Gazette*, Part II, vol. 93, no. 23, 1192, 9 December 1959.

76 Television Broadcasting Regulations, 1987, s. 4 (effective 1 September 1987). Modest changes to the prior regulations which affect ethnic or remote stations only have not been considered here.

77 Crean, *Who's Afraid of Canadian Culture*, 49.

78 A.W. Johnson, "Presentation to the CRTC Hearing on Canadian Content" (1981), 5.

79 *Canadian Broadcasting and Telecommunications: Past Experience, Future Options*, 25.

80 RSC, 1985, c. B-9, s. 3(d).

81 See generally *Caplan-Sauvageau Report*, chapter 5. On English-language television 98 per cent of all available drama programming is foreign, and 98 per cent of viewing time goes to foreign programs. Eighty per cent of drama viewing of French-language television is devoted to foreign programs (ibid., 94). The president of the CBC reported the following ratios of exhibition time to actual viewing of Canadian programs generally: CITY-TV, 40/10; CHCH, 45/10; Global, 42/28; CTV, 50/42; CBC (Toronto), 68/62. See Johnson, "Touchstone for the CBC," 27–8.

82 Section 4(e) of the regulations, for example, qualified events such as the World Series or Academy Awards as basically Canadian.

83 SOR 84–364, s. 1.

84 See Frieman, "Canadian Content," 24.

85 The CRTC proposed to lower the quotas in return for a fixed budget committment of Canadian programming in 1986. This initiative was recently abandoned. See Public Notice, CRTC, 1987–8, 9 January 1987, 4. For an explanation of how broadcasters can satisfy Canadian content requirements with programs designed to be unrecognizable as Canadian, see Ellis, *Split Screen*, 132–6.

86 Applebaum-Hébert report, 281–2.

87 Caplan-Sauvageau report, 38–9. See also Ellis, *Split Screen*, 172–7.

88 See generally Beke, "Government Regulation of Broadcasting." From 1974 to 1984, pre-tax profits ranged between 17 and 20 per cent: Caplan-Sauvageau report, 448. See generally Babe, "Regulation of Private Television Broadcasting, 562, 580; Spry, "Decline and Fall," 215; and CRTC, *Annual Report, 1986–87*, xi. Pre-tax profits in private television declined from $180 million in 1985 to $84.7 million in 1989 and $16.4 million in 1990 (CRTC, *Annual Report 1990–1991*, 21). It is unclear whether this decline might be greater were it not for the protective quotas. Ellis reports that CanWest-Global continues as an unusually profitable enterprise, but CTV has not done as well. See David Ellis, *Networking* (Toronto 1991), 94, 175.

89 See "CBC Program Cuts 'Dismaying,' Says Author of Task Force Report," *Globe and Mail*, 5 March 1987, quoting Gerald Caplan. See also *Globe and Mail*, 15 November 1986, for an example of the latest "get tough" policy statement by the new CRTC chairman.

90 Caplan-Sauvageau report, 38–9.

91 See generally Globerman, *Cultural Regulation in Canada*.

92 See Babe, "Regulation of Private Television Broadcasting," 585–6. Note that the "capture theory" does not necessarily entail any bad faith on the part of the regulators. For a criticism of this explanation, see W.N.H. Hull, "Captive or Victim: the Board of Broadcast Governors and Bernstein's Law, 1958–68," *Canadian Public Administration* 26 (1983), 544.

93 This is a particular version of the capture theory, which suggests that regulation is a "product" that is traded in the political market. It predicts that concentrated interest groups will make effective demands for regulation in their interest, and that the government will be more willing to supply such regulation to them because they are the groups whose relevant behaviour – voting and political contributions, for example – is likely to change according to how the regulatory issue is resolved. For a general description of this and other capture theories and some useful references, see Richard Posner, "Theories of Economic Regulation," *Bell Journal of Economics* 5 (1974), 335.

94 I am at a loss to explain their continued success at having independent task forces adopt this belief. See, for example, Caplan-Sauvageau report, 469–71.

95 RSC 1985, c. B-9, s. 3 read: "It is hereby declared that (a) broadcasting undertakings in Canada make use of radio frequencies that are public property and such undertakings constitute a single system, herein referred to as the Canadian broadcasting system, comprising public and private elements." The 1991 act, 38–39 Eliz. II, c. 11, s. 3, reads: "the Canadian Broadcasting system ... comprising public, private and community elements."

96 Caplan-Sauvageau report, 148, note 8.

97 The single-system approach reflects the history of broadcasting policy in this country. In particular it represents an attempt to graft a public service model onto a well-entrenched dominant commercial model. See Williams, *Television*, 32–5. For other criticisms see Crean, *Who's Afraid of Canadian Culture*, 24; Applebaum-Hébert report, 273; Liorn Salter, *Methods of Regulation* (Ottawa 1986), 80–1; and Salter, *Issues in Broadcasting* (Ottawa 1986), 18–19.

98 "[Former Minister of Communications Marcel] Masse sees no conflict between industrial and cultural objectives, saying 'It's always possible to have a good profit and to use good Canadians to have it." Barbara A. Moes, "Marcel Masse: Getting His 'Act' Together," *Broadcaster* 44 (January 1985), 22, 23.

99 See generally Caplan-Sauvageau report, 38–41, and Applebaum-Hébert report, 282–3.

100 See *Re CTV Television Network Ltd. and CRTC et al.* (1982), 134 *Dominion Law Reports* (3d series), 193 (Supreme Court of Canada).

101 See *Decision CRTC 86–1086, Global Communications Ltd.*, 14 November 1986.

102 There was a similar proposal in the Caplan-Sauvageau report, 581. It is, in part, dependent upon the introduction of new specialty Canadian channels on the basic tier, and these proposals do not strike me as viable. The report (559) concluded that the demand for basic cable service is "relatively price insensitive, at least up to monthly rates of $12 and that there could be considerable flexibility in repricing the service."

103 Such a suggestion was considered and rejected unconvincingly by the Caplan-Sauvageau task force. See Caplan-Sauvageau report, 469–71.

104 Broadcasting Act, RSC, 1970, c. B-11, s. 3(d).

105 While a dramatic increase in VCR use is predicted in the Caplan-Sauvageau report, the authors do not appear to grasp its significance in terms of channel capacity needs.

106 See Caplan-Sauvageau report, chapter 13. Programming for TV Canada would have included: children's programming, repeats of Canadian programs, National Film Board productions, arts productions and documentaries, programs in the other official language, and generally increased representation by regions and independent producers. In my opinion, with some modification, this would be a useful programming strategy to be pursued on the basic CBC channel. Cable companies could offer repeat programming on existing channel capacity; such programming could be provided to them and broadcast by them free of charge. The new network proposals were endorsed by the minister of communications. See *Globe and Mail*, 6 February 1987.

107 See also Caplan-Sauvageau report, 301–4.

108 There is evidence that public service broadcasting can have an impact on the audience. See W. Brian Stewart, "The Canadian Social System and the Canadian Broadcasting Audience", in Benjamin D. Singer, ed., *Communications in Canadian Society* (Toronto 1975), 63.

109 See Applebaum-Hébert Report, 296.

110 See ibid., 279, 289. The Canadian justice minister calmly explained the 10-word meaning of a 100-word proposed amendment to the federal constitution. Then a TV-London announcer cut in just as the television screen plunged into darkness. "Due to previous program commitments," he explained, the station was forced to discontinue its coverage of the constitutional conference; at the same time he promised that the verbatim broadcast would continue at 10 A.M. the next day. The previous program commitment turned out to be a five-year-old episode of *Barney Miller*, playing in the *Video Hits* time slot. After the sitcom, the same announcer surfaced again, this time warning that the midnight showing of Dallas would not be available for the next two nights. "Instead, we present in its place a two-part *Kojack* special". *The Jeffersons* appeared soon afterward.

111 It was, however, predicted that only CFPL-London would survive if the Applebaum-Hébert recommendations were adopted. CFPL-London disaffiliated from CBC as of September 1, 1988. See Bender, "Report on Arts 'Naive, Old-Fashioned,'" *London Free Press*, 12 November 1982.

112 On narrowcasting as the best strategy for public broadcasting, see Katz, "Public Broadcasting and the Arts," 262. See also Pierre Juneau, "Public Broadcasting in the New Technological Environment: A Canadian View," address given in Luxembourg, 16 July 1983.

113 See Susan Crean, "What Applebert Said," *This Magazine* (February 1984), 24.

114 Another proposal, modelled loosely on BBC-4, would be to appoint regional commissioners, allot each a budget and time quota, and give them discretion to purchase independent Canadian productions for exhibition on the public service.

CHAPTER 4   BROADCASTING AND CANADIAN CULTURE

I would like to thank Robert Young of the Department of Political Science at the University of Western Ontario for his helpful comments on an earlier version of this essay.

1 Raymond Williams, *Keywords: A Vocabulary of Culture and Society* (London 1983), 87.
2 Clifford Geertz, "Art as a Cultural System," *Modern Language Notes* 91 (1976), 1473.
3 Alfred L. Kroeber and Clyde Kluckhohn, *Culture – A Critical Review of Concepts and Definitions* (New York 1963), 357.
4 T.S. Eliot, *Notes Towards the Definition of Culture* (London 1958), 19.
5 Theodor W. Adorno, *Prisms*, translated from the German by Samuel and Shierry Weber (London 1967), 19, 22.
6 For example, Paul Audley, *Canada's Cultural Industries* (Toronto 1983).
7 Margaret Atwood, "Just What Are We Getting Into?" *Globe and Mail*, 5 November 1987.
8 W.L. Morton, *The Canadian Identity* (Toronto 1961), 18–19.
9 George Grant, *Lament for a Nation* (Toronto 1965), 70.
10 A headline in the *Globe and Mail* on 23 December 1988 read: "Language Bill Given Royal Assent."
11 CRTC Decision 87–904; *CBC Newsletter*: note to staff, English Networks, 17 December 1987.

CHAPTER 5   A SWEET HOPE OF GLORY IN MY SOUL

1 Dallas Smythe, *Dependency Road: Communications, Capitalism, Consciousness, and Canada* (Norwood, NJ 1981).
2 B. Jules-Rosette, "The Conversion Experience: The Apostles of John Maranke," *Journal of Religion in Africa* 7: 2 (1976), 132–64.
3 James L. Peacock, "The Southern Protestant Ethic Disease," in J. Kenneth Morland, ed., *The Not So Solid South: Anthropological Studies in a Regional Subculture* (Athens, Ga. 1971), 108–13.
4 The tense used throughout this account is what anthropologists call the "ethnographic present." The epilogue deals with developments since 1988, including the coming of Vision TV.

5 PTL is the Praise the Lord Ministry.

6 We are grateful to our student, Christine Noon, for pointing this out.

7 Victor W. Turner, "Betwixt and Between: The Liminal Period," in *Rites of Passage: In the Forest of Symbols* (Ithaca 1967), 93–111; Turner, *The Ritual Process* (London 1969); Arnold Van Gennep, *The Rites of Passage*, translated by Monika Vizedom and Gabrielle L. Caffee (Chicago 1960).

8 Television has its own conventions and "ritualized forms," in part dictated by the demands of the clock, in part by the use of colour, the close-up shot, the low definition of the picture, the small size of the screen, and the ability of its audience to walk out and switch channels. Because of the power of the u.s. market, the message has certainly tended everywhere in the west to accord with American conventions but it is, arguably, in part dictated by the medium as much as by ethnic, national, and cultural differences. Hymn, sermon, and appeal must all fit into thirty or sixty minutes. A certain amount of repetitiveness, the use of predictable formats, and relatively brief internal sequences compensate for the short attention span of an audience free to chat and roam about the house. A stress on climax, rather than on lengthy preliminaries and conclusions, would seem to meet many of these technical needs.

9 Gregor Goethals, "Religious Communication and Popular Piety," *Journal of Communication* 35: 1 (1985), 149.

10 Michael G. Kenny, *The Passion of Ansel Bourne: Multiple Personality in American Culture* (Washington 1986).

11 William James, *Varieties of Religious Experience* (New York 1906).

12 Kenny, *Ansel Bourne*, 72–3.

13 Susan F. Harding, "Convicted by the Holy Spirit: The Rhetoric of Fundamental Baptist Conversion," *American Ethnologist* 14: 1 (1987), 167–81.

14 See Hope Evangeline, *Daisy: The Fascinating Story of Daisy Smith, Wife of Dr. Oswald J. Smith, Missionary Chaplain and Founder of the People's Church, Toronto* (Grand Rapids 1978); Lois Neely, *Fire in His Bones: The Official Biography of Oswald J. Smith* (Wheaton, Ill. 1982).

15 Neely, *Fire in His Bones*, 93.

16 Ibid., 160.

17 Razelle Frankl, *Televangelism: The Marketing of Popular Religion* (Carbondale and Edwardsville, Ill. 1987), 31.

18 Neely, *Fire in His Bones*, 187, 221.

19 Ibid. 9, 288.

20 Peter G. Horsfield, *Religious Television: The American Enterprise* (New York and London 1986).

21 George Gerbner and K. Connoly, "Television as New Religion," *New Catholic World* (April–May 1978), 52–56.

22 Reginald W. Bibby, *Fragmented Gods: The Poverty and Potential of Religion in Canada* (Toronto 1987), 36.

23 Ibid.

24 These figures are taken from the 1981 census.

25 Charles R. Wright, *Mass Communication: A Sociological Perspective*, 3d ed. (New York and Toronto 1986), 46–8.

26 Frankl, *Televangelism*.

27 Pierre Bourdieu, *Distinction*, translated by Richard Nice (London 1986).

28 We are grateful to Michael Carroll and Theodore Yanow for pointing out some of these intertextual political messages in the culture of taste.

29 The relative absence of liminality in mainstream North American religion has alienated many representatives of relatively high-status, politically liberal segments of society as well as conservative elements with little symbolic capital. Individuals of the former category, however, are more likely to be drawn to eastern religions, astrology, and various "New Age" phenomena than to fundamentalism.

30 A number of Christian broadcasters (and would-be Christian broadcasters) have recently petitioned the CRTC for permission to operate exclusively Christian stations and networks, being dissatisfied with the interfaith requirements imposed on Vision TV. The press mentioned *100 Huntley Street* as a party to this request, but *The People's Church*, perhaps significantly, is not. See *Globe and Mail*, 17 October 1992.

CHAPTER 6   INFLECTING THE FORMULA

1 John Fiske, *Television Culture* (London 1987), 110.

2 Information about American series television in this essay comes from entries in Alex McNeil, *Total Television: A Comprehensive Guide to Programming from 1948 to 1980* (New York 1980). Information about British programs to 1982 is from Leslie Halliwell, with Philip Purser, television critic for the *Sunday Telegraph*, *Halliwell's Television Companion*, 2d ed. (London 1982). Details about Canadian programming are from Mary Jane Miller, *Turn Up The Contrast: CBC Television Drama since 1952* (Vancouver 1987).

3 Miller, *Turn Up the Contrast*, 55–66; and see two interviews with John Kennedy, head of TV Drama for a decade, ibid., 357–73.

4 Horace Newcomb, *TV: The Most Popular Art* (Garden City, NY 1974).

5 In mid-season *Storefront Lawyers* was given a new male character and retitled *Men at Law*. The change in emphasis is clear. Presumably

the combination of 1960s activism and a team of lawyers that included a woman did not get the necessary ratings.

6 Confirmed by interviews with thirty-five makers and decision-makers in Mary Jane Miller, "Rewind and Search: Conversations with Makers and Decision Makers in CBC English Television Drama" (unpublished).

7 Half-hour adaptations in several episodes of Canadian novels and the brilliant filmed anthology with recurring characters, *Cariboo Country*.

8 In order, the reviews in the British Film Institute's microfilm collection are by W. Marshall, *Daily Mirror*, 27 June 1969; Charles Herbert, *Daily Sketch*, 27 June 1969; *Communist Morning Star*, 5 July 1969 (it had a very good television critic at the time); and *The Times*, 22 August 1969. Other critics saw it as a cops and robbers show, with a "mean streets" loner protagonist, and as very violent or even as film noir.

9 Contrast the section on *Wojeck* in Miller, *Turn Up the Contrast*, 23–68.

10 Miller, *Turn Up the Contrast*, 34–41.

11 See, for example, Brian Johnson with Pamela Young, "Legal Eagles and the Law of the Jungle," *Maclean's*, 23 February 1992, 53–4.

12 Carrie, "a young ambitious and attractive criminal lawyer. Leon, a passionate civil rights lawyer and a quirky romantic ... Chuck, a maverick and engaging streetwise fighter [who] pursues the big cases": CBC Television press release, 13 May 1986.

13 Specifically, Andrew Borkowski, "Attack of the 100 Channel Universe: TV distribution in the 21st Century," *Scan: The Publication of CBC Television Producers and Directors*, specifically volume 5, numbers 4, 5, and 6 (January–February, March–April, and May–June 1992).

14 Diane Smith, *Starweek*, 10–17 January 1987. But compare also McEwen to Jennifer Fisher, *T.V. Guide*, 3 January 1987: "The law tends to reflect its society, so without being self-conscious about it, this series will be very Canadian."

15 Conversation with Maryke McEwen, February 1988. McEwen also showed me the reports of their visit to Los Angeles. The "bible" is the series of guidelines issued to new writers to orient them to the premises and the probable development of the series over the following season.

16 This sort of detail is highlighted for would-be writers of scripts in a copy of the series "bible" of 1988–89 given to me by executive producer Maryke McEwen.

17 John Haslett Cuff, *Globe and Mail*, 26 September 1987, saw it differently. Citing this and other episodes he wrote, "The episodes always seem to flatten out and dribble to a close"; "Too little cut and thrust in courtroom," etc. It seems to me that what he wanted was *L.A. Law*.

18 Clayton Ruby, "Who Would You Want in Your Corner?" *T.V. Guide*, 18 April 1988.

19 Jeffrey Miller, "TV Lawyers Reflect Country's Culture," *Lawyer's Weekly*, 8 April 1988.

20 Paula Kilig, *Law Times*, 29 January-4 February 1990, 10.

21 Interviews, 5 January 1985, with writer William Deverall, director Peter Yalden-Thomas, and producer Maryke McEwen.

22 Deborah Hastings, "*L.A. Law* Fights to Regain Form," *The Standard* (St. Catharines, Ont.), 1 February 1992.

23 Sid Adilman, *Toronto Star*, January 16, 1992; Peter Gzowski, "Steamy 'Street Legal'," *Canadian Living*, April 1991.

24 See Fiske, *Television Culture*, chapter 5, "Active Audiences," 62–83; and R. Allen on reader response theory in *Channels of Discourse: Television and Contemporary Criticism* (Chapel Hill 1987).

CHAPTER 7   POPULAR CULTURES OF OLYMPIC SPORT
IN CANADA AND THE UNITED STATES

1 C. Mukerji and M. Schudson, eds., *Rethinking Popular Culture* (Berkeley 1990); S. Kutler and S. Katz, eds., "The Promise of American History: Progress and Prospects," *Reviews in American History* 10 (1982), 1–423; Joseph Gusfield and Jerzy Michalowicz, "Secular Symbolism: Studies of Ritual Ceremony and the Symbolic Order in Modern Life," *Annual Review of Sociology* 10 (1984), 417–35; Gary Fine, ed., "Sociology and Popular Culture" *Journal of Popular Culture*, 11 (1977), 379–526; Herbert Gans, *Popular Culture and High Culture* (New York 1974).

2 Clifford Geertz, "Blurred Genres: The Refiguration of Social Thought," in C. Geertz, ed., *Local Knowledge: Further Essays in Interpretive Anthropology* (New York 1983); Lawrence Grossberg, Cary Nelson, and Paula Treichler, eds., *Cultural Studies* (New York 1992).

3 Joseph Gusfield, *The Culture of Public Problems* (Chicago 1981); Arjun Appadurai and Carol Breckenridge, "Why Public Culture?" *Public Culture Bulletin* 1: 1 (1988), 5–10.

4 Pierre Bourdieu, *Distinction: A Social Critique of the Judgement of Taste*, translated by Richard Nice (Cambridge, Mass. 1984). See also Bourdieu, "Program for a Sociology of Sport," translated by John MacAloon, *Sociology of Sport Journal* 5 (1988), 153–61.

5 Marshall Sahlins, *Culture and Practical Reason* (Chicago 1976).

6 Bruce Kidd is the most informed and articulate observer of Canadian transformations of Olympic ideology. See, for example, his "The Philosophy of Excellence: Olympic Performances, Class Power, and the

Canadian State," in S.-P. Kang, J. MacAloon, and R. DaMatta, eds., *The Olympics and Cultural Exchange* (Seoul 1988), 343–70.

7 John J. MacAloon, "The Ethnographic Imperative in Comparative Olympic Research," *Sociology of Sport Journal* 9: 2 (1991), 104–30; and MacAloon, "Missing Stories: American Politics and Olympic Discourse," *Gannett Center Journal* 1: 2 (1988), 111–42. For theoretical treatments of the role of metaphor in cultural and political life, see George Lakoff and Mark Johnson, *Metaphors We Live By* (Chicago 1980) and James Fernandez, *Persuasions and Performances: The Play of Tropes in Culture* (Bloomington 1986).

8 Victor Turner, *The Forest of Symbols* (Ithaca 1967).

9 Fernandez, *Persuasions and Performances*, 186–213.

10 Donald Macintosh, *Sport and Politics in Canada: Federal Government Involvement since 1961* (Kingston and Montreal 1987), 174; and Donald Macintosh and David Whitson, *The Game Planners: Transforming Canada's Sport Systems* (Kingston and Montreal 1990). Laurence Chalip, "The Framing of Policy: Explaining the Transformation of American Sport" (PH.D. dissertation, University of Chicago 1988) is the only text offering any serious parallel for the U.S.

11 For fuller accounts see MacAloon, "Missing Stories," and Chalip, "Framing of Policy."

12 See, for example, Pierre de Coubertin, *Universités transatlantiques* (Paris 1890); Hervé Varenne, *Americans Together* (New York 1977); and Michel Crozier, *The Trouble with America* (New York 1985).

13 As noted earlier, the effect is sometimes a matter of linguistic habits. Even well-informed political analysts can fall into discussing the "Americanization" of Canadian sport without pausing to note the radical difference in the Olympic field occasioned by federal non-engagement in the United States. See Kidd, "How Do We Find Our Own Voice in the 'New World Order'? A Comment on Americanization," *Sociology of Sport Journal* 8: 2 (1992) 1788–84, and my response in MacAloon, "Ethnographic Imperative."

14 See John MacAloon, "Steroids and the State: Dubin, Melodrama, and the Accomplishment of Innocence," *Public Culture* 2: 2 (1990), 41–64, for a full analysis.

15 *Report of the Commission of Inquiry into the Use of Drugs and Banned Practices Intended to Increase Athletic Performance* (Ottawa 1990).

CHAPTER 8   WHOSE NATIONAL PASTIME?

1 Several historians have outlined this American colonial phenomenon; the most comprehensive treatment is Robert Henderson, *Ball, Bat*

and Bishop: The Origin of Ball Games (New York 1947). See also Jennie Holliman, *American Sports: 1785–1835* (Durham, NC 1931); David Quentin Voigt, *American Baseball: From Gentleman's Sport to the Commissioner System* (Norman, Okla. 1966); and Harold Seymour, *Baseball: The Early Years* (New York 1960).

2 American immigration into southwestern Ontario after 1815 is clearly documented in Fred Landon, *Western Ontario and the American Frontier* (Toronto 1967), 46–61.

3 Ibid., 1–22, 134.

4 This analogy has been applied in similar contexts to other immigrations westward. See, for instance, my investigation of German-Americans passing through Louisville, Kentucky, on their way west in the 1850s (Robert Knight Barney, "German-American Turnvereins and Socio-Politico-Economic Realities in the Antebellum and Civil War Upper and Lower South," *Stadion* 10 [1984], 143–44).

5 *Sporting Life*, 5 May 1886; Nancy B. Bouchier and Robert Knight Barney, "A Critical Examination of a Source on Early Ontario Baseball: The Reminiscence of Adam E. Ford," *Journal of Sport History* 15: 1 (1988), 88.

6 Ibid., 85–86.

7 Peter Leslie Lindsay, "A History of Sport in Canada, 1807–1867," (PH.D. dissertation, University of Alberta 1969), 79; *Clipper*, 22 June 1861.

8 Canadian baseball clubs carefully observed rules changes made from year to year by the NAPBBP and the NLPBBC. For example, the Ingersoll *Chronicle* (18 March 1875) reported the changes emanating from the NAPBBP's convention in Philadelphia. Likewise, the Woodstock *Sentinel* (20 November 1886) described rules changes created by the National League for play in 1887. Many nineteenth-century Ontario newspapers published comments on how American rules changes would affect local play.

9 Several baseball historians have chronicled the Knickerbockers' historic contribution to the game. Among the most detailed accounts is Melvin L. Adelman, *A Sporting Time: New York City and the Rise of Modern Athletics, 1820–1870* (Urbana 1986), 121–83.

10 Lindsay, "Sport in Canada," 79.

11 *Railton's Directory for the City of London, C.W. (Canada West) 1856–1857*, (London 1856) 25; Ingersoll *Chronicle*, 27 July 1860.

12 *Clipper*, 17 July 1869. This newspaper was well aware of Woodstock's place in Canadian baseball. In August 1864 the Woodstock Young Canadians played host to a meeting to promote a Canadian "national" baseball association, the advertised playing rules of which copied

those of the National Association of Baseball Players in the United States (see, for instance, *Clipper*, 14 September 1864; Hamilton *Times*, 24 August 1864; and Ingersoll *Chronicle*, 26 August 1864). In 1864 the *Clipper* reported a match game challenge issued by the Woodstock Young Canadian Baseball Club to the Brooklyn Atlantics, then the reigning American Champions; the game, played in Rochester, New York, in September 1864, resulted in a lopsided American victory, 75–11 (*Clipper*, 4 September and 1 October 1864).

13 See Adelman, *A Sporting Time*, 145–83. The path towards professionalism in baseball commenced with the phenomenon of "substitution" (gaining the services of a skilled player for one game), led rapidly to the practice of "revolving" (a player's breaking an agreement in mid-season to join another club), and concluded with signed contracts for services. For early comments on substitution, see *Spirit of the Times*, 13 September 1856. For early comments on revolving, see *Brooklyn Eagle*, 4 August 1866 and *Spirit of the Times*, 11 March 1871.

14 Several historians have examined the Cincinnati Red Stocking experience. See, for instance, Joseph S. Stern, Jr., "The Team that Couldn't Be Beat: The Red Stockings of 1869," *Cincinnati Historical Society Bulletin* 27: 1 (1969); Robert Knight Barney, "Of Rails and Red Stockings: Episodes in the Expansion of the National Pastime in the American West," *Journal of the West* 17: 3 (July 1978); Voigt, *American Baseball*, 23–34; and Seymour, *Baseball: The Early Years*, 56–8.

15 William Humber, *Cheering for the Home Team: The Story of Baseball in Canada* (Erin, Ont. 1983), 28–9.

16 Ibid., 29.

17 See George Sleeman Collection, Regional Collections, D.B. Weldon Library, University of Western Ontario. Sleeman's personal papers include several letters to and from ballplayers on the subject of payment for services rendered to the Maple Leafs.

18 Humber, *Cheering for the Home Team*, 29–30.

19 Several historians have recorded the success of the London Tecumsehs in the 1870s. See, for instance, Humber, ibid., 30–44; and Henry Roxborough, *One-Hundred-Not-Out: The Story of Nineteenth-Century Canadian Sport* (Toronto 1966), 112–16. For a penetrating insight from a primary source, see Tecumseh Baseball Club of London, *Tecumseh Minute Book*, 22 June 1868–1 May 1872, Regional Collection, D.B. Weldon Library, University of Western Ontario.

20 See Humber, *Cheering for the Home Team*, 39–41.

21 Voigt, *American Baseball*, 76.

22 See Humber, *Cheering for the Home Team*, 39–43.

23 Bruce Prentice of the Canadian Baseball Hall of Fame in Toronto compiled this data on Canadian minor league growth and development. I am grateful to him for allowing me access.

24 Evelyn Janice Waters, "A Content Analysis of the Sport Section in Selected Canadian Newspapers: 1926 to 1935" (Master's thesis, University of Western Ontario 1981), 56, 60, 64, 70, 74.

25 The Stanley Cup and the National Hockey League came into existence in 1892 and 1917 respectively.

26 The saga of Jackie Robinson's short-lived career with the Montreal Royals and his subsequent promotion to the Brooklyn Dodgers is best captured in the scholarly work of Jules Tygiel, *Baseball's Great Experiment: Jackie Robinson and His Legacy* (New York 1983).

27 Larry Millson, *Ballpark Figures: The Blue Jays and the Business of Baseball* (Toronto 1987), 137.

28 Buzzy Bavasi's first position as general manager of a ball club was in Montreal with the Royals during the 1948 and 1949 seasons. He subsequently became "Big League" as general manager of the Brooklyn Dodgers from 1950 to 1957, the Los Angeles Dodgers from 1958 to 1967, and the San Diego Padres from 1968 to 1973.

29 Millson, *Ballpark Figures*, 125.

30 Ibid., 131.

31 Ibid., 134–5 and 284–6. Here Millson describes the terrifying effect on Blue Jay finances of the lower value of the Canadian dollar against its American counterpart.

32 Ibid., 9. According to Millson, *Fortune* magazine's assessment was less, putting the value of the Blue Jay franchise at between $36 million and $40 million. Roger Noll's assessment of between $40 million and $45 million (u.s.) was made at a time when the noted Stanford University economist was serving the Players' Association in a review of the financial status of all major league clubs.

33 Millson, *Ballpark Figures*, 136.

34 Jacques Barzun, *God's Country and Mine: A Declaration of Love Spiced with a Few Harsh Words* (Boston 1954), 159. Commentators often cite Barzun's pronouncement to underscore the importance of baseball in American culture. For one example, see Douglas Wallop, *Baseball: An Informal History* (New York 1969), 22,

35 W.P. Kinsella, *Shoeless Joe* (New York 1982), 213.

36 Statistics on Canadian participation in baseball at various levels in 1988 reflect a total registration figure in excess of 200,000 individuals, roughly broken down as follows: Little League Baseball, 54,000; Babe Ruth baseball (played only in the province of British Columbia), 2,500; all other levels and categories of amateur baseball, 147,000. I

am indebted to Joe Shea (Calgary) Little League Baseball of Canada; Al Elliott (Vancouver), Babe Ruth Baseball of Canada; and John Hamilton (Ottawa), Canadian Federation of Amateur Baseball, for the information noted above. The statistics for participation in fast pitch and slow pitch softball for 1988 are startling. Slightly over 2 million Canadians, almost 10 per cent of the total population, played softball; of those, 210,000 were registered in league play leading to local, regional, provincial and national championships. The 210,000 figure was split almost evenly between males and females. I am indebted to Gail Gibson (Ottawa), Softball Canada, for the participation statistics noted above. Hockey and its ersatz forms (ringette and ball hockey) include approximately 500,000 registered players (there is little organized hockey played in Canada featuring non-registered players). For participation statistics relevant to forms of hockey, I am indebted to Dennis MacDonald (Ottawa), Canadian Amateur Hockey Association; Wes Clarke (Ottawa), Ringette Canada; and Althea Arsenault-Sharkey (Toronto), Ontario Ball Hockey Association.

CHAPTRE 9   AMBIVALENCE AT THE FIFTY-FIVE-YARD LINE

A version of this essay appeared in Helen Holmes and David Taras, eds., *Seeing Ourselves: Media Power and Policy in Canada* (Toronto: Harcourt Brace Jovanovich 1992). Reprinted with permission of the author.

1 Frank Cosentino, "A History of Canadian Football 1909–1968," (M.A. thesis, University of Alberta 1969), 1.

2 Ibid., 11.

3 Nancy Howell and Maxwell L. Howell, *Sports and Games in Canadian Life: 1700 to the Present* (Toronto 1969), 80–1, 195.

4 Bruce Kidd, "Sport, Dependency, and the Canadian State," in Hart Cantelon and Richard Gruneau, eds., *Sport, Culture, and the Modern State* (Toronto 1982), 293.

5 Robert A. Stebbins, *Canadian Football: The View from the Helmet* (London, Ont. 1987), 109–10.

6 See, for example, the 19 March 1984 training rosters for each CFL team in Terry Jones, *Canadian Pro Football '84* (Markham, Ont. 1984).

7 Stebbins, *Canadian Football*, 110.

8 Ibid., 116.

9 Steve Simmons, *Calgary Herald*, 8 December, 1986.

10 Stebbins, *Canadian Football*, 191–2.

11 Canadian Broadcasting Corporation, "Inside Track," CBC radio, 13 October 1986.

CHAPTER 10 MOUNTIES, MUGGINGS, AND MOOSE

1 I am indebted to Thelma McCormack of York University for the phrase "deep template" in her response to my essay, since it neatly sums up the sense I am trying to convey.

2 Lionel Rubinoff, "National Purpose and Ideology," in Andy Wainwright, ed., *Notes For a Native Land* (Toronto 1969), 43–8.

3 Ibid., 45.

4 Frank Davey, "Critics' Folly," *Canadian Forum* (November 1986), 40.

5 Ibid., 40.

6 Northrop Frye, "Conclusion," in Carl F. Klinck, ed., *A Literary History of Canada: Canadian Literature in English*, 2d ed., 3 vols. (Toronto 1976), 3, 318–32.

7 D.G. Jones, *Butterfly on Rock* (Toronto 1970), 6.

8 Alan Stratton, *Rexy!* (Toronto 1981).

9 Rubinoff, "National Purpose and Ideology," 47.

10 Margaret Atwood, *Survival: A Thematic Guide to Canadian Literature* (Toronto 1972), 245.

11 Robin Mathews, *Canadian Literature: Surrender or Revolution*, ed. Gail Dexter (Toronto 1978), 120, 121; Pierre Vallières, *White Niggers of America: The Precocious Autobiography of a Québec "Terrorist,"* translated by Joan Pinkham (New York 1971).

12 Pierre Berton, *Why We Act Like Canadians: A Personal Exploration of Our National Character* (Toronto 1982); Jim Christy, "History in the Underground," *Globe and Mail*, 11 July 1988.

13 Richard Paul Knowles has pointed out in that it is the role of education to deconstruct, though it has not been the practice of Canadian education to do so.

14 Malcolm Ross, *The Impossible Sum of Our Traditions: Reflections on Canadian Literature* (Toronto 1986), 201.

15 John Gray with Eric Peterson, *Billy Bishop Goes to War* (Vancouver 1981).

16 Chad Evans, *Frontier Theatre: A History of Nineteenth-Century Theatrical Entertainment in the Canadian Far West and Alaska* (Victoria, BC 1983), 9.

17 San Francisco *Herald*; cited ibid., 76.

18 Brian D. Johnson, with Pamela Young, Ann Finlayson, and Roy Shields, "TV Boils Over," *Maclean's*, 22 September 1987, 38–40.

19 Mary Jane Miller, *Turn Up the Contrast: CBC Television Drama since 1952* (Vancouver 1987), 102.

20 Ibid., 104, 105.

21 Richard Carpenter, "Ritual Aesthetics and TV," *Journal of Popular Culture* 3 (1969), 54.

22 Miller, *Turn Up the Contrast*, 106.

23 John Lazarus, "An Omen for Us in 'Murder, She Wrote'?" *Vancouver Sun*, 20 October 1987.

24 Pierre Berton, *Hollywood's Canada: The Americanization of Our National Image* (Toronto 1975).

25 John Powell, "Report on RCMP Recruitment," *The World at 6*, CBC Radio, 28 March 1988.

26 Quoted in Kenneth Freed, "The Mounties (Almost) Always Get Their Man," *New York Times*, 7 February 1988.

27 Ibid.

28 Sharon Pollock, *Walsh* (Vancouver 1973; reprinted with revisions, 1974).

29 Hugh Fraser, "Women Get Foothold in Pre-school TV," *Vancouver Sun*, 13 November 1987.

30 See Ernest Thompson Seton, *Wild Animals I Have Known* (New York 1898); *Lobo, Rag, and Vixen* (1899); and stories by Charles G.D. Roberts.

31 Margaret Atwood, "The Animals in That Country," in Gary Geddes and Phyllis Bruce, eds., *15 Canadian Poets Plus 5* (Toronto 1970), 294.

32 Dennis Lee, *Alligator Pie* (Toronto 1974), 21.

33 Barbara Gamarekian, "Canadian Musical Puts National Hero on Stage," *New York Times*, 17 May 1980; Mel Gussow, "Theatre: Capital Sees 'Billy Bishop Goes to War,'" *New York Times*, 13 March 1980.

34 Allan Massie, "Canadian Ace Lands," *The Scotsman* (Edinburgh) 15 November 1979.

35 Bryan Johnson, "Billy Bishop Brought Down to Earth," *Globe and Mail*, 17 February 1979.

36 Rubinoff, "National Purpose and Ideology," 47.

CHAPTER 11   SYNCRETIZING SOUND

1 Paul Oliver, *Songsters and Saints: Vocal Traditions on Race Records* (Cambridge, UK 1984); Dorothy Scarborough, *On the Trail of Negro Folk-Songs* (1925; reprinted, Hatboro, Pa. 1963), 33–64.

2 George Mitchell, "Rosa Lee Hill," *Blues Unlimited*, 60 (1969), 4.

3 Peter J. Welding, "An Interview with Carl Martin," *78 Quarterly* 1: 2 (1968), 31.

4 David Evans, "The Johnnie Temple Story," *Blues Unlimited*, 56 (1968), 8.

5 John Cohen, "The Folk Music Interchange: Negro and White," *Sing Out!* 14: 4 (1964), 42–9; William R. Ferris, Jr., "Racial Repertoires among Blues Performers," *Ethnomusicology* 14 (1970), 439–49; John

S. Otto and Augustus M. Burns, "John 'Knocky' Parker – A Case of White and Black Musical Interaction," *John Edwards Memorial Foundation Quarterly* 10 (1974), 23–6; and Tony Russell, *Blacks Whites and Blues* (New York 1970).

6 David Evans, "Black Musicians Remember Jimmie Rodgers," *Old Time Music* 7 (1972–73), 12–14.

7 Peter J. Welding, "Ramblin' Johnny Shines," *Living Blues* 22 (1975), 29.

8 J. Nicholas Perls, "Son House Interview, Part One," *78 Quarterly* 1: 1 (1967), 60.

9 Bengt Olsson, *Memphis Blues and Jug Bands* (London 1970), 23–4.

10 Paul Oliver, *Conversation with the Blues* (New York 1965), 46.

11 Jeff Titon, ed., *From Blues to Pop: The Autobiography of Leonard "Baby Doo" Caston* (Los Angeles 1974), 25.

12 Neil V. Rosenberg, "Biblio Discographies: The 'Whitehouse Blues' – 'McKinley' – 'Cannonball Blues' Complex," *John Edwards Memorial Foundation Newsletter*, 4: 2 (1968), 46.

13 Neil V. Rosenberg, "Big Fish, Small Pond: Country Musicians and Their Markets," in Peter Narváez amd Martin Laba, eds., *Media Sense: The Folklore-Popular Culture Continuum* (Bowling Green 1986), 149–66.

14 Roderick E. Deihl, Michael J. Schneider, and Kenneth Petress, "Dimensions of Music Preference: A Factor Analytic Study," *Popular Music and Society* 9: 3 (1983), 42.

15 Neil V. Rosenberg, *Bluegrass: A History* (Urbana, Ill. 1985), 259–69.

16 Norm Cohen, "'I'm a Record Man' – Uncle Art Satherley Reminisces," *John Edwards Memorial Foundation Quarterly*, 8 (1972), 18.

17 Michael Taft, "The Lyrics of Race Record Blues, 1920–1942: A Semantic Approach to the Structural Analysis of a Formulaic System" (PHD dissertation, Memorial University of Newfoundland 1977), 145.

18 Rosenberg, *Bluegrass*, 363–5.

19 See Neil V. Rosenberg, "'Folk' and 'Country' Music in the Canadian Maritimes: A Regional Model," *Journal of Country Music* 5 (1974), 76–83; Michael Taft, "'That's Two More Dollars': Jimmy Linegar's Success with Country Music in Newfoundland," *Folklore Forum* 7 (1974), 99–120; Taft, "Computer Database of 75,000 Song Citations from the Young Cooperators Song Columns in the *Western Producer*, 1927–1975" (computer database, Social Sciences and Humanities Research Council of Canada, grant no. 410–85–0032).

20 See, for example, Phyllis R. Blakeley, "Music in Nova Scotia, 1605–1867. Part II," *Dalhousie Review* 31 (1951–52), 223–30.

21 Sheilagh S. Jameson, with Nola B. Erickson, *Chautauqua in Canada* (Calgary 1979), 110.

22 Taft, "Computer database of 75,000 song citations."

23 See John Bridges and R. Serge Denisoff, "PMS in Retrospect: A Look

at the First Six Volumes," *Popular Music and Society* 7: 1 (1979), 4.
An exception is Richard D. Dixon, "Music in the Community: A Survey
of Who Is Paying Attention," ibid. 37–56.

24 E.A. Howes, *With a Glance Backward* (Toronto 1939), 52–73.

25 Lester B. Sellick, *Our Musical Heritage* (Hantsport, NS 1984), 52–54.

26 Benoît L'Herbier, *La Chanson Québécoise* (Montreal 1974), 28
(my translation).

27 See also Bob Coltman, "Habitantbilly: French-Canadian Old Time
Music," *Old Time Music* 11 (1973), 9–13 and 12 (1974), 9–14; Nor-
mand Cormier, Ghislaine Houle, Suzanne Lauzier, and Yvette
Trépanier, *La Chanson au Québec* (Montreal 1975); and Miles
Krassen, "An Analysis of a Jean Carignan Record," *Canadian Folk Music
Journal* 2 (1974), 40–4.

28 Ronald Caplan, "The Function of Narrative Obituary Verse in Northern
Cape Breton (1894–1902)" (MA thesis, St. Mary's University,
Halifax 1988).

29 Michael Taft, *A Regional Discography of Newfoundland and Labrador,
1904–1972* (St. John's 1975), vii.

30 Peter Narváez, "Country and Western in Diffusion: Juxtaposition and
Syncretism in the Popular Music of Newfoundland," *Culture & Tradition* 2 (1977), 107–14.

31 Neil V. Rosenberg, "Introduction," in Michael Taft, *Travelling the Out-
ports: Two Studies in Newfoundland Itinerant Culture* (St. John's 1981),
2–3.

32 Michael Taft, "Of Scoffs, Mounties and Mainlanders: The Popularity
of a Sheep-Stealing Ballad in Newfoundland," in Narváez and Laba,
eds., *Media Sense*, 77–98.

33 Robert B. Klymasz, "'Sounds You Never Heard Before': Ukrainian
Country Music in Western Canada," *Ethnomusicology* 16 (1972),
372–80.

34 See Paul Dimaggio and Michael Useem, "Social Class and Art Consumption: The Origins and Consequences of Class Differences in Exposure to the Arts in America," *Theory and Society* 5 (1978), 143; and
Nicholas Tawa, *A Music for the Millions: Antebellum Democratic Attitudes and the Birth of American Popular Music* (New York 1984).

35 Herbert Halpert, "Preface," in Taft, *A Regional Discography*, vi.

36 See Herbert Halpert, "Vitality of Traditional and Local Songs," *Journal
of the International Folk Music Council* 3 (1951), 35–40.

37 Sheldon Posen, *For Singing and Dancing and All Sorts of Fun* (Toronto
1988). I found the same phenomenon in Saskatchewan; Michael
Taft, *Discovering Saskatchewan Folklore: Three Case Studies* (Edmonton
1983), 23–42.

38 Taft, "Computer database of 75,000 song citations."

39 James R. McDonald, "Bob Dylan: Biograph – A Journey into Life," *Popular Music and Society* 10: 3 (1986), 91.

40 Martin Laba, "Problems in Canadian Folklore Studies," *Canadian Folklore canadien* 7 (1985), 202.

41 Dimaggio and Useem, "Social Class and Art Composition," 156.

CHAPTER 12 OUR HOUSE, THEIR HOUSE

1 R. Bruce Elder, "The Cinema We Need," *Canadian Forum* (February 1985) 32–35.

2 Obviously, this goes beyond the clichéd depiction of Canada as female and its sexist connotation of that femininity as passive. The Oedipal dilemma functions for either gender. And the young Sandy is far from passive.

3 Quoted in Peter Morris, *Embattled Shadows: A History of Canadian Cinema 1895–1939* (Montreal 1978), 175.

4 Quoted ibid., 57.

5 See Pierre Veronneau, "The First Wave of Quebec Feature Films: 1944–1953," in Pierre Veronneau and Piers Handling, eds., *Self Portrait* (Ottawa 1980), 54–63.

6 "Documentary Films: World War II," in Seth Feldman and Joyce Nelson, eds., *Canadian Film Reader* (Toronto 1977), 55. Although as many as four hundred films were produced in this style at the NFB during the Second World War, a useful and certainly a seminal example would be *Churchill's Island* (Stuart Legg and Tom Daly, 1942), the board's and Canada's first Academy Award winner.

7 "The Innocent Eye" is in Feldman and Nelson, eds., *Canadian Film Reader*, 72.

8 See, for instance, his "Men of Vision: Some Comments on the Work of Don Shebib," in Feldman and Nelson, eds., *Canadian Film Reader*, 208–16.

9 R. Bruce Elder, "On the Candid Eye Movement" in *Canadian Film Reader*, 93.

10 Stuart Legg's *Coal Face, Canada* (1940), the first film made in this country by the British team who were to form the core of the National Film Board, was an attempt to use non-actors to recreate the world of unemployed youth in a Nova Scotia mining town.

11 Feldman and Nelson, eds., *Canadian Film Reader*, 217–34.

12 Elder, "The Cinema We Need," 35.

13 As Alan Gedalof of the University of Western Ontario correctly pointed out in a response to this essay, the American fantasy is discredited even within the film's plot. Butch is exposed as a fraud, a poseur who has stolen his mother's car, a superficial Don Juan fleeing in terror

at the prospect of having impregnated his California girlfriend. Building upon Gedalof's suggestion, I would argue that all this points to Butch as a victim of his own cultural creation, that impossible American adolescent image referred to earlier in this essay. Ironically, then, it is Butch who faces the cultural confusion inherent in not making it as an American teenager. Sandy, an alien (or a potential alien) to the image of adolescence, is far less its victim.

14 Ann McKinnon, "Sandy Wilson: First Features, Canadian Wives, American Cousins: An Interview," *Cinema Canada* 120–121 (July–August 1985), 21.

CHAPTER 13   WIVES, WHORES, AND PRIESTS

1 Chantal Hébert, "Burlesque in Quebec: A Cultural Product Imported from the United States or a Phenomenon of Cultural Integration?" presentation to a conference on American popular culture in Canada, University of Western Ontario, 4–6 May 1988, 9.

2 Ibid., 3.

3 B. Tomachevsky, "Thématique," in Tzvetan Todorov, ed., *Théorie de la Littérature* (Paris 1965) (my translation).

4 For example, see Dan Ben-Amos, ed., *Folklore Genres* (Austin 1976).

5 Alan Dundes, "Jokes and Covert Language Attitudes: The Curious Case of the Wide-Mouth Frog," in *Language in Society* 6 (1977), 141–7.

6 Hébert, "Burlesque in Quebec," 8.

7 The focus on structure is forced precisely by the fact that we have at our disposal only story outlines; for outlines are nothing other than structures.

8 See, for example, Tzvetan Todorov, "Les transformations narratives," *Poétique. Revue de théorie et d'analyse narrative* 3 (Paris 1970), 322–34; Claude Bremond, *Logique du Récit* (Paris 1973); Algirdas Julien Greimas, "Un problème de sémiotique narrative: les objets de valeur," *Langage* 31 (Paris 1973), 13–35.

9 This number represents every occurrence of a legend with a priest collected for the Archives de Folklore de l'Université Laval. See Charline Poirier, "L'image du prêtre dans la tradition légendaire du Québec: Essai d'analyse formelle et sémiotique" (MA thesis, Laval University 1981).

10 Ibid., 160–74.

11 Ibid., 6.

12 Ibid., 65 (my translation).

13 A memorate is a legend in which the narrator plays a role. It could be told in the first person, or it could have been witnessed by the narrator. A fabulate is a narrative that allegedly happened to a person

known to the narrator or a person known to someone known to the narrator.

14 Collection of Irene Audet, *Apparition d'une âme de prêtre*, Narrator Eugénie Minville, Gaspésie, Quebec.

15 Poirier, *L'image du prêtre*, 168.

16 Ibid., 168.

17 Ibid., 171.

18 Ibid., 172–3.

19 Carol Gilligan, *In a Different Voice* (Cambridge, Mass. 1982), 62, 29.

20 Ibid., 43–4.

21 We can safely assume, on the basis of Gilligan's research (based as it is on Lawrence Kohlberg's results, for example in "Moral Stages and Moralization: The Cognitive-Developmental Approach," in Thomas Lickona, ed., *Moral Development and Behavior: Theory, Research and Social Issues* [New York 1976]), that – these results having a cross-cultural validity – our Quebecois man and the American man would show similar ways of thinking. This suggests that an examination of the two burlesques, taking the difference in narrative voice as our focal point, would be appropriate and useful.

22 Ibid., 62.

23 Hébert, "Burlesque in Quebec," 8.

CHAPTER 14   THE CANADIANIZATION OF
AN AMERICAN FAIR

Sections of this paper were derived from a larger study entitled "World's Fairs and the Constitution of Society: The Ideology of Expo 86," presented to the annual meeting of the Canadian Ethnology Society, Edmonton, 16 May 1986, and subsequently published in Michael M. Ames, *Cannibal Tours and Glass Boxes: The Anthropology of Museums* (Vancouver 1992), 111–31. I have benefited greatly from discussions with Julia D. Harrison and David Jensen, who bear no responsibility for the final result.

1 Stephen Godfrey, "Expo's Canadian Content Questioned," *Globe and Mail*, 29 June 1985.

2 Marjorie Nichols, "Dizzy Doings Down at Expo," *Vancouver Sun*, 31 May 1985; Nichols, "Clearing the Stench at Expo," ibid., 6 June 1985.

3 Pete McMartin, "What Has Michael Bartlett Wrought?" *Vancouver Sun*, 14 June 1985.

4 Gordon Hamilton, "Bartlett's Operation: On Time, On Budget," *Vancouver Sun*, 6 June 1985.

5 Gordon Hamilton, "Expo Sold National Emblem Along with Souvenir Rights," *Vancouver Sun*, 10 October 1985.

6 Stephen Godfrey, "'Bazooka' Approach Used In Expo 86 Ad Campaign," *Globe and Mail*, 26 October 1985.

7 Michael M. Ames, "Is the McDonald Hamburger a Work of Art? A Discourse on Popular Aesthetics and Unpopular Curators," *Parachute* 49 (December – January – February 1987–88), 22–27.

8 Moira Farrow, "Managers' Style At Expo Criticized," *Vancouver Sun*, 25 November 1986.

9 David Lowenthal, *The Past Is a Foreign Country* (Cambridge, UK 1985).

10 "Design Brief Main Hall: Canadian Pavilion Expo '86," 4 February 1985.

11 In a survey of twelve North American and European pavilions, plus China, at Expo 86, Diane Bennett, University of British Columbia Museum of Anthropology researcher, counted 889 images of people; of those, only 21 per cent were of women. Most of the women were shown in the traditional female roles of nurses, stewardesses, keyboard operators, etc. There were no images of women as scientists in these pavilions, though both the United States and Canada pavilions showed women as astronauts. Diane Bennett, "The Culturally Conditioned World of Expo '86: Gender Splitting at a World's Fair" (University of British Columbia Museum of Anthropology manuscript 1986).

12 "Design Brief Main Hall: Canadian Pavilion Expo '86," 4 February 1985 (emphasis added).

13 Michael J. Powell et al. *Official Souvenir Guide, Expo 86* (Vancouver and Victoria 1986).

14 "Expo Draw World Record," *Real Estate Weekly* 8(44), 28 September 1984.

15 Bonni Raines Kettner, "Supers Battle," *The Province*, Vancouver, 12 July 1985.

16 John Cruickshank, "Expo's Space Race: Three Superpowers Use Fair to Build Up Their Prestige with Showcase Technology," *Globe and Mail*, 29 March 1986.

17 Kettner, "Supers Battle," *The Province*, 12 July 1985.

18 The Canada pavilion measured 10,869 square metres, compared with 5,000 square metres for the four U.S. pavilions and 2,750 square metres for the Soviet pavilion.

19 Max Wyman, "Introduction," in Max Wyman, ed., *Vancouver Forum I: Old Powers, New Forces* (Vancouver 1992), 17.

20 "Planner Has Beef with Floating McDonald's," *Vancouver Sun*, 23 July 1985.

21 Pete McMartin, "Rare Treats or Not, McDonald's You Have with You Always," *Vancouver Sun*, 5 May 1986.

22 David Hartline, "Expo: You Rate It ... Tops!" *The Province Magazine*, 15 June 1986.

23 Ann Rees, "Layoffs Hit Expo," *The Province*, Vancouver, 22 June 1986.

24 "Frontier Outlook Leans to 'Loan Gun'" *The Province*, Vancouver, 6 October 1985. Needless to say, Pattison has his eastern Canadian counterparts.

25 Philip Resnick, "Neo-Conservatism on the Periphery: The Lessons from British Columbia," *Australian-Canadian Studies* 5: 2 (1987), 7.

26 Michael Sasges, "A Fair Appeals, Firms Give ..." *Vancouver Sun*, 12 April 1982.

27 Paul McKay, "The Less-Than-Holy Roman Empire," *Globe and Mail*, 9 April 1988.

28 Robert C. Coates, "Denison Mines Chief Leaves a Legacy of Accomplishments," letter to the editor, *Globe and Mail*, 9 April 1988.

29 McKay, "Roman Empire."

30 Brian O'Neill, "Too Risky a Venture: Hibernia Will Cost the Taxpayer Billions the Rock Could Better Use Elsewhere," *Globe and Mail*, 18 July 1988.

CHAPTER 15   CULTURE FOR SALE

1 "Canada Discovers Itself," *Time*, 5 May 1967, 34–5.

2 Geoffrey Wall and Natalie Zalkind, "The Canadian National Exhibition: Mirror of Canadian Society," in Geoffrey Wall and John Marsh, eds., *Recreational Land Use: Perspectives on Its Evolution in Canada* (Ottawa 1982), 311–21.

3 Geoffrey Wall, "Outdoor Recreation and the Canadian Identity," in Wall and Marsh, eds., *Recreational Land Use*, 419–34.

4 World Commission on Environment and Development (the Brundtland Commission), *Our Common Future* (New York 1987).

5 Geoffrey Wall and John Sinnott, "Urban Recreational and Cultural Facilities as Tourist Attractions," *Canadian Geographer* 24 (1980), 50–9.

6 Geoffrey Wall and Christopher Knapper, *Tutankhamun in Toronto* (Waterloo 1981).

7 Geoffrey Wall and Colleen Roberts, "The Economic Impact of the Tutankhamun and Van Gogh Exhibitions," in William S. Hendon, Nancy K. Grant, and Douglas V. Shaw, eds., *The Economics of Cultural Industries* (Akron, Ohio 1984), 66–77.

8 Clare Mitchell and Geoffrey Wall, *Impacts of Festivals: A Comparative Analysis*, report prepared for the Ontario Ministry of Citizenship and Culture (Waterloo 1986).

9 Geoffrey Wall and Alison Woodley, "Souvenir Sales: A Case Study on the North Shore of Lake Superior," in *Proceedings of the Northern Tourism Conference: Focus on Communities and Resources* (forthcoming).

10 Pierre L. van den Burghe and Charles F. Keyes, "Tourism and Recreated Ethnicity," *Annals of Tourism Research* 11 (1984), 343–52.

11 Geoffrey Wall and Barbara Oswald, "Cultural Groups as Tourist At-tractions: A Comparative Study," *Cahiers du Tourisme*, série C, no. 138 (Aix-en-Provence 1990).

12 Pierre Berton, *Hollywood's Canada: The Americanization of Our National Heritage* (Toronto 1975).

13 Hugh Winsor, "Canada's New Tourism Campaign in u.s. Features Nightlife," *Globe and Mail*, 19 February 1986.

CHAPTER 16   MADE IN AMERICA

My thanks to my colleague John Ingham, who read an earlier draft and suggested how to strengthen the essay's thesis.

1 I employ here the definition of nationalism presented by Elie Kedourie: "Nationalism is a doctrine invented in Europe at the beginning of the nineteenth century ... Briefly, the doctrine holds that humanity is naturally divided into nations, that nations are known by certain characteristics which can be ascertained, and that the only legitimate type of government is national self-government." Kedourie, *Nationalism* (New York 1960), 9.

2 "What is proposed here, in short, is a functional definition of nation-ality. Membership in a people essentially consists in wide comple-mentarity of social communication. It consists in the ability to communicate more effectively, and over a wider range of subjects, with members of one large group than with outsiders." Karl Deutsch, *Nationalism and Social Communication: An Inquiry into the Foundations of Nationality* (Cambridge, Mass. 1967), 97.

3 The term "popular culture" I take to refer to the things of the mind held in common by ordinary people. It may be used to mean the various artistic forms that people consume (sensational literature or rock music, say), sometimes abbreviated to "PopCult," placing it primarily in the field of entertainment. Or it may mean the attitudes, values, myths, rituals, and arts prevalent in ordinary life. For a brief discussion of popular culture from a somewhat different per-spective, see Winfried Fluck, "Popular Culture as a Mode of So-cialization: A Theory about the Social Functions of Popular Cultural Forms," *Journal of Popular Culture* 21: 3 (1987), 31–46.

4 Canada, *Parliamentary Debates on the Subject of the Confederation of the British North American Provinces* (Quebec 1865), 86.

5 The quoted phrases and taken from *Le Monde*, 20 December 1887, and the London *Advertiser*, 9 October 1893, respectively.

6 I have spoken about this ethos in Paul Rutherford, *A Victorian Authority: The Daily Press in Late Nineteenth-Century Canada* (Toronto 1982), especially 156–89.

7 For a discussion of ideas and behaviour see, for example, Paul Rutherford, "A Portrait of Alienation on Victorian Canada: The Private Memoranda of P.S. Hamilton," *Journal of Canadian Studies* 12 (September 1977), 12–23; D. Livermore, "The Personal Agonies of Edward Blake," *Canadian Historical Review* 56 (March 1975), 45–58; Michael Bliss, "Pure Books on Avoided Subjects: PreFreudian Sexual Ideas in Canada," Canadian Historical Association, *Historical Papers 1970*, 89–108.

8 P.B. Waite, "Sir Oliver Mowat's Canada: Reflections on an Un-Victorian Society," in Donald Swainson, ed., *Oliver Mowat's Ontario* (Toronto 1972), 12–32.

9 For a discussion of Canadian opinion, see R.C. Brown, "Canadian Opinion after Confederation 1867–1914," in S.F. Wise and R.C. Brown, eds., *Canada Views the United States: Nineteenth-Century Political Attitudes* (Toronto 1967), 98–120.

10 Alison Prentice, *The School Promoters: Education and Social Class in Mid-Nineteenth Century Upper Canada* (Toronto 1977), 53.

11 Blair Fraser, "Our Hush, Hush Censorship: How Books Are Banned," *Maclean's*, 5 December 1959, 24–5 and 44.

12 James Gray, *Booze: The Impact of Whiskey on the Prairie West* (Toronto 1972), 20–37.

13 See Frank Abbott, "Cold Cash and Ice Palaces: The Quebec Winter Carnival of 1894," *Canadian Historical Review*, 69 (1988), 167–202.

14 See, for example, John S. Marsh, "The Evolution of Recreation in Glacier National Park, British Columbia, 1880 to Present," in Geoffrey Wall and John Marsh, eds., *Recreational Land Use: Perspectives on Its Evolution in Canada* (Ottawa 1982), 62–76.

15 Among writers in the United States, Canada had already acquired a reputation as the abode of Nature. James Doyle, *North of America: Images of Canada in the Literature of the United States 1775–1900* (Toronto 1983).

16 Paul Rutherford, "The People's Press: The Emergence of the New Journalism in Canada, 1869–1899," *Canadian Historical Review*, 56 (June 1975), 167–91.

17 On the transformation of American advertising, see Daniel J. Boorstin, *The Americans: The Democratic Experience* (New York 1973), 137–45, and on the Canadian imitation see H.E. Stephenson and C. McNaught, *The Story of Advertising in Canada: A Chronicle of the Years* (Toronto 1940).

18 *Printer and Publisher*, August 1895, 1.

19 *Le Monde*, Paris, 28 September 1892.

20 M.E. Nichols, *The Story of the Canadian Press* (Toronto 1938).

21 Mary Vipond, "National Consciousness in English-Speaking Canada

in the 1920s: Seven Studies" (PHD thesis, University of Toronto 1974), 394.

22 See George Parker, *The Beginnings of the Book Trade in Canada* (Toronto 1985), which carries the story up to the end of the nineteenth century.

23 Mary Vipond, "Best Sellers in English Canada, 1899–1918: An Overview," *Journal of Canadian Fiction* 24 (1979), 108.

24 Robert Bothwell, Ian Drummond, and John English, *Canada 1900–1945* (Toronto 1987), 190–1.

25 Samuel Moffett, *The Americanization of Canada* (New York 1907; reprinted Toronto 1972), 109.

26 This paragraph is largely based on Alan Metcalfe's excellent monograph *Canada Learns to Play: The Emergence of Organized Sport, 1807–1914* (Toronto 1987).

27 Chantal Hébert, "Burlesque in Québec: An Easy Cocktail to Digest," *Journal of Canadian Culture* 1: 1 (Spring 1984), 78, 82.

28 Moffett, *Americanization of Canada*, 114.

29 For an interesting discussion of the nature of the mythology of individualism in Canada, see Allan Smith, "The Myth of the Self-Made Man in English Canada, 1850–1914," *Canadian Historical Review* 59 (June 1978) 189–219.

30 John C. Weaver, "Canadians Confront American Mass Culture, 1918–1930," (paper delivered at the 1972 annual meeting of the Canadian Historical Association), 14. Hobson probably exaggerated just how commonplace British products were.

31 This rapid expansion of the "car culture" probably would not have happened otherwise. See Donald F. Davis, "Dependent Motorization: Canada and the Automobile to the 1930s," *Journal of Canadian Studies* 21 (1986), 106–32.

32 "During the Dempsey-Tunney fights the newspapers devoted more space and ink to each contest than they had previously thought justifiable for the Tokyo earthquake of 1923, which killed 90,000, or the Florida hurricane of 1926, the most disastrous storm of the century." James H. Gray, *The Roar of the Twenties* (Toronto 1975), 106. Gray's book contains a chapter on the sports and games madness of the decade on the prairies.

33 On the takeover of hockey, see John Herd Thompson with Allen Seager, *Canada 1922–1939: Decades of Discord* (Toronto 1985), 188–90. Their chapter "The Conundrum of Culture" is an excellent survey of the cultural scene in the 1920s.

34 Frank Cosentino, *Canadian Football: The Grey Cup Years* (Toronto 1969), 94–99.

35 It is only fair to add, though, that amateur sport was still very much alive in this period: for example, the Edmonton Grads, a women's

basketball team, earned a reputation as the best team on the continent. See "The Golden Age of Sport" in *The Crazy Twenties 1920–1930* (Toronto 1978), 93–101.

36 Weaver, "American Mass Culture," 14.

37 See J.A. Stephenson, "American Periodical Literature," in H.F. Angus, ed., *Canada and Her Great Neighbor: Sociological Surveys of Opinions and Attitudes in Canada Concerning the United States* (Toronto 1938), 152–72, and Mary Vipond, "Canadian Nationalism and the Plight of Canadian Magazines in the 1920s," *Canadian Historical Review* 58 (1977) 43–63.

38 On the rise and fall of Canadian movies, see Peter Morris, *Embattled Shadows: A History of Canadian Cinema 1895–1939* (Montreal and Kingston 1978).

39 Margaret Prang, "The Origins of Public Broadcasting in Canada," *Canadian Historical Review*, 46 (1965), 4.

40 Frank Peers, *The Politics of Canadian Broadcasting 1920–1951* (Toronto 1969), 56–8.

41 See Carl Berger, "The True North Strong and Free," in Peter Russell, ed., *Nationalism in Canada* (Toronto 1966), 3–24, and George Altmeyer, "Three Ideas of Nature in Canada, 1893–1914," *Journal of Canadian Studies* 11: 3 (August 1976), 21–36.

42 This tradition has received much attention in accounts of English Canada's literary history: see Alec Lucas, "Nature Writers and the Animal Story," in Carl F. Klinck, ed., *Literary History of Canada: Canadian Literature in English* (Toronto 1966), 364–88, and T.D. MacLulich, "Reading the Land: The Wilderness Tradition in Canadian Letters," *Journal of Canadian Studies* 20: 2 (Summer 1985), 29–44.

43 Douglas L. Cole, "An Enquiry into the Success of the Group of Seven," *Journal of Canadian Studies* 13: 2 (Summer 1978), 77.

44 This story was told best by an indignant Pierre Berton in *Hollywood's Canada: The Americanization of Our National Image* (Toronto 1975). The fact is, however, that Hollywood's fabrications about Canada were not that unusual: they fit the traditions both of movie-making and of Canada as Nature.

45 Joyce Nelson, *The Colonized Eye: Rethinking the Grierson Legend* (Toronto 1988), 50–1.

46 For a general discussion of this maturing mass culture, see John N. Ingham, ed., *Assault on Victorianism: The Rise of Popular Culture in America 1890–1945* (Toronto 1987), especially 55–6 and 165–8.

47 See Lary May, *Screening Out the Past: The Birth of Mass Culture and the Motion Picture Industry* (New York 1980), which charts the development of this Hollywood approach and emphasizes the importance of its Jewish makers who had a talent for fusing different styles and selling the result to the millions.

48 There is an excellent monograph on advertising in the 1920s and 1930s: Roland Marchand, *Advertising the American Dream: Making Way for Modernity 1920–1940* (Berkeley 1985).

49 MacMechan was an English professor at Dalhousie University in Halifax. S.E.D. Shortt, *The Search for an Ideal: Six Canadian Intellectuals and their Convictions in an Age of Transition 1890–1930* (Toronto 1976), 47.

50 Susan Mann Trofimenkoff, *Action Française: French Canadian Nationalism in the Twenties* (Toronto 1975), 71–83.

51 Quotations from A Censor, "The Censorship of Moving Pictures," *Dalhousie Review* 1 (April 1921), 39–40, and Weston Gaul, "Censors in Celluloid," *Maclean's*, 15 June 1940, 10. See also Malcolm Dean, *Censored! Only in Canada* (Toronto 1981), 28–37.

52 MacMechan, "Canada as a Vassal State," *Canadian Historical Review* 1: 4 (December 1920), 347.

53 Some American magazines, *Liberty* being an outstanding example, avoided the tariff by publishing a Canadian edition. See J.A. Stevenson, "American Periodical Literature," in Angus, *Canada and Her Great Neighbor*, 152–72. On the effort by Canadian magazines to win protection, see Vipond, "Plight of Canadian Magazines," 43–63.

54 Indeed, Grierson, recommended that the Canadian government not endeavour to compete with Hollywood in the future. The post-war NFB was dogged by charges of pro-Communism (Grierson, who had left, was himself a target), a reduced budget, and by the loss of its theatrical outlets. See Gary Evans's sympathetic account, *John Grierson and the National Film Board: The Politics of Wartime Propaganda 1939–1945* (Toronto 1984), and the highly critical analysis by Joyce Nelson in *The Colonized Eye*.

55 Data from Elliott-Haynes, *Program Report*, February 1950 (available in box no. 6 of the broadcast ratings collection of the Moving Image and Sound Archives, National Archives of Canada, Ottawa).

56 See Angus, *Canada and Her Great Neighbor*, 383–449.

57 Cited in Mildred A. Schwartz, *Public Opinion and Canadian Identity* (Scarborough, Ont. 1967), 74.

58 Canada, Royal Commission on National Development in the Arts, Letters, and Sciences (the Massey Commission), *Report* (Ottawa 1951), 18.

59 Ibid., 7.

60 For a discussion of this 'revolt of the highbrows,' see Bernard Ostry, *The Cultural Connection: An Essay on Culture and Government Policy in Canada* (Toronto 1978), 51–60. The Canadian revolt was actually part of a wider North American movement. To sample the ideas of American highbrows, see Bernard Rosenberg and David Manning

White, eds., *Mass Culture: The Popular Arts in America* (New York 1957).

61 Roland Marchand, "Visions of Classlessness, Quests for Dominion: American Popular Culture, 1945–1960," in Robert H. Brenner and Gary W. Reichard, eds., *Reshaping America: Society and Institutions 1945–1960* (Columbus, Ohio 1982), 170.

62 There are some valuable discussions of the trends in Canada's popular culture from 1945 to 1970 in Bothwell, Drummond, and English, *Canada since 1945*, 109–20, 165–75, 253–66, 332–7.

63 Alexander Ross, *The Booming Fifties: 1950–1960* (Toronto 1977), 43. Ross's book has some marvelous stories about the moods of the 1950s, not the least being his chapter on "The Discovery of the Teenager."

64 M.C. Urquhart and K.A.H. Buckley, *Historical Statistics of Canada* (Toronto 1965), series T1–24, 571.

65 Hugh A. Stevenson, "Crisis and Continuum: Public Education in the Sixties," in J. Donald Wilson, Robert M. Stamp, and Louis-Philippe Audet, eds., *Canadian Education: A History* (Scarborough, Ont. 1970), 483.

66 George Grant, *Lament for a Nation: The Defeat of Canadian Nationalism* (Toronto 1965).

67 Jerry Goodis, *Have I Ever Lied to You Before* (Toronto 1972).

68 Canada, Royal Commission on Newspapers (the Kent Commission), *Report* (Ottawa 1981), 216.

69 Knowlton Nash, *Prime Time at Ten: Behind-the-Camera Battles of Canadian TV Journalism* (Toronto 1987), 209.

70 Canada, *Report of the Task Force on Broadcasting Policy* (Ottawa 1986), 96.

71 This did not happen overnight, since the press was initially very suspicious of this brand of "cultural socialism." See Robert Ayre, "The Press Debates the Massey Report," *Canadian Art* (August 1951), 25.

72 The definitive study of the politics of television in the 1950s and 1960s is Frank Peers, *The Public Eye: Television and the Politics of Canadian Broadcasting 1952–1968* (Toronto 1979).

73 *Canada Year-Book 1952–53* (Ottawa 1953), 848; and *Public Accounts of Canada 1990–91*, vol. 3, (Ottawa 1991), IV–104.

74 J.L. Granatstein, *Canada 1957–1967: The Years of Uncertainty and Innovation* (Toronto 1986), 143. Granatstein's book has a superb chapter on the first ten years of the council.

75 The key event was the passage of the Fitness and Amateur Sport Act in 1961, though there had been earlier initiatives going back at least to 1937. For a brief overview, see Jean Harvey and Roger Proulx, "Sport and the State in Canada," in Jean Harvey and Hart Can-

telon, eds., *Not Just A Game: Essays in Canadian Sport Sociology* (Ottawa 1988), 93–119.

76 Briefly put, the amendments stipulated "that advertisements published in non-Canadian newspapers and periodicals but aimed primarily at Canadian readers cannot be deducted, for tax purposes, as a business expense." A Canadian outlet meant a corporation three-quarters owned by Canadians and incorporated here. There were some exemptions, the most famous being *Time* magazine, though that exemption disappeared in 1976. Kent Commission, *Report*, 56.

77 For a discussion of this phenomenon see Ostry, *Cultural Connection*; *Report of the Federal Cultural Policy Review Committee*, (Ottawa 1982); and the highly critical appraisal by George Woodcock, *Strange Bedfellows: The State and the Arts in Canada* (Vancouver 1985).

78 Woodcock, *Strange Bedfellows*, 71.

79 For a recent and interesting expression of this sense of achievement, see Robertson Davies, "Signing Away Canada's Soul: Culture, Identity, and the Free-Trade Agreement," *Harper's* (January 1989), 43–7, where he explained to Americans what the flap over free trade in the Canadian election was all about.

80 Gaile McGregor, *The Wacousta Syndrome: Explorations in the Canadian Langscape* (Toronto 1985). I find her argument so exaggerated and convoluted as to be unbelievable.

81 Quotation from the CBC's "Memorandum" to the Royal Commission on Broadcasting (the Fowler Commission), 15.

82 Quoted in *CBC Times*, 23–29 January 1960, 27. That attitude was endorsed by Fowler as well: "our distinctively Canadian culture" apparently embraced "'everything from hockey and lacrosse to the Group of Seven and Andrew Allan's radio drama," and included sports announcers, ice-skaters, poets, musicians, in short all who contributed to "the whole way of life of the Canadian people." Fowler Commission, *Report* (Ottawa 1957), 66, 76 (the definition was taken from the brief of the University of British Columbia).

83 For an extensive survey of the ingredients of the teleromans, see Line Ross and Helene Tardiff, *Le Téléroman québécois, 1960–1971. Une analyse de contenu*, cahier 12, Laboratoire de recherches sociologiques, Université Laval (Quebec 1975).

84 There was an additional irony to the migration of CBC-TV producers, because these were the very people whom the corporation made into stars: see Alexis Barris, *The Pierce-Arrow Showroom Is Leaking: An Insider's View of the CBC* (Toronto 1969), 103–6.

85 I have pursued the story of early television at considerable length in Rutherford, *When Television Was Young: Primetime Canada 1952–1967* (Toronto 1990).

86 See chapter 8, "The Distinctiveness of French Broadcasting," *Report of the Task Force on Broadcasting Policy*, 205–56. See Richard Collins, *Culture, Communication and National Identity: The Case of Canadian Television* (Toronto 1990), for a lengthy discussion of Canadian programming and Canadian tastes in the 1970s and 1980s.

87 For a sample of these studies, see Barry K. Grant, "'Across the Great Divide': Imitation and Inflection in Canadian Rock Music," *Journal of Canadian Studies* 21: 1 (Spring 1986), 116–27; Robert A. Wright, "'Dream, Comfort, Memory, Despair': Canadian Popular Musicians and the Dilemma of Nationalism, 1968–1972," ibid., 22: 4 (Winter 1987–88), 27–43; Seth Feldman, ed., *Take Two: A Tribute to Film in Canada* (Toronto 1984); Mary Jane Miller, *Turn Up The Contrast: CBC Television Drama since 1952* (Vancouver 1987). Miller's book is an extensive and sophisticated elaboration of the Canadian difference in drama. The difference is a major theme of the essays in the present volume by Seth Feldman, Mary Jane Miller, Andrew Lyons and Harriet Lyons, and Reid Gilbert.

88 "The documentary tradition, the tradition of telling it like it is, has been at the heart of Canadian film from its beginnings": Morris Wolfe, *Jolts: The TV Wasteland and the Canadian Oasis* (Toronto 1985), 80.

89 One historian, John Herd Thompson, has written an interesting and generally sympathetic critique of *The King Chronicle*, which appeared in March 1988: "'Writing History with Lightning': Mackenzie King's Television Biography," *Canadian Historical Review* 69: 4 (1988), 503–10.

90 Wolfe, *Jolts*, 83.

91 See, for example, the pieces by Margaret Atwood, Michele Landsberg, Martin Katz, Jerry Goodis, and Rick Salutin in Laurier LaPierre, ed., *If You Love This Country: Facts and Feelings on Free Trade* (Toronto 1988).

92 See Jerry Bowles, *A Thousand Sundays: The Story of the Ed Sullivan Show* (New York 1980), 147–52. I recognize that *The Beachcombers* might also count as an exception.

93 Joel Garreau, *The Nine Nations of North America* (Boston 1981). Garreau divided the Canadian portion of the continent into Newfoundland and the maritimes (which became part of "New England"), Quebec, southern Ontario (as part of the "Foundry," including the old industrial heartland of the United States), the grain-growing areas of the prairies (attached to the American midwest as the "Breadbasket"), the rest of the prairie provinces and mountainous British Columbia (with their American counterparts in the "Empty Quarter"), and the British Columbia coast joined with the American

west coast (in "Ecotopia"). His claims are exaggerated, but they do highlight the pluralism of the continent.

94 Regarding country music, see Tommy Hunter's interesting autobiography (with Liane Heller), *Tommy Hunter – My Story* (Toronto 1985).

95 Neil Postman, *Amusing Ourselves to Death: Public Discourse in the Age of Show Business* (Toronto 1986).

96 I am indebted to John Ingham for the phrase "Fortress Canada."

97 William H. McNeill, *Polyethnicity and National Unity in World History: The Donald G. Creighton Lectures 1985* (Toronto 1986), 6. McNeill identified himself as a world historian, and justifiably so on the basis of a range of books covering the history of civilizations over many centuries, including *A World History* and *Plagues and Peoples*.

98 Quotation taken from the jacket blurb for William Kilbourn, ed., *Canada: A Guide to the Peaceable Kingdom* (Toronto 1970). There is more of this kind of rhetoric in Kilbourn's own introduction.

99 Thus Alan Herscovici claims, in *Second Nature: The Animal-Rights Controversy* (Toronto 1985), 24: "This discussion has special significance for Canada, a northern country where much of the land is best suited to raising animals or harvesting wildlife and other natural resources. There aren't many parts of Canada where soybeans or grapefruits will grow; not even potatoes grow in Newfoundland. If these fundamental physical and cultural realities are not acknowledged, it is difficult to understand what half a century of debate on the 'Canadian identity' has been about."

100 See, for example, Hildegard Hammerschmidt, "Images of Canada in Advertising," *Journal of Canadian Studies*, 18: 4 (Winter 1983–84), 165–7, and Michael Ames, "Cultural Productions: The Case of Expo 86," in this volume. A 1986 survey undertaken for Tourism Canada revealed that Americans thought their outdoors was as splendid as Canada's. This finding apparently has led officials to adopt other approaches in attracting American visitors. See Geoffrey Wall's essay in this volume.

101 Morton's book grew out of three public lectures to an American audience at the University of Wisconsin and a presidential address to the Canadian Historical Association. They were published in Canada by the University of Toronto Press in 1961. Another example, though it is more of a textbook than a simple interpretation, is Donald Creighton's famous *Dominion of the North: A History of Canada*, initially published in 1944 by Macmillan of Canada.

102 See Alan Smith, "Metaphor and Nationality in North America," *Canadian Historical Review* 51: 3 (1970), 247–75.

103 One of the best examples of this sort of amalgam, full of all manner of cliché, is Pierre Berton's *Why We Act Like Canadians: A Personal Exploration of Our National Character* (Toronto 1987), a 1982 book reprinted for the free trade debate.

104 Fulford was referring to both cultural nationalism and feminism, citing especially the example of Margaret Atwood. Robert Fulford, *Best Seat in the House: Memoirs of a Lucky Man* (Toronto 1988), 187.

105 See in particular Innis, *Strategy of Culture*, 1–20, and Dallas Smythe, *Dependency Road: Communications, Capitalism, Consciousness, and Canada* (Norwood, NJ 1981).

106 Margaret Atwood, *Survival: A Thematic Guide to Canadian Literature* (Toronto 1972).

107 Tony Wilden, *The Imaginary Canadian: An Examination for Discovery* (Vancouver 1980), 2.

108 Similarly, Rick Salutin, writing the "Perspectives" column in the *Globe and Mail's* "Broadcast Week" (28 January – 3 February 1989), argued that the sympathetic treatment of the police in shows like *Hill Street Blues* (then appearing on CITY-TV in Toronto) cultivated a hostility to reports that suggested the police might be at fault. That he saw as one cause of complaints directed against a CITYPulse reporter who had been covering the shooting death of a black teenager, Wade Lawson, by the police. "There is no comparable TV series that personalizes and emotionalizes for us the experiences, say, of black teen-agers growing up in Peel Region."

CHAPTER 17   AMERICAN POPULAR CULTURE AND THE CANADIAN STATE

1 Royal Commission on National Development in the Arts, Letters, and Sciences (the Massey Commission), *Report* (Ottawa 1951).

2 *Report of the Federal Cultural Policy Review Committee* (Ottawa 1982) and *Report of the Task Force on Broadcasting Policy* (Ottawa 1986).

3 *Butler* v. *The Queen* (1992), 89 *Dominion Law Reports* (4th) 449; *Glad Day Bookshop, Inc. and Jearald Moldenhauer* v. *Deputy Minister of National Revenue for Customs and Excise*, unreported, 14 July 1992, Ontario Court of Justice.

4 N. Robin Morgan, "Theory and Practice: Pornography and Rape," in N. Robin Morgan, ed., *Going Too Far* (New York 1978), 163–9; Gloria Steinem, "A Clear and Present Danger," *Ms.* (November 1978), 53–4, 75–8.

5 See *Pornography and Prostitution in Canada: Report of the Special Committee on Pornography and Prostitution* (the Fraser report) (Ottawa 1985);

and U.S. Department of Justice, *Attorney General's Commission on Pornography and Prostitution: Final Report*, 2 vols. (Washington 1986).

6 *Pornography and Prostitution in Canada*. See also Thelma McCormack, "Deregulating the Economy and Regulating Morality: The Political Economy of Censorship," *Studies in Political Economy* 18 (1985), 173–85.

CHAPTER 18 AMERICAN POPULAR CULTURE IN CANADA

1 Harold Adams Innis, *The Strategy of Culture* (Toronto 1952), 20.

2 Paul Audley, *Canada's Cultural Industries* (Toronto 1983); *Report of the Task Force on Broadcasting Policy* (Ottawa 1986).

3 See *Report of the Federal Cultural Policy Review Committee* (Ottawa 1982).

4 Dick Hebdidge, *Hiding in the Light* (London and New York 1988), 181–208.

5 See Frederic Jameson, "Postmodernism, or the Logic of Late Capitalism," *New Left Review* 146 (1984); and Jean Baudrillard, "Design and Environment: or How Political Economy Escalates into Cyberblitz," in *Towards a Critique of the Political Economy of the Sign* (St. Louis 1981).

6 Key texts include Arthur Kroker, *Innis/Grant/McLuhan* (Montreal 1986); John Fekete, *The Critical Twilight* (London 1977); Paul Heyer, *Communication and History: Theories of Media, Knowledge, and Civilization* (Westport, Conn. 1988); and Donald Theall, *The Medium is the Rear-view Mirror* (Montreal 1971).

Index